SINGLEHANDED SAILING

THOUGHTS, TIPS, TECHNIQUES & TACTICS

Another aspect of singlehanded sailing—the afternoon nap. *(Courtesy Andrew Madding)*

SINGLEHANDED SAILING

THOUGHTS, TIPS, TECHNIQUES & TACTICS

ANDREW EVANS on *Foolish Muse*

INTERNATIONAL MARINE / McGRAW-HILL EDUCATION

Camden, Maine • New York • Chicago • San Francisco • Lisbon • London • Madrid
Mexico City • Milan • New Delhi • San Juan • Seoul • Singapore • Sydney • Toronto

4 5 6 7 8 9 QFR 21 20 19 18 17 16
ISBN 978-0-07-183653-1
MHID 0-07-183653-5
E ISBN 0-07-183654-3

Library of Congress Cataloging-in-Publication Data is available from the Library of Congress.

McGraw-Hill Education books are available at special quantity discounts to use as premiums and sales promotions or for use in corporate training programs. To contact a representative, please e-mail us at bulksales@mcgraw-hill.com.
This book is printed on acid-free paper.

Questions regarding the content of this book should be addressed to
www.internationalmarine.com
Questions regarding the ordering of this book should be addressed to
McGraw-Hill Education
Customer Service Department
P.O. Box 547
Blacklick, OH 43004
Retail customers: 1-800-262-4729
Bookstores: 1-800-722-4726

All photos courtesy of the author unless credited otherwise.

DEDICATION

THE CAPITAL
AND VANCOUVER ISLAND

TIMES COLONIST • SUNDAY DECEMBER 30 2007

Editor: Denise Helm · Telephone: 380-5333 · E-mail: localnews@tc.canwest.com

TC B1
Classified, B3
Colour comics, B5
Weather, B12

SAILORS TAKE ON STORMY SEAS

The freighter Maersk Bering and a sailboat make their way through whitecaps just off Trial Island yesterday as yet another storm hit the area with winds forecast up to 70 kilometres per hour.
Debra Brash/ Times Colonist

This book is dedicated to my wife Sharon, who tells me to "go sailing" every time I get underfoot. This is why I can sail so often. *(Courtesy* Victoria Times Colonist*)*

CONTENTS

FOREWORD

I met Andy when he came to help out my preparations on *OceanPlanet* for the 2004–2005 Vendée Globe. A nice guy and good sense of humor—after all, he's Canadian.

In many ways he represents all those who have become successful solo sailors on their own nickel: learning slowly from a mix of hard-earned experience, digging up obscure info, and sharing with each other.

It's not like this sort of experience is falling off trees. While a lot of jabber about singlehanded sailing can be found on discussion forums and the odd magazine articles, this is the first collection of the varied aspects of the sport put together in one place. It takes thousands of hours of sailing to get the kind of knowledge contained in this book. It also takes a lot of experimentation and a willingness to be wrong nine times before getting it right on the tenth.

There are many recipes for successful solo sailing—as many as the actual sailors who do it. And there are many different levels of personal priorities. However many, many of the same mistakes are made over and over by those new to the sport, and by those who simply think they have it already figured out. Most of those mistakes can be prevented by carefully analyzing what Andy has put together.

This is good stuff, and I'm especially glad that he did it, because now I don't have to.

Cheers,
BRUCE SCHWAB

Bruce Schwab is a lifelong marine services professional and two-time solo circumnavigator. Schwab has won many crewed, doublehanded, and solo sailing races, including the 1996 Singlehanded Transpac aboard Rumbleseat. *After completing his first circumnavigation in the 2002–2003 Around Alone Race, Schwab came to Portland, Maine, to refit* OceanPlanet *for the 2004–2005 Vendée Globe Race. On February 25, 2005, Schwab became the first American in history to officially finish the Vendée Globe, and currently holds the American solo circumnavigation record of 109 days and 20 hours.*

CHAPTER 1 **INTRODUCTION**

If I were the richest man in the world, I'd have a bigger boat and newer sails. But on a Saturday afternoon with only God and the wind, I wouldn't be any happier than I am right now.

Another great day on the water. *(Courtesy* Victoria Times Colonist*)*

Over the past ten years I've gone singlehanded sailing close to a thousand times. I started just four days after getting my first boat and have rarely looked back. Included are more than 250 individual races. In total, it adds up to perhaps 4,000 hours of singlehanded sailing—a reasonable start.

With all of the times that I have left the dock, I have never—not even once—had a bad day on the water. I've had days when things went wrong: difficult things, expensive things. I've shredded several spinnakers. I've hit rocks and cracked the hull. I've broken my mast. I've had days when the wind blew more than most could handle, and I've had days when it didn't blow at all. But I have never had a day when I wished I were somewhere else. I have never had a bad day sailing.

Sailing gives me a sense of joy that seems rare in life. I imagine it is something like what the monks in Tibet achieve. It is certainly the sense that the

Dalai Lama seems to show every time he laughs.

But not all sailing gives me this feeling, only singlehanding. I have raced many times with a full crew but found myself frustrated more often than not. Why is this? I've had some great crewmates, friendly people who were fantastic to spend time with. Perhaps I found it too exhausting, as skipper, to be responsible not only for my own actions but also for the actions of every other person on the boat.

When I'm alone, I rarely need to consider what I'm doing. The boat just reacts to my desires—automatically. One day I was sailing alongside another yacht and the skipper told me that I "wear my boat like a glove." So I guess it could be said that, for me, sailing alone is like putting on a comfortable bodysuit that reacts to my every whim, but sailing with a crew is like wearing a suit of armor, in which every move must be considered, communicated, then performed. It's just too much work.

I do know that if singlehanded sailing were not possible, I wouldn't sail at all. I'd take up some other hobby—perhaps jigsaw puzzles.

With this number of trips under my keel, it is reasonable to guess that I am one of the more experienced singlehanded sailors in the world. Not in miles, but certainly in the number of times I've left the dock, and the number of tacks, number of gybes, spinnaker launches and douses—and number of learning experiences.

By nature, I have a real interest in efficiency. I have always tried to find the best, most efficient way to perform any task. Over the past decade I have looked at every aspect of singlehanded sailing and tried to find the best way to do it on my boat. This compulsion gets right down to how long should I pause during a tack to do the least work hauling in the sheets, and it even includes a detailed plan for how to urinate. I've taken every action down to a precise science.

I'm also not at all shy about asking other sailors questions. I get some funny looks at the bar and some nasty comments on the forums, but I would rather look stupid and learn than look smart and remain stupid. When I speak to other skippers, I don't just ask, "Do you use a spinnaker?" I say, "Tell me the exact steps you take to pull the halyard, guy, and sheet to raise the spinnaker without fouling it." My Olson 30 is named *Foolish Muse*, and my forum name is Foolish. Some have pointed out that this seems appropriate.

This book is the result of my almost "academic" study of the techniques of singlehanded sailing.

It is also the result of trial and an incredible number of errors. For my first eight years of sailing, I can confidently say that something went wrong every time I went out—every single time. It got to the point where if I was returning to the dock and something bad had not happened yet, I knew that it still would happen. I have always pushed my boat and myself to the limit. Of course things will go wrong when pushed.

Every time something went wrong, I took it as a learning experience. Most times it took making the same mistake over and over again before I figured out a better way. Raising the spinnaker is a good example. I'd had too many broaches to count before finding the perfect method. Because of these I now know exactly how far the water will come into my cockpit on a broach and no longer have any fear, or even concern, about broaching. But since the day that I figured it out, I have not had a single broach in any wind conditions. When my autopilot quit last spring, I took it as a great chance to relearn the basics. I finally discovered a way to gybe the spinnaker with just a bungee cord on the tiller. I'd been working on that problem for ten years.

But I am not finished. That things have stopped going wrong is only an indication that I need a faster boat to start the learning process again.

The purpose of this book is to impart these many, many lessons to interested readers in the form of tips, techniques, and tactics. In some cases I will go into a painful level of detail. My intention is that new singlehanders should not have to go through the trial and error phase that I did. If he or she can learn from my mistakes before they leave the dock, they can push their boat further and create their own, new mistakes. After reading this book, and with perhaps one or two thousand hours of practice, every sailor should be able to wear their own boat like a glove.

MY HEROES

The singlehanded community is fairly small, and a few names are well known. In my office hang autographed posters of Dame Ellen MacArthur and Sir Robin Knox-Johnston. It seems that of any activity in the world, singlehanded sailors have the best odds of being knighted. Even my good friend Jeanne Socrates, who at age 70 became the oldest woman to sail nonstop around the world alone, was invited to a reception with the Queen at Buckingham Palace.

My greatest admiration goes to everyone who has left the dock on their own, personal voyage. Some of these skippers have met their goals, while others have not. One circumnavigator stayed at sea for more than 1,000 days, while another singlehanded sailor ended her voyage after just a week. But they have all been successful in undertaking a significant life adventure. They all have stories to

My autographed poster from Dame Ellen MacArthur, who broke the record for the fastest solo circumnavigation in 2005.

Jeanne Socrates celebrates receiving the Blue Water Medal from the Cruising Club of America. *(Courtesy Anne Hammick)*

My signed photo of Sir Robin Knox-Johnston, the first man to sail non-stop around the world singlehanded, aboard his 32-foot ketch, *Suhaili*.

tell, and they are all worthy of our admiration. Off-shore singlehanded sailing is a challenge taken by just a tiny percentage of experienced sailors. In our over-protective society, it is one of the few activities where an individual is responsible for his own safety. For this reason alone, every singlehanded sailor made it onto my hero list the moment they left the dock.

My dream started back in 1989 when I read John Hughes's *The Sailing Spirit* about the BOC Challenge (forerunner of the Around Alone and Velux 5 Oceans races). I followed the races very carefully in a time before the Internet, when the only news came as a recorded voice over an expensive long-distance telephone call. I plotted the positions with colored lines on a world map. Eleven years later I said to my wife, "If I'm going to sail around the world, I'd better get a boat," and this adventure began.

A BIT MORE ABOUT ME

By profession I am a lawyer and Chartered Financial Analyst, but mostly I am president of a small company in the solar power industry. I live in Victoria, British Columbia, on the West Coast of Canada, and sail out of the Royal Victoria Yacht Club. I am blessed that this is the only region of a cold country where I can sail year-round.

WHY DO WE DO IT? WHAT OTHERS HAVE SAID

Here is a quote from Jerry Freeman on the Solo Offshore Racing Club website (www.offshoresolo.com):

> For most of us normal yachties the prospect of spending 20 to 30 nights alone at sea is so far off the scale as to be impossible to contemplate. A recent gathering of singlehanders provided an ideal opportunity to study these rare creatures in their natural habitat before they dispersed for their hibernation.
>
> Is it a macho thing, this solo ocean racing?

If so why is it that two of the biggest boats were sailed by the two most petite lady skippers? They will claim that solo yacht racing is a cerebral sport like chess; brawn is not required and if it is you must be doing something wrong so have a nap and try again. What other sport is there where the contestants out-sleep each other?

From this group, it seems the overriding qualification for solo sailing is advanced age, being a paid up member of the 'Last Chance' brigade. Time is running out as the years of procrastination accumulate towards a crisis. Grandpa, casting off the responsible years of family and school fees, enjoys a financial second wind. The prospect of dying and not knowing becomes more scary than the prospect of going.

The legend of the oldest race goes back to 1960 when men were made of sterner stuff and by gum they had to be. That's the trouble with young people, no respect, they just toddle across the Atlantic like it was a Sunday school outing. Where is the drama, the passion, how are they going to get a book deal out of 21 days and no problems?

The art of tuning a cat's whisker on the wireless has been lost in the mists of time as the Iridium phone connection brings Mum and Dad into the cabin with the clarity and convenience of normal conversation. There's not even Test Match cricket on short wave of the BBC World Service to endure, all gone! What about enjoying a pipe of Condor 'ready rubbed' and a glass of fine claret under the spray hood to

celebrate a good day's run? You can forget that. We are all athletes now.

Numerous reviews have been written about an earlier edition of this book that was published online. Here is my favorite, from *The Watchorn,* which both provides a preview of this book and touches upon the spirit of singlehanding.

This month I'd like to switch gears and get a little philosophical with you about boating. I was recently reading a lengthy article titled "Singlehanded Tips," written by Andrew Evans, who has logged more than 3,000 [now over 4,000] hours of singlehanded sailing in the last ten years. The article is a great read. I highly recommend it to anyone interested in the mental and physical effects that singlehanded sailing can have on an individual, or for those who are toying with the idea of rigging your vessel for singlehanded operation.

The subject that interests me most in this article is the underlying desire for these eccentric boaters to try singlehanded sailing in the first place. Yes, at times everyone has a reason for taking their boat out by themselves and partaking in a little solo cruise, but this type of sailing is a far cry from bashing through fifteen-foot seas with a triple reef in the main and sixty-knot winds trying to knock the boat over on her ear. And to do this by yourself, with no one there to relieve you at the wheel or to make you a hot cup of coffee when you are tired, must require a hearty individual indeed. If these men and women weren't finding their thrills sailing they would probably be getting them by fighting the Taliban in Afghanistan or base-jumping off of cliffs. I guess some people see a mountain and just have to climb it.

I wonder if some people have a natural inclination towards danger. Certainly the idea goes against Darwin's thoughts; natural selection does not favor those who stick their necks too far into the fire. And yet I have known too many people who simply must do something dangerous in order to truly feel alive. Is this rush of adrenaline really worth the chance of perishing in Arctic waters during a heavy storm? Being the polar opposite of these adrenaline junkies, I guess I really cannot say. I can tell you I'm jealous every time I read literature like the aforementioned article, and can't help but daydream of what it must truly be like to fight tooth and nail for every second of survival. I can also tell you that it simply must be better to feel those fleeting moments of danger and survive them than to have never felt them at all. Andrew Evans, I salute you.

D.H. jr

... and now, nothing more,
I want to be alone with my essential sea ...
I don't want to speak for a long time,
Silence! I want to learn,
I want to know if I exist.
—Pablo Neruda

CHAPTER 2 THE MENTAL CHALLENGES

Many sailors consider "shorthanded sailing" comparable to "singlehanded sailing." In my view, having two people on the boat is no different from having eight. This is not because of the physical difficulties. The reasons are entirely based on the mental and emotional challenges facing a singlehander that the crew of a doublehanded or fully crewed boat will never see. Mental challenges occur during even the shortest trips. Emotional challenges can appear on trips as short as eight hours but more likely after 12 hours or a day.

The Internet has become the best resource to prove this point. Skippers in around-the-world races post daily videos on the web. These videos show sailors who are physically, mentally, and emotionally exhausted from days without adequate sleep. It is obvious that they are working with significantly less than full mental faculties. The picture is completely different on doublehanded or crewed boats, where sleep is possible. Solo sailors are forced into complex decision-making processes at the very time when they are least able to perform. As Ellen MacArthur conveyed in her incredible story in *Taking on the World*:

> It was more than just physical exhaustion; it was causing more pain inside than I had ever felt before. I clenched my teeth and threw my head down against the hard, wet floor and wept. I cried like a baby till I was so numb with the cold that the pain was dulled. Shivering and weak, I crawled into the cabin and slept in my waterproofs, curled up in a ball in the footwell by the engine.

Or as John Hughes wrote in *The Sailing Spirit*:

> The tears ran unabated down my face as I watch *Turtles*, the boat carrying my girlfriend, my mother, and my close friends turn and scuttle back to the shelter of Newport Harbor. The image of that parting will never leave me. It came almost two hours after the starting gun was fired to signal the start of the BOC race, two hours of beating to windward that had left me physically and emotionally exhausted.

In the Singlehanded Transpac logs, a sailor commented:

> Last thought for now: it is so beautiful out here, I am finding myself crying over every happy memory I have with family and friends. I don't know why that's going on.

Another Transpac memory:

> I spent two solid hours bawling half way to Hawaii. Every sad possibility crossed my mind. 'What was in the half-way package that my wife gave me? Was it a note that she was leaving me? Was it a note that she was dying?' I knew that these were both incredibly ridiculous concepts, but I'd been alone for more than a week with very little sleep and no contact from home, emotions can run wild.

In *Sea of Dreams,* Adam Mayers wrote:

> John Dennis turned fifty-eight on the fleet's third day back at sea after the Bay of Biscay storm. The boyish glee he'd felt on leaving Newport was long gone and he felt old, tired, depressed, and guilty about the toll the trip was taking on his family, something he had not fully considered before he set sail. He had expected to miss them, but had not expected the pangs of loneliness to outweigh the pleasure of the journey. Phone calls and e-mails became painful stews of anticipation and regret.

In a later chapter, when Dennis was forced to retire from mechanical problems, Mayers continues:

It was over; John Dennis was not going to sail around the world. "I'm so drained, I don't have any tears left," he said, "It is a dream and I know now I am never going to achieve it. I'm devastated."

Two months into his second westward circumnavigation attempt, Glenn Wakefield accidently snagged and drowned a wandering albatross with his fishing line. Glenn recorded what is undoubtedly the most poignant video of any singlehander in history. His fragile emotional state could easily be compared to what a man would face with the death of a child, rather than a sea bird. I have never in my life seen a man cry in this way—but it reflects my own experience after many days at sea.

A couple of weeks later Wakefield described his attitude as being as happy as a ten-year-old boy while he watched a whale playing nearby.

As far as I know, singlehanded sailing is the only sport where one needs to be physically, mentally, *and emotionally* ready, just to finish. I have read many books on sailing the great races. I have never read that the skipper in the Volvo Ocean Race broke down and cried. It just does not happen. This is the difference between singlehanding and crewing, even with just two on board.

Consider how rare it is in modern society for someone to be totally alone and totally self-reliant. This does not mean reading a book with a family member in the next room or even being out for an afternoon hike in the woods with the dog. Being totally alone means the sailor must rely completely on his own abilities with no recourse to any physical, mental, or emotional assistance from any other person.

Some might counter that with radio, cell phone, or satellite phone a singlehander is never alone and can always call for assistance. This is true in the long term but has no standing for the hundreds of things that do go awry and require immediate resolution. A VHF serves no purpose when a boat is broached and the cockpit is half full of water. A cell phone won't help with strong winds and a lee shore.

A single-sideband (SSB) radio cannot unwrap a spinnaker, and it sure as heck won't cuddle up after hours in the cold wind.

In one race with a 20-knot wind, I wrapped my spinnaker around the forestay when attempting a gybe. I was about 3 minutes from the rocks, but because the spinnaker was half out, I could not turn up. I went to the bow and got the chute down with about 30 seconds to spare. After the race, the skipper of a crewed boat told me that they were just about to come to my aid when I got the mess sorted. I could only ask him, "What were you going to do?" My actions alone were the only possible source of a solution to the problem. If I couldn't do it, the boat was lost.

The singlehanded sailor must understand that he is completely, 100% self-reliant. It is up to him alone to solve every problem that he faces, whether it's a simple knotted line or a life-threatening danger. I believe that this is why we are rare. One only needs to look at a single/doublehanded race, regardless of whether it's a 2-hour club event or a professional around-the-world adventure. There will be ten doublehanded boats for every singlehander. The reason is not that the doublehanders are physically incapable of sailing their boat alone. The reason is that only the singlehanders are willing to take on the challenge of 100% self-reliance. This can be a very uncomfortable position. It is such a rare situation that most people will never face it.

STRESS AND COPING

Several studies have concentrated on the specific stresses of long-distance, singlehanded sailing. Glin Bennet performed an in-depth, real-time study of thirty-four competitors in the Observer Transatlantic race (forerunner of the OSTAR and Transat races). Each competitor was designated by a letter A to Z. (See Bibliography on page 233 for the full citation for this and other quoted matter in this book.)

Sailing in general is an exhilarating activity most of the time. However, when a man has to spend hours on end at the helm, is cold, soaked through, seasick, hungry, uncertain about his ability to handle the boat in all conditions, and does not know his position, he is liable to make mistakes observing lights and landmarks, reading his charts, and planning rational courses of action. This is borne out by numerous personal accounts reported to me, and is in line with experimental work on the effects of fatigue on performance.

Visual Disturbances

R reported on day 10: "Spots before my eyes when looking at the sky. I feel my tactics in staying south and east so long may have backfired with this weather and more or less put me out of the competitive race." He was sleeping adequately but feeling tense and physically uncomfortable. On day 26 "spots before my eyes again. Not serious and only occasional. I think I've been spoiled by all that calm weather. Conditions have not been all that rough but I'm really exhausted."

Day 35: "Usual spots before eyes when tired. Three days of gales and storms. Very miserable. Poor progress." He had little sleep during this period, made errors in navigation and sail handling. A tape recording made at the time records his distress and despair in the most poignant fashion.

T was setting his twin foresails for the first time in the race at about noon on day 33 in good visibility when he saw an object in the water. "A baby elephant," he thought. "A funny place to put a baby elephant." A little later, looking at the same object: "A funny place to put a Ford Popular." He accepted these observations without question until on closer inspection he realized that the object was a whale. This occurred three days before arrival, and he was feeling alert, just trying out a maneuver for the first time.

Much more complex visual experiences were reported in the qualifying trip. K had been continuously at the helm for 56 hours because of bad conditions and was making do with only occasional snacks. He saw his father-in-law at the top of the mast. They were aware of one another's presence, and the experience was in no way alarming.

Sailing his 52-foot trimaran up from the Bay of Biscay around Ushant, A could not put into any harbor west of St. Malo, and because of the treacherous coast and the shipping he could get little rest. Further he had only one day's food remaining, to last for six days. He was lying on his bunk when he heard a man putting the boat about on to the other tack. He had "seen" nothing at that point, but when he went up on deck to investigate, the man passed him in the passageway coming down as he went up. The boat had indeed been put about and was on the correct course.

Amongst singlehanders the difference between sleeping and waking was often blurred, even when apparently well rested, so what was a premonition while awake and what was a dream dreamed in sleep was hard to distinguish.

What is striking are the frequency and range of the psychological phenomena reported. Taken out of context, they might be said to provide evidence of severe mental disorder, but what is their significance in context? Is there something special about the business of singlehanded sailing that makes such phenomena common, or are they due to some peculiarity in the sailors themselves?

Experimental work on sensory deprivation and sleep deprivation shows that gross disorders of perception and thinking processes can be produced quite reliably. Further, these reactions are more likely if the subject is fatigued or anxious. The sustained exposure to the elements, the seasickness, and a lack of nourishment certainly contribute to the development of fatigue. Sensory deprivation also occurred, but mainly in the form of seduced patterning. The whine of wind in the rigging, the steady noise of the waves, the lack of anything on the surface of the sea or in the sky, especially in foggy conditions, all reduce the sensory input and increase the likelihood of the development of visual and auditory experience from within.

Published accounts of perceptual disturbances which would lead the subject to disaster suggest that insight generally prevents total destruction. For instance, a very weary sailor on another occasion was close to the Belgian coast and saw two men on the shore beckoning him and pointing to the harbor entrance. He did not go in for some reason but anchored offshore. In the morning he woke after a long sleep to find only rocks along that stretch of coast. On the other hand one is not likely to have many records from the very fatigued whose insight was totally suspended.

It is hoped that those who have to maintain a high level of function in adverse physical conditions will come to recognize the subtle ways fatigue can place them at risk and take measures to protect themselves.

Hallucinations

Hallucinations are fairly common among single-handers. This is a predictable byproduct of lack of sleep and an unfamiliar environment. During the Singlehanded Transpac, I climbed on deck in the middle of the night to find three men crouched at the bow as I sailed down a river in Germany. They were ignoring my commands. After a couple of minutes I sat down in the cockpit and realized that something was wrong. I gained hold of my senses and thought, "Wow, that must be an hallucination."

During the 2002 Transpac, Mark Deppe reported:
I had my first set of lucid dreams in awhile last night. A lucid dream is unlike any normal kind of dream. It is so vivid and detailed that it is very close to being awake. But the most interesting aspect is that the dreamer is aware that he is dreaming, and can control how the dream develops.

I've only experienced lucid dreams a handful of times, and most always on a boat or ship after a week or so. In my case, being extremely fatigued helps initiate the special conditions required to enter the lucid state, since you must remain aware of the fact you are dreaming without actually waking up. It's a very fine line. The dream rivals reality in how detailed and lifelike it is. My favorite thing to do while lucid dreaming is to fly. Since I can control any aspect

of the dream, I can move my body about freely without any of the normal constraints of gravity. Fun stuff.

The famous psychologist Carl Jung was himself a sailor and often used boating analogies. Dr. Matthew Fike included an entire chapter about singlehanded sailors in his 2014 book *The One Mind: C.G. Jung and the Future of Literary Criticism.*
The unconscious is to the sea as consciousness is to a boat; those who wish to make psychological progress must dip their oars into the unknown. . . . Messages from the depths filter up to consciousness because solitude on the sea is conducive to psychic phenomena. . . . Solitary voyage on the sea removes barriers between the conscious mind and the unconscious. Quoting from Jung's work, "It is something that we cannot tell anybody. We are afraid of being accused of mental abnormality—not without reason, for much the same thing happens to lunatics. . . . Isolation causes an activation of the unconscious, and this produces something similar to the illusions and hallucinations that beset lonely wanderers in the desert, seafarers, and saints."

Fike continues:
The wanderer is unable to tell anyone about his inner pain because that degree of self-revelation is not part of the Anglo-Saxon warrior's heroic ethic. Repression is the rule, but spending time alone on the sea causes an activation of the unconscious, which enables the repressed material to surface as hallucinations. These are shadowy personifications of the unconscious and weird ghostly shadows that flit about in place of people, but their appearance means that the wanderer is moving toward momentous alteration of his personality.

A common parallel is that many lone sailors have experienced an undeniable inner order to wake up when their boats have been in danger, usually from an approaching ship. Such an order indicates that the isolation and sensory deprivation of lone voyaging enable, exactly as Jung recognized, greater communication between the conscious mind and the unconscious. Here again is ostensibly objective evidence that an unconscious process responds to an actual physical condition. It is not just that the unconscious is the portal to all knowledge but also that some higher part of oneself—an aspect of oneself normally hidden from consciousness—has an investment in the physical body and does not want it to be crushed by the hull of a passing ship.

Hearing Voices

While crossing the Pacific, I heard distinct voices inside the boat. It sounded like a group of people having a conversation in a foreign language, as if over a radio broadcast. I have never had this experience with short voyages, so it is not simply because of water on the hull. Fatigue must play a role.

This is a very common phenomenon on long-distance voyages, as Mark Deppe, aboard the J/120 *Alchera*, wrote in the 2008 Transpac logs:

I've started hearing voices again. Seems to happen every Transpac at some point. I could swear there's a radio with a talk show tuned in, located somewhere in the forward berth under the spinnaker that I have spread to dry from the last dunking it took. And in the sound of the water going by outside the hull, I hear what sounds like party conversations going on very faintly.

In the 2010 race, Deppe wrote about a similar experience:

Got to go, it sounds like there's an argument going on in the forward berth, and someone else is knocking on the outside of the hull for attention. There's another voice that keeps saying "Got Milk?" "Got Milk?" over and over again, I wish it would get its milk and shut up.

Al Hughes, sailing on the Open 60 *Dogbark*, reported that he heard things, too:

Dogbark has had a relatively slow trip for her so far, but the skipper is showing signs of cracking. I remember this from the first trip,

I start hearing things, like a radio playing or voices in the background. After a while you can start talking to them, strange but true. I guess it is a little bit of sleep deprivation, near constant stress, and limited contact with others. It sounds like the solo sailor's lament or dream, depending.

I know of one skipper who searched his boat for stowaways during the 2006 Transpac.

In his second study (see Bibliography, page 233), Glin Bennet carefully analyzed the stresses faced by Donald Crowhurst in his ill-fated attempt in the first around-the-world-race. Bennet based his study on the research in the book *The Strange Last Voyage of Donald Crowhurst* by Nicholas Tomalin and Ron Hall:

It is perhaps the most completely documented account of a psychological breakdown. His [Crowhurst's] speculative writings begin proper off the southern part of South America while he is waiting to "re-enter" the race. He becomes aware of the tremendous reception awaiting him, the BBC coming out to meet him, and he finally retreats from reality altogether. Until the last few days of course he is sailing his boat competently and navigating with adequate precision, and later when he was apparently totally preoccupied with his thoughts he was able to send messages in Morse code concerning his arrival home. These are all relatively complex tasks which one might not expect of someone as detached from reality as presumably Crowhurst was. Or does it mean that someone apparently absorbed with their own thoughts does have a greater ability to switch back into contact than is generally supposed?

On the whole, the evidence points to a breakdown in the face of an utterly impossible situation: a tumultuous homecoming with national television and radio coverage as the winner of a unique contest, through a deception that was certain to be discovered. The disgrace would be too big for many to bear, but for Donald Crowhurst this was to have been the triumphal moment of a life that until now had been marked by many false starts and failures. This success had possibly been achieved in his mind from the moment he first thought of circumnavigation. The realities of the voyage had proved too much for him, and when after the first fortnight of the voyage success seemed to be slipping out of reach, he began to manipulate the realities until he had adjusted the world to match his requirements. Then in his mind he gained mastery over the world, over the universe, over god, until there was no longer any point in remaining in the world which most people regard as real.

One of the functions of tragedy in the theater is to present an intensified view of ordinary life. With the story of Donald Crowhurst we have such a story but, alas, one that is true. The crisis and the breakdown occurred on the high seas, but the steps which led to it in the first place and the remorseless way in which he became more firmly caught in the trap are clearly discernible, and the parallels with ordinary life are not hard to find. *Individuals will make their own interpretations, but one powerful message that comes through from this story is the need to provide those in distress with the opportunity to express their real feelings when all around them the barriers are going up and the avenues of escape are closing.*

Read the second half of the last paragraph one more time, just to absorb it again.

I strongly recommend that every singlehander read *The Strange Last Voyage of Donald Crowhurst* and *The Long Way* by Bernard Moitessier. I have never seen an instance where the line between insanity and genius was so fine.

H.E. Lewis and coauthors undertook a detailed, real-time study of the participants in the 1960 Observer Singlehanded Trans-Atlantic Race from Plymouth, England, to New York, United States, and reported:

The men have certain features of reported mood pattern in common. On the whole they tended consistently to be calm and relaxed rather than irritable and excitable, to feel keen to do well

rather than regretful at having started, and to be confident rather than scared.

There is even more resemblance among the men in the pattern of interrelation between their moods than there is in the mood profile itself. Thus the positively toned emotions tended consistently to occur together, and likewise the negatively toned ones. Calmness, relaxation, self-sufficiency, keenness, confidence, and physical freshness were closely related to each other in all the records, and conversely excitability, irritability, tension, boredom, loneliness, exhaustion, and fear waxed and waned together.

There are three important concepts to understand from the study. First is that positive emotions build on themselves to create even greater positive emotions; likewise negative emotions build on themselves to create even worse negative emotions. The "highs" are higher and the "lows" are lower.

Second, while the highs are wonderful, it is important to get a handle on the lows. I strongly suggest that on long-distance voyages, every skipper understand the practice of mindfulness discussed in detail in Chapter 15.

Third, the very reason we undertake this bizarre thing called singlehanded sailing is to experience all of its wonder—both the good and the bad. At the end of a particularly intense emotional outburst, the skipper should think to himself, "Oh, this is what Andy was talking about. I'm a real singlehanded sailor now." A skipper cannot join the pantheon of greats until he has faced and overcome an emotion never experienced before. It's every bit as important as launching a chute in 30 knots.

Neil Weston and coauthors performed a detailed psychological assessment of five singlehanded sailors entered into the 2006–07 Velux 5 Oceans round-the-world race. They report:

All skippers stated that poor yacht performance as a result of light winds was one of the most difficult stressors to deal with.

Although much of the responsibility for the poor progress lay outside their control, skippers would spend a lot of time and energy trying to find wind and get the yacht moving. These efforts would subsequently result in less sleep, greater physical exhaustion, and emotional instability.

As noted above, singlehanders face their greatest stress not in storms but rather in calms. I believe that David Maister's study on waiting is applicable:

Uncertain Waits Are Longer than Known, Finite Waits. The most profound source of anxiety in waiting is how long the wait will be. For example, if a patient in a waiting room is told that the doctor will be delayed thirty minutes, he experiences an initial annoyance but then relaxes into an acceptance of the inevitability of the wait. However, if the patient is told the doctor will be free soon, he spends the whole time in a state of nervous anticipation, unable to settle down, afraid to depart and come back. The patient's expectations are being managed poorly.

A good example of the role of uncertainty in the waiting experience is provided by the "appointment syndrome." Clients who arrive early for an appointment will sit contentedly until the scheduled time, even if this is a significant amount of time in an absolute sense (say, thirty minutes). However, once the appointment time is passed, even a short wait of, say, ten minutes, grows increasingly annoying. The wait until the appointed time is finite; waiting beyond the point has no knowable limit.

Solo Waits Feel Longer than Group Waits. One of the remarkable syndromes to observe in waiting lines is to see individuals sitting or standing next to each other without talking or otherwise interacting until an announcement of a delay is made. Then the individuals suddenly turn to each other to express their exasperation, wonder collectively what is happening, and console each other. What this illustrates is that there is some form of comfort in group waiting rather than waiting alone.

The most successful predator introduced to hunt down unproductive and anxiety-producing wait times has been the Blackberry. Aptly dubbed the "Crackberry" by some, this device lets people be productive in the most naturally unproductive locations, like waiting in line. I guess this would apply to text messaging on phones or other things that can be done silently in lines.

These studies indicate that calms of indeterminate length cause the greatest stress to singlehanders. With a crew there are others to talk and joke with. By oneself there is nothing that can be done to improve the situation. A simple, inexpensive hand-held video game might be the best solution to this problem. A small game of Tetris can keep one occupied for hours.

Neil Weston and coauthors provided the following as stress-coping mechanisms from their study:

Using social support (e.g., team, family, friends, supporters, organizers) enabled skippers to deal with the difficult environmental conditions, isolation, and possible threat stressors. Anshel (1996) suggested that such emotion-focused coping approaches are more likely under low perceived controllability situations. Nevertheless, although the present findings provide partial support for this assertion, the skippers also employed other problem solving (e.g., staying calm), appraisal (e.g., rationalizing the situation), and approach-focusing efforts (on controllable factors) to deal with these uncontrollable environmental stressors.

Boredom

Surprisingly, boredom can set in even when sailing conditions are perfect and the boat is moving at top speed. I was very bored in the steady trade winds a few days out of Hawaii. The boat was steering itself perfectly. There were no steps that I could take to increase performance, so I had nothing to do. During an afternoon radio chat, one of the other skippers mirrored my thoughts exactly when he commented, "I never expected to be so bored."

A skipper is advised to bring numerous books on any voyage. Modern society does not train us how to sit still and do nothing. It is much more difficult than most people know.

I have found tremendous relief by listening to audio books. The website www.librivox.org contains thousands of classic books in the public domain and free to download. I will never have a chance to actually read massive volumes such as the 1,946 pages in 135 chapters of *Moby-Dick*. But I was very happy to listen to it over 24 hours, 37 minutes. Another fascinating book was *The Eventful History of the Mutiny and Piratical Seizure of H.M.S. Bounty: Its Causes and Consequences* running 10½ hours. Both of these go well beyond their movie versions. Virtually all of the classic novels can be found at Librivox, and skippers will find them welcome friends on long voyages.

Emotional Inertia

"Fear paralysis" is a well-understood phenomenon in which a person is in such fear that he or she is unable to move. I know of one sailor who experienced this during the famous Fastnet storm. He was so paralyzed that his crew moved him below, where he simply curled up on the bunk for the duration of the storm.

I have developed a different theory that seems to be applicable to singlehanded sailors or others who perform dangerous tasks alone. This theory is based on my own experience and what I have learned from others. "Emotional inertia" occurs in a highly stressful situation in unfamiliar circumstances. The result of the inertia is that the singlehander continues to actively sail the present course and hope for the best, even if the course will lead to certain doom, rather than take a potentially dangerous action required to resolve the situation.

There are three keys to recognize in this situation. First, the singlehander continues to actively sail the boat, trim the sails, and steer the present course.

Second, the present course will lead to certain doom. There is no question, at least in the skipper's mind, that the course will lead to a very bad, dangerous, or even life-threatening situation. Sailing into a rock, losing the rig, and so on are perfect examples of this type of situation.

Third, the skipper is unwilling or unable to take whatever action is necessary to rectify the situation because of a fear of the danger of that action. The skipper simply "hopes for the best." In some cases the required action will be extreme, but with foresight it is still preferable to the doom that will result on the existing course. Note that I said "with foresight." What matters is that the skipper perceives that doom is certain.

The best example is a boat heading for rocks in high winds. The only way to avoid the rocks is to gybe, but this action will bring the boat even closer to the rocks before sailing clear. The skipper must make an immediate choice between the certainty of hitting the rocks in 3 minutes or gybing with the potential of hitting the rocks immediately or hopefully sailing clear. But the skipper faces emotional inertia. Unable to make the choice to gybe, the skipper sails on to doom on the rocks.

I've included this concept because a sailor who is aware of the concept of emotional inertia will be able to avoid it. When facing this type of dilemma, the skipper should think for a moment, "This must be that emotional inertia problem. I'd better snap out of it and do something!"

I have faced the rocks dilemma twice in my sailing career. The first time I was unwilling to gybe and ran on the rocks. After developing the theory of emotional inertia, the second time I was aware of the dilemma and did an immediate gybe and sailed clear.

As one becomes more skilled, the starting point for emotional inertia moves further out on the scale but still remains in effect. Following are two examples involving highly skilled sailing experts. I believe that they faced emotional inertia in what can only be described as the most extreme circumstances.

Derek Hatfield faced emotional inertia approaching Cape Horn, as described in the book *Sea of Dreams* by Adam Mayers:

As dawn broke on Friday, March 7, Hatfield saw a red light winking ahead to his right, about two and a half miles away. He had been at the helm for almost twenty-four hours and was so exhausted he could barely think, so he was not able to comprehend immediately what his eyes were telling him. As the realization sank in, fear squeezed the breath from his lungs. He would later say this moment was the most terrifying in his life. "It still makes me shiver thinking about it," he says.

Hatfield knew he was looking at the glow of a lighthouse. But if this was the Horn, the lighthouse should be on his left, not his right. If it was the Horn, it meant he was driving towards assured destruction, for to the left there could only be the jagged shards of volcanic rock. Driven by hurricane force winds, he would be dead very quickly, joining the thousands of others who had perished here.

Over the next fifteen to twenty minutes, the red circle of light drew closer as *Spirit of Canada* surfed barepoled towards its fate. The light transfixed Hatfield, and he wondered whether these were his last moments on earth. He tried to change course and sail towards the light in the hope that as he got closer he would be able to see it more clearly and maneuver around it. But try as he might, he couldn't do it. This wind and wave combination was such that as he altered his course the waves threatened to capsize his boat. When collision seemed certain, the light slipped by and receded into the night. . . . He had passed the Diego Ramirez Islands, a small chain of rocky outcrops . . . thirty miles west of the horn.

I believe that Pete Goss also experienced emotional inertia, as he described in his fantastic book *Close to the Wind*:

An hour later the wind suddenly increased . . . up to forty knots . . . I would never be able to reduce sail in time—the boat was on edge and it would be too much to ask the autopilot. . . . The front two thirds of the boat was out of the water, the bow was up and she was touching twenty-seven knots as the gusts swept in from nowhere. . . . What a prat! I was trapped by my own stupidity. She was over canvassed and yet there was no way I could put the boat back on autopilot so that I could go forward and reduce

sail. All I could do was helm and hope for the best . . . whatever happened now I must keep clear of the runner—the rig was going to go for sure.

[Note that I had included "hope for the best" in my emotional inertia theory before reading Goss's account.] A few hours later Goss's boat did a Chinese gybe and broached, pinning the mast to the water. Luckily the rig survived, but the spinnaker was destroyed. Continuing the story:

I was determined to make the most of the experience. As the last tatter of spinnaker disappeared into the hatch—£4,500 down the drain, I decided I wouldn't be so stupid again.

Given the very high probability of losing the rig under these conditions (certain doom), it might have been better to take some other action while reducing sail in a somewhat orderly manner, but Goss had only "hoped for the best."

I can only think of a person being led to a firing squad. Any action, any action at all, is preferable to this certain doom. Contrary to what the movies show, there is no dignity in being shot. When we are alone on a boat, we don't even need to consider how an action might look to others.

The problem of emotional inertia is less likely on crewed boats because at least one member of the crew will step up and make the necessary suggestion that leads to a decision. But this is the type of situation where the singlehander should slap himself across the face and "snap out of it!"

SLEEP

Sleep is one of the most discussed topics in singlehanding. Most of us can stay awake 24–36 hours on a short voyage, but for anything longer, sleep is a necessity.

For a beginning singlehander, going belowdeck itself can be a challenge. We have grown accustomed to driving a car, where we don't take our eyes off the road for more than 3 seconds. How could we possibly sleep while the boat continues to move?

I suggest that a new singlehander practice going below during short afternoon trips, even when there is really no reason at all. He or she should go below for 5 minutes at a time to perform a specific task, like checking the charts, making coffee, or practicing knots. He must resist the urge to stick his head on deck for at least 5 minutes. After a few days of this, the time belowdeck can be increased to 20 minutes while cooking an entire meal—and eating it. Do not use any electronic monitoring during this period. Turn off the radar, AIS, or Sea-Me active radar transponder. It takes a person time to become accustomed to sailing on faith alone for 20 minutes, but it must be done. Electronic monitoring aids are just that—aids. They must not become crutches and must not supplant the skipper's instincts.

One piece of advice is that if the skipper can hear the motor of a ship, he should look around. Whales may be able to hear ships 50 miles away, but humans can hear ships only half a mile away.

Once the skipper has become accustomed to 20 minutes below, a duration during which he could have run into any amount of floating debris, the idea of spending an hour or more below without looking around becomes less stressful. At this point the electronics can be reactivated. It has long been held that it would take 20 minutes for a ship to come over the horizon and hit a sailboat. So this is as long as one should sail on faith alone.

Approaches to Sleep

It is well known that a person cannot "store" sleep in a bank to use at a later date. However, it is highly advisable for a singlehander to get the most sleep possible for two nights before a voyage to be well rested when leaving the dock. Studies have shown that athletic performance is determined more by the quantity and quality of sleep taken two days, rather than one day, in advance of an event. Based on this, I make sure to get at least two very good nights of sleep before any voyage. This means that I do not drink any alcohol in these days (alcohol keeps me awake), I get to bed early (I am a lark-type sleeper rather than an owl), and I will even take a sleeping pill so that I sleep soundly all through the night. I make sure that my boat is fully prepared two days in advance to reduce stress, and I definitely avoid the prerace parties that most sailors attend.

I know that adrenaline will keep me from sleeping the first night at sea when I will probably be in a high-traffic area anyway. Starting the voyage well rested ensures that missing one night of sleep is not debilitating.

Once underway, a common method of keeping watch is to get out of the bunk every 20–30 minutes to take a quick look around the horizon and at the compass, then go back to sleep again. The idea is to get back to the bunk before becoming completely awake so that it is easy to fall back into deep sleep. This is much like a land-bound person waking in the middle of the night to urinate, then climbing back into bed and back to sleep. With this technique, the skipper is not intending to work the boat at all but is simply checking for hazards. I use this technique, and Derek Hatfield used it in the 2002 Around Alone race; he set an alarm at 20 minutes. He would wake up, check around the boat, then go back to sleep for another 20 minutes. After a few days he found the alarm unnecessary.

I use three tips to make this technique workable. First, I find that getting out of, and back into, a sleeping bag in my cramped bunk belowdeck requires too much effort. It takes too long and tends to bring me fully awake. So I have set up a sitting hammock in the cockpit made from a sailbag (see photo next page). This is a very comfortable place for me to sleep, facing backward with my head against the main hatchway and my bum just slightly above the cockpit sole. In this position I barely need to move to look all around at the horizon. I can also reach the autopilot and all three sheets to make small adjustments if necessary. Modern singlehanded racing boats have built-in cockpit houses to cover the skipper next to the hatchway for the same purpose. I have taken voyages of up to five days sleeping only in my hammock.

Second, I have a small kitchen alarm clipped to my harness. It is important that the alarm automatically resets to 20 minutes after each activation. If it takes concentration to reset the alarm, once again it wakes me too much.

Third, I eliminate electronics that might wake me unnecessarily. The ocean is a really big place. I don't care if a ship passes 20 miles away or even

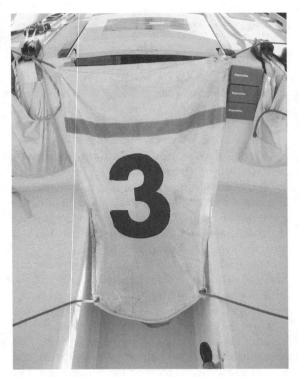

My cockpit sleeping hammock, made out of an old sailbag, faces aft and allows me to reach the autopilot and sheets should minor adjustments be necessary.

5 miles away. I only want to know if a ship is passing less than 1 mile away. Radar and AIS alarms should be set for the skipper's own level of comfort. This also refers to the autopilot's wind-shift alarm. My autopilot has a built-in 15 degrees wind-shift alarm that can't be adjusted. I have found this to be too tight a range. On a gusty run, the wind will shift back and forth by 15 degrees many times during the night. All these electronic alarms not only wake the skipper, but keep him nervously on guard, waiting for the next alarm. This problem led to my hallucinations during the 2006 Singlehanded Transpac. I have since disconnected the wind-shift alarm altogether.

Polyphasic Sleep

Dr. Claudio Stampi is considered the world's greatest expert on polyphasic sleep for singlehanded sailors. Through his Chronobiology Research Institute he has lectured many times on this topic, and his methodology is often used by top-performing racers. The two basic ideas behind this technique are reducing the total time sleeping each day from a normal 8 hours to 5 hours or less, and sleeping in short naps with productive times between naps. (Note: It is important to read this entire section, including the rebuttals to Stampi's techniques. Hallucinations are a wonderful thing!)

Ellen MacArthur was one of those racers using Stampi's method, as described in "MacArthur is Caught Not Napping" (*The Sunday Times*, January 20, 2005):

> The ocean never sleeps and nor does Ellen MacArthur. At least, that is how it seems during her race to become the fastest sailor to circumnavigate the world singlehanded. . . . Sleep represents something of a Catch 22; she knows that she must sleep in order to achieve the mental and physical condition to keep making good time but that each time she does, she is losing time.
>
> MacArthur wears a monitoring device on her arm and the data is sent to Boston to be analyzed by Claudio Stampi, the chrono-biologist with whom she has worked for the past five years.
>
> From the start, on November 30, until January 12, she averaged 5.54 hours sleep a day. But from January 6 to the 12th, MacArthur averaged just 3.9 hours. "Under normal circumstances this would already represent quite a sacrificed sleep allowance in comparison to the two-week transatlantic race in 2000, where Ellen averaged 4.2 hours per day," Stampi said. "But this low sleep quota will have an even more dramatic impact on someone who is particularly fatigued having been at sea for 50 days."
>
> MacArthur's sleep patterns are usually feverish, mostly divided into ten or 20 minutes, but napping is one of her strategies. According to Stampi, for the 94 days of the Vendée Globe in 2000–01, MacArthur averaged 5.7 hours sleep a day, divided into nine naps. "When you have to go from an average of 7½ hours a day to Ellen's average of 5½," Stampi said, "we have seen from many experiments that it is actually better to divide those fewer hours into multiple naps." . . .

Another of Stampi's suggestions is the "Sunday Strategy; that is the strategy of once a week, declaring a different day—like a vacation day, or half-day," Stampi said. "That is both psychologically as well as from a sleep perspective. Sleep seems to be extremely plastic. One day is enough to put you back to a very good level.

"Ellen, from a sleep physiology perspective, is a normal person. Where she is exceptional is in her drive and discipline. You will never find a day without sleep with Ellen. Not every sailor can do that. Some will stay a day, two, sometimes three, without sleep at all. The benefits of even a short nap are disproportionate to the duration."

According to Mayers in *Sea of Dreams*, Brad Van Liew used this technique in the 2002 Around Alone race. Brad had taken part in a sleep study at Harvard University Medical School, where he learned that he could operate in the eightieth percentile of alertness with just 4½ hours of sleep. During the race he had a 45-minute sleep every 4 hours.

Dr. Stampi teaches sailors how to perform best on minimal sleep. The secret is learning how to power nap ("pulling an Einstein"). His research included base-testing cognitive performance with a normal 8-hour sleep. Then he had all subjects shift to 3-hour routines, divided into three groups. A month later, the group that had one long sleep of 3 hours showed a 30% loss in cognitive performance. The group that divided its sleep between nighttime and short naps showed a 25% drop. But the polyphasic group, which slept exclusively in short naps, showed only a 12% drop.

Stampi divides sleep into REM sleep (important for memory and learning) and non-REM sleep (restores energy). Non-REM sleep itself has four stages: one, light slumber; two, the onset of real sleep (heart rate and breathing slow); three and four, deep (slow-brainwave) sleep that is most restorative.

Sleepers generally follow a 90-minute cycle through these stages with REM between each cycle. Under this theory, the body needs slow-wave sleep first and achieves this in the first 3 hours. If only 4 hours of sleep are possible, the body will still achieve 95% of slow-wave sleep while missing most of the REM and stage-two sleep.

This suggests that slow-wave sleep is the most critical. That sleep is more valuable at the beginning of the sleep cycle than at the end. So a singlehander who takes more naps is recharging more efficiently than with a single longer sleep.

Stampi notes that a skipper must nap wisely by tailoring times and lengths to the body's particular requirements. For example, sleep peaks normally occur in midafternoon and early morning, but it is not desirable to sleep in the early evening. This made scientific sense to him: humans tend to feel sleep pressure at those times.

His research showed that afternoon naps had the most valuable slow-wave sleep, important for recharging the body. Sailors should try to get at least some of their quota then. Skippers should try to get their body "in phase" and cycle accordingly, so that no time is wasted simply lying in the bunk with eyes wide open.

According to the testing, there are two types of people: morning people, or "larks," and evening people, or "owls." Larks are good at taking short naps but are not as efficient at night and prefer a regular routine. Owls appear to cope better with irregular schedules but prefer longer naps. For example, Ellen MacArthur is a lark and tends to spend 60% of her sleep in naps of less than an hour. Mike Golding, on the other hand, is an owl. Only 23% of his sleep time was devoted to naps of less than an hour. But both sleep about the same amount while racing, between 4.5 and 5.5 hours on average.

An excellent video on Claudio Stampi and polyphasic sleep is available on YouTube. Search for "Polyphasic sleep study."

It is difficult to jump into polyphasic sleep on the first day of a long voyage. Here are some techniques for adapting to a polyphasic sleeping schedule, adapted from www.sleepingschedules.com:

- Determine a personal circadian cycle, i.e., when the body wants to sleep and when it wants to be active. Every person has an individual circadian rhythm with peaks and dips in alertness, when they are normally asleep and normally awake. This forms the basis of sleep times in the polyphasic system. As mentioned above, most people are a lark or an owl.

- Staged transition: Some have found that staging the transition over three to nine days helps them adapt. Start with one (shorter than usual) core sleep at night and one afternoon nap. Move to two sleeps at night separated by a task, along with the afternoon nap. Increase to three sleeps, etc., depending on lark or owl status.
- Core sleep is the one longer sleep period each 24 hours. Most researchers suggest that this be when the skipper normally goes to sleep. For example, I (a lark) normally go to bed at 10 P.M. and can fall asleep in just a few minutes.
- Use an alarm to wake up, and never sleep past the alarm.
- Turn on a bright light to activate the body when waking. This simulates morning. Get out of the bunk immediately. Do not stay in the bunk and daydream, even if awake.
- Do not attempt to sleep between 6 P.M. and 8 P.M. Stampi refers to this as the "forbidden zone." He suggests that our ancient ancestors used this period to ensure safety before sleeping, so it is instinctive that we not sleep during this period.
- Avoid caffeine before scheduled sleep. It is important not to miss a sleep period if it will lead to reduced performance later.

The polyphasic approach does have critics. As reported in a paper by John Caldwell, the U.S. military has studied fatigue countermeasures:

Each individual nap should be long enough to provide at least 45 continuous minutes of sleep, although longer naps (2 hours) are better. In general, the shorter each individual nap is, the more frequent the naps should be. The objective remains to acquire a daily total of 8 hours of sleep.

The Canadian Marine Pilot's trainer's handbook also expresses concerns:

Under extreme circumstances where sleep cannot be achieved continuously, research on napping shows that 10- to 20-minute naps at regular intervals during the day can help relieve some of the sleep deprivation and thus maintain minimum levels of performance for several days. However, researchers caution that levels of performance achieved using short naps to temporarily replace normal sleep are always well below that achieved when fully rested.

Dr. Piotr Wozniak has studied polyphasic sleep and does not believe it is possible to perform adequately using Stampi's techniques. Another excellent counterview is expressed in a video on YouTube titled "Polyphasic Sleep Experiment," where the best line is "I can't tell if I've been getting sleep or not. I don't know. I might be. I've got memory gaps. I want some pancakes."

The following is excerpted from http://ftp.super-memo.com/articles/polyphasic.htm:

The theory behind the polyphasic sleep is that with some effort, we can entrain our brain to sleep along the ancient polyphasic cycle and gain lots of waking time on the way, mostly by shedding the lesser important stages of sleep.

EEG measurements indicate that humans are basically biphasic. There is a single powerful drive to sleep during the night and a single dip in alertness in the middle of the day. The cycle can be prodded and shifted slightly on a daily basis. The degree of the shift requires a precise timing of the phase-shifting stimulus. In other words, with a stimulus such as light, physical activity, or social interaction, we can move the period of maximum sleepiness slightly. Although the precise measurements speak of the possible shift of up to 3 hours in a single day with a single strong stimulus, it is hard, in practice, to shift one's circadian rhythm by more than 1 hour per day.

An increasing portion of the population use the alarm clock to do the job that should naturally by done by sunlight. This is not a healthy solution and is usually forced by our electrically lit lifestyle with evening TV, evening reading, evening Internet, evening partying, etc.

The well-defined effects of natural sleep affecting stimuli on sleep patterns lead to an instant conclusion: the claim that humans can adapt to any sleeping pattern is false. A sudden shift in the schedule, as in shift work, may lead to a catastrophic disruption of sleep control mechanisms.

It appears that polyphasic sleep encounters the precisely same problems as seen in jet lag or shift-work. The human body clock is not adapted to sleeping in patterns other than monophasic or biphasic sleep. In other words, the only known healthy alternatives are: (1) a single 6–8 hour sleep block in the night, or (2) a night sleep of 5–7 hours combined with a 15–90 min. siesta nap.

Through sleep deprivation, polyphasic sleepers can increase the number of naps during the day to three. However, the pattern of one night sleep and three daily naps is highly unstable and can be maintained only with a never-ending degree of sleep deprivation.

The above findings lead to a conclusion that it is not possible to maintain a polyphasic sleep schedule and retain high alertness and/or creativity!

The answer to the question "to sleep or not to sleep polyphasically" will depend on your goals and your chosen criteria. You may want to sleep polyphasically if you want to maximize the frequency of a waking activity (e.g., monitoring the instruments and the horizon in solo yacht racing). Yet you will definitely not want to sleep polyphasically if you want to maximize creative output, alertness, or health. Only when approaching substantial sleep deprivation can a polyphasic schedule be superior to a biphasic schedule in that respect.

Stampi's methods are primarily targeted at minimizing sleep deprivation. When speaking about Ellen MacArthur, he puts his research in a nutshell: "What Ellen is doing is finding the best compromise between her need to sleep and her need to be awake all the time." Stampi has shown that polyphasic sleep can improve cognitive performance in conditions of sleep deprivation as compared with monophasic sleep: Individuals sleeping for 30 minutes every 4 hours, for a daily total of only 3 hours of sleep, performed better and were more alert, compared to when they had 3 hours of uninterrupted sleep. In other words, under conditions of dramatic sleep reduction, it is more efficient to recharge the sleep "battery" more often.

With the above rebuttals in mind, it appears that sleeping in short naps spaced throughout the day is superior to a single sleep of just 3 hours but is still far less than ideal. A polyphasic sleeping schedule might be the best compromise between a need to sleep and a need to be awake, but it is nothing more than that. Given that the very reason a singlehander would use this method is to ensure that the boat remains in control, short naps are what he would want and need anyway. Under stressed conditions, no singlehander is likely to get 3 straight hours of sleep in any case.

THE 3:00 A.M. EFFECT

This is another of my original concepts in the field of human psychology. I think it vital for all singlehanders to understand what I call the 3:00 A.M. effect. I refer to it often in this book and when discussing offshore singlehanding with any group. **The 3:00 A.M. effect refers to the absolutely brainless, blind, clumsy oaf that every skipper becomes at some point in the night.**

For me, this effect occurs between 1 and 4 A.M. For other skippers, it might occur earlier or later depending on their own circadian rhythms. Up until 1:00 A.M., I can function quite normally and make intelligent decisions, even if I am tired. After 4:00 A.M., I can wake up and start my day with full alertness. But between those times, and particularly right at 3:00 A.M., I can barely function.

A couple of things to note. First, when I say "barely function," I am referring to normal activities such as

(continued on page 21)

Here is a poem about my first long-distance race, singlehanded against crewed boats. I was on my Tanzer 22 *Foolish Laughter* on Lac Deschene and the Ottawa River. I was given two mementos for my efforts: the first for hitting three different rocks, the second for being "the keenest sailor in the race."

THE FOOLISH 50 MILES (with apologies to Robert Service)

There are strange things done 'neath the moon and sun
By the men who ply the waves.
Leaving wives at home they face the foam
That will blow them to their graves.

Lac Deschene has seen keen men
But the keenest it ever did see
Was the stalwart Captain of *Foolish Laughter.*
I know him, for that man is me.

It was the ninth month of ought one,
the day the fateful race started.
I said to the wife "Oh, it'll be fun"
As I kissed her and happily parted.

With a promise of rain I raised genny and main
And headed out of the harbour.
But the wind came up fast and struck hard at the mast
As I moved from port tack to the starboard.

"Shorten sail!" yelled the Captain, "Aye Aye!" said the Mate
"We will do whatever we can!"
But the die had been cast when the crew rushed the mast.
For the entire crew was only one man.

The genny was doused and a reef in the main
When I first grounded on that lee shore.
The impact was that of a slow moving train,
And who knew that I'd do it twice more.

I raised centre board up and the boat spun around
When I hit hard rock like a shot.

With the meter destroyed how fast could I go?
I could no longer measure a knot.

A long beat up river, under storm jib and main
I settled down to my course
I had just poured black coffee, when it started to rain.
Oh Lord, could it get any worse.

I raised number one on the down river run.
At surfing the T doesn't fail.
The sky grew quite dark when I rounded S Mark
And then came the crack of the hail.

The wind gusted up to 48 knots
And my heel reached 60 degrees.
The jib came down fast, mainsheet out to the last
As I waited for much calmer seas.

Beating up the North shore, could I take any more
Of the wind and the cold and the hail?
I poured my next cup, taking time to look up
And my gaff hook slipped over the rail.

Many men have faced grief upon Blueberry Reef
And I was to join that fine crowd.
It was more like a shudder, kicking c-board and rudder
The boat moaned, but not really out loud.

Up river again as the darkness it came.
I passed boats loaded with crew.
"A great adventure!" I shouted, they laughed in return.
I still had so much left to do.

Should I have chosen to stop when the genny went "POP"
And parted two feet from the head?
I touched ground once more as I neared the South shore
Seeking shelter from the gusts that I dread.

Pure joy made me shiver racing back down that river
And the moon and the stars did appear.
It was 10:59 when I crossed the end line,
And put away all of my fear.

So what's to become of this brave, naive man.
Will my days be happy ever after?
If you come near the lake bend an ear to the West.
On a clear night in a 10 knot breeze,
You can just make out the sound,
Of *Foolish Laughter.*

checking the sails and making small adjustments, scanning the horizon for hazards, pushing buttons on the autopilot, checking the radar and AIS. These activities are so commonplace to the singlehander that they do not require full wakefulness. Therefore the mind and body simply do not fully wake up.

Think of getting up in the middle of the night to visit the toilet at home. A person can walk to the bathroom, turn on the lights, pee, flush, turn off the lights, walk back to bed, and fall back asleep in an instant. Was that person ever really awake? Would that person have been able to recognize if something minor had changed in the bathroom?

But the 3:00 A.M. effect is overridden in crisis situations. At home, a fire in the middle of the night will bring the person to full wakefulness and full alertness instantly.

The best example I can give of this is what Jessica Watson faced when she collided with a ship (discussed in detail in Chapter 10, See and Be Seen). At 1:46 A.M., Jessica checked her radar and AIS and scanned the horizon, but she failed to see a ship only 1 mile away. Just 4 minutes later, after the collision, Jessica was fully alert and able to make phone calls and radio calls and, more importantly, to take control of her stricken yacht.

During the investigation, Jessica stated categorically that she had not been feeling fatigued. I believe that the 3:00 A.M. effect is not necessarily related to fatigue. It is simply a basic circadian rhythm that tells our body and mind they are not needed. This probably goes back to evolutionary times when humans' predators would most likely attack in the evening and early nighttime hours. At 3:00 A.M. our body and mind shuts off because we are least likely to be attacked by a saber-toothed tiger. What does this mean for the singlehanded sailor? The answer is that he must set up his boat and systems to compensate for his own 3:00 A.M. stupidity. Elsewhere in this book I discuss handling lines to prevent tripping in the middle of the night. I also discuss setting the radar and AIS alarms appropriately.

The real answer is quite simple. Before darkness falls, the singlehander should set up everything on the boat—every sail, every line, every electronic system—so that it can be properly managed by a brainless, blind, clumsy oaf.

In the middle of the afternoon when sailing with the big spinnaker in 30 knots of wind, I consider myself an elite athlete. But when sailing offshore at 3:00 A.M., I have been that brainless, blind, clumsy oaf many times. The only saving grace is that I know it's coming and I set up the boat to compensate.

CHAPTER 3 SAILBOAT DESIGN AND SETUP

WHAT BOAT TO LOOK FOR

The best boat for singlehanding is the one that the skipper already owns. Owning a boat is 80% of the way to singlehanding so in owning a boat, any boat, the skipper has taken the first large step. There is a boat for every budget: the Cal 20 *Black Feathers* was purchased for just $1,000 but completed the Singlehanded Transpac. The first, last, and only criterion for the beginner is to get a boat and get out on the water. Unfortunately, it is virtually impossible to be a singlehander without owning a boat. No one is going to lend a boat to be taken out alone.

The worst boat is the one that will be purchased "next year." I know of too many wannabes who spend their time searching for the perfect boat but never get out on the water. I've had many conversations with these dreamers, asking me what boat they should buy, doing months of research on one boat, then another. It seems they can name every design and model, but they never pull away from the dock. Until they do so, they are only pretenders. But the moment they get out on the water, they can become singlehanded sailors. A person who misses even one season for lack of a boat is a dreamer, not a sailor.

When searching for a boat, the singlehander has a terrific advantage over the crewed boatowner. Most modern boats, built within the past ten years and thus the most expensive, are the least suitable for singlehanding. Older fiberglass boats, built twenty to thirty years ago, have the design features that are best suited to singlehanding. (In Chapter 4 we take a closer look at several high-performance, specialized, and rather expensive boats built specifically for singlehanded racing.)

KEY FEATURES OF A SINGLEHANDING SAILBOAT

The key features of a singlehanding sailboat are outlined in the following sections.

Helm

Choose a tiller rather than a wheel. A tiller is almost a requirement for singlehanding, for several reasons. First, a tiller is designed to be used while sitting; a wheel is designed to be used while standing. There will be times when the singlehander is at the helm for hours on end. The ability to sit is paramount. Second, it is easy to control a tiller between the knees while standing or under a leg while sitting. These techniques are necessary when pulling sheets during a tack or when raising a halyard. Third, a tiller can be operated from the front or side, while a wheel is designed to be used from behind. It takes gymnastic abilities to extricate oneself from behind modern wheels that stretch from rail to rail. The singlehander must be able to move around the cockpit very quickly to control lines. A tiller is preferred regardless of the size of the boat. Even the most modern Class 40 and Open 60 designs include a tiller. Fourth, a windvane works better with a tiller than a wheel. Friction is greatly reduced and the force from the windvane is more directly transmitted to the rudderstock. Finally, a tiller opens up more space in the cockpit and eliminates the cables and quadrant belowdeck that are subject to wear and breakage and take up useful space. At anchor the tiller can be raised vertically, leaving the whole cockpit free.

Cockpit

Choose small rather than large. The singlehander must be able to reach and control all major lines while at the tiller, even if this means stretching forward with the tiller between the knees. Modern racing boats have massive cockpits designed to hold six or eight crewmembers, with winches on the cabintop ten or fifteen feet away from the tiller. These are wholly unsuitable. Older-style cockpits are compact and crowded with just two crew. These are the best choice.

Mast

Choose strong and secure. When things go wrong, a singlehander will put far more stress on the mast than a crewed boat. The boat will broach more often, and there will be times when the spinnaker is dragging in the water. These events are common and must not break the mast. Many modern boats have spindly masts that snap under the slightest pressure.

Single Backstay without Running Backstays

Runners add complexity at the very moment—while tacking or gybing—that the skipper needs simplicity. A runner is allowed only if it does not get in the way during a tack or gybe, even if it is entirely ignored, and if using the runner incorrectly will not cause damage to the sails or mast. At night, in high winds and tight waters, adding two extra lines to a tack or gybe is insane. Modern boat designs seem to add an unending number of control lines. For the singlehander, the fewer lines the better.

Below Deck

Simplicity is best. An amusing feature of modern boat designs is two heads, even on boats less than 40 feet. Some think there must be a head for the owner's family along with a separate head for their guests. Obviously only one head is required for a singlehander. A two-burner stove is ideal, rather than a big galley. A small navigation station with minimal instruments is better than something designed

like the *Starship Enterprise*. Once again, the singlehander prefers a simple boat. This is in contrast to modern complex boat designs, so by its very nature, the ideal singlehander's boat will be less expensive than a comparable crewed boat.

Rudder Design

A key reason why autopilots burn a significant amount of power is that some boat designs are hard to steer. The sad truth is that some boats are too heavy and have poorly designed or unbalanced rudders. One should carefully assess the suitability of a particular boat for long-distance singlehanding before buying it, and a big part of this is the hull/rudder/steering system. Avoid a full-keel, barn-door-rudder bruiser that weighs as much as an island.

BOAT SETUP

Jacklines

I start with jacklines because I consider them the most important gear on my boat. As a serious singlehander, I alone am responsible for my life. I sail in the North Pacific, where the water temperature is never above 12°C (54°F). If I become detached from the boat more than a few hundred yards from shore, I'm dead. It's that simple.

Jacklines should be made from strong, flat webbing. Do not use a rope line or tubular webbing because it will roll under foot. The jacklines must be mounted so that the singlehander can walk from the bow to the stern without unclipping the harness. It is completely unacceptable to use jacklines that require unclipping when passing the shrouds or sheets. On my boat the shrouds are slightly inboard, so I run the jacklines outside the shrouds and jibsheet but inside the lifelines.

The jacklines can run very close to the bow. However, they must stop well short of the stern, so that the skipper will not drag even an inch behind the boat should he start to fall overboard. It is impossible to pull oneself back up a line with the boat moving at 5 knots. Add the length of the tether to the back of the jacklines to see the total length. Then either shorten your tether or shorten the jacklines.

MULTIHULLS

A quick note to say that multihulls require a skill set that is well beyond the scope of this book and, I believe, well beyond the abilities of all but the most experienced singlehanders. The issue is that cats and trimarans have a nasty tendency to flip. Once overturned, there is no way to bring them back upright. Performance multihulls are sailed on the razor's edge. It takes an experienced helmsman to keep them under control. An autopilot cannot reliably perform this role, but singlehanding relies on an autopilot. So there is a necessary contradiction.

Several years ago a major transatlantic race was held with monohulls and multihulls. Although the weather was typical for the race, 40% of the multihulls capsized and required rescue. To me it is puzzling that one would enter a race with a 40% (or even 5%) chance of needing rescue.

As I have mentioned elsewhere, self-sufficiency is the bedrock of singlehanded sailing. The skipper should be able to get to port under all but the most extreme circumstances. I don't believe that an extra strong blast of wind is sufficient reason to require rescue.

Stability on a multihull is a world apart from a monohull—a multihull's heel angle and limits of positive stability are much lower than a monohull's, so the edge they sail on is very narrow, and once they flip they stay inverted, unlike a monohull, which is designed to right itself. *(Courtesy Unlocker.com)*

Because jacklines are such a vital piece of equipment, I suggest leaving them permanently mounted on the boat. Do not remove them after returning to the dock, because the temptation will be to not replace them the next sunny sailing day. Because nylon jacklines deteriorate in the sun, they should be purchased annually.

The Pacific International Yachting Association has set the following standards for jacklines on crewed boats:

Jacklines with a minimum breaking strength of 4,500 pounds (2,040 kg) shall be fitted each side from cockpit to bow such that crew can clip on before leaving the cockpit. Jacklines shall be attached to fittings equal to the full strength of the attached jackline.

Safety snap-on line and harness for each crew member. The recommended assembly shall be ready for use, all components attached. Load-bearing components, including attachment fittings, shall withstand a static load of at least 700 kilograms (1,543 lb.). The safety line shall attach to the harness at chest level and the harness shall support the upper back.

Falling overboard is obviously a rare occurrence. I put out a request to learn about sailors' experiences and received several replies. The following responses come from different skippers and thus may be conflicting.

Craig Horsfield fell off of his Mini Zero during the 2009 Pornichet Select, a 280-mile race off the French Coast. This is a three-day race near shore that crosses fishing grounds, meaning that sleep is virtually impossible. Undoubtedly this added to the problem. "It was not a good experience," Horsfield reported. "The whole thing happened so ridiculously slowly in my mind. It seemed to take forever. You're getting towed along on the leeward side. You try to get back on your boat and you just can't."

It started on the afternoon of the third day, in a beautiful 10-knot breeze. Horsfield walked up to the bow to clear a line before setting the spinnaker. The boat rolled slightly and he fell overboard. "The jib was down because I was setting up for the spinnaker. I thought it was there and you instinctively lean on the sail. I just fell overboard."

Being dragged along, halfway down the starboard side with his tether caught on the shroud base, Horsfield's first act was to tuck his knee up to his chest and pull his boots off. They were completely full of water. Horsfield actually bought boots too large with just such an incident in mind. After this, his life jacket inflated and was limiting his arm reach. He used his knife to puncture and deflate it.

Horsfield realized that if he unclipped his tether and was not able to hold on to a stanchion, he was lost. He was wearing an integrated Spinlock life vest with harness and crotch straps. He could feel the vest pulling up and is quite sure that the crotch straps kept it on.

Eventually, the boat rolled slightly and he was able to get a leg on board. With tremendous effort he pushed himself up over the lifelines. He estimates the event took 10 minutes in total. That's 10 minutes of dragging beside the boat. He always keeps a sealed bag of clothes, and now quickly changed into warm clothing.

In 1999, Harvey Schlasky and a crew member sailed in the Doublehanded Farallones Race out of San Francisco. They had rigged jacklines from pulpit to pushpit the entire length of the boat. When knocked over, the crew member was thrown across the boat and dragged alongside it. He was able to climb back on board. Unfortunately, Schlasky's tether slid to the end of the jacklines, so he was dragged behind the boat and perished.

Several OSTAR sailors also faced challenging overboard experiences. Sailor A says:

In the OSTAR I got washed overboard whilst changing headsails. I was hanging over the upper guardrail—bashing against the hull as we continued at 5 knots under main in around 25 knots of wind. I have a second shorter lifeline on my harness and used this to attach myself under the lower guardrail to the jackstay, before releasing the longer one, and slipped back on board—very quickly! I did have the benefit that a Contessa 32 has a low freeboard.

Sailor B says:

I was washed overboard in a very bad storm on OSTAR 76 about 1,000 miles west of the Scillies. I was hove-to with a storm jib and fully reefed main. My wind-speed indicator (analogue in those days of course) had been on the stops at its limit of 60 knots for most of the night. I was sitting in the cockpit in the early hours, having decided to remove all sail and run under bare poles. I was trying to work out the best way of going about it when a breaking wave knocked down my 32-foot Pioneer 10. She had been coping with the huge waves until the breaking one arrived. I was washed straight over the side as she capsized and when I eventually surfaced, I was very relieved to find my harness was still attached and in one piece. The next problem was to get back on board. I was over the port (lee) side with my tether attached to its anchorage point on the cockpit sole. One option was to work my way round to the stern and use the Aries to climb back aboard but I didn't fancy that as it meant detaching from the lifeline. While pondering the problem, the solution presented itself because the next big wave rolled the boat. I was able to wait for the next wave and when the boat rolled towards me, I grabbed a stanchion base and got a leg on to the boat, then as it rolled upright I slid in under the guardrail.

I was lucky to be able to get back aboard and two things made it possible: 1) the boat was not moving forward as the sails were trashed by the capsize and she had been hove-to; 2) because of the huge waves and the boat being broadside on to them she was rolling heavily. The strange thing is that in a flatter sea, I would have had much greater difficulty getting back aboard.

If a singlehander goes over the side with the boat under way with any forward speed and the boat is being controlled by a windvane or autopilot, it would be nigh on impossible to get back on board without a means of bringing the boat head to wind. With a windvane such as an Aries, one could arrange to have control lines over the stern and bring her head to wind. I can't think of a way to do it under electronic autopilot. It is a nightmare scenario to imagine being over the side and being towed along by a boat doing 6 or 7 knots.

Andrew Bray, editor of *Yachting World* writes:
I have been involved in several man overboard trials. It may seem illogical but it is much easier getting back on a moving boat than a stationary one—unless that is you are unfortunate enough to fall over to windward. There are two reasons for this. 1. The freeboard is less as the boat is heeled towards you. 2. As you are towed on your lifeline your body is on or near the water's surface. Once, when being towed at about 5 knots, I was able to hook an arm and a leg over the rail and roll in under the guard wires. For the AZAB 75 and OSTAR 76 (also in a Pioneer 10) I rigged weighted lines, one each side from about midships to the stern so that when deployed they would hang about two feet below the surface. These were held on deck by some light twine, the theory being that I could reach the line in the water, yank it to break the twine and have a loop in the water to help me step (delicately) back on board. Luckily I never tested it.

Tether

A tether should use proper, strong carabiners like those used by mountain climbers or ones properly made for sailing harnesses. The skipper must be able to clip and unclip the tether quickly, for two reasons. First, if it requires two hands, there will be many times when the skipper forgoes clipping on simply because one hand is busy on the tiller or holding a sheet. I will repeat this sentiment several

times in the book: a singlehander is just as likely to fall off the boat on a nice day, when nothing significant is happening but is just off guard for a fraction of a second, as on a stormy day with high winds when being extra careful. It is on one of those nice days when you might just skip clipping on if it is the least bit difficult. Human nature is such that people will avoid "unnecessary" work unless it is made as simple as possible.

Second, the skipper must be able to unclip with just one hand in situations where the other hand is busy. For example, if the tether gets caught on a cleat in the middle of a spinnaker gybe, it is much easier, and in the end probably safer, to unclip rather than leave the spinnaker pole swinging across the boat. I am not so unrealistic to think that the tether must be worn every second of every voyage. The easier it is to clip on and clip off, the more likely it is that the skipper will wear it more of the time.

Each tether should have two clip points. The long one reaches across the boat or allows the skipper to walk upright. The shorter one is used when sitting or crawling to the bow.

Some boaters insist on locking carabiners. I have no problem with these as long as they can be quickly and easily fastened and unfastened blindly with one hand. In nine years of running all over my boat dragging my tether, I have never had a carabiner detach from the jacklines or my harness, so I don't feel that a locking mechanism is necessary. I have heard of situations where the jackline runs alongside a sheet and the carabiner catches onto the sheet. My suggestion is to move the jackline to a new position where this cannot happen.

Some races insist on a quick-release mechanism for the clip. I disagree with this concept. First, I have never seen a quick-release mechanism that can be easily fastened with one hand. If this can't be done, the tether won't be used for the reasons mentioned above. Second, I cannot imagine any circumstances in which I would want to be detached from the boat. Even if I am thrown overboard and dragging injured beside the boat, this is a much better situation than watching the boat sail away. I can see the safety advantage of a quick release on a crewed boat, but not when singlehanding.

A centerline tether runs behind the mast.

My homemade harness fits me perfectly—it is snug across the chest and crosses with an X on the back.

The tether must be long enough so that the skipper can move from rail to rail in the cockpit without unclipping during normal tacking or gybing. After a tack, it is necessary to unclip from the leeward jackline and clip to the windward jackline in order to walk up the windward side of the boat.

A solution to this is to use two tethers—one clipped on each side of the boat. Both tethers must still be long enough to reach across the boat. After each tack and when settled on the new course, the skipper can just clip onto the windward tether.

A different configuration is to skip the jacklines and use a longer tether fastened to the center of the deck aft of the mast. This tether must be long enough to reach both the bow and stern but once again not so long as to allow the user to drag behind the boat. This system works only if the mainsheet and traveler are on the transom so that the skipper need not unclip for every tack.

A Tether Does No Good If Not Worn

I will say it again, over and over and over. A singlehander is just as likely to fall off the boat on a nice day when nothing significant is happening but is just off guard for a fraction of a second as on a stormy day with high winds when being extra careful. It could be having a loose line roll underfoot or, like Craig Horsfield, leaning against a sail that isn't there. Horsfield agrees with me on this point and he has the hard-earned experience to prove it.

I have listened to many experienced singlehanders say that they wear a tether only in rough weather. These are the same people who don't see the necessity of wearing a seat belt in a car or a helmet on a motorcycle. In my mind, they all equate to the same thing. I am willing to take the risks of singlehanded sailing. But I would feel dammed stupid watching the boat sail off into the North Pacific Ocean because I tripped on a loose sheet.

Lifelines

In my discussions with Craig Horsfield, who had such tremendous difficulty climbing back on board, we realized that wire lifelines were a primary cause of his problem. It was nearly impossible for him to climb over the lifelines. Now that races are allowing for Dyneema or Spectra rope lifelines, this would be a better and safer choice. A singlehander carrying a knife could easily cut the lifelines and roll directly on deck rather than having to push up 18 or 24 inches over the lifelines.

Handrails

A singlehander must be able to work up to the bow, even in very rough conditions. But the distance from the mast to the bow is very much a no-man's land. On a typical boat there is nothing solid to hold onto on the foredeck. Lifelines are not sturdy and do not provide a stable grip. In fact it is very common for singlehanders to avoid the bow during

Handrails like the ones I mounted on the foredeck give sailors a place to hold on to while working on the bow.

a storm, leaving up a jib that is too large for the wind.

A set of handrails mounted on the foredeck will solve this problem. I've mounted handrails along the toe rails on both sides of the boat. I can crawl to the bow under any rough conditions to change the jib for a storm jib.

Sail Control Setup

Lines in General

Crewed sailing boats have made tremendous advances for tuning all aspects of the mast and sails. This has led to an incredible number of control lines mounted around the boat. With a full crew, it is possible to handle these lines, but a singlehander must concentrate only on key lines that create the most significant change. Lines that only offer incremental advantages should be avoided—the skipper does not have the time or energy to manage them all. A small number of lines provide 95% of the control possible from a significantly greater number. The singlehander should accept this 95% and disregard the remainder.

Lines are also a threat to the safety of the sailor. They get tangled at the very instant the skipper is attempting to drop a spinnaker in 30 knots of wind, or they wrap around the skipper's boot when stepping from the cockpit to the cabintop, so the number and length of lines should be reduced as much as possible. Especially at night, lines are a threat everywhere around the boat. It is impossible to eliminate all lines, but it is possible to make them manageable. The only way is to store lines in exactly the same place every time.

Halyards

It is commonly thought that all halyards should be led to the cockpit. This is certainly true for the jib and spinnaker but is not necessary for the mainsail.

The main halyard can be left on the mast because it is usually the first sail raised and the last dropped. On most sailing days the singlehander raises and lowers the main only once. Typically the skipper is at the main halyard with the motor running and the boat flat on the water. The main is usually the heaviest and most physically difficult sail to raise, so we don't want to add extra turning points in the halyard that require extra effort. Even in the worst possible weather, it is still safe to take the few steps from the cockpit to the mast to put in a reef. When reefing the main, the skipper must be at the mast to tie it up anyway. Having the main halyard right next to the reefing line on the mast is very convenient. It makes it possible to drop the main and tighten the reef lines from one position. (For more on reefing, see Chapter 9, Sail Handling and Sailing Techniques.)

One problem with having the main halyard on the side of the mast is the difficulty of reefing in a heavy wind when the halyard is on the leeward side. If the boat is heeling 45 degrees, it is awkward to handle the halyard from the bottom side. In these cases I just tack first so that I'm on the top again.

Some skippers believe that leading the main halyard and reef lines back to the cockpit is preferable, but I am not a proponent of this idea. Their methodology requires that they "grind" the main down and "grind" the reef lines in place. I find it much faster to release the mainsheet so there is no pressure at all on the sail, then simply drop the main by hand and pull the reef lines by hand, then jump back to the cockpit to trim the mainsheet back into place. I have watched fully crewed boats struggle for several minutes grinding a reef into place while I complete mine in under 30 seconds.

The jib and spinnaker halyards are used in tandem and are used much more often than the main halyard, so they should be led to the cockpit. The halyard clutches should be mounted where they can be reached with the tiller held between the legs, even if it is a stretch. The day will come when a really beautiful spinnaker run turns into something stronger than the autopilot can handle—or the autopilot will have quit altogether. The skipper must be able to drop the spinnaker while steering the boat. Since the spinnaker drop requires both hands, steering with the knees is necessary. The singlehander should make these measurements at the dock standing in the cockpit with the tiller between his knees. How far he can reach is the limit of where the jib and spinnaker halyard clutches should be mounted.

Storing the halyards of a raised sail is an important consideration for both convenience and safety. The best way to store halyards is in a rope bag positioned directly under the halyard clutch. This serves two purposes. First, it stores the halyard safely out from underfoot, as it is not possible to trip on a halyard tucked inside a bag. Second, it allows the halyard to run free when the sail is dropped. The skipper should not have to worry about the halyard jamming during a drop.

Line must not be coiled inside a rope bag because the coil would tangle on itself inside the bag. Rather, the line should be shoved into the bag starting with the bitter end. Simply shove the line into the bottom of the bag, one handful at a time, until the entire line is inside. This puts the end of the line at the bottom, and the entire line will come out without tangling.

Because halyards are always stored in their bag in the same place on every voyage, the skipper instinctively learns to avoid them in the dark. Even if he does catch a halyard on his foot, he will know exactly how to shed it in the dark because he will have done it dozens of time in the light.

Halyard Locks

Halyard locks are, for a singlehanded sailor, perhaps the worst idea I have ever heard. In the Volvo Ocean Race one boat had to send their bowman up the mast in high winds when their halyard lock jammed. How would a singlehander manage this crisis?

Winches

Self-tailing, two-speed winches are vital to the singlehander. A significant amount of sheeting is performed with one hand, and it is impossible to put the entire body weight into cranking, as a crew normally can. Spend the money to purchase a good set of winches. They are used more than any other mechanical device on the boat, so they must work well. Also keep the winches well-greased. This will have a significant impact on their performance.

Jibsheets

Virtually all sailing is done sitting on the windward (high) side of the boat, and the bulk of maneuvering the boat is done by hand, rather than with an autopilot. So set up the sheets to operate from the windward side while maintaining one hand on the tiller.

Jibsheet winches should be mounted just in front of the normal, high-side seating position where they can be operated easily with one hand while the other remains on the tiller. Most winches come with a strong intended mounting direction, i.e., they are designed to mount in a particular direction. On a typical boat with winches on the leeward side, the winch would be aimed forward. However, on a singlehanded boat, the sheet will come up from the leeward side to the windward side, so the winch must be aimed toward the leeward side. (The installation manual for the winches indicates the strong direction.)

A permanent turning block on the leeward side of the boat is required to bring the jibsheet from the leeward side to the windward side. Thus, when sailing on a starboard tack, the active jibsheet runs down the port side of the boat to a turning block, and then up to a winch on the starboard side next to the skipper. It is very handy if the turning block has a locking mechanism that allows the sheet to be locked even when removed from the winch. There will be times when the winch is needed for other purposes, such as for the spinnaker sheet.

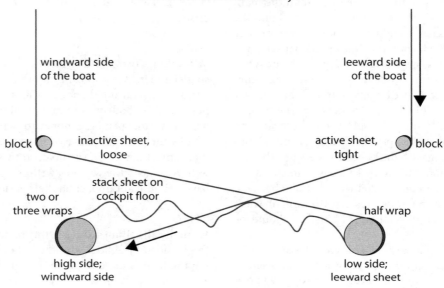

I use a single continuous sheet, 60 feet long;
sheet is tied at the clew of the jib.

windward side
of the boat

leeward side
of the boat

block

inactive sheet,
loose

active sheet,
tight

block

stack sheet on
cockpit floor

two or
three wraps

half wrap

high side;
windward side

low side;
leeward sheet

Cross-sheeting of a continuous jibsheet.

Jibsheets are used continuously on any voyage, even the shortest. A new pile of sheet is formed with every tack. These piles are never neat and get in the way of any activity in the cockpit. A very easy method to reduce the length of loose line in the cockpit is to use a single, continuous sheet. This is rarely seen on boats but is incredibly practical. It eliminates the entire sheet piled in the cockpit. A single, continuous sheet is longer than one usual single sheet but much shorter than two sheets.

To create a continuous jibsheet, start with one end tied to the clew of the jib. Run the sheet backward through the turning blocks on the leeward side of the boat, around the windward winch with three wraps, around the leeward winch, through the blocks on the windward side of the boat, and tie the remaining end to the sail clew. When measuring for the length of the continuous sheet, ensure that it is just long enough to ease the jib completely when sailing on a deep run.

It's important to ensure there are no twists in the continuous sheet before starting this process, using

the method described above. It is also important to wrap the sheet three times around the windward winch and half wrap around the leeward winch. This puts the exactly correct number of twists into the line. Thus the line laying in the cockpit will remain twist-free during the sailing trip.

It takes practice to become accustomed to using the continuous sheet method. But once mastered, it is clearly the better approach.

Spinnaker Sheets

Because of the potential for trouble, it is even more important that the spinnaker sheet be run back to the singlehander sitting at the tiller. It may be possible to run the spinnaker sheet directly from the spinnaker sheet block across the boat to the jibsheet winch on the windward side of the boat. My boat has a second set of winches on the cabintop. I use these winches for the spinnaker sheet and guy during the launch. After the spinnaker is raised, I move the sheet back to the jib winch on the windward side and take my position at the tiller. I leave the guy on

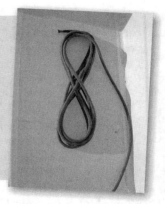
the cabintop winch. When singlehanding, the guy is used much less than the sheet and is rarely needed in emergencies. (In fact, in most cases, having the guy slightly out of reach stops me from using it in emergencies, which is the best thing.)

Craig Horsfield on his Mini 6.50 has a great idea for his spinnaker sheet while navigating or sleeping below. He has mounted a cleat for the spin sheet inside his cabin. If he wakes up to the autopilot straining, he can instantly blow the sheet. This is much easier than sorting out the mess of a broach.

Tweaker Lines (Twings)

Tweaker lines, or twings, are small-diameter lines that run along the spinnaker sheet at the widest point on the boat. They are used to pull the sheet and guy into the boat and add control. They are invaluable to the singlehander because they can

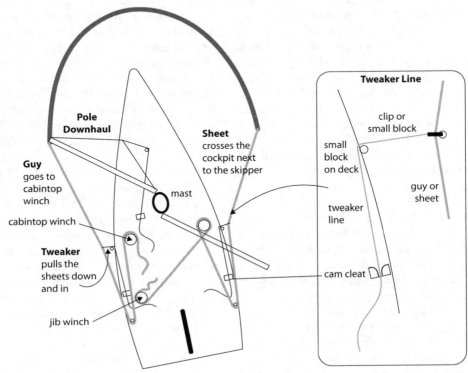

Spinnaker lines and tweaker line setup.

control the sheet and guy when the spinnaker pole downhaul is released for gybing in higher winds. I use them often. (For more on tweaker lines, see Chapter 9, Sail Handling and Sailing Techniques.)

Cleats

Another tripping threat is hardware, particularly cleats. These should be moved away from the main walking areas. A cleat that is directly underneath the lifelines is less likely to trip than a cleat inboard by just a couple of inches. Other hardware should be grouped to create avoidable areas, rather than scattered randomly around the deck. Leave open paths from the deck to the cockpit when mounting hardware. After just a few days on the water the skipper will intuitively learn to follow the open paths.

Rope Clutches

As boats have become more complicated with a greater number of lines, the number of rope clutches has grown significantly. Some sailors have spread these clutches across the deck in an attempt to keep the lines neat. But this takes up the entire deck space, leaving no room to walk. It is very important that adequate walking space be left on both sides of the boat and on the cabintop. It would be virtually impossible to walk on top of lines with the boat healed at 30 degrees because the lines will roll underfoot. In conjunction with the earlier comments about reducing the number of control lines, clutches must be interspaced and overlapped to reduce the overall footprint and leave a significant amount of walking space.

Mainsheet and Traveler

As with the jibsheet, the mainsheet must be positioned to be worked constantly by the skipper sitting in the normal position on the high side of the boat. I use the mainsheet more often than any other line, as I trim or ease for each small variation in wind strength. I usually leave it resting over one knee so that it is not lost in the tangle of lines in the cockpit. With a strong puff, I can instantly ease the sail and keep the boat upright. (I often hear of crewed boats having a dedicated mainsheet trimmer. To me, this just means a significant delay in each adjustment because the crewman must wait to see how the helmsman reacts to each puff before adjusting the sheet. In my early sailing days, I remember telling my mainsheet trimmer, "If I grunt, it means you need to ease!" In a car, it would be the equivalent of having one person handle the steering wheel while another person holds a foot on the gas pedal. It just doesn't make sense.)

For the traveler, a windward sheeting system is invaluable. Once again, this allows the skipper to manage the sail from one position on the high side of the boat.

Sails

Singlehanding causes significantly greater wear to sails than crewed sailing. The key reason is that there are many times where a sail is left to flog for extended periods while something more important, or even critically dangerous, is sorted out. I was once entering a narrow channel hoping to keep the spinnaker up from a run to a beam reach with the wind blowing at 20 knots. Both the sheet and guy got away, and the chute was streaming from the masthead straight out the side. For several minutes it was impossible to turn downwind without running into rocks. Only after passing the channel marker was I able to turn, activate the autopilot, and douse the sail. The spinnaker was flapping wildly during this time and undoubtedly suffered extensive wear. A crew would have pulled the chute down immediately, but it was impossible alone.

In other cases, the mainsail will be flogging wildly while it is reefed in 40-knot winds, or you may have to quickly smash the genoa into a ball and shove it belowdeck when 10-knot winds suddenly gust to 20. Neatness and proper sail packing take a distant second place to safety when the skipper is on a bucking, wet foredeck in such a situation.

High-tech, Mylar, or Kevlar sails are fantastic if properly handled by a crew but will crack and break under the flogging conditions typical for a singlehander. Watching a $5,000 sail split would bring tears to any sailor's eyes. These plastic sails are also nearly impossible to repair. Mylar repair kits are available to mend small splits, but once

That's me repairing a high-tech genoa that split down the leech when I was halfway between San Francisco and Hawaii.

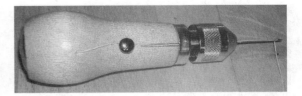

A basic awl makes sail repair much easier than needle and thread.

patches are being applied over older patches, it can be assumed that the sail has finished its life. Experience has shown that extensive singlehanding will destroy these sails beyond use in one or two years. The trouble with high-tech sails is that they go from practically perfect to completely useless in an instant. There is no middle ground.

Unless the singlehander has money to burn, standard Dacron sails are the only choice for singlehanding. Although Dacron does not hold its perfect airfoil shape past the first few seasons, at least it will still be workable for many years. Dacron sails are also very simple to repair with a sewing machine, an awl, or even a needle and thread on the high seas. The expense of a few trips to the sail loft for repairs will convince the singlehander to learn these skills.

With Dacron, it is even possible to unstitch old repairs and start fresh. This is often necessary at key stress points, such as batten pockets, which will split open under flogging conditions. (Specialty sewing machines are available for sails at a reasonable price, but even cheaper are old sewing machines from the 1960s. These have metal gears necessary for sail repair. Modern machines with plastic gears are useless.)

An awl with fine, waxed thread is excellent for hand sewing. It is much better than a standard needle and thread for repairs in the middle of a sail because it is worked mainly from one side. It can also push through multiple layers of sailcloth at seams and edges. You can learn more at www. speedystitcher.com.

Mainsail Reefing

The main must have at least two, or preferably three, reef points. The first reef point will be used very often. The second reef point is used a few times a year, and the third reef point once every year or two. It is impossible to predict the weather or the wind. A day that starts with a nice breeze can turn into a gale at any moment with little warning. A singlehander must be prepared to deal with these changes in a seamanlike manner. This means properly reducing the main and jib. It would be irresponsible to leave the dock without being able to reduce sail for any wind conditions.

LAZYJACKS

One of the greatest difficulties in singlehanding is raising and lowering the mainsail. The main will flop around wildly until it is completely raised and the boom will bang violently inside the cockpit. A topping lift from the top of the mast to the end of the boom prevents damage from the boom, but it does not help in managing the sail.

An additional problem is neatly folding the mainsail for storage on top of the boom. I've watched this to be a challenge for a crew of four. It borders on impossible for a singlehander.

Lazyjacks solve both of these problems. These are a network of lines that run from a single point high up on each side of the mast to multiple points on both sides of the boom. Lazyjacks should be designed to be detached from the boom and secured on the mast when the boat is underway. They are known to get tangled with the mainsail battens when hoisting the sail. Some larger boats use fabric

Lazyjacks help keep the mainsail on top of the boom when dousing.

Wichard hanks have snaps that make them easier to use with one hand.

covers on the boom to hold the sail. These are a problem because it is very difficult to work with reef lines while reaching under the fabric.

Jib and Genoa Setup

The key to the foresail is that it must go up and come down easily from the cockpit. This usually means that hanks are preferable to a headstay foil.

When raising the jib on a headstay foil, even with a pre-feed, it is likely to jam, and the singlehander must rush to the bow, free the sail, and rush back again to pull on the halyard. When the jib is dropped, a foil will not let it fall to the deck on its own. Hanks solve both of these problems. Hanks rarely jam on the way up and will quickly drop by at least a few feet when the halyard is released. It is very simple for the singlehander to grab armfuls of genoa and pull the sail down onto the deck when using hanks.

In my experience, Wichard snap-on hanks are preferable to piston hanks. The piston type requires two hands to hank on or off—one hand to pull the piston and one hand to move the hank onto or off the forestay. This can be dangerous or even impossible when crouched in a bouncing pulpit. Wichard hanks can be easily clipped on or off with one hand while the other is holding on to the boat. The small ends of a piston hank are also impossible to grab with gloved hands—not an issue with Wichard hanks—and the piston hanks will seize with salt, again not an issue with Wichard hanks.

Wichard hanks have a drawback for boats using an asymmetrical spinnaker. If the jib is still up, the spinnaker sheet may get caught in Wichard hanks as the spinnaker is gybed. This is a known problem on Mini 6.50 boats. This is only a problem with asymmetrical spinnakers, not with symmetrical chutes.

Regardless of the type used, hanks on all sails should be positioned in the same direction so that the singlehander knows, even in the dark, which direction is used to hank on or hank off a sail. On my boat all sails—the genoa, jib, and storm jib—all hank on from port to starboard.

A handy device is a line run up the forestay, woven between just a few of the hanks, to the head of the sail. This line is run through a block on the deck and back to the cockpit. When the halyard is released, the skipper can pull this line to pull down the foresail.

Although rarely seen, reef points on the foresail are a good idea. These are common on the Mini 6.50 boats. Changing jibs underway is difficult and exhausting, particularly when the wind is increasing. It is unlikely that a singlehander will want to reduce from a #1 to a #2 for a slight increase in wind strength, although such changes are common on a crewed boat. It is more likely that a singlehander will drive the #1 past its suggested wind range or will jump to a #3 before its required wind strength. Reefing a genoa 3 feet up from the bottom will make the jump from a #1 to a #2 sail size much easier. The same practice holds for the move from a #3 to a #4.

The tack position on a reefed foresail should not be at deck level. The entire foot of the reefed sail should be at least 6 inches (15 cm) above the deck. Otherwise water will collect in the bundle of material at the foot of the reefed sail. A short line should be used from the tack of the sail to the boat. In addition, small drain holes with proper grommets should be positioned along the sail a few inches below the reef points.

I do believe that a singlehander should use the largest sails designed for the boat. Some have suggested that we not use an overlapping genoa but stick with a jib for ease of tacking. I want my boat to sail as fast as it is designed, so rather than sacrifice speed, I have learned how to use the designed sails.

Roller-furling sails are a great convenience for the cruising singlehander. The key advantage is that it is easy to reduce sail from as much as a genoa to a tiny handkerchief with just the pull on a line. Obviously this completely eliminates the problem of dropping and bagging the foresail. I know of several round-the-world singlehanders who have used roller-furling sails successfully. But there is a disadvantage: roller-furling sails are cut for their fully extended position. They lose their aerodynamic shape and wing effect the moment they are rolled part way, which is why many racers won't use them.

Larger boats have used two roller-furling sails to prevent this sail shape issue. A second forestay is positioned a few feet back from the headstay. Of course every new solution its own problems. The largest headsail must be tacked through the relatively small gap between the two forestays. This is not an issue on long voyages but is inconvenient in short tacking situations. As well, sailors go to great lengths to reduce weight up the mast. (Refer to Chapter 5 on this topic.) It is not appealing to leave a large sail permanently mounted all the way up to the top of the mast—a significant amount of weight that must be counterbalanced at the keel.

This problem is avoided if the entire rolled sail, including its foil, stay, and roller, can be dropped to the deck as one complete unit. This is an incredibly neat and efficient way to store a sail on deck.

Twin roller-furling jibs are convenient but add a huge amount of weight aloft.

A self-tacking jib is a real convenience for the singlehander. Many modern fractionally rigged racing boats use a larger mainsail with a jib, rather than a genoa. Self-tacking jibs slide from side to side during tacking and require no effort at all. Only when sailing on a reach is any adjustment made to the jibsheet.

Jib Downhaul

In situations where the wind or waves might rise to a level where the singlehander does not want to crawl to the bow, it is easy to rig a cockpit-maneuvered jib downhaul. This is probably only applicable in offshore or extreme weather situations that pose a significant risk on the foredeck.

Before raising the jib, tie a downhaul line to the halyard shackle. Feed this line through just a few of the jib hanks on the forestay. Run the downhaul through a snatchblock at deck level and back to the cockpit where it can be tied to any convenient fitting. Once the halyard is popped, pulling the downhaul will bring the jib right down to the deck.

Unfortunately the problem with this system is in getting the jib to fall to the deck and not in the water. Even if the boat is hove-to, the top half of the jib will fall in the water on the leeward side. Once again this is what I know from hard learned experience. The only way to get the entire jib on the deck is to sail head-to-wind and very quickly pull the downhaul before the boat turns off. And of course even if the sail is down on the deck, it will still fall overboard with the first wave. So it must be tied to the foredeck, which still necessitates a crawl to the bow.

Positioning the Autopilot

It must be possible to operate the autopilot from the tiller position. During a typical sail there are times when the autopilot is turned on and off for just a few seconds. For example, at the start of a race the skipper will be hand steering but may need to rush to the bow to skirt the jib. Using the autopilot for just a 10-second spurt is very typical, even in a cruising situation where the skipper just needs to find his coffee cup. Autopilots are covered in detail in Chapter 6, Self-Steering Systems.

Spinnakers
SPINNAKER SOCKS

I am not a fan of spinnaker socks. First, they are just not necessary on 20- to 40-foot boats. A skipper who follows the detailed instructions in this book will never get into trouble with a spinnaker in any wind conditions. Also, there are several drawbacks to socks. The first and most obvious is the extra lines and sock itself are prone to fouling at the top of the mast. Second, a singlehander should do everything possible to reduce weight up the mast. A bunched-up sock has a lot of weight and wind resistance. The third and worst issue is that the skipper must move to the bow to work the sock. It is easy to imagine using a sock on a nice sunny day with a moderate breeze. But what happens when the wind increases to 20 knots against a current and the waves are a choppy 4 feet high? Is this the time for a sailor to be standing on the bow with arms raised overhead? It is very easy to drop the chute directly into the cockpit under these conditions, but difficult to use a sock. And finally, socks are slow. When I'm near a mark, I want to be able to raise or drop my chute with the same speed as any crewed boat. A spinnaker sock makes this idea preposterous.

My lack of faith in spinnaker socks was augmented by Stanley Paris, during his attempt to break the record as the oldest person to solo circumnavigate on the 63-foot *Kiwi Sprit*. The hoop on Stanley's sock broke during the spinnaker launch. Later, the wind came up to 30 knots and the lightweight spinnaker tore apart. While Stanley was trying to douse under these conditions, the sock got caught in the upper spreader. When it popped loose, Stanley fell on his back onto an extrusion of the deck. "The area just below my left scapula was in as much as any pain I have ever experienced. I lay still for a few minutes testing my lungs and then started to get going. I could feel a rib cracking in my back. Crawling was out, as my left arm could take no weight. A few more actions and I collapsed for several hours in the cockpit."

RAISING THE SPINNAKER ON LARGER BOATS, WITHOUT A SOCK

In the past, boats often secured the length of the spinnaker with wool ties or rubber bands that broke

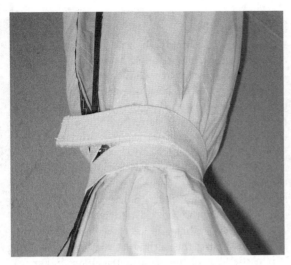

An elastic strap with Velcro every six feet up the spinnaker luff allows for controlled launches. *(Courtesy UK Sails)*

off when the spinnaker filled. This littering has been outlawed in racing and is pretty dumb for cruisers. UK Sails came up with an elastic strap-and-Velcro combination that is sewn every six feet along the luff of the chute. The spinnaker is bundled with these straps and raised in a long sausage. When the pole is pulled back into the wind and the sheet trimmed, the Velcro pops open from the foot to the head. For asymmetric spinnakers, the same effect is achieved by heading up to put the bowsprit into the wind.

Top-Down Spinnaker Furling

Top-down furlers for asymmetrical spinnakers are a new idea, made possible by the invention of the antitorsion cable that turns the top swivel of the furling system at the same rate as the bottom roller. In addition, Profurl has developed Spinex, a sphere that spins freely around the cable to protect the light-weight spinnaker fabric from damage or from jamming while being furled. This system is being evaluated by Class 40 skippers as an alternative to a sock.

Spinnaker Net

A spinnaker net is used to prevent wraps around the forestay. Nets are usually homemade from light webbing material, with sail hanks to connect to the forestay. The net is stretched between the forestay

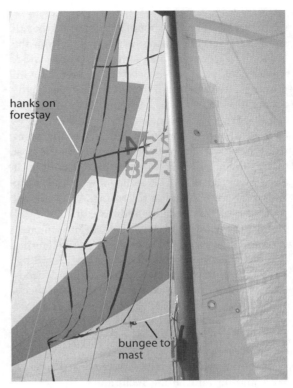

hanks on forestay

bungee to mast

My spinnaker net is hanked on to the forestay. A light shock cord connected to the mast allows the net to be pushed to the side during a gybe.

and mast. The biggest problem with nets is that they become a tangled mess when stored below deck. They should be tied in a nice bundle before storage. Another issue is that the net is in the way of the spinnaker pole uphaul (sometimes known as topping lift) during a gybe. My net has a very light bungee cord to connect to the mast. This bungee cord allows the net to be pushed out of the way by the uphaul during the gybe. It defeats the purpose of the net if it must be disconnected from the mast in order to gybe.

Spinnaker Design

The Figaro Beneteau II (for more on this boat, see Chapter 4) uses spinnakers that are designed to be "stable" for singlehanded sailing. I contacted Rick McBride with Leitch and McBride Custom Sailmakers in Sidney, British Columbia. McBride explained the differences between a stable and a flat spinnaker. The skipper should keep in mind that all spinnakers act like a wing, with air flow from the luff to the leech, even when sailing deep downwind.

A stable spinnaker is designed to be used with minimal attention to sail trim. It will fly even as the apparent wind oscillates back and forth in normal conditions. A flat spinnaker, in contrast, requires constant trimming or will collapse. A stable spinnaker has greater cord depth. This allows the boat to sail higher or lower without the sail stalling. It also has a more elliptical leech, allowing the luff to fold over on itself without collapsing. A flat sail will collapse if the leading edge folds over at all.

Like the wings in a jet airplane, a flat spinnaker is faster but is more prone to stalling or collapsing than a stable spinnaker designed for singlehanding. This tradeoff between speed and stability depends on how much the skipper is able to work the sheets over hours at a time. The accompanying drawings are highly exaggerated. In reality a stable spinnaker has a cord depth only a few percent greater than a flat chute.

Handling spinnakers is covered in Chapter 9, Sail Handling and Sailing Techniques.

LETTERBOX SPINNAKER DOUSING

Dousing is not difficult when the spinnaker is protected behind the mainsail. But on a reach in higher winds it can be a greater challenge since the chute will pull back to the stern quarter. On a large boat the force would be unmanageable. Richard Du Moulin works with a letterbox dousing method that maintains control of the large spinnaker on his Express 27 *Lora Ann*.

Du Moulin pulls the lazy sheet of his spinnaker through a slot between the mainsail and boom. He runs the sheet to a snatch block on the windward rail, just aft of the shrouds, then aft to a winch. The snatch block helps to keep the spinnaker from jamming against the outhaul at the back of boom. When the tack of his asymmetrical spinnaker (or the guy of a symmetric chute) is released, the entire sail is pulled through the slot down into the main hatch. It is important to pull the clew of the spinnaker through the slot before releasing the halyard. Otherwise the foot can end up in the water.

For singlehanders, running the spinnaker over the boom will add an extra modicum of control during the most difficult part of the high-wind take

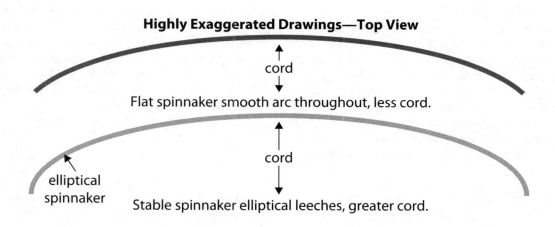

Highly Exaggerated Drawings—Top View

cord

Flat spinnaker smooth arc throughout, less cord.

cord

elliptical spinnaker

Stable spinnaker elliptical leeches, greater cord.

A flat spinnaker may be faster, but the elliptical leech of a stable spinnaker allows the luff to fall over on itself without collapsing, a big help to the singlehander, who cannot devote himself exclusively to trimming the spinnaker.

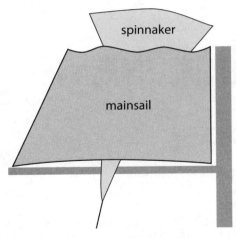

A letterbox douse pulls the spinnaker through the slot in-between the boom and the loose-footed mainsail.

Door handles make excellent cup holders, especially when within reach of the tiller.

down. It might allow for better two-handed hauling or free one hand momentarily to untangle the halyard. The skipper must pre-check for any boom fittings that will catch on the chute.

Miscellaneous Boat Setup Ideas

The key idea to boat setup is placing controls that are used minute to minute within reach of the singlehander sitting at the tiller. Items that are used less often require the singlehander to stand up in the cockpit, and items that are usually used just once per trip require the singlehander to leave the cockpit.

Over time I have added many convenience items to the boat. For example, I have a coffee cup holder right next to the tiller.

If I am hand steering for several hours, it is nice to have my coffee within reach. I've also added a holder for my GPS unit, so that I don't drop it in the cockpit or overboard (which I've done).

I have attached cloth bags just inside the main hatch for items that I am likely to use only once each trip. I can put sunglasses, sunscreen, a spare knife, gloves, and my GPS when not in use inside these bags that can be accessed just by stepping to the hatch.

Think about what you use during a voyage, and find your own way to store it appropriately.

A handy pocket in the cockpit is helpful for holding my radio, GPS, cell phone, or iPod.

FOUR BOATS DESIGNED FOR SINGLEHANDING

Singlehanding makes up a tiny amount of the total sailboat market. There are very few boats designed specifically for the singlehander, and all have been designed for racers with none for cruisers. I will take a closer look at the Figaro Beneteau II, the Mini

Designed by Marc Lombard specifically for singlehanding, the Figaro II, at 10.1 meters (33 feet), is a high-performance offshore racer. *(Courtesy Marc Lombard)*

6.50, the Class 40, and the IMOCA 60. This is not intended as an instruction manual on sailing these high-performance racers—just an introduction for the dreamer.

FIGARO BENETEAU II

Only one dedicated singlehanded design is being built in production quantities: the Figaro Beneteau II, designed by Marc Lombard specifically for the Figaro racing series. At 10.15 meters (33 feet) this falls in the middle of my coverage range of 20- to 40-foot boats. It is reasonably priced new, and there is an active market for used boats. A number of boats are even available to lease for a single racing season (www.classefigarobeneteau.com). Thus it is worth looking at in more detail. This is a serious racing boat designed to cross oceans. However, given that the lessons learned from racing any type of vehicle (car or bicycle) are later transferred to nonracers, it is interesting to examine the design decisions made with this model.

La Solitaire du Figaro (www.lasolitaire.com) is a well-developed series of singlehanded races taking place over four weeks in June each year. The races run between various ports in France, with longer legs to Ireland and back. This is a true open ocean event. The Bay of Biscay is considered to have some of the roughest waters in the North Atlantic.

This is a one-design event open only to the Figaro II. Many of the world's best known single-handed skippers enter the series, but it is also open to amateurs, so I consider it to be a good representation of the keen sailor's abilities.

SINGLEHANDED SAILING SCHOOL

The only formal singlehanded racing school that I am aware of is the Artemis Offshore Academy, which uses the Figaro II to train sailors. John Thorn provided the following description:

> The Artemis Offshore Academy is a UK training program of excellence for British shorthanded sailors, providing a structure to bring talented sailors up through the ranks. Designed to help them win major offshore solo and shorthanded races in the future, the ultimate goal is to put a British sailor in a strong position to win the Vendée Globe.
>
> The academy offers a unique scholarship to race on the Figaro circuit each year with a fully funded campaign. In a natural progression to the top of the sailing world the sailors will then most likely move into IMOCA 60 racing.
>
> The academy has a Development Squad of eight members as well as two associate members. The Development Squad sailors are selected at the selections trials held once a year at the Weymouth and Portland National Sailing Academy. The associate members are sailors who already have funded campaigns but wish to train alongside the academy. The training program is run from November to April in La Grande Motte (France) at the prestigious Figaro training Centre D'Entrainement Méditerranéen (CEM). The race program includes official and unofficial Classe Figaro events in France and RORC (Royal Ocean Racing Club) races in the UK.

Unfortunately, the Artemis school is only available to selected members and is not open to paying students.

Our interest is not in the race series but in the boat itself. I had a long discussion with designer Marc Lombard (www.marclombard.com) about his baby. In particular, I asked him to compare how he designed it to be a singlehanded boat versus a crewed boat of the same size. I also spoke with skipper Murray Danforth, perhaps the only North American Figaro II owner, and with Charles Darbyshire, Project Director of the Artemis Offshore Academy, which trains singlehanded sailors in the UK (see sidebar). He commented, "These people train like Olympic athletes, much more than an amateur."

Lombard explained that the design team met with a group of highly skilled skippers of the older Figaro model to ask for their requirements for the race series. Naturally there were differing opinions on every aspect of the boat. In many cases the majority ruled, but in others the team had to rely on their own expertise in meeting conflicting desires.

Final boat cost played a significant role in the design. The Figaro II is intended to be within the price range of the average sailor, not solely for sponsored professionals. With a length of 10.1 meters (33 ft.), the beam was established at 3.4 meters (just over 11 ft.) to control costs.

The boat had to meet a basic minimum weight of 3 tons empty to meet ISO (International Organization for Standardization) Category A requirements for open-water stability. The final design came in at 3,050 kilograms (6,724 lb.). There are two 240-liter (63.5 gal.) water ballast tanks on each side for upwind power. The designers were not allowed to use larger tanks because stability would be threatened if the boat was sailed with a crew of six in other races. (Note that the much smaller Mini 6.50s have tanks of up to 450 liters [119 gal.] of water ballast—see discussion of the Mini 6.50 on page 43.)

For upwind sailing, the water ballast can be transferred from side to side via gravity in about 15 seconds, controlled by levers in the cockpit. The process is to open the valves and allow the water to flow, then close the valves again, just before tacking. The ballast is not so great as to overly tip the boat during this process. If the tank is empty, a pump can fill it in about 4 minutes. A scoop drops below the boat for this purpose or to empty the tanks. (For more on water ballast, see Chapter 5, Keeping the Boat Upright.)

Lombard explained that with the Figaro II, the difference between skilled and unskilled sailors becomes apparent when sailing upwind. The boat responds quickly to changes in sail trim. To excel, the skipper must have a strong theoretical knowledge and a lot of practice in differing conditions. The twin rudders provide control regardless of boat heel while beating to windward.

The boat has a single backstay, without runners. This was requested by the skippers to avoid tangling with the sails. The mainsail has a traditional shape without a large headboard as has more recently become popular. The mainsail will slide past the backstay in higher winds. In lighter wind, the backstay can be eased to allow the main to pass under. Marc mentioned other recent boat designs with no backstay. The single backstay allows the fractional, double-spreader mast and main to be adjusted as necessary for optimal trim in upwind racing.

The mainsail is large (36 square meters, or roughly 388 sq. ft.) and has two standard reef points. The fractional foresail is only 28 square meters (just over 300 sq. ft.). Marc described this as desirable for fewer headsail changes, a benefit to singlehanders.

The cockpit was designed so that all the major controls can be accessed by the skipper while at the helm. The jibsheets cross over the cockpit to the windward side of the boat for easily making adjustments while seated.

For downwind racing, the hull has a wide, flat stern with twin rudders. This was a particular requirement for singlehanding as the boat is often run by autopilot. The design allows a skipper to launch and gybe a spinnaker in 30 knots of wind with the autopilot in full control. The hull shape is incredibly stable in these conditions. Marc explained that the boat becomes more stable the faster it goes downwind. He commented that the twin rudder design will stop any broach in its early stages. Broaches are very rare in these races, even when the boats are pushed to their limits. As a user, Murray Danforth confirmed this stability. He commented that the rudders really dig into the water and grip it very tightly. A narrow hull with single rudder would be much less stable. Watch the YouTube video "Rough Weather—Corentin Douguet Sailing crazy Figaro" for a great view of sailing in 55 knots of wind. Note in particular (1) the skipper's light hand on the tiller, (2) how the autopilot is able to hold course when he is on the bow, and (3) the stern view showing the twin rudders' grip on the water.

There was debate among the skippers over the choice between symmetrical and asymmetrical spinnaker. In the end, majority ruled and the symmetrical chute was chosen. According to Lombard, the Figaro is a tactical race where skippers want a complete range of options in their route. Symmetrical spinnakers allow for much deeper sailing and thus more routing options.

I asked Charles Darbyshire how they train his students to gybe a spinnaker in 30 knots of wind. This is something they practice extensively. His first answer: "Very quickly." They use twin sheets and guys and twin foreguys (pole downhauls). Most important, they make no wasted movements. Darbyshire contrasted them with an expert crew on a Mumm 30: the singlehanded skipper only makes one trip to the bow and one trip back to the cockpit, performing all necessary tasks during this one trip, grabbing lines along the way fore and aft. The skipper gybes the main first, then moves forward to gybe the pole. (The entire process is described fully in Chapter 9, Sail Handling and Sailing Techniques.) On a crewed boat, there ends up being a few trips to the foredeck to accomplish the complete gybe.

Darbyshire pointed out that the spinnaker design for the Figaro II is much more stable than on another performance boat of similar size. A key to gybing is completing the entire maneuver at the fastest point of sail, while surfing down a wave when the pressure on the spinnaker is least. Problems will occur if the skipper is delayed past this brief window of opportunity.

An NKE autopilot package is usually used on the boat, but skippers can install any brand desired. The autopilot controls are usually mounted next to the main hatchway, but again this is up to the individual. Most skippers use a remote control for all autopilot functions, including gybing from the foredeck. Darbyshire noted that the performance settings of each racing boat are set individually, after many hours of personalized testing. The racers even change the autopilot's gain settings for upwind and downwind legs of a race to get the maximum performance.

MINI 6.50

Craig Horsfield is one of North America's most successful Mini sailors. Originally from South Africa and now living on the U.S. West Coast, Craig travels often to race on the European circuit. Some of his recent accomplishments include:

- Mini 500 L'Escala
- Pornichet Select 6.50
- Mini Pavois
- Trophée Marie-Agnès Péron
- Mini-Fastnet
- Demi-Clé 6.50
- Mini Transat 6.50 (2009; tenth place in 2013)

The Mini 6.50 is the smallest purposely designed open ocean race boat. At just 6.5 meters (just over 21 feet) and 3 meters (9.8 feet) at the beam, it is truly a pumpkin seed. Because the Mini is such a specialized boat, I was interested in discussing what it is like to sail it rather than spending time on the technical specifications.

I asked, "How would a singlehander feel stepping off of a 30-foot cruiser onto a Mini?"

"It's like a rocket ship when you're on deck and a coffin when you're lying down inside and you're scared," he replied. "It's fast, agile, and really fun to sail, but it's spartan."

Like a sports car speeding through an old French town, the boat is agile enough that the skipper can put it where desired on the waves. When the boat

Mini 6.50s are built to plane—notice how it scoots along on the back portion of the hull. *(Courtesy Eliza Chohadzhieva)*

is planing at 18 knots on the back third of the hull, it bounces over the waves, but the twin rudders dig in and maintain control. Horsfield can even let go of the tiller for a few seconds to take a drink under these conditions. It handles better with much larger sails in front. He often sails in 25 knots with three reefs in the main but still has the big 78-square meter (840 sq. ft.) spinnaker off the bow. Skippers are pushing the boats much harder than earlier generations, and the big spinnaker actually lifts the bow out of the water.

With the pumpkin seed hull shape, it is important not to bury the bow in a wave. "It's just not long enough to survive." If the water comes over the bow by more than 2 feet, it will lead to a crash situation and spin out in one direction or the other. "Hopefully to windward, because to leeward is terrible." Excess baggage is stacked in the transom to keep the bow up. If the situation is looking bad, Horsfield pushes the helm down and encourages a windward broach rather than the alternative. The boat is strong enough to handle any crash he can throw at it. With patience the boat will sit and shake itself for a while but eventually turns back down again.

The NKE autopilot can handle the boat in most conditions, but it can't manage the top end of the big spinnaker in rough weather, like a quartering sea. "Sleeping in 25 knots with the big spinnaker can't be done." As mentioned earlier, Horsfield leads the spinnaker sheet to a cleat below deck so that he can blow it in a hurry if he senses problems while navigating or sleeping, then climb on deck to sort it out. This is easier than climbing out of the cabin after a broach.

Under these tough conditions, the NKE autopilot with a hydraulic ram uses a tremendous amount of power. (His former linear-drive Raymarine pilot used significantly less.) The gain needs to be wound up to the maximum, so the pilot is using 250 watts or more. This is unsustainable for anything other than short durations.

Upwind the boat is "terrible. It just pounds. It's fat, short, and its hull speed is 5¼ knots. It's not pleasant and it's wet. It's horrible. The Transat went upwind for five days in the middle of the Atlantic when we should have been in the Trades. It was throwing some nasty weather. It's horrible up wind." The big Dacron main with 1.6 meter headboard allows the skipper to twist off and dump a lot of wind.

The boat has reefable jibs because of the limited allowed sail inventory (see photo on page 119). One night in 40 knots of wind Horsfield sailed with the storm jib and three reefs in the main. It was just "pounding, pounding and wet, wet, wet." The pilot can drive but with ear plugs and music it's still possible to sleep.

On his second Transat and with an Automatic Identification System (AIS) unit, Horsfield was much more comfortable sleeping below. The fishing boats turn their AIS units off so their competitors can't see where they are fishing. But in the open ocean all the commercial ships use it. Horsfield used the 10-mile warning alarm to wake up.

On a reach the Mini has great form stability. The gennaker is nearly the size of a code zero. Absolutely everything below is stacked on the windward side. Even empty containers are filled with seawater and tied to the lifelines. Super-keen racers will empty their spare gear out of a dry bag and fill it with sea water. "There is absolutely nothing on the leeward side, not even a chart."

Surprisingly this level of commitment is not required upwind. The hull speed of 5¼ knots can be reached without stacking, so the extra effort serves no purpose. In high winds it is simpler to put another reef in. The boat goes just as fast.

Horsfield sails with 100 watts of solar panels and a 100-watt methanol fuel cell for power. The fuel cell is nice and quiet. He ran it 10 hours a day over the 25 days of the Transat, which was as much as the 20 liters (5.3 gal.) of fuel he carried allowed for. He says he should have taken 30 or more. To compensate for the lack of power, Horsfield ran the autopilot when the conditions were sufficiently stable for him to turn down the gain. Otherwise, he hand steered for 12–16 hours a day.

In spite of the 73 entrants in the 2013 Mini Transat fleet, Horsfield only saw three other competitors after the first day of racing. One was only a light in the distance. Another he saw at the Canaries for a day, and the third stayed in sight for a week so that the two racers could compete aggressively against each other until the last day when all bets were off.

Down below, Horsfield's use of the word "coffin" was appropriate. Several years ago I sat below in Drew Wood's brand-new carbon Mini. The cabin was so black that it actually absorbed light. A shiny dime dropped on the floor could be lost forever. Today even the most serious racers make a weight sacrifice and paint the ceiling white. The cabin would be unlivable otherwise.

Although the boat has quarter berths, in reality they are simply a cover on top of the foam required for flotation and are only used for stacking equipment. Skippers sleep by laying an inflatable cushion over the stack of sails or anything else underneath. If the wind is low, they even sleep on the windward side on deck, still wearing their harness and tether. In higher wind they can sit on the cockpit floor.

Even over the 25 days of the Mini Transat, cooking falls to a level that I consider below minimal: a handheld Jetboil is used to heat 1 liter of water in about 2 minutes. This is poured into a freeze-dried food packet or oatmeal for breakfast. I'll repeat the fact that the stove is *handheld*—it is not mounted or gimballed in any way. To avoid burns, Horsfield always wears his foul-weather pants when performing this operation—always. He holds the stove in his left hand and keeps his right hand on the gas shutoff.

In a previous race he had one get out of control and had to throw the whole thing overboard. And I'll repeat that his meals are 100% freeze-dried or oatmeal with fruit thrown in—for twenty-five days!

There is no chart table or even a proper seat in the cabin of a Mini. All course plotting and navigation is done before the race starts. All the waypoints and possible exit points are loaded into the GPS at the dock. Horsfield had small laminated sections of charts for every waypoint or possible port that he might need if abandoning the race, but never looked at a chart for the race itself.

During the Mini Transat, race organizers transmit a once-daily weather report developed by a private meteorologist for each block of the ocean. The Mini SSB radios receive but do not transmit. Horsfield marked weather fronts with wax crayon on a North Atlantic chart. This was his only source of weather other than VHF conversations with a passing ship. During the Transat the only radio reports given about competitors is their ranking and distance to finish, not their actual position.

By rule, the Mini is unsinkable. The required internal foam will keep the boat afloat, if only at the level of the deck. During the 2013 Mini Transat the Italian boat *Umpa Lumpa* came off a wave and hit an unknown floating object. The bottom of the boat split open and it sank to the deck in 3 minutes. Thankfully, seven large support sailboats follow the racers to provide rescue in such situations. An inordinate number of skippers were picked up in this race, and a few boats, but not skippers, were lost. The race was held later than usual in 2013, and the North Atlantic was much rougher than expected.

Horsfield keeps five knives within easy reach: one on his lifejacket, another in his pants, one on each tiller, and one on the boom vang. "When you need a knife you want it in easy reach." In a recent race, when his spinnaker pole broke he cut the tangled guy to douse the spinnaker. The cost of a guy is much lower than the cost of the chute.

Horsfield concludes: "A Mini Transat is a $100,000 problem. It's doable for most people. A Class 40 is a $1 million problem and you can put a heater in the cabin."

THE CLASS 40

I spoke with Joe Harris, one of North America's preeminent Class 40 skippers and owner of the Akilaria RC2 *Gryphon Solo 2*. In preparation for the 2014–15 Global Ocean Race, Harris's racing pedigree is notable:

- 4 Transatlantic crossings
- 9 Newport-Bermuda races
- 5 Marblehead-Halifax races
- 5 Bermuda 1–2 races
- 2 Atlantic Cup races
- More than 60,000 nautical miles of open ocean sailing over 30 years in five boats

When I asked Harris to describe the Class 40, his first word was "powerful." The hull is "a big slice of pie, forty feet long and thirteen feet wide with an articulating prod on the bow. . . . My job is to control that power and transfer it to forward thrust."

The boats have forward and aft ballast water tanks on each side, holding 750 liters (198 gal.). With both tanks full, the boat can be sailed in up to 20 knots of true wind with full 72-square meter (775 sq. ft.) main and 43-square meter (463 sq. ft.) Solent jib (nonoverlapping #1 jib on the fractional rig). All of this adds up to significant righting moment and a tremendous amount of power that gives the boat rapid acceleration and an ability to plow through rough offshore seas.

Typically, upwind the skipper first fills the windward forward water ballast tank to get the bow down. As the breeze climbs above 15 knots, the aft tank is filled to help control heel angle. Above 20 knots of true wind speed, the boat is getting overpowered. The first move is to reduce sail area one reef and change from the Solent to a staysail. Then another reef in the main and a move down to the ORC #4.

Reefing is a long process. The boat is first sailed down 5 degrees. Otherwise, with the extra-narrow keel, it would lose momentum in short order. The jib is trimmed accordingly, and the main is luffed by releasing the traveler. The cunningham is connected to an eye in the luff and the mainsail is pulled down. Then the outboard reef line is winched in at the deck. The process takes 6–7 minutes. Shaking

A Class 40 surfing down a wave. *(Photo by Billy Black, courtesy Joe Harris)*

out the reef takes longer because the main must be winched up to the top level. The big square-top sail with full battens is very heavy.

Harris typically sails upwind with the B&G autopilot set to true wind. Hitting target speeds requires fairly constant attention to trimming the main. "Traveler up, traveler down, and opening the sail at the top. The boat really likes the traveler up and easing the sheet for twist. Even though it looks like its spilling air, this creates lift and is fast." Class 40s are oriented toward reaching and running. They are not known for optimum upwind sailing, especially without anyone on the rail.

Upwind, the smaller jib can be dialed in and set. As a fractional rig with the jib at only 60% of the main, it is the shape of the main that is the key to speed. Harris keeps an eye on the autopilot and tiller, watching the amount of weather helm. Boat speed reacts almost immediately to excess weather helm, so watching the knotmeter is just as effective. On a reach, it is more typical to allow the boat to swing slightly, with normal 10–15 degrees of oscillation in wind direction.

When singlehanding, the autopilot rams are connected at all times, even while in neutral. Joe mentioned how light and responsive the tiller feels when the rams are detached.

The 2014–15 Global Ocean Race will have singlehanders, doublehanders, and crews of four all racing together. I asked how a singlehander would compare to the full crew. Harris referred me to doublehanded skipper Emma Creighton. Her blog mentions giving up only 20 minutes over 6 hours

when racing against a fully crewed boat. Perhaps another 5% to 10% would be given up by a singlehander, due to lack of weight on the rail, longer sail changes, and of course the need for sleep.

Harris finds that he is constantly moving around the boat. He is not one to sit in place for extended periods. I think this is more a statement about his personality than a requirement of the boat. He is always checking things. During the Transat Jacques Vabre (5,000 miles over 20 days) he had to remind himself to sit and steer. The Class 40 is a boat in which skipper steering is faster than the autopilot in light air, particularly upwind. Harris describes: "autopilot on—adjust the sails—autopilot off and I'm driving. It's a continuous loop in light wind."

The 40 is certainly a more lively boat than the larger Open 50 that Harris spent some time with. It was powerful enough to crush through the waves and gave him a sense of security. The Class 40 is a frisky horse on which you've got to stay one step ahead and don't get one step behind. Wipeouts happen more often.

Comments from Harris's blog on the 2013 Bermuda 1–2: "The first 24 hours have been a bit trying as the remnants of tropical storm Andrea left a large and messy sea state that was difficult to punch through. *GS2* led the fleet out into a nasty sea state. The boat would rise up over a giant swell and launch itself airborne, only to return to the sea with a shattering pancake-like smash that left me looking for something broken. Repeat. Repeat."

Off the wind in power-reaching conditions, the 40 is nearly as quick as the 50, largely due to the evolution in hull shape and the recent additions of chines. Harris sails the second generation Akilaria (his decision for this is described below). A few third-generation boats are now on the water. He feels that there might be an incremental but not significant increase in boat speed. Harris prevailed in his two races against third-generation boats so far but recognizes that the vessels were still in tune-up mode.

The A2 masthead asymmetrical spinnaker is flown from a sock. The bowsprit articulates to windward, allowing the boat to be sailed as deep as 160 degrees true, at least 10 degrees beyond that of the usual asymmetrical. When raising the sail he heads deep downwind to 170 degrees so the socked spinnaker is covered by the main. The sheet is kept loose. He raises the sock from the mast, then runs back to the cockpit and heads up by 15 degrees using the autopilot, sheets in, and then the chute catches and he is flying. The autopilot can be overwhelmed by the spinnaker in a big puff. It's necessary to keep an eye out for squalls.

Dousing the 190-square meter (2045 sq. ft.) spinnaker by lowering the sock can be a challenge in big air. Under rough conditions he leads the sock control line through a snatch block up to the forward deck and sits down, well harnessed in place with the waves breaking overhead. He pulls the sail down right into his lap. This is a technique also used on the Open 60s.

More recently, Class 40 boats are starting to look at top-down furling systems. These eliminate the sock by furling the spinnaker around an antitorsion cable. This fiber cable is the critical part of the system. It runs from a top swivel at the masthead to the furling drum on the end of the bowsprit. The cable is stiff enough that it will not twist as the sail is unfurled or furled—thus it's called an antitorsion cable. This keeps the bottom, middle, and top of the cable all turning at the same speed to roll the sail evenly from the top down.

On a jib furling system, the luff of the jib is connected to the furler for its entire length. With a spinnaker system, only the head and tack of the sail are connected. As the furler is rolled, the sail is coiled around the antitorsion cable from the top down to the bottom. Once it is fully rolled, the halyard is released and the entire sail drops neatly to the deck.

Harris's main halyard runs to the cockpit. His foresail halyards, including the spinnaker, run to the mast and around a winch. He feels this is crucial, and it has been copied by others. He can hoist the spinnaker as far as possible by hand and then winch up the last few feet. This is particularly effective for the code zero, which has a two-part halyard and requires the winch for luff tension. He also thinks this is critical for dousing. He leaves one wrap around the winch and can walk to the bow, trailing the halyard behind him to capture the sail as it falls.

I asked if the Class 40 requires more or less physical effort than his former Open 50. He answered that the 40 is much more sensitive to stacking of weight. He spends at least 10 minutes on each tack moving sails and other bulk from side to side. "Everybody stacks maniacally, every tack, every gybe." This is incredibly taxing to do repeatedly. Everything onboard is packed into waterproof duffle bags marked with the contents. Every bag, including the sails, becomes stackable. The tacking process starts with moving the stack. Three quarters of the way through, he opens the valves to transfer the water ballast. At this point the leeward rail is underwater and the boat is very unstable, trying to turn up into irons. Then he tacks and reconfigures for the new heading.

Although the Class 40 has a seemingly large amount of space below, the actual living area is very small. The space under the cockpit is too cramped to be of practical use, and the forward area is for sail storage. The cabin area is tight quarters. Harris uses a single burner Jetboil stove to heat hot water for dehydrated astronaut food.

Harris matches my own feeling of having spiritually gained from singlehanded sailing. He readily admits to the addiction. "Solo sailing is a lot of grunt work and you're wet and tired. Then the sun comes out and the breeze goes aft to make it all worthwhile."

Class 40 Construction

The Class 40 got its official start in 2005 with the unveiling of class rules and a broad outline of design features. The acceptance of a boat midway between the Mini 6.50 and the Open 60 was immediate. Within months, fifty-four boats were launched, and an astounding twenty-five lined up for the 2006 Route du Rhum. One of the class founders, Michel Mirabel, commented, "We wanted to create a class for enlightened amateurs and a race circuit accessible to all. A class which enables all good sailors to fulfill their dream of offshore—easily, for pleasure, and without bankrupting themselves, or spending months in the yard on a complicated prototype."

As such a new class, the 40s have been built to the most modern designs from the start. Thus they have not had the intergenerational increases in boat speed that larger Open 60s have achieved over the past three decades. Although they all are designed to box rules, the Class 40 is a tighter box with many of the rules aimed at avoiding a spending war between skippers.

I asked Harris one of the most basic questions: how does a singlehander decide on one boat over another when each manufacturer is claiming the best boat?

Even within the box rule, budget remains the starting point. An off-the-shelf, production-design Class 40 costs nearly $1 million before being race ready. For a custom-design the team must be prepared to nearly double the boat budget.

Harris pointed at two new custom creations from designer/skipper Sam Manuard. *GDF Suez* triumphed in the 2013 Transat Jacques Vabre, and *Mare* in the 2012 Atlantic Cup. Harris felt that both had better acceleration out of tacks and pointed a bit higher upwind, which he had previously mentioned was a weakness in the Class 40s. Harris's budget meant a custom solution was out of reach, reducing his choice to currently designed production models. He looked at the performance success of the three designs by comparing various race results. The boats that he felt offered the highest level of performance were the Farr Kiwi 40, the Akilaria RC2, and the Pogo S2.

Next, he considered design and construction factors. Harris had worked as a boatbuilder through his twenties and had a good idea of what to look for. (A skipper without this background would be wise to hire an experienced and trusted professional to assist in these comparisons.) He examined the

materials, the thickness of the laminates, the structural grid of the fore-and-aft longitudinal framing and transverse framing, how the deck was fixed to the hull, the mast step, the rudders, and rudderposts. "All of the one hundred details and areas of stress."

Regarding the Pogo S2, which was least expensive of the three, Harris thought the ergonomics and layout were quite good, but he felt it was not as strong nor as well built or finished as the other choices. On the other hand, he thought the Kiwi 40 was extremely well built, with beautiful glass work and attention to detail—"almost a custom boat"— but the inside ergonomics failed completely. He also thought that it might be difficult to manage a boat being built in New Zealand, literally on the other side of the world. Finally, Harris felt the Akilaria RC2 construction was second to none. He was also pleased with the ergonomic interior layout and bulkhead placement. This brought the RC2 to the top of his list.

Before the final decision, Harris made a trip to England and sailed an RC2 sister boat in the Solent. He was thrilled with the performance over a two-day sail and made his decision then and there to buy. Then Harris hired Josh Hall (Race Director of the Global Ocean Race) to help project-manage the building. In his position with the GOR, Hall has numerous relationships with key suppliers throughout Europe who have all become Race Partners with the GOR. He was able to substantially lower the cost from these suppliers, a real benefit for the project.

Harris used the Marc Lombard design for the production hull and deck but customized winch placement, running rigging, and the navigation station. In the end Harris feels that he got good value for his money and will be competitive against the later generation and custom-designed boats when sailing around the world in the Global Ocean Race.

Lombard had selected MC-TEC, a builder in Tunisia. With Harris in the United States and Hall in France, it was much easier for Hall to keep an eye on the build process with a quick flight across the Mediterranean. Harris would certainly recommend this arrangement to any skipper. Harris and Hall had planned to commission and sail the boat out of Tunisia. But just a few weeks before it rolled off the line, the country underwent a revolution at the start of the Arab Spring, causing travel problems. The build schedule was delayed only two weeks, but a wise decision was made to move the commissioning to France.

IMOCA 60

Although a 60-foot boat is well beyond the financial range of most skippers and well beyond the range of coverage of this book, I wanted to know what it's like to sail an IMOCA (International Monohull Open Classes Association) 60 (formerly known as an Open 60).

I spoke at length with Ryan Breymaier, considered one of the most prominent and successful American shorthanded sailors in the professional ocean racing circuit today. Breymaier's experience and pedigree are unmatched. He started offshore sailing while at St. Mary's College in Maryland, United States, where he quickly became one of the top racers. While this taught him the concepts of speed, from a singlehanded point of view the other activities he undertook were more important. He often delivered 40- to 55-foot boats between races, offshore and singlehanded without an autopilot. After college he spent 14 years ocean racing in boats between 50 and 80 feet before he stepped onto an IMOCA 60. These early experiences were invaluable, setting him up for his current level of success in the sport: since he had sailed large boats from the start, he didn't face the usual apprehension of moving up to a larger boat. Over the past three years Ryan has accelerated his program, aiming at the 2016 Vendée Globe. His accomplishments include:

- 2010, 5th place in the Barcelona World Race (nonstop, doublehanded circumnavigation)
- 2011, 6th place in the IMOCA World Championship
- 2012, 1st place in the Atlantic Cup in a Class 40
- 2012, 2nd place in the Transat Québec Saint-Malo
- 2013, world speed record holder, New York to San Francisco, onboard a VOR 70

I asked Ryan to speak about what it is like to sail an IMOCA 60 compared to a 30-foot cruiser. He is so utterly comfortable sailing these huge boats at high speed that it was difficult for him to make the comparison, so I had to press him with individual questions. The best comparison came at the end of our talk. I told him that with the big spinnaker in high winds, I can get my Olson 30 up to 12½ knots. At that speed the boat is really humming; I'm on the edge of my seat and the boat is on the edge of control. Breymaier said that he feels the exact same sensation on an IMOCA 60, the only difference being that the boat is surfing at 28 knots. It's the same hum of the boat, the same twitchy helm, and the same feeling of sailing on the edge.

Breymaier's main focus throughout the interview was how the boats are set up for ease of singlehander control. This entails every aspect of design—from changing sails, to sail balance, to the feel of the helm.

For example, on a typical 30-foot boat, changing the headsail involves dragging the sailbag from below, easing the sheet, struggling to pull down the existing jib, unhanking, flaking, folding, and stuffing it into a sailbag, and then unfolding, hanking, and hauling up the new jib. There is a lot of material open to the wind.

The sails on an IMOCA 60 are simply too large to work this way. It would be impossible to handle a sail that is lying open on the deck. It is nearly impossible to wrap one's arms around it, let alone lift its 70-kilogram (155 lb.) weight. So the process is entirely different. First, in anything other than light winds, the boat is headed dead downwind. Unlike on a smaller boat, it is impossible to use the roller furler in higher winds. The existing foresail is rolled up tight on its furling unit. Then the entire sail and furler is dropped onto the deck. The foresails are always stored tightly rolled on their furler, even on the deck. They are stored in bags 6 feet long and 18 inches in diameter (2 m by 50 cm). The heaviest weighs 155 pounds (70 kg), which is at the limit of what one person can move alone. The sails are stored in the bow, on the windward side of the boat. Only after the boat is turned downwind is the new sail carried on deck. Breymaier described this as the most labor-intensive job on the boat. It can only be done by brute force (see photo page 54). Once on deck, the sail is held in place with ratchet straps secured to pad eyes in predetermined locations. The new sail is raised in a tight roll. The halyard—with a locking mechanism—is raised and then tightened on a 3-to-1 downhaul purchase with a coffee grinder and a big winch. Only after the sail is up and secure is the roller furler unwound, always sailing dead downwind.

Once the sail is out, the boat is turned to the correct direction and the sail trimmed. Obviously this is an extensive and time-consuming process to move from a deep run to sailing close-hauled. While still downwind, the foresail is trimmed roughly to its final trim, or even a bit further. Then the boat is brought back to course slowly. When the desired course is reached, the sail gets its final trim to perfection. Hopefully this is an easing of the sail rather than a grind against the full power of the boat. The entire process of changing from one foresail to another takes 15–30 minutes. Just rolling up a gennaker takes 4 or 5 minutes of constant grinding in second gear on a size 65 winch. Breymaier emphasized that it is entirely too dangerous to attempt a sail change when sailing into the wind. He bears away to dead downwind nearly always. This is a far cry from the 48 seconds it takes me to change hanked on foresails on my Olson 30 while close-hauled.

Of course everything works fine when well planned. I asked Ryan what he does when things go wrong. His answer was that the skipper is better off doing nothing than doing something in a half-planned way. If a squall catches the skipper off guard, it would be a mistake to attempt to change the sails during the squall. Even if he was able to roll up a sail during the squall and then attempt to lower the furled sail to the deck, "if the top of the sail unrolled a little bit or if it dropped in the water, then you would have a real issue on your hands." And of course a "real issue" with a jib that measures 130 square meters (1,400 sq. ft.) is a lot different from effort required by the small sails that most skippers are used to working with. Brute strength just will not work on a 60-foot boat. It is futile to try. The better approach is to ride out any squalls with the existing sails and change them after it passes.

On a 60-foot boat, retrieving a jib from the water becomes a Herculean task for a singlehander. Note the jib is still connected via the tack and sheet. (Courtesy Ryan Breymaier)

Of course it is best to make the right decisions in the first place.

Just after he rounded Cape Horn in the double-handed Barcelona World Race, a metal swivel at the top of his roller-furling jib broke, dropping the sail overboard. Breymaier put the boat into irons and let it drift backward, allowing the sail to stream off the bow while connected at the tack and sheet. It took the two-man crew more than 15 minutes to drag the sail back on board. Breymaier does not want to contemplate what it would have taken single-handed. Because the sail is so large, it could not be packed up from the soggy mess on deck. The only way to save it was for Breymaier to climb the mast and reattach the stay. They used another halyard to hoist the sail back up and then drop it onto the deck in a somewhat more orderly stack.

The mainsail is similar: "It takes a long time in a slow gear on a winch to make anything happen." When I asked Ryan how long it takes to raise his mainsail, he laughed. "You would hope to never, ever, ever have to pull it up from all the way down to all the way to the top." He did it doublehanded during the Barcelona World Race when they needed some repairs at the top of the sail. With two people it took 10 minutes or more of constant grinding to get it all the way up. He guessed it would take 15 minutes with one person. Just to go from the second reef to the first reef takes 10 minutes of constant grinding

IMOCA 60 design features include a canting keel with bulb attachment well out to windward; a daggerboard lowered on the leeward side and raised above deck and visible on the windward side; twin rudders spread wide under the hull; short tiller steering, even on a 60-foot boat; a wing-shaped mast that rotates 50 degrees in each direction; and outriggers (deck spreaders) that keep the shroud base wide, giving less compression and allowing for a lighter, rotating mast. Not visible are halyard locks on the foresails and a 3-to-1 purchase on the main halyard. *(Courtesy Nico Martinez)*

when sailing downwind. "Everything you do, you plan out well in advance and make sure you have a really good reason for doing it." The halyard on an IMOCA 60 is 3-to-1. When heading downwind with the sail against the shrouds, it is very difficult to raise the sail even one reef point. So it is necessary to head up and luff as much as possible to raise the sail past the spreaders. Brute strength is never an option. If possible, it is better to wait for wave action to reduce the pressure on the sails and take a couple of quick turns on the winch. (Breymaier mentioned that a key reason for wing masts on some IMOCA 60s is that they don't have spreaders or shrouds, reducing the difficulty of pulling a sail down to reef.)

Steering the boat in anything over 8 knots of wind is just not done. Breymaier and his crew did a lot of testing comparing the autopilot against hand driving and found that 80% of the time, the autopilot is better, even in large wave conditions. Although hand steering might be advantageous for a short time, the autopilot becomes advantageous on average over a longer period.

Sail balance takes on a whole new meaning on the 60s. They have perfect sail balance with *no*

weather helm at all. The rudders are balanced and the sails are balanced: the full main with the big jib, one reef with the #2, two reefs with the #3. "You can steer up or down and there is never any resistance to push against. You can't drive against the weather helm because there isn't any."

I was able to confirm Breymaier's statement about weather helm with Merfyn Owen, partner in Owen Clarke Design and one of the world's most famous racing yacht designers. Unlike most race boats, built for windward/leeward round-the-buoys courses, the IMOCA 60 is built for open ocean racing. Therefore pinching to windward is not a required feature. For this reason, the boats are designed with dagger-boards that twist the entire boat toward the wind, offering excellent pointing ability. This allows the skipper to ease the jibsheet slightly to increase speed. At the same time, the rudders, the main source of weather helm on most boats and a source of considerable drag, are designed rather small. (A more in-depth discussion on IMOCA 60 foils is presented in Chapter 5, Keeping the Boat Upright.)

The only balance problem is occasional lee helm downwind because the gennaker (a cross between a genoa and spinnaker) is so big compared to the mainsail. Breymaier's spinnaker measures a whopping 425 square meters (4,575 sq. ft.) as compared to the 170-square-meter (1,830 sq. ft.) mainsail.

Everything on the boat is built to have balance. I asked if the autopilot could handle the boat if it got out of control, and Ryan answered, "With twin rudders firmly planted in the water they just don't get out of control." Even with a big spinnaker up in 35–40 knots of wind, the pilot will drive the boat in flat water and the correct sail plan, i.e., three reefs and a storm jib. The autopilot is capable of maintaining control in 40-foot waves and 60 knots of wind. The risk is greater that the spinnaker will blow out than the pilot will lose control. Breymaier always uses the autopilot set to true wind direction when sailing downwind. This is an obvious indication of his confidence in the autopilot. Smaller units would not be able to handle a dramatic change in apparent wind if the boat suddenly sped up and the apparent wind moved forward. The autopilots on these boats have a 3D-sensor from a guided missile system tracking the boat's motion in all six axes. It learns how much rudder to apply in every situation. Breymaier's NKE autopilot has seven different adjustable variables, each of which has three different adjustments with ten different settings, for a total of 210 parameters of control. (In contrast, famous French skipper Michel Desjoyeaux commented that he usually sails in compass mode because it requires him to pay constant attention to the wind and make adjustments more often.)

Breymaier noted that the Volvo Ocean Race crewed boats are not built with the same level of balance as the IMOCA 60s because they depend on a helmsman to constantly maintain heading and crew to constantly adjust trim. These boats are built to be unforgiving for driving or sail trim, the exact opposite in design philosophy compared to the singlehanded IMOCA 60s. The IMOCA 60s reward getting the sail trim and angle of heel right and then leaving the boat in the sweet spot.

I asked Ryan how the pilot can handle sudden changes, such as with raising the spinnaker. He replied that the pilot is the first thing to work on. He would switch the autopilot to compass mode to follow a straight course regardless of what happened to the apparent wind direction when the boat suddenly accelerated. "In compass mode you could hit the boat with a train and it would still go straight." If the pilot is set to compass mode deep downwind with high damping and maximum power, it will not follow the jump in apparent wind direction when the spinnaker catches. After the sail is up and running, the pilot is adjusted to the correct course and the sails are trimmed for the new point of sail.

The spinnaker is put up in a sock. A winch is used to raise the sock part way, and once the spinnaker catches, the sock runs up by itself. The chutes used on this type of offshore boat have a cloth weight at least twice as heavy as a spinnaker on a typical inshore boat of the same size. It is unlikely to explode when flogging when the sock is brought back down, which can take up to 2 minutes.

At this point I asked, "How do you handle it when things get out of control?" He replied, "If you Chinese gybe [broaching downwards and gybing the main, rather than broaching on a round-up]

the boat when going downwind or if you auto-tack going upwind, then you've got a big problem on your hands." With the water ballast and canting keel both on the wrong side of the boat, the mast is over at 70 degrees with the leeward side of the boat underwater and the skipper walking on the side of the cockpit wall with "a mountain of boat beside you . . . From there you have to get everything rolled up, stored or socked—whatever, so that you can get the boat back on its feet and sailing again."

Jean Le Cam (a multiple winner of the Vendée Globe) gave this advice: "If you have that problem and the boat Chineses, go inside, make yourself a cup of tea, drink it, relax, and then twenty minutes later go outside and calmly sort it out. Nothing is going to break. It doesn't do you any good to be stressed out about it. Just relax, take a deep breath, calm down, and then methodically fix the problem."

Breymaier has gone through the Chinese gybe process at least five times and has auto-tacked three times, so he has the experience to go through this calmly.

Breymaier emphasized that everything on these boats is built to a size and strength such that nothing is going to break with any mistake—the mast, the boom, the shrouds, everything, even down to the mainsail battens, are built at least 30% stronger than an inshore boat of the same size. The backstays have a strength factor of 7-to-1. (Note: Just two months after this interview Breymaier broke the mast on *Hugo Boss*.)

Breymaier said that the one thing all French sailors have in common is they don't get excited on boats. "If something goes wrong they laugh, light a cigarette, and very methodically get back to getting it fixed. That attitude is certainly not an Anglo-Saxon or a North American attitude, but it's absolutely crucial to sailing big boats by yourself."

"Loick Peyron said it best: 'sailing around the world in and of itself is not very difficult. But sailing around the world very quickly and safely to win a race is one of the hardest things there is.' This is something that the public doesn't always grasp when following the Vendée. If you look at the last race you have two guys out in front—the most highly trained racers of their generation; then you

Down below, the IMOCA 60 more closely resembles the cockpit of a starship fighter than anything recognizable as a sailboat. *(Courtesy Ryan Breymaier)*

Repairs underway on an IMOCA 60—the singlehanded racer has to be a master of all trades, jury-rigging repairs of all kinds. *(Courtesy Ryan Breymaier)*

have a group of six or seven guys who have been doing this for a very long time but have gotten to the age when they are not keeping up physically or their boats are a few design cycles behind; and behind them you have the gentlemen adventurers who don't have the boats or the experience to really compete." Just as in Formula 1 auto racing, the opportunities for the gentlemen adventurers are going away in the upper class of sailing. The top tier is fully professional now.

The IMOCA 60s are complex. With a canting keel, water ballast, and daggerboards, there is a lot to consider and a lot of changes to make with any maneuver. There is much more to these boats than trimming the sails and steering. "At 3:00 in the morning, it is very easy to forget that the forward, port side water tank is full."

When it comes to sailing to the best possible speed over an extended race, Breymaier thought that my analysis (see Chapter 15, Maintaining a Winning Attitude for the Duration of a Long-Distance Singlehanded Race) was right on the money. No quarter is given for anything other than full participation. All of the boats establish their polars with a crew of three or four driving by hand, racing against other boats in short races. The singlehanded skipper is still expected to sail to those polars, alone with not another boat in sight.

To help with this, the original sailing performance software was developed for use on the IMOCA 60s by Adrena. With this software, the skipper is constantly aware of how fast the boat is sailing relative to its polars. The skipper is kept constantly aware of how he is doing on all aspects of boat speed. In its simplest explanation, the software uses the current boat speed and direction, along with the current wind speed and direction, to tell him "you are sailing at 85% of polar speed."

I asked Ryan if it is possible to trim constantly, as they do in the Volvo Ocean Race. He replied that the VOR is a series of short races, not an around-the-world race. "If you trimmed like that on an IMOCA 60, the mainsheet would be dead in fifteen days. You are not going to carry and change four mainsheets over the course of a race."

The sails are a handful on the IMOCA 60. *(Courtesy Ryan Breymaier)*

of adjustment depends on the length of the cycle in wind fluctuations. If the cycle lasts less than 10 minutes, the skipper can stay below and press buttons on the autopilot to head up or down by a few degrees and the speed will remain at a high percentage of maximum. If the cycles last a half hour or more, the skipper keeps the true-wind angle but goes outside and trims the sails slightly. The skipper gets a feel for the cycle of wind fluctuations from watching closely.

Roland Jourdain noted that the average speed of these 60-foot boats in the Southern Ocean was 16 knots in 2004, 17 knots in 2007, and 18 knots in 2008. The last Vendée made a leap of 3 knots in average boat speed from 19 to 22. The amount of money going into this and the expectations of the people driving these boats continues to expand. Breymaier mentioned that the IMOCA boats he started on six years ago are well behind in technology and boat speed today. In fact, a modern Class 40 can sail as fast downwind as an older 60.

I commented that the newest IMOCA 60s have a completely enclosed cockpit, making it look more like the pilothouse of an aircraft carrier. Breymaier agreed. There is the constant noise and vibration of a train, but the rest of the time it's like camping. "You feel like a train driver or an aircraft pilot. You have a nice display that is showing where you're going and you have the pilot controls right by your hand. You can just sit there and play with the pilot to drive the boat the whole time if you want to. Except for those times when you have to put on your foul-weather gear and get wet so you can go out and trim the sails." This is why there is so much protection on the newest boats. The skipper can trim all the sails without ever being exposed to the spray or rain. This is the future of the IMOCA 60s: the skipper will be able to make all adjustments without getting wet.

But is there a happy medium between going below to forecast weather for 8 hours straight and constantly trimming as the VOR racers do? The answer is to set the sail trim up for perfect balance and set the autopilot to true-wind angle. With this the pilot drives the boat optimally, and then the skipper only has to watch for changes in wind strength or direction. "If the wind drops a little you come up 3–4 degrees and if the wind strengthens you bear away 3–4 degrees." The type

CHAPTER 5 **KEEPING THE BOAT UPRIGHT**

MINIMIZING HEEL IMPROVES UPWIND PERFORMANCE

Keeping the boat upright is not about avoiding sinking. It is all about upwind performance. As a singlehander on a standard sailboat, especially an ultralight like the Olson 30, I have a huge handicap racing against crewed boats in anything over 10 knots of wind. That handicap is leeway. Since I do not have four heavy men sitting on the rail, my boat heels more than the crewed competitors when beating into the wind. The result of the extra heel is that I drift significantly more to leeward. This chapter is based on my attempt to understand and correct the problem.

The following excellent explanation of the effect of boat heel on leeway is adapted from the website of Waypoint Amsterdam, a highly respected Royal Yachting Association sailing school in Amsterdam, Netherlands.

The keel and rudder of a sailboat are there to steer and to resist sideways forces. They do this by generating lift from the water flowing over them in the same way that an aircraft wing generates lift, though on a boat the keel and rudder are vertical so the lift goes sideways.

Although the wings on aircraft are asymmetrically shaped to be more curved on top, a wing with a symmetrical section will also generate lift by being set up to have an angle of attack to the fluid flow.

When a boat is sailing, the force that the sails generate can be divided into a driving component in line with the boat and a sideways component at 90° to the boat. The sideways force makes the boat slip to leeward so the boat actually travels at a small angle downwind of its heading. The boat's leeway has given the keel an "angle of attack."

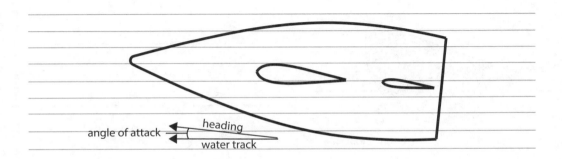

A sailboat's driving force is not all forward, there is a sideways component—known as leeway—that accounts for boats not heading precisely where steered, giving the keel an "angle of attack."

In essence, the boat is not pointing in the direction that it is traveling. For example, if the boat is sailing perfectly toward a distant tower on port tack at a course of 270°, a line from the center of the transom to the bow would actually be pointing at a slightly higher angle, perhaps 273°. In this case the angle of attack is 3°. It is the angle of attack that allows a symmetrical keel to provide lift, just like an asymmetrical wing. In this case the lift provided by the keel is the same 3°, allowing the boat to travel at 270° rather than 273°.

The impact of speed: one of the most commonly used phrases in sailing is "speed is your friend." This is because the amount of lift produced by any foil is a square of the speed. If the boat doubles in speed, the lift increases by four times. This is the reason why it is vital to gain speed as quickly as possible coming out of each tack. If a boat sailing at 6 knots drops down to 3 knots while tacking, not only is the boat falling behind in distance traveled, but has cut its ability to point by three quarters. The reason why singlehanders practice tacking is not to reduce the few seconds it takes to tack but to maintain or quickly regain as much speed as possible after the tack is finished. Because of the squared factor, even a small drop in speed has a big impact on lift.

Heeling effect on the keel: the lift that a foil [in this case, the keel] generates is perpendicular to its surface. If a boat is upright any lift generated by the keel acts horizontally. As the

boat heels, the lift forces from the foils move away from the horizontal.

From the diagram we can see that as the angle of heel increases the horizontal force decreases. The lift of the keel actually brings it even closer to the surface of the water, creating even more heel. The accompanying table shows how the horizontal force from a foil depends on the angle of heel.

For heel angles up to 15°, the horizontal force is much the same as the lift force. [Later in this chapter we note that boat designers aim at 15° as their optimum heel angle.] As the boat heels to 20° and beyond, the horizontal component of the lift force starts to fall off more rapidly. By

Horizontal Force on a Keel in Relation to Angle of Heel

Angle of Heel	Horizontal Force
0	100%
5	100%
10	98%
15	97%
20	94%
25	91%
30	87%
35	82%
40	77%
45	71%
50	64%
55	57%
60	50%

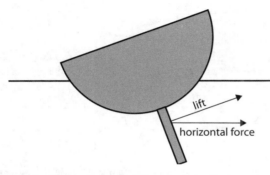

The angle of lift force from the keel changes as the boat heels.

the time the boat is heeling over at 60° only half of the lift force is going in the direction that we need.

Heeling effect on the rudder: as the boat heels the horizontal component of the rudder's lift is also reduced. If the weather helm and boat speed are constant then we need to increase the rudder angle to generate more lift so that the horizontal component stays the same. At 25° of heel the rudder has to generate about 10% more lift than it did when vertical to produce the same turning force; if we push the boat to 40° we're asking the rudder for 30% more lift.

Increasing the angle of heel also has the effect of increasing the weather helm. This needs more turning force from the rudder to counteract it just as the effective turning force it produces is being reduced. The result is that as the boat heels we find ourselves winding on more and more rudder to keep her running true. Because of the two-pronged impacts, the rudder angle that we need increases even more quickly than the table of horizontal force for heel angle would suggest.

Increasing the lift generated by the rudder also increases the rudder's drag. So as we heel the boat we get more drag from the rudder for a given turning force. Drag slows the boat down, and slowing the boat down increases leeway.

To put the above explanation into the simplest terms, excess boat heel absolutely destroys the ability to point when beating into the wind. There is nothing quite as depressing as watching myself tack well above other boats, only to slip far below them by the first turning mark. It also means that at a crowded starting line, I must pinch up or else I will fall onto the boats below me. Of course, pinching reduces speed, and I am soon at the back of the pack sucking dirty air. The result of all this is that I can never win a race against crewed boats in more than 10 knots of wind. In more than 15 knots I'm dead last.

It is important to understand that the angle of excess boat heel is not really noticeable while sailing. I look at the heel of my own boat and look at the other boats and I can't see any difference. But as the chart above indicates, just a 5-degree increase in heel has a substantial effect on leeway. The effect of a 10-degree difference in heel is massive! Naturally I take steps to reduce heel by changing my headsail from a #1 to a #3 or by reefing earlier than crewed boats, but this simply means that I have smaller sails and am traveling slower anyway.

Singlehanders who do not race against crewed boats, probably 99% of my readers, may be wondering: why this is so important? Would a man wear his best polished brogues to run 26 miles, even if it was not a marathon competition? Would a woman wear spiked heels for a hike in the woods? Both are possible, but they are certainly not efficient. The purpose of this book is to teach efficiency in sailing. Although the methods discussed below are a significant step beyond what most would look for in a cruiser, they should certainly be considered in any boat destined for singlehanding.

STACKING

For standard design boats, stacking is the simplest means to replace rail meat. As discussed in Chapter 4, high-performance racers from the Mini 6.50 to the Class 40s and even the IMOCA 60s stack every piece of equipment on the windward side with every tack. Ellen MacArthur said that it took her several hours to finish each tack. This is even done with the Volvo Ocean Race boats. One sailor spoke of how it took 10 minutes with their entire crew to complete a tack. Nine of those minutes were spent moving absolutely everything to the windward side. They went to the extreme of shifting every coffee cup.

For a singlehander, I think that shifting every coffee cup is going beyond the necessary into the ridiculous, even the detrimental. A singlehander's time is better spent elsewhere—like sailing the boat.

However, I do think that some of the especially heavy items on board can be moved in a few minutes for tacks that will last an hour or longer. For example, spare sails, an inflatable life raft, inflatable dinghy, water jugs, and boxes of canned food could all be stacked. The skipper should think about what is being carried for the voyage. Perhaps 25 gallons (94.6 L) of water is stocked on a trip to Hawaii. This alone weighs more than 200 pounds (about 90 kg). The life raft required for the Singlehanded Transpac weighs another 75 pounds (34 kg), and the dinghy that will be used to row to shore weighs 50 pounds (about 23 kg) more. If we add in some canned food and the sails, we're approaching the weight equivalent of three men on the rail.

It is easy to disregard this effort as unnecessary. But look again at the horizontal force table presented earlier. A reduction in heel from 20 degrees to 15 degrees increases the horizontal force by 3%. A singlehander is on the open ocean—he will not notice that he is giving away forward movement. But when next to a fully crewed boat and within ¼ mile of travel distance, the skipper will recognize that something is seriously wrong. A ridiculous question: would a skipper carrying three men on the boat tell them to sit below on the cabin floor rather than on the windward rail?

The boat should be set up in advance for this stacking activity. For example, loops of spectra can be mounted inside, at the hull-deck joint, to hang water jugs. (I use the bolts from my toe rail for this purpose.) The skipper should imagine what effort will be required to reach into this tight corner in rough seas. Velcro might be easier to connect than hooks. Lee cloths on the quarter berths can be used to hold the sails, life raft, and dinghy on the high side. The main consideration is that all of this weight must be very secure. Having a sail slip from the windward quarter berth to the cabin floor is inconvenient. Having a water jug break off would be a much greater mess.

It is much less effort to shift the weight just before tacking, i.e., it is easier to drop 600 pounds from the windward side to the leeward side than the opposite. The boat will heel an extra amount during this time. The autopilot should be turned down a few degrees to offset the leeward weight attempting to roll-tack the boat by itself. But the alternative is that the boat would heel extra after the tack is completed but before the skipper can shift the ballast to the high side.

SPECIALIZED BOAT DESIGN CHANGES

Boat designers have taken substantial steps to minimize boat heel and improve pointing, particularly with high-performance singlehanded boats. These steps include water ballast, canting keels, daggerboards, and the newest Dynamic Stability Systems (DSS)—which is covered on page 65.

Water Ballast

When I started investigating concepts of keeping the boat upright, I was only looking at one thing—getting the keel vertical so that it acted properly as a wing and minimized leeward drift. My conversation with Geoff Van Gorkom made me realize that I was far too limited in my thinking.

Van Gorkom is a well-known boat designer in Rhode Island. He has a particularly long history designing boats in the 28- to 35-foot range with water ballast integrated into the original design. He has also designed water-ballast systems to be retrofit into existing boats, including the Olson 30.

The VG-Mount Gay 30 was the first boat that Van Gorkom designed with integrated water ballast. The Mount Gay 30 class boat originated as the Whitbread 30, a smaller version of the Whitbread 60 that was used in the Whitbread Round the World Race (forerunner to the current Volvo Ocean Race). The original design was conceived as a box-rule boat that could be handled with a limited crew. It allowed for water ballast to compensate for the lack of three or four bodies on the rail. Although the Mount Gay 30 class has faded, the boat remains an excellent forerunner to later water-ballast designs.

Water ballast is carried in built-in tanks inside the hull on either side of the boat at the widest beam. A typical boat, such as the VG-Mount Gay 30, has a ballast tank capacity of 300 liters (about 80 gal.) on each side, which weighs about 300 kilograms (about 660 lb.), the same as three burly crew sitting on the rail. The boat sails optimally at 15 degrees of heel upwind. The water ballast reduces heel by 3–4 degrees in 12–15 knots of breeze, bringing heel into the desired range.

To fill the tanks, a scoop pipe is lowered out the bottom of the hull while the boat is moving. The speed of the boat forces water up the scoop into the

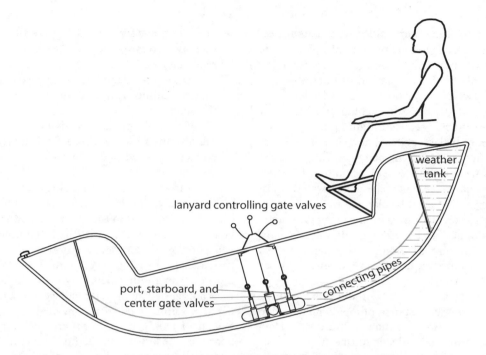

weather
tank

lanyard controlling gate valves

connecting pipes

port, starboard, and
center gate valves

Water ballast tanks allow the singlehander to shift ballast when tacking; they reduce the heel angle when sailing to windward, improving the forward drive of the boat. Gate valves are opened by means of lanyards in the cockpit.

tank, although a pump might be required toward
the end. This process can take a few minutes. The
skipper knows the tank is full when water comes
out the deck vent. Once the tank is full, the scoop
is drawn back flush with the hull. The deck vents
allow air to enter or exit the tank to offset the flow of
water. My friend Bruce Schwab suffered an explo-
sion of the leeward tank on his Open 60 during the
Around Alone when he forgot to open the air vent
during a gybe. Afterwards he installed a foolproof
auxiliary air vent.

Large-diameter pipes connect the port and
starboard tanks. To tack, the skipper uses levers in
the cockpit to open valves and allow the water to
flow downhill to the leeward side tank. As the tank
fills, the boat will lean well over to leeward, often
putting the rail underwater. This forces the boat to
round up like a roll tack on a dinghy, thus assist-
ing an experienced user with an immediate tack.
If the tack is delayed, the skipper has to fight extra
weather helm as the boat attempts to round up on

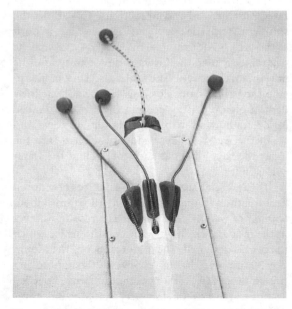

The gate valves that control water movement in the water ballast tanks
are opened and closed via lanyards and cleats at the base of the cockpit.

its own. While the water is flowing, the mainsheet is eased to reduce pressure on the sail and keep the boat somewhat upright. Once all the water is in the leeward tank, the boat is steered through the tack, leaving the water on the new windward side.

Because of the delay in tacking and the water on the leeward side reducing righting moment and speed, water-ballast systems are impractical for short-distance, round-the-buoys racing against crews. A tacking duel would be impossible. Van Gorkom emphasized that tacking with water ballast is a challenge that must be planned well in advance compared to a crew running from one rail to another. On the Mount Gay 30, tacking takes 40 seconds, including shifting the ballast. These systems are best suited for distance races with several miles between each maneuver.

If a crash tack is required without sufficient time to shift the water ballast first, pumps can be used to slowly bring the water to the windward side. Having water on the leeward side in this circumstance has a very bad effect on boat speed. In windy conditions a crash tack might pin the boat on its side until the water can be shifted.

On most boats the tanks on each side are separated into forward and aft sections. This allows the skipper to trim the boat by using either one or both of the tanks. For example, in bumpy seas it may be desirable to keep the forward tank empty and the bow out of the waves. The tanks also have baffles to stop the ballast from sloshing. In one notable incident, a Figaro sailing deep in high winds danced up on its bow after hitting a moderate wave and all of the water ballast suddenly sloshed into the forward tank. The boat had stopped but the water ballast hadn't.

The essential question: is 3–4 degrees of reduced heel worth carrying an extra 300 kilograms (about 660 lb.) of weight? The answer is a resounding yes in the moderate or high-wind conditions for which the boat is designed. The performance of the Mount Gay 30 improves 10% to 15% with this slight reduction in heel. Van Gorkom taught me what I needed to understand—reducing heel actually has three different impacts on overall performance:

- First, it orients the keel more vertically, thereby increasing the wing effect and reducing leeway.
- Second, it orients the sails more vertically, thereby adding greater power and speed to the boat.
- Third, with the greater speed of water passing over the keel, the wing effect is increased and leeway is reduced even further.

This threefold impact of keeping the boat upright is what really improves performance. Of course, each impact feeds into the others in a cycle. As the boat travels faster, the sails can be trimmed more efficiently, generating even more speed, which in turn adds to the wing effect on the keel and reducing leeway in another step.

Another benefit of water ballast is that the skipper can dump it when not needed. Imagine the benefit of telling three burly crew to jump overboard for the last run to the finish line. In light air water ballast might not be needed at all. If the winds change during the race, water can be pumped in or out for the conditions. Even in heavy air it might be beneficial to dump the ballast for downwind runs, catapulting the boat to surf city.

In essence, water ballast can turn a light boat with limited righting moment into a powerhouse built for maximum speed in high winds. This is why water ballast is used on Mini 6.50 proto boats, Class 40s, and IMOCA 60s. In light winds these open ocean boats dump their ballast to become nimble. In the 40-knot winds of the open ocean, they load up on ballast to become stable racing machines.

The stability factor cannot be overstated for another reason. In a chop or in heavy seas, a light boat is bounced back and forth with each wave. This decreases the ability of the keel to establish a hydrodynamic flow. It also pumps the sails, constantly powering up and then dumping wind. But adding 300 kilograms (660 lb.) of weight stabilizes the boat in a certain direction and with a certain amount of heel, enabling the skipper to properly set the sails and drive forward in a steady direction. Substantial speed is gained because of this stability.

Canting Keels

I asked Geoff Van Gorkom to compare systems that might be appropriate for a boat like mine. Would he choose water ballast or a canting keel? He pointed me to an Open 30 boat that he had designed in 2007. A canting keel has greater righting moment. This is because the weight of the bulb is much farther outboard than the weight of water inside the hull. Also, a canting keel can be significantly lighter than a fixed keel, reducing the weight of the boat as a whole.

His very simple Open 30 design has a 750-kilogram (about 1,650 lb.) keel (lead bulb with a high-ductile-strength iron fin). The cant is controlled by a block and tackle system with 6:1 purchase and lines running aft to the cockpit and through jammers. When tacking, the skipper eases the line down. Suddenly dropping the keel would result in damage. If a rush tack was required, the keel could be pulled up from the low side using the winch in moderate winds. Referring to the Open 30 *OverProof*, which has a canting keel and daggerboards, Van Gorkom commented that the owner is overjoyed with the performance and the way that the foils "talk to each other." He felt it would be an ideal boat for single-handed sailing.

On larger boats, hydraulic systems are used to move the keel. As it cants to the side, the forward keel bearing is lifted and the aft keel bearing is lowered. Thus the canted keel always has a 5-degree angle to the water flow, giving it an angle of attack. Like a wing, there is lift on the keel. However, this lift is on the windward side of the boat, causing the boat to heel farther to leeward. This reduces the righting moment because it is lifting on the windward side of the boat; the boat heels over more quickly and there is less sail force drive.

Merfyn Owen, partner in Owen Clarke Design, as mentioned previously, one of the best-known and most experienced designers of singlehanded racing boats today, has written an article describing an instance in which the canted keel can lead to loss of control. If the bow plows underwater and the boat tilts downward farther than the lift of the canted keel, it is possible that the lift of the keel is reversed, now on the top side of the keel (it is normally on the underside) pushing the bow down. This in turn can lead to an instant reversal in flow over the rudder from one side to the other, leading to an uncontrollable bear-away. This can be counteracted by adding buoyancy in the bow to ensure the bow does not dive in the first place.

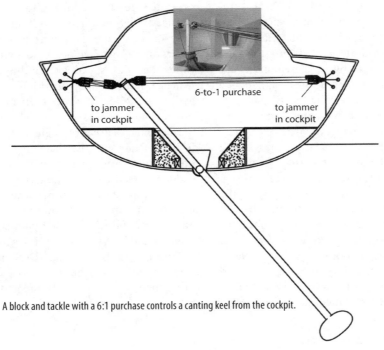

A block and tackle with a 6:1 purchase controls a canting keel from the cockpit.

RUDDER LOAD

I had a long technical discussion with Owen that touched upon rudder load. I first needed to understand sailor Ryan Breymaier's comment that the IMOCA 60 does not have weather helm.

Owen explained there are two main reasons why typical race boats have weather helm. First, many boats have a deliberate amount of built-in rake in the mast, loading up the rudder as a lifting foil. This is done because the surface area of the keel, and thus the wing effect, is limited. By adding extra load to the rudder, the boat points as high as possible to get the first cross after the start or be first at the mark on a typical windward/leeward race course. The rudder is used as part of the upwind foil area. The profile view of the boat's design shows the rudder is deliberately loaded in order to make up for a small keel. This reduces leeway and improves pointing toward the weather mark.

On an IMOCA 60, the skipper is not as concerned with getting to the weather mark as a round-the-buoys racer. Offshore skippers prefer to reduce rudder area in light air. The design is aimed at driving the boat downwind with greatest efficiency. The skipper balances the rake of the mast so that the rudder does not receive excess load. Even when sailing upwind, the IMOCA 60 skipper foots off slightly to get maximum speed. After all, the weather mark might be 600 miles away, and the wind will certainly shift during the voyage. It is not worth pinching in these conditions. For these reasons the rudder is not designed as a part of the upwind foil area. The IMOCA 60 gets all the lift it needs from a very-high-aspect, very efficient asymmetrical daggerboard. Designers prefer to get the lift from a special-purpose lifting foil, i.e., the daggerboard, rather than using the rudder for the dual purpose of steering and lifting. If the daggerboard is positioned vertically in the water, it provides nearly all of the lift required to make the boat point with a very small amount of added drag. Rudders, positioned at the stern and being low-aspect foils, are not nearly as efficient as the purposefully designed daggerboard. "You need them, but you'd love not to have to need them," Owen said about rudders. Since the IMOCA 60 is designed for a specific type of sailing, the rudder loads are relatively small.

Second, the rudder blade itself is designed to reduce load. On a typical boat the center of effort on the rudder blade is positioned aft of the rudder shaft. On the IMOCA 60, by changing the shape of the rudder and moving more of the surface area forward, the center of effort on the blade is much closer to the rudder shaft and the load is significantly reduced.

For most racers, the feel of the tiller is important for understanding the trim of the sails. Designers of round-the-buoy racers build this feel into the shape of the rudder. On the 60s, however, the autopilot steers the boat so there no reason to design feel into the rudder. The autopilot does not need feel, and the skipper is rarely holding the tiller in any case.

In smaller boats, the force on the rudder blade is a linear function of the angle of the blade to the water: doubling the angle results in doubled force. If the typical weather helm of 5 degrees is doubled to 10 degrees, then the force on the helm is doubled from 3 kilograms (6.6 lb.) to 6 kilograms (more than 13 lb.)—an amount that is certainly manageable.

But boat speed has a much more dramatic effect on rudder load. In addition to the linear effect of rudder angle, the force on a rudder is also a function of boat speed—squared. Round-the-buoys racers up to 40 feet don't normally exceed 1.25 times their hull speed, even in high winds at their fastest point of sail. The IMOCA 60s can easily get up to 2.25 or 2.5 times their hull speed. Going upwind at 10 knots with a helm load of 3 kilograms and 5 degrees of angle on the rudder would feel fine. Then we raise the gennaker and go flying down waves and surfing at 25 knots. When we suddenly need to make a big adjustment to drive down a wave to avoid broaching, we will face at least 6 times more force on the rudder because of boat speed and the doubled helm angle. Suddenly there would be a total of 15 times more load, or 45 kilograms (99 lb.) of force. Designers take major steps to reduce weather helm so that skippers can drive their boat at the extreme end of the performance requirements. It would do no good to build

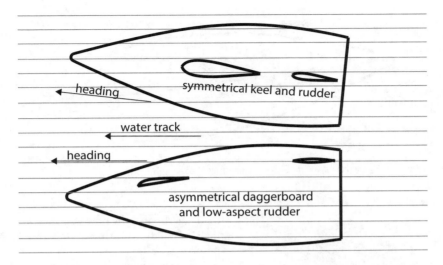

An exaggerated comparison showing the underbody of a typical monohull with fin keel and rudder and the consequent leeway versus a daggerboard with offset rudder, an arrangement that greatly reduces leeway.

in a small amount of weather helm for sailing at 10 knots if it would break the skipper's arm in a 25-knot broaching emergency.

WHAT DOES THE DAGGERBOARD DO?

With the IMOCA 60, we can look at daggerboards in their most extreme case. Using these boats as an example, we can best understand exactly what a daggerboard achieves. On a typical boat the keel and rudder (see the diagram) work as lifting foils—notice that the boat is not actually pointing in the direction of travel. The skipper sailing toward a distant tower sees that a line from the center of the stern to the bow is actually pointing a few degrees to leeward.

As discussed earlier, the angle of attack between the direction the boat is moving and the direction the boat is pointing gives rise to the wing effect of the keel that reduces leeward drift. On the IMOCA 60, the daggerboard completely replaces the wing purpose of the keel and rudder. The daggerboard is aimed 3–5 degrees toward the bow of the boat. This effectively twists the boat toward the bow and eliminates the angle of attack on the keel. That is, the boat is now pointing in the same direction that

the boat is moving. Rather than fighting against the water, the boat is now slicing through it like a dart. Obviously this is faster.

On the 60s, the daggerboard is so well designed that it actually lifts the boat to windward, rather than simply reducing leeward drift.

Imagine looking down on the plan of a 60-foot boat flat in the water. The centerline of the boat runs from the bow to center of the transom. When the boat is heeled and rolls onto the chine, the effective centerline of the boat shifts to leeward. The centerline of the boat is a line from the bow to the rudder.

If the boat is narrow, the difference between the two centerlines is not large. On a beamy 60, the angle is much wider. If the daggerboard is positioned so that it offers positive leeway, the wider hull is lined back up with the direction of travel of the boat. The heeled centerline is now pointing in the same direction as the boat is travelling. The flow of water down the hull is symmetrical, and there is less drag.

In explaining the purpose of the daggerboard, Owen suggested that we think of a typical sailboat where we could twist the keel independently of the hull. We could thus improve the wing effect of the

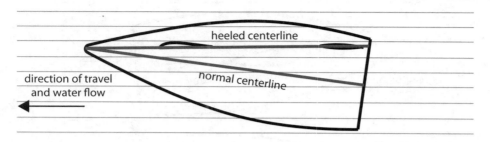

Daggerboards shift the heeled centerline of the vessel, resulting in less drag.

Computer-generated cross-section of an IMOCA 60 daggerboard.
(Courtesy Merfyn Owen)

keel and point the boat where we want to go. Since the asymmetrical daggerboard creates lift only on one side (the daggerboard is 3–5 degrees off parallel to the centerline of the boat), the boat no longer needs to make leeway to activate the wing effect. The angle of the daggerboard is tuned to the lift provided by the keel. The daggerboard is raised or lowered to change its lift force. Upwind the entire daggerboard is used. When footing or reaching, the board is raised partially. Going faster increases the load on the daggerboard in the same way as described earlier for the rudder. To offset this, designers would either need to build a stronger/heavier daggerboard or raise it up to reduce the load. Remember that the daggerboard is asymmetric.

An additional benefit of the daggerboard is that with the board in place and the bow pointing higher, we can maintain the same apparent wind angle by easing the jibsheet and opening the slot. Imagine we are back on the water sailing toward a tower in the distance. Without the daggerboard the bow would be pointing a few degrees to leeward. Once we drop the daggerboard, the bow will lift to windward and the boat will be pointing in the same direction that the boat is sailing, i.e., toward the tower. Now we can ease the sheets for more speed. We are effectively footing slightly off of a beat. If we did not ease the sheets, the telltales would quickly show that we are not trimming aerodynamically.

This is a difficult concept. Imagine sailing upwind without the daggerboard. The instruments in the cockpit show an apparent wind over the boat of 30 degrees. However, we know that our bow is pointing to leeward 3 degrees. So the actual apparent wind in relation to our direction of travel is 27 degrees. We put the daggerboard down and the bow swings to windward by 3 degrees. By putting the daggerboard down we are effectively twisting the hull underneath the sail plan. Thus we can ease the sails by the same 3 degrees. The boat is still heading at the same point and the sails have not seen a change in the apparent wind direction (when looking at the direction the boat is traveling, not the direction the boat is pointing). The boat has twisted underneath the sail plan. Owen had a Hallelujah moment when this concept finally clicked.

The best way to understand this is to draw a jib alone. On a second sheet of paper, draw the hull. Lay the hull on top of the jib, with the meeting point at the bow. Put a tack through both sheets of paper at the bow. Now, imagine that the daggerboard has been dropped. The hull points up farther (swing the hull drawing counter-clockwise), but the jib stays in the same position. It can be seen that the jibsheet can be eased for the new position of the hull.

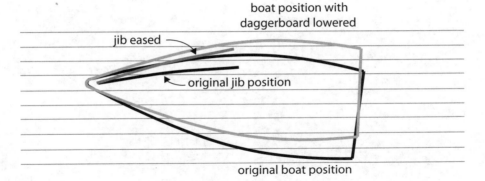

boat position with
daggerboard lowered

jib eased

original jib position

original boat position

Once a daggerboard is deployed, the hull can point higher, effectively twisting the hull shape toward the direction of travel. Once the hull aligns higher, the jibsheet can be eased, improving boat speed.

So we have two effects from the daggerboard: reduced hull drag through the water and eased sheets for a faster point of sail. "Now you're smokin'!" I asked if the skipper could not simply tighten the sheets and point even higher. Owen replied that this would quickly lead to the inefficiencies of pinching. The boats were designed to be fastest at the optimum upwind point of sail and not to be pinched beyond that. "It's strictly a VMG [velocity made good] thing."

Of course, the daggerboard adds drag, but this is offset by its benefits. All of the lift is achieved by the daggerboard.

DYNAMIC STABILITY SYSTEMS

The most recent advance in the field of keeping the boat upright is the Dynamic Stability System (DSS) invented by British yacht designer Hugh Welbourn. In brief, the DSS is a wing that juts horizontally out the leeward side of the boat at the waterline. When the boat heels to leeward, the wing is underwater providing lift, just like an airplane wing. In light winds the wing is simply retracted back into the hull.

As this is written, the DSS is considered a radical change by many designers who are questioning its effectiveness. However, in the past few years we have seen Moths, Lasers, and even the massive America's Cup boats all riding on foils. The DSS is simply using the same concept in different form.

The DSS performs three main tasks:

Most efficient in high winds, the Dynamic Stability System (DSS) wing juts out from the hull on the leeward side. *(Courtesy Infiniti Yachts)*

- It effectively makes the boat wider.
- By lifting on the leeward side, it keeps the mast pointing up and the keel pointing down.
- It lifts the entire boat higher in the water.

The DSS wing is custom designed for each boat, but the target that Welbourn has set is to reduce heel by 5% sailing upwind, keeping the boat flatter. The DSS group has not found a significant improvement in VMG for boats racing round-the-buoys in flat water, but they did extensive testing with a 40-foot racer in rough water and consistently received VMG gains of 5%, 7%, or even 10%.

Adding to effective beam increases stability and

Seen just below the water line, the DSS wing widens the boat's effective area and allows the boat to sail flatter and higher in the water. *(Courtesy Infiniti Yachts)*

makes the boat feel bigger overall. Typically users comment that sailing with the DSS makes it feel like they are on a boat 10–15 feet longer. The DSS dramatically smoothes the motion of the boat by adding stability in all three dimensions from wave action, whether from long waves or a short chop. "It is smoother in roll and pitch. And when you go over and down and around a wave, you have less steering action required," Welbourn said. Every racer knows how waves can slow the boat, so the standard practice is to bear off slightly. With the DSS, the effective widening of the hull reduces the impact of wave action and allows the boat to point higher. For example a 30-foot boat is more affected by wave action than a 40-foot boat. It is certainly a benefit if the 30-foot boat can be made to sail like a 40-foot boat. The real benefit comes from reduction in pitching and bouncing around in waves. This smoothing the action of the boat was found in Welbourn's very first radio-controlled boat testing, then replicated in tank testing and again on real boats.

The DSS also improves the action of the sails by reducing boat-heel bouncing that occurs from fluctuations in wind speed or wave action. Because boat heel can be maintained at a more stable level, the sails can be properly set for maximum power at that heel angle without needing to constantly trim and ease the sails in wind and waves. The righting moment of the boat is substantially improved,

The DSS wing adds considerable width, and thus stability, to a sailboat. *(Courtesy Infiniti Yachts)*

resulting in more power overall. Because everything isn't bouncing around so much, the rig has a chance to work more efficiently. This was proven on a 40-foot boat. The VMG gain was consistent. When sailing upwind, the skipper will not feel the boat is sailing quicker, but the improvement in stability results in the 5% to 10% increase in VMG mentioned earlier.

For singlehanders using an autopilot, one of the most dramatic effects of this smoother running through and around waves is the reduction in steering required, resulting in a significantly reduced power drain. This was tested in lumpy seas near Australia. Even in situations with lower wind, if the sea is lumpy the stability is improved and efficiency of the sails and keel enhanced.

A Mini 6.50 with the DSS wing extended. *(Courtesy Chris Tutmark)*

A cross section of the DSS wing—the hydrodynamic foil shape is designed to provide maximum lift. *(Courtesy Chris Tutmark)*

The DSS is currently being tested on a new Mini 6.50. While the normal Mini has a beam of 3 meters (almost 10 ft.), the new boat was built at less than 2 meters (6.5 ft.), making it the lightest Mini anywhere by a substantial margin. (The Mini box rule allows for a maximum beam of 3 meters. The 2-meter beam with foil extended out on one side remains within this box.) This narrower hull planes better downwind and improves the ability of the boat to sail upwind—a noted weakness of the standard Mini design. The improved performance also allows for reducing rig size, saving another 40 kilograms (88 lb.) and using smaller sails. Tests have shown the DSS-modified-Mini to run in 12 knots of wind at the same speed as other Minis in 20 knots of wind.

The Mini's wing does not tuck completely into the hull. If it is not wanted, the skipper simply sticks it out slightly on the high side. On other boats the wing tucks in flush with the hull, shaped to match the curve of the hull. Welbourn emphasized that in this way the wing is available when required but does no harm if tucked away when not needed. (On a boat like my Olson 30, Welbourn estimated that the wing would protrude 1.8 meters in use, nearly doubling the beam of the boat at the waterline.)

A common comparison is the canting keel. Welbourn considers the wing to be fail-safe. If a canting keel breaks, "you are having a very bad day at the office." If the DSS wing breaks, "you've still got a normal boat." The DSS structure is mounted between two bulkheads and the hull casings. These are separate units so that even if they are damaged, water will not flow into the hull. If hit, the leading edge of the wing will crumple to the point of the internal support spar before the board itself breaks.

All of the DSS boats up to 40 feet have used a line with a 2-to-1 purchase to extend the wing manually. Pulling it out is easy with no load. On smaller boats the wing slides on a graphite surface. A winch is necessary if it is extended at moderate speed. At a high boat speed it would become stuck, with two or three tons of load holding it in place. Larger boats use a motor and substantial bearing system. The 100-foot maxi *Wild Oats XI* has a custom-designed, triple-bearing system allowing the wing to be extended even at 25 knots.

DSS's Effect on Righting Moment and Lifting Power

As mentioned, in addition to widening the hull, the other two main benefits of the DSS design are righting moment and lifting power. In brief, greater wing span equates to greater righting moment. Greater chord length (width of the wing) gives greater lifting power.

The question of the additional drag from the foil is often raised. However, the effect of the wing raising the boat in the water reduces hull drag so much that the reverse is actually true. Overall drag is reduced using the system. As mentioned, the longer the chord length of the DSS foil, the greater is the lift created.

For Welbourn's Quant 28 design, the DSS wing lifts nearly 80% of the total displacement of boat and crew. Even on a light displacement 36-foot boat, the wing still lifts 50% to 60% of the displacement when sailing downhill at 25 knots. These are astounding but real numbers. "This is where we are getting the real speed gains. It is more efficient to take displacement on dynamic lift rather than planing lift or by shoveling the water out of the way. This is why hydrofoil boats go so fast. They are taking all the weight on an efficient lift to drag configuration," Welbourn commented. *Wild Oats XI* is using a foil just 2.5 meters (8 ft.) long. "They're very effective upwind anyway. Downhill they have problems. Last year in the Sydney-Hobart they stuffed the bow into waves at speed and nearly killed themselves. They are looking at ways to lift the boat out of the water. Once you find ways to have the boat supported dynamically, it isn't affected by the seas so much, even going downhill."

Typically the foil is moved from side to side as the tack is completed so that it is already extended on the new heading. Coming out of a tack, it is important to gain speed as quickly as possible before steering up to the proper course. Wing efficiency goes up as the square of the speed, so an additional tenth of a knot has a significant effect.

The same process is followed when gybing in rough water so that the boat is gybed directly onto the stability of the foil.

Depending on their design, some boats use a single foil that moves from side to side. As mentioned, other designs have two separate boards, allowing either or both to be in or out at any time. In construction of a boat, the DSS cannot be considered on its own. The loads added to the rig and foils are considerable, pushing well past the original design constraints and requiring an upgrade to the chainplates, shrouds, and mast itself.

The DSS wing is custom-designed, giving consideration to the intended purpose of the boat. Is the intended purpose to achieve lift or increase righting moment? The system would be different for a round-the-buoys racer compared to a round-the-world racer. The designer looks at the cost of the drag of both the chord length and wing span in determining the best design for each boat. Chord length of the wing adds to lift, while span adds to righting moment. An ultralight like my Olson 30 would benefit most from a longer span to improve righting moment. Because the boat is already so light, additional lift from chord length might not have the same payback.

A DSS wing is usually thought to offer the

The boat on the left has a DSS—notice how the hull is lifted out of the water, compared to the boat without DSS on the right. *(Courtesy Dynamicstability-systems.com)*

greatest benefit to boats with a narrow hull. When a low-drag, skinny boat is needed upwind in light air, the foil is retracted. On the other hand, when a wider hull is better for planing, the foil can be extended to provide these benefits. It is like having two boats in one to match whatever conditions are faced. It turns a skinny boat into a powerful boat without adding permanent weight in the keel or temporary weight with water ballast.

A crucial aspect of the design is the dynamic nature of the wing, which depowers the board and prevents overloading as the boat speeds up. This is necessary because the amount of lift increases very rapidly as speed increases. The shape of the wing and its position in the hull create this dynamic feature. As the boat speeds up, the foil causes the stern to lift. The bow remains in the water, however. With the stern lifted, the entire boat is tilted a couple of degrees bow-down; this reduces the angle of the wing to the passing water, thereby reducing the lift coefficient of the wing in direct proportion. It falls into balance naturally. There is never a situation where the wing is providing more and more lift until the boat crashes down.

If more lift is provided than is needed for the boat's righting moment, then the wing lifts right to the water surface and loses all effect. In fact, the wing effect drops quickly in the top foot of water because water above the wing is pushed up into the air rather than acting as a uniform fluid for the wing to flow inside.

As mentioned repeatedly, boats are best sailed at 15 degrees of heel. At further heel the lift of the foil moves toward the side rather than upwards. Nonetheless, the DSS wing foil is always improving righting moment. At less heel, the foil is within the top foot of water where the wing has less effect.

Over the years, other attempts at such a lifting foil have been made. Some had added flaps on the trailing edge or required the skipper to pull them partially in and out as conditions changed. The DSS design is either full-on or full-off with no attention required once deployed. With the dynamic nature of the design, the foil doesn't require any further attention from the skipper until a tack or gybe. Hugh has some 300,000 miles of offshore sailing under his keel and understands that simplicity of design is important.

In the end, it all comes down to speed. I asked Welbourn what the DSS could achieve for my Olson 30 on a reach. Right now with a good strong wind I can get up to 9 knots for long periods of time. Welbourn said that with the DSS, speeds of at least 15 knots would be expected—an order of magnitude faster. He noted, "The Infinity 36 will do wind speed sailing downhill. If it's blowing 25 knots the boat will go 25 knots." Two-sail reaching is where the boat is really transformed. "Most boats just fall over. We don't. We just keep going faster."

I asked how I would manage the foil on my Olson 30 in 25 knots of wind, sailing at 155 degrees apparent with the big spinnaker? Welbourn said that even with the boat so flat, the foil should be extended on the leeward side because it gives a lot of freedom to move the boat around. "You can sail pretty much where you want to. Instead of having that tiny window where you sail the boat to keep the pace up, suddenly you find you can move it around and come up or down. It gives a *way* wider sweet spot." Normally under these conditions, I would have to keep the boat within a tiny range of apparent wind in order to plane at 12.5 knots. The DSS would increase that range to 20 degrees or more. "You can keep bearing off until the wing comes out of the water and you don't need it. But if the speed drops you head up slightly and the board just kicks in again." Under these conditions Welbourn thinks my boat speed would jump from planing at 12 to "way over 18."

In low-wind conditions, the foil is retracted into the boat and not used at all. "The Swiss lake boats are sailing most of the time in 4–5 knots of breeze," Hugh noted. "They are a very skinny, low-drag boat that is effective in light winds. But once there is a breeze the boat has the added stability of the wing. It is really the two boats in one scenario."

DSS is a simple and comparably cheap approach doing almost everything better than a canting keel; you can compare it with any existing system—canting keels, water ballast, or whatever. On big racing yachts crossing oceans close reaching with two sails, downwind with kites etc., it is the system to have, no doubt.

ONE SAILOR'S EXPERIENCE WITH A DSS

Michael Aeppli sails a Quant 30 sport boat lake racer equipped with the DSS wing. Aeppli is an avid proponent of the DSS and answered my questions as I searched for a reality check on the claims.

Q. Are you using the DSS primarily to provide righting or lift/planing?

A. You cannot separate these concepts above 7 knots of speed. It provides lift that helps for righting moment and planing as well as heel angle.

Q. The Quant 30 brochure indicates that the DSS provides sufficient lift to more than compensate for the additional drag of the foil. Do you find this to be true?

A. Absolutely, the boat is lifted 40 mm to 60 mm. In extremis if everything works for you—with this boat you sail up to 80% faster than any, even taller modern sport boat.

Q. The brochure describes the DSS as offering the most improvement on a reach. But standard races are beating/running. Do you find that the DSS offers substantial improvement when beating?

A. Yes, it does for other reasons: the whole boat moves less, roll and pitch is reduced, aero- and hydrodynamics work better. But the difference upwind to comparable boats is not as great as if you can bear off and open the sails a bit. As soon as you can go substantially over 7 knots you are off and gone. You always have to think that lift on the foil rises with the square of speed. The curve of lift-production is a parabola and benefits start at 7 knots of flow around the foils whether on big or small boats. If you build a 100-foot race yacht you go over 10 knots constantly, you can benefit from the system (producing lift) almost all the time. The bigger the boat the better the system works.

Q. Are you able to achieve a measurable improvement in boat heel using the DSS? How much?

A. Upwind the DSS provides about 5 degrees of heel reduction. On a sport boat like we have it is not relevant as we sail the boat like a dinghy not like a yacht.

Q. Are you able to achieve a measurable improvement in reduced leeway using the DSS? How much?

A. Leeway happens when we sail too slow, so on our boat we live with the "speed is your friend" philosophy. This means that upwind we are better off to sail deeper but much faster so we eliminate leeway and end up with a better VMG than pointing higher but sailing slower.

Q. The brochure says "the foil that rights and lifts the boat allows it to sail nearly 100% faster than comparable conventional boats" Really? 100%?

A. I would say that this can happen. If you compare with a modern type of European sport boat, the Esse 850 which is the benchmark here for the last 6 years, then I would say downwind you can sail easily double speed at peaks and your VMG is constantly 60% to 70% higher. Thanks to DSS you minimize downwind drag so much that you still accelerate when the hull resistance of conventional boats get disproportionately high. I had a situation during a race in Geneva: we sailed with wind from the side, direct course two-sail reaching. Next to us was a modern 18-footer with an oversize rig. As long as wind speed was over a solid 12–13 knots, we sailed the same speed as faster boats. Later the wind was getting weaker, and we couldn't really use the foil 100% so the 18-footer got away slowly.

Q. Have you had any problems with the DSS?

A. No problems so far, as on little boats you can easily remove things from the foil. You have to look after the DSS just as you would look after a fin keel or rudder on conventional boats.

SPEEDDREAM—THE WORLD'S FASTEST MONOHULL

Brian Hancock is one of the most experienced sailors in the world, with more than a quarter million miles under his keel, both singlehanded and crewed. Brian is currently working on the SpeedDream project to develop the world's fastest monohull. The concept of SpeedDream has three aspects that I find particularly interesting: a radical canting keel to shift weight to the windward side, daggerboards, and the DSS.

Canting Keel. In the past, keels have canted 30 or even 45 degrees. SpeedDream takes this to an entirely new level with a cant of 85 degrees, literally taking the entire keel and bulb right out of the water. In this case it's wrong to speak of the keel as a foil. It is simply a weighted appendage that makes a monohull boat sail like a multihull with the windward hull flying. (Of note is that multihull boats have rounded hulls that carve into the water. The SpeedDream has flattened hull sides designed to bring the boat up to plane when heeled with the keel flying.)

Daggerboards. The daggerboards are short and narrow, only 4 feet long and 13 inches wide under water. They are asymmetrically shaped to provide maximum lift. Hancock expects the daggerboards on the 50-foot version to be only 10 feet by 18 inches. With such small foils, it should be obvious that this boat is designed to work at high speed. We talked about how the boat would be difficult to handle in a crowded starting line against standard designs. At low speeds the boat will have significant leeward drift.

DSS. A DSS foil is being added to the Speed-Dream boat to provide more lift and stability. The SpeedDream team limited the size of the DSS so that the boat would not pull right out of the water and be impossible to control.

The current SpeedDream boat is 28 feet long. However, plans are in the works for 50- and 100-foot versions that are expected to break monohull speed records. For the 100-foot version, they are looking at a computer-controlled canting/telescoping keel providing instantaneous reaction time. I mentioned my distaste for breakable technical equipment, but Brian reminded me that they are pushing the limits of speed and are willing to face this drawback.

THE MAST

The discussion in this chapter has focused on changing the weight distribution of the hull and below. Of course, it is also possible to reduce heel with improvements on the other side of the weight calculation: the mast. For example, moving from aluminum to a carbon fiber mast would cut the upper weight in half. One can imagine the difference in leverage achieved by reducing the weight of the entire length of the mast on a 30-foot boat.

FINAL THOUGHTS ON SYSTEMS TO IMPROVE BOAT PERFORMANCE

As one of the more active singlehanded, short-distance racers, I'll offer my thoughts about the various systems discussed in this chapter. I compete in many 3- to 4-hour races each year and even some round-the-buoys beer-can races. Tacking and gybing is a significant part of these. I have had many tacking duels against crewed boats with 10 or more tacks in rapid succession. Even at the club level, one blown maneuver can destroy any chance for victory.

I know that I can tack faster than any crewed boat in the world, as I don't require prep time for crew to get into position. I simply think "tack," and it is done. For the racing that I do, any system that delays my ability to tack instantly, such as water ballast, would be unsuitable.

Tacking and gybing are my busiest times on the boat. I would design a system to ensure the ballast or wing shift can be done with one quick movement. I should be able to pop one line and let go, and this one movement should be enough to complete the move. When I'm stuck in the middle of a crowded starting line, I am far too busy sailing the boat to perform even one extra task.

Although a small percentage of singlehanded skippers will move to highly specialized, single-purpose boats, most skippers want something that can meet all their needs: some cruising, some beer-can club racing, and the occasional highly competitive offshore adventure race. Any system to improve boat performance should meet all of these criteria.

CHAPTER 6   **SELF-STEERING SYSTEMS**

ALTERNATIVE SELF-STEERING SYSTEMS

Shock-Cord Sailing
Shock-cord sailing is for every singlehander.

I put this first because it is essential for every singlehander, and if I left it until last most readers would just skim over it and not learn these techniques. Shock-cord (or bungee-cord) sailing is important because it is guaranteed that at some point the autopilot will fail or the windvane will break. Neither of these pitfalls is an excuse to stop sailing. I find it ridiculous that a significant voyage (such as a major transatlantic race costing hundreds of thousands of dollars) would be halted because of autopilot failure. These techniques work perfectly well, are virtually idiot proof, and require only five dollars' worth of materials.

As a second consideration, crewed boat racing rules insist that boats not use any type of autopilot or windvane. Hand steering by the compass at three in the morning is extremely difficult, even on a fully crewed boat. The techniques described below do not contravene any racing rules because they work solely by making use of the wind on the sails and nothing more.

Although these techniques were developed many years ago for full-keel boats, I have tested them and found that they work perfectly well on modern, fin-keel boats. My Olson 30 is considered to be especially twitchy. If these alternate self-steering techniques work on my boat, they are likely to work on most other boats. (I have a video of these techniques on YouTube. Search for *"Foolish Muse self-steering."*)

Upwind Steering with the Tiller Line System
Beating into the wind is the easiest. Simply lashing the tiller in place and making some minor adjustments to sail trim ensures the boat continues on its course with only slight variation. It is amusing that in most races, the singlehander can eat on upwind legs whiles the boat steers itself, while on crewed boats the sailors eat on downwind legs when the boat is flat.

I recommend not using a commercial tiller-locking device. These are certainly more expensive and they do not work nearly as well as my own tiller line, which takes about 5 minutes to create.

This quick method is appropriate for short-term use when beating into the wind, but will fail with a significant wind shift or change in wind speed. Here's how to do it. Cut a length of quarter-inch line about 3 feet shorter than the beam of the boat at tiller point. Tie a foot of surgical tubing or shock cord (bungee cord) to each end of the line. (Surgical tubing is better than shock cord because it stretches more consistently as it is extended out.) Then tie some sort of hook at each end of the tubing, attaching this to the toe rail or a cleat on each side of the boat, about 1 foot back from the tip of the tiller. (See the illustration on next page and the photo on page 75.) It should take a little tension to wrap the line one time around the tiller and more tension to wrap the cord around the tiller twice. To use this device, sail the boat by hand until it is beating perfectly into the

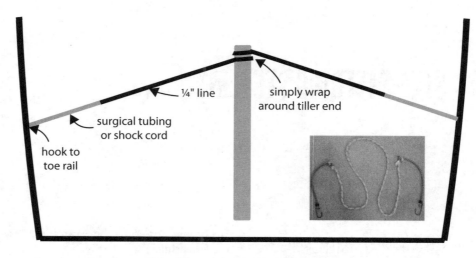

Construct a self-steering system for sailing to windward with quarter-inch line and surgical tubing. Once you have the sails trimmed perfectly using hand steering, tie off the self-steering line—you may have to make minor adjustments as the surgical tubing stretches at first. If the boat rounds up, ease the mainsheet rather than adjusting the tiller line.

wind. The sails should be trimmed perfectly with the telltales flying. Wrap the line one time around the tip of the tiller (or twice in higher winds or even three times in very high wind if necessary). The tiller line should have enough grip to hold the tiller without slipping. Then make off the other end of the line to the other rail. Make sure that the tiller line is holding the tiller exactly in the same position as when you were hand steering. This usually involves some adjustment because the stretch of the tubing lets the tiller drop. The beauty of using a stretchy tiller line is that it allows for small adjustments by pulling on the line without having to remove it from the tiller.

Let go of the tiller and watch. Most likely the boat will round up slowly. When hand steering, the usual tendency is to have more weather helm than necessary, even if the skipper follows my previous advice about eliminating pressure on the helm. When the boat rounds up, ease the mainsheet slightly—just an inch at a time—because it is the mainsail that is pulling the boat up. As the mainsheet is eased, at some point the tiller line will do its job and the boat will sail perfectly on its own.

This system works because the tiller, held

slightly to windward, is trying to steer the boat down. Every time the boat sails down, the mainsail catches more wind and tries to pull the boat back up again. When the boat heads up, the mainsail luffs and stops pulling the boat up, and the tiller steers the boat down again. The boat will sail an elongated S shape through the water, sailing up and down again. With a bit of adjustment this S shape can be eliminated and the boat will sail perfectly straight. A variation of 5 degrees on either side of straight is acceptable and indicates the system is working very well. Make tiny adjustments to jib and mainsail trim and tiller position until the perfect combination is achieved.

The important part of this technique is to *not* tighten the mainsheet when the mainsail luffs. Normally when hand steering you tighten the mainsheet when the mainsail luffs—this is a very typical reaction. But when using the tiller line, tightening the mainsheet pulls the boat up past the point where the tiller line has control. This would be pulling the boat up past its normal beating position. Instead, let the mainsail luff until the boat falls down again and the mainsail catches. It requires self-control to allow the mainsail to luff, but it is important.

I leave my tiller line rigged all the time. The autopilot can quit at any moment and the tiller line lets me keep on racing.

The tiller line system works best in consistent, moderate winds. With this system, as with hand steering, changes to the tiller position are required with changes in wind strength. The tiller must be pulled more to windward as the wind increases, and dropped to leeward as the wind drops. Otherwise the boat will quickly sail off in the wrong direction. Such changes are easily made by slipping the tiller line's position over the tiller.

I keep my tiller line system rigged all the time. I have learned from numerous experiences that the autopilot can fail at any moment, for any reason. In fact it failed in the middle of a race just yesterday when a fuse blew. It was nothing for me to wrap the tiller line in place while I went below and discovered the problem. If I hadn't had the tiller line mounted, I would have had to heave-to in the high winds of the race. As it was, the autopilot failure did not cost me even a second in my race finish time.

Storm Jib Steering System

The tiller line system described above works only when beating into the wind. On a reach the boat would just round up, so a more elaborate system is needed. The storm jib system described here works from beating close-hauled to a broad reach of around 120 degrees true. It still works past this point but becomes less reliable. Additionally, the storm jib system is a long-term solution that can be used for hours or days on end in any conditions. Singlehander Tony Skidmore used this method as

his sole means of self-steering on a 17,000 mile voyage in a 24-foot sloop.

The storm jib system requires only a few feet of surgical tubing, a storm jib (or staysail), and two snatch blocks. The usual jib/genoa and mainsail are used to drive the boat at speed.

The following steps must all be completed for the system to work. The steps are ordered here only for clarity. It takes only 5 minutes to set up the boat to use this method. During this setup time, use the simple tiller line steering method described previously to beat into the wind. After setting up, bear off to a beam reach for the best use of the storm jib system.

Tie 3 feet of surgical tubing in a loop and attach a short line. Run this line through a turning block on the *leeward* side of the boat even with the tip of the tiller and around the leeward winch (see illustration, next page). Slip the surgical tubing over the tip of the tiller. It should be tight enough that it pulls strongly on the tiller. The line on the winch is used to adjust the tension of the tubing.

Attach the tack of a storm jib or staysail to the toe rail or bow cleat on the *windward* side of the boat a foot or two back from the bow. Use a spinnaker halyard to raise the storm jib tight. (On *Foolish Muse* the storm jib has its own stay. That may not be true for other boats.) Run a small line, such as a spinnaker sheet, from the clew of the storm jib to a block on the *windward* toe rail near the shrouds. Run the sheet back through another block on the *windward* toe rail even with the tip of the tiller (see illustration). Pull tight on the sheet and wrap it around the tiller just in front of the surgical tubing. I find that wrapping the sheet over itself two or three times holds it in place securely. The tension of the sheet on the windward side of the boat should offset the tension of the tubing on the leeward side.

The storm jib is now parallel with the boat's centerline. As the boat sails downward, wind pressure on the storm jib is reduced and the surgical tubing pulls the tiller down, bringing the boat back up. As the boat sails up, wind pressure on the storm jib increases, and the sheet pulls the tiller up, sailing the boat back down again. Use the line from the tubing to the winch to adjust the tension of the

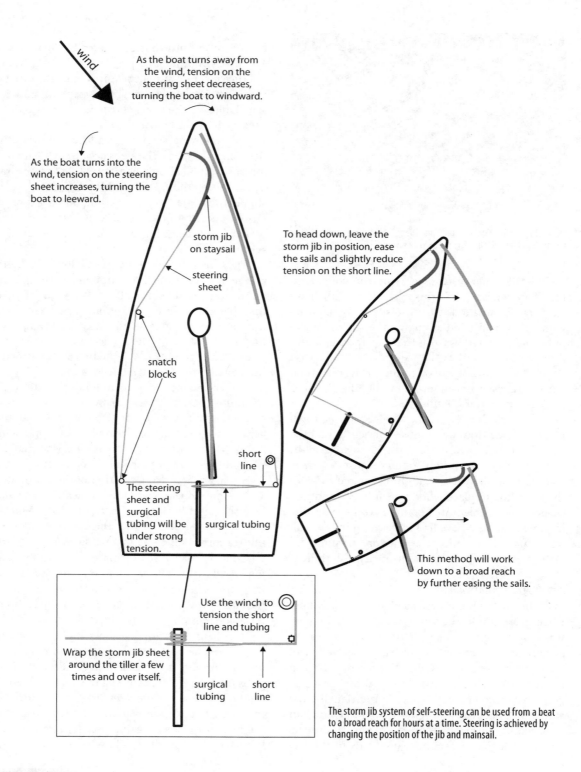

wind

As the boat turns away from the wind, tension on the steering sheet decreases, turning the boat to windward.

As the boat turns into the wind, tension on the steering sheet increases, turning the boat to leeward.

storm jib on staysail

steering sheet

snatch blocks

The steering sheet and surgical tubing will be under strong tension.

short line

surgical tubing

To head down, leave the storm jib in position, ease the sails and slightly reduce tension on the short line.

This method will work down to a broad reach by further easing the sails.

Use the winch to tension the short line and tubing

Wrap the storm jib sheet around the tiller a few times and over itself.

surgical tubing

short line

The storm jib system of self-steering can be used from a beat to a broad reach for hours at a time. Steering is achieved by changing the position of the jib and mainsail.

tubing on the tiller. Use the sheet and the forward block position to adjust the tension of the storm jib.

On the first attempt, pull on the tiller and ease the mainsheet and jibsheet to drop to a beam reach. *Important:* the storm jib is used only to keep the boat sailing in a straight line. It is the jib and mainsail that determine the direction of the boat. Thus the jib and main must be properly trimmed for a beam reach because the storm jib will not override the basic sail trim. At first, ease the jibsheet and mainsheet well past their usual sailing position. Tighten them slowly until the boat starts to head up. Then ease them again. With small adjustments the boat can be steered with amazing accuracy.

To change course, under normal conditions it is not necessary to adjust the storm jib or the tubing. The boat direction can be changed simply by adjusting the sail trim in or out. Pull the sails nearly all the way in to head up to a close reach. Ease the sails out to lay off to a broad reach. As mentioned, I have found this method works well down to 120 degrees true. At 130 degrees true the system stills works but the boat will swing through a wider range.

The storm jib and tubing tension do require adjustment with a significant change in wind strength. In high winds two loops of surgical tubing can be used to increase the tension on that side of the tiller.

The storm jib method works amazingly well in all conditions and can hold a course better than most human drivers. It does not require any power and certainly makes less noise than an autopilot. Even the skipper of a boat with the most advanced electronic autopilot should consider using the storm jib method in open water.

Downwind Poled-Out Jib Steering System

The storm jib system just described operates effectively down to a broad reach. After this point, we move to the poled-out jib system of self-steering. This approach works all the way down to a dead run at 180 degrees but it is most effective at 145 degrees.

This method works only when sailing downwind with a genoa, not with a spinnaker. The poled-out jib (or poled-out storm jib in high winds) steers the boat.

Setup in the cockpit is the same as with the storm jib self-steering system. The surgical tubing and tension line is set up exactly the same on the leeward side of the boat, although it may require more tension.

A jib (or storm jib) is raised on the forestay along with the genoa. The genoa will be on the leeward side of the boat and the jib on the windward side. The skipper must interweave the sail hanks to ensure that both sails can be raised to their full tension. The jib usually has a shorter luff than the genoa, so two halyards are needed to raise both sails simultaneously.

A spinnaker pole or whisker pole is used to pole the jib out very far forward on the windward side of the boat. The end of the pole is only a foot or two back from the forestay, and the jib will fly well in front of the boat (see illustration, next page).

A sheet is run from the clew of the jib back to a snatch block (or spinnaker sheet block) on the toe rail on the windward side, even with the tip of the tiller. The sheet is wrapped around the tip of the tiller, in front of the tubing. Even in moderate winds, the sheet is under significant tension. It requires strength to wrap it around the tiller, and the surgical tubing must be under sufficient tension to hold the tiller in the center of the boat. In high winds two loops of surgical tubing can be used to increase tension.

When this system is in use, as the boat heads up, the poled-out jib catches more wind, pulling the tiller to windward and heading the boat down. As the boat drops down, the poled-out jib sheds wind, allowing the tubing to pull the tiller down and head the boat up again.

Of course, the sails must be properly trimmed for the desired heading. With this system, the poled-out jib is used to adjust the boat heading, unlike in the storm jib system upwind. If the pole is pulled back about 3 feet from the forestay, the boat will drop down to sail between 170 and 180 degrees. In this case the genoa is completely blanketed by the mainsail, so the boat could be sailed with no genoa at all. As the boat nears 180 degrees, the poled-out jib collapses, allowing the boat to head up.

If the pole is eased to about 1 foot from the forestay, the boat will head up to sail between 135

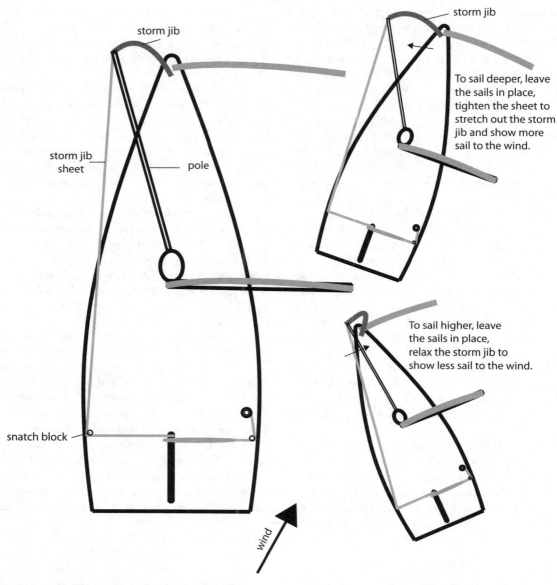

storm jib

storm jib sheet

pole

snatch block

storm jib

To sail deeper, leave the sails in place, tighten the sheet to stretch out the storm jib and show more sail to the wind.

To sail higher, leave the sails in place, relax the storm jib to show less sail to the wind.

wind

The poled-out jib system of self-steering is most effective around 145 degrees off the wind. Steer by changing the amount of storm jib showing to the wind—to sail deeper, tighten the jibsheet to expose more of it to the wind; to sail higher, slacken the jibsheet.

degrees and 145 degrees. In this case the genoa fills and the boat will sail at optimum speed. The range of control of the poled-out jib is very small, about 3 feet in total. Very small adjustments to the jib-sheet thus change the heading.

In light to moderate winds, it is best to use a poled-out jib in this system. In strong winds a poled-out storm jib should be used. Using a storm jib in light or moderate winds is unwise because the storm jib must be stretched out completely to have the desired effect on steering. In that configuration it will continue to have pull even if the boat is at 180 degrees, risking an accidental gybe.

Sheet-to-Tiller Systems

Other methods of self-steering have been developed using either the jib or the main as the force for the steering power, rather than a storm jib as described above, with the same surgical tubing on the opposite side. These systems require a few more blocks and lines, but not a storm jib. In one such system, a line is connected to the mainsheet midway between the traveler and the boom, run out to a block on the windward toe rail, and back to the tiller, with surgical tubing providing opposing force. An excellent description with photographs is provided on "Augustine—A Pearson Ariel Page" located at http://solopublications.com/sailariq.htm.

A benefit of this system is that the skipper need not shift a storm jib from side to side with each tack. A disadvantage of the system is that the large sails are very powerful and must be carefully balanced.

For greatest efficiency, any self-steering system should not require either the jib or main to luff for the system to steer the boat to back off the wind. Obviously, allowing a sail to luff slows the boat down considerably. The benefit of the storm jib self-steering system is that only the storm jib luffs. This does not slow the boat.

AUTOPILOT OR WINDVANE?

Whether it is better to use an autopilot or windvane is a long-standing debate among singlehanders. But in reality, the choice has already been made; it is just up to the skipper to determine what type of sailing he will do and what type of boat he will do it on. Then the choice becomes obvious.

In my own situation, I prefer an electronic autopilot system for the following reasons.

Although I dream of long ocean passages, in reality, 51 weeks a year my sailing involves 3- to 5-hour trips within 20 miles of my home club. This requires maneuvering in relatively tight waters, i.e., leaving the harbor and raising the sail under motor power, tacking out of the bay and up the strait, returning home and gybing down the strait with all

of the maneuvers reversed, dropping the sails, and returning to my slip. Each of these steps requires precise boat control and steering. I estimate that on a typical fun sail, I adjust the autopilot 30–40 times, even more during a race. An autopilot is ideal for this type of day-to-day sailing. It activates immediately, adjusts with the push of a button, and responds rapidly. A windvane cannot offer this level of flexibility.

However, for long passages, the windvane can easily become the preferred solution. For example, once into open water on a large lake or wide strait, it may be 3 hours between tacks. On the open ocean it may actually be several days between course changes. In these cases, the benefit of the autopilot's immediate flexibility is overtaken by the windvane's mechanical simplicity and directional reliability. Losing a minute or two during a tack is unimportant if only done a few times each day. When heading in one particular wind direction for several hours at a time, a windvane can hold that direction very accurately without limit, with no power draw or noise. An autopilot has a constant power draw, and the unremitting hum becomes extremely annoying. The singlehander will come to despise the sound of the autopilot belowdeck. After several days it can lead to insanity.

The decision is also influenced by the type of boat. I sail an ultralight (an Olson 30) that surfs easily downwind. In these situations the boat takes off down a wave at nearly the same speed as the wind. A windvane must have a reasonable apparent wind passing over the boat. If my boat starts to surf there is virtually no apparent wind, and the windvane will lose its grip. This is the reason why modern, ocean-going racing boats always use an electronic autopilot. They all surf, and a windvane simply will not work.

On the other hand, a heavy cruising boat rarely picks up and surfs down a wave. It always experiences an apparent wind, regardless of the point of sail. A windvane is effective most all the time.

As a further consideration, autopilots are rated depending on the weight of the boat. If conditions are rough and the wind is strong, an autopilot may be overtaxed steering a heavy boat. In contrast, a windvane is set up for the size of the boat rather than displacement and is less affected by rough conditions.

Thus the choice between autopilot and windvane has already been made for most single-handers. It depends solely on the type of boat and the type of sailing to be done. If the majority of sailing is active maneuvering within a few hours of the home port, an autopilot is by far the better choice. For a long ocean voyage, the autopilot is preferable only for light racing boats. The wind-vane is the better choice for cruising yachts. Many long-distance sailors do not make a choice—they take both a windvane and autopilot. The autopilot is used when motoring and in light, downwind, or beam-reach conditions. It is also useful during sail changes, tacking, or gybing. Otherwise, the wind-vane silently does all the work.

TONY GOOCH'S COMPARISON AUTOPILOT VS. WINDVANE

Tony Gooch is another of my great heroes. In 2002, Tony left the Royal Victoria Yacht Club on a solo, non-stop circumnavigation. During his trip he did an in-depth comparison between windvane and autopilot. Below is an article written by Tony and published in *Cruising World* magazine in January 2004.

In 1995, my wife, Coryn, and I sold the Arpège 29 we'd sailed for 16 years, during which time we'd crossed the Atlantic and Pacific oceans. In her place, we bought a 42-foot German-built alumi-num sloop, named her *Taonui*, and proceeded to log more thousands of miles. Then in September 2002, I set off on my attempt to sail solo, nonstop around the world, starting and finishing in British Columbia. On that voyage, which I intended to complete as quickly as I prudently could, I planned to make extensive use of an autopilot.

Based on my experience two years earlier on a solo voyage from Cape Town, South Africa, to England via Cape Horn, I felt that a good, powerful autopilot would do a better job than a windvane, particularly when running before the wester-lies in the Southern Ocean. With this in mind, I upgraded *Taonui's* Simrad autopilot drive unit to the manufacturer's HDL2000L model. To drive it, I installed the latest Simrad AP22 and J300X control units, and I also added the necessary electronics to enable the AP22 to steer a course relative to a chosen apparent-wind direction.

When we bought *Taonui*, she had a Monitor windvane that had already seen 30,000 sea miles. *Taonui* has a long keel, a keel-hung rudder, and tiller steering, and this windvane, which we affec-tionately called Albert, did a fine job of keeping a steady course in all manner of seas and winds.

Taonui leaves Victoria on its round-the-world voyage. Note the uncluttered deck, free from any late-night tripping obstacles, and the well-thought-out placement of the radar. (*Courtesy Tony Gooch*)

I have a great regard for Albert, but without wanting to seem disloyal after many thousands of miles, I felt that the upgraded Simrad autopilot, nicknamed Otto, achieved longer daily runs.

The force of wave action on the hull and changes in the apparent wind will cause a windvane to steer a course that weaves from side-to-side. In theory, because it's set to follow a chosen compass heading, an autopilot steers a dead-straight course. I even installed a new RFC 35 fluxgate compass that would give the control unit more accurate information. In fact, of course, the actual track steered by the autopilot also weaves from side-to-side. A soft key on the new Simrad control unit allows you to view the actual course (as distinct from the chosen course), and I was surprised at the amount of yawing it displayed. In the early days of singlehanded ocean racing, the boats were steered by windvanes, but as the yachts became longer and faster and able to accelerate more quickly, the changes in the apparent wind became too rapid for a windvane to handle. Today, these racing machines regularly hit sustained speeds of 20 to 30 knots and need sophisticated electric/hydraulic autopilots acting directly on their rudderstocks.

Taonui is 42 feet long and displaces about 15 tons, fully loaded with her full bilges and deep, long keel, she's a very comfortable offshore cruiser, and Albert [the windvane] can certainly handle any speeds she's likely to achieve, even "surfing" downwind in a Southern Ocean gale. Albert follows the apparent wind. If I set the sails for maximum speed for the wind that's blowing, Albert will keep *Taonui* sailing at her fastest speed for that wind. The wind rarely blows steadily from exactly the same direction; it always oscillates five to 10 degrees, and of course, it's subject to actual shifts in direction. None of which troubles Albert. Otto follows a chosen compass heading. He doesn't know about wind shifts, and when they do occur, the boat will be sailing at less than its maximum speed. I felt that when wind oscillations are small, these probably wouldn't have a big effect, but a 10-degree wind shift would certainly result in a loss of speed, which, if I were asleep, would go unnoticed until the change in the boat's motion woke me.

(continued)

Tony Gooch performed an extensive comparison of autopilots versus windvanes during his 2002 solo circumnavigation.

Under the influence of the wind and waves, both Albert and Otto deviate from side to side of the desired or, in Otto's case, the selected course. Albert's deviations are wider, but he delivers a higher speed. The objective when passagemaking is to maximize the number of miles made good toward a selected point.

So which system is better?

The Contest

On a six-month nonstop circumnavigation, I had plenty of time and opportunity to compare the performances of the two steering systems. I ran tests in which I would set *Taonui* on a steady course relative to the wind, with first the windvane (Albert) steering for an hour, then with Otto the autopilot at the helm for an hour.

If the wind strength or direction changed, I abandoned the test and started again. I wanted to see which steering system yielded the most miles made good in an hour in as near as possible the same wind and sea conditions. If the wind was between 38 and 85 degrees apparent, I set the autopilot to steer a course relative to the apparent wind. The autopilot can't steer off the readout of the apparent wind if it's aft of the beam, so with the apparent wind between 90 and 180 degrees, I had the autopilot steer a compass course. I tracked *Taonui's* performance by GPS, and to get a readout of miles made good to two decimal places, I set a course to a waypoint that was less than 100 miles away. Before I started the clock running, I would trim the sails

for maximum speed, then not touch them for the two hours of the test.

Observations

Although the autopilot steers a straighter course, in most of the tests, the windvane yielded more miles made good. The windvane reads the small oscillations in the apparent wind and adjusts the course to keep the sails driving at maximum efficiency. With the wind aft of the beam, the autopilot tries to steer a compass course, and the changes in the apparent wind result in the sails performing at less than maximum efficiency. The differences are small, but over a long passage, they do add up: If my average speed for the circumnavigation had been 5 percent slower, I would have taken 186 days instead of the actual 177 days.

With the wind forward of the beam and the autopilot steering to a set apparent-wind angle, there wasn't much to choose between the autopilot and the windvane, though it was clear that the windvane yielded more miles made good at the smaller apparent-wind angles. If the wind was between 85 and 95 degrees apparent, it was better to set the autopilot on a fixed compass course, and with this, the autopilot yielded more miles made good than the windvane.

I also ran a number of tests, which aren't recorded here, in which I sailed on a close reach and close hauled with Otto steering a compass course. The autopilot's inability to "read" the wind reduced the speed and miles made good, when compared to those achieved by the windvane, by about a third. The reason for this is that a windvane acts like a helmsman and keeps the sails performing at maximum efficiency by following the wind as it oscillates and/or as the boat rides up and over the waves. The autopilot tries to force a fixed course, and the sails are inevitably luffing or overtrimmed relative to the changing wind.

BOTTOM LINE

Boats up to about 30 feet can be steered by an autopilot that connects directly to the tiller, and some models of light-performance autopilots can be connected to the hub of a steering wheel. These units are adequate for motoring, but they're not strong enough for extensive use offshore. Ocean-going boats longer than 30 or 32 feet will typically have an electric or hydraulic linear-drive ram connected to the rudderstock below deck. This requires fitting a strong mounting base, running electrical cables, and mounting control units. The cost of *Taonui's* upgraded Simrad system was $4,300, not including taxes. Installation cost only $450 because the mounting place was built when the boat was constructed and we could use much of the old wiring. To fabricate and install a mounting base, run wiring, and fit the autopilot components would take 25 to 30 man-hours and cost roughly $1,500 to $2,000, for a total cost of around $6,000. By contrast, a new Monitor windvane costs $3,500 to $3,800, depending on whether the boat has wheel or tiller steering, you can fit it on the stern of almost any sailboat, and it's a do-it-yourself installation. An autopilot draws a current of 3 to 5 amps, which on most boats is generated by the engine-driven alternator. Most windvanes are

reasonably bulletproof in construction, but if something does fail, they're relatively easy to repair. The sacrificial tube between the pendulum strut and the water vane is designed to break in the event of a collision or excessive load. It's easy to replace.

I had only one such breakage on this trip. During 110,000 miles of sailing, Albert's only other breakages were a worn-out bushing, a compression fitting on the actuator shaft—which was an easy fix on a drill press—and the loss of the water vane. Before my first circumnavigation, I replaced the pendulum, and every three or four years I've replaced the turning blocks for the windvane control lines. In contrast, a couple of years ago, a hydraulic seal broke on my old Simrad, and I had to return it to the factory for repair. Since then, I've carried a spare drive unit (costing $2,150). An autopilot's electronic control units are usually trouble free, but if they do fail, they're black boxes. Aesthetically, a windvane is more pleasing. It makes no noise, requires no feeding, and works in harmony with the wind and waves. An autopilot makes a noise, requires the running of an engine or generator to supply its energy, and uses force to overcome the pressure of the wind and the waves. Based on the tests I ran, a windvane delivers more miles made good. On a long passage, this is what it's all about.

Having said all this, I would always carry both an autopilot and a windvane, if for no other reason than an autopilot is needed when motoring. For shorthanded sailing, it's essential to have two independent self-steering systems in case one fails. But, if I could have only one, I'd choose a windvane for offshore passagemaking.

USING A WINDVANE

A windvane is really useful only in ocean sailing where you expect to be on the same point of sail for hours or days. A windvane should be considered a device to hold a course relative to the wind, rather than a means of steering the boat or changing course, so it is not used for tacking or gybing. Before the windvane is engaged, the boat should be set on the desired course relative to the wind and the sails should be set so the boat is balanced and can be steered with only a little pressure on the tiller. The most common mistake in using a windvane is carrying too much mainsail, which causes the boat to round up into the wind.

Section 4 of the *Manual for the Monitor Self-Steering System* sets out the best practices for using a windvane on various points of sail. This excellent manual can be downloaded at http://www.selfsteer.com/pdfs/MonitorManual.pdf.

A windvane works best and outperforms an autopilot when sailing with the wind forward of the mast in any wind strength. On a beam reach, an autopilot outperforms a windvane, especially in light winds. In heavy winds (20+ knots), a windvane outperforms an autopilot on a beam reach. In light winds aft of the mast, an autopilot yields higher speed and distance made good; as the wind strengthens above 12 knots true, the windvane is superior. Of course, if the wind shifts, the windvane follows the wind and speed is maintained; with an autopilot the boat stays on a constant compass course (unless driven by a wind-direction sensor), and the boat speed drops.

Using a windvane, small (say 5-degree) course

SCANMAR'S ADVICE FOR SUCCESSFUL WINDVANE SAILING

The Scanmar website www.selfsteer.com discusses three keys to successful windvane steering.

THE BOAT

As different as sailboats are in appearance, rigging, size, speed, performance, etc., it is obvious that the properties of the yacht will influence the performance of the vane gear. Any characteristic that contributes to balance and makes it easy to trim the boat to stay on course helps the performance of the vane gear. Any characteristic that makes it easy to steer the boat back on course after a deviation is positive. Thus moderate size (30'–55'), moderate displacement, moderate keel, reasonable rudder response, and an easily balanced sail plan are some important contributing factors.

THE OPERATOR

Top windvane performance requires a balanced boat. Although true for autopilots also, vane gears are especially affected by gross errors in choice and trim of sails. An inexperienced skipper can smother the performance of the best vane gear.

Balancing the boat for self-steering involves setting things up so that the boat has a tendency to stay on the desired point of sail. If a wave or a change in the strength of wind takes the boat off course balanced trim should produce a tendency for the boat to return to course by itself. Through years of experience we have found that the common mistake by first-time vane sailors is to over-changes can be made by changing the angle of the vane and the set of the sails. For greater course changes, it is best to disengage the vane from the tiller, steer the boat onto the new course, adjust the sails as needed, make sure that the boat is balanced and little pressure is needed on the tiller to maintain course, then set the angle of the windvane vertical, then reconnect the control lines from the windvane to the tiller. After this, watch the boat's performance and make small adjustments as needed. To emphasize an earlier comment, a windvane can't be used to change course. It is a device to maintain a chosen course relative to the wind.

Windvane Choices

Windvane steering systems are manufactured by several companies. When selecting one, the key issue is to ensure the unit is built to manage the size and weight of the boat. Windvanes obviously can't have an electronic failure like an autopilot, but still they can break. Luckily, most units are built so that key breakable parts are simple to replace while underway. Experience has shown which parts are most likely to break, and singlehanders are advised to carry several spares.

One only hears of catastrophic failures of windvanes under the most severe conditions, when the boat has rolled or when another component such as the boom, mast, or a large solar panel has dropped on the windvane.

Note that the components of a windvane can also form the basis of an emergency rudder system. Most races accept a windvane to meet emergency rudder requirements.

canvas and over-sheet. The sailors that get the fastest and best results are those that have spent some time trying to balance their boat for self-steering without a vane gear prior to getting one.

Although good vane gear can be quite forgiving, the best performance will be achieved when the vane is only asked to make small corrections to keep a well-balanced boat on track. Usually, the new vane sailor will find that a bit of experience leads to great improvements. The vane actually teaches you a lot about sailing and trimming your boat.

THE POINTS OF SAIL

The particular point of sail is of importance to the performance of a vane gear. Most boats can be trimmed to self-steer by themselves when going hard to weather. Consequently, most vane gears will work well when beating. Running or reaching are trickier. When the boat is moving downwind its own speed forward causes a loss of apparent wind, which weakens the signals from the air vane sensor. In light winds they can become outright erratic as the air vane gets affected more by the boat's rolling than by the wind.

A reach can be difficult if the wind varies a lot in strength. A hard puff can induce a lot of weather helm. A temporary lull can cause a lot of lee helm. In either case it may require quite a bit of rudder to keep the boat from rounding up or bearing off.

As stated, some boats are easier to balance to overcome these problems. The operator can do a lot to minimize them also. The myth that vane gears do not steer downwind is simply not true provided they are reasonably designed, engineered, and operated.

HOMEMADE WINDVANES

An online group supports building windvanes at home. The site's founder Walt Murray died in 2006, but the site can be downloaded as a zip file from http://tinyurl.com/4mvxpg6/. Numerous designs are presented with highly detailed plans and precise building descriptions. Most of these could be built by any handyman with a decent workshop.

At my yacht club, several boats have been fitted with homemade windvanes. This is obviously a common approach. An online forum is also available for any discussions concerning windvanes: http://www.cruisenews.net.

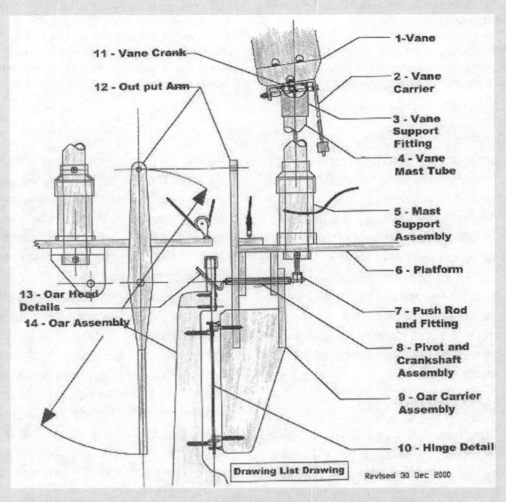

Diagram of a homebuilt windvane from Walt Murray's website on the same topic. *(Courtesy Walt Murray)*

Scanmar has an off-the-shelf attachment for their Monitor windvane. The M•RUD essentially attaches a small spare rudder to the regular windvane mounting tubes already installed on the boat. Robin Davie used this system to sail some 2,300 miles in the Around Alone race. It can be used to steer by hand, with the windvane itself, or with an autopilot. The emergency rudder is smaller than would be required to steer the boat aggressively, so it may be necessary to reduce sail, but the rudder will get the skipper back to port. It is important to install and test the emergency rudder system before leaving on a voyage.

AUTOPILOTS

There are several well-known manufacturers of autopilot systems. Some are more prevalent in Europe, and others in North America, and they range in price. I will not attempt to compare the different systems, but the following general statements should be held as gospel truth.

First, every system will break. There is no question about this. Therefore, the location of repair services is just as important as the initial purchase. I am especially lucky that a Raymarine service center is only a kilometer from my home. A single-hander would not want to wait three or four weeks for service when the autopilot breaks during racing season. A two-day turnaround is invaluable. Before making a purchase, carefully search the manufacturer's website for a local service center. A quick phone call can confirm whether service is actually performed on site or whether they ship repairs to the other side of the world. I also know from experience that it is a good idea to develop a personal relationship with the repair technician, who might then hand over a new unit rather than make you wait while he is busy working on commercial systems costing many times the price of a small boat autopilot.

Second, every system can communicate with common instruments from other manufacturers via a common protocol such as NMEA. While this is true, mixing components from different manufacturers is significantly less than optimal. This

will be noticed when the autopilot does not react as quickly as expected with a wind shift or when a cross wave swings the boat around. Every autopilot manufacturer has developed its own communications protocol, and each system works best within itself. I strongly recommend against mixing instruments from different manufacturers. In a recent round-the-world race, an IMOCA 60 skipper withdrew because his various computer systems were not talking to each other. What did this cost him—a million dollars or more?

Third, I can speak from hard-learned experience that problem solving becomes nigh-on impossible with mixed systems. The technician from Company A will say the problem is with Company B. A call to Company B will only lay the blame back on Company A. And absolutely nobody in the marine electronics world will have experience with the exact mixture of components installed on the boat. The problem will only be solved, if it is ever solved, by the skipper's own efforts at trial and error. This is not too bad at the dock, but the situation is a lot less fun 100 miles offshore.

Fourth, every system proudly advertises its "hard-over time," i.e., the time it takes for the ram to move from inner to outer limit. This is useless information. I don't care how fast the ram moves. Other than while tacking, an autopilot never needs to move more than a few inches even in the worst wave conditions. Infinitely more important is that it move intelligently. There is nothing more frustrating than watching the tiller stick in the wrong position and waiting for the autopilot to figure out what to do. Before making a purchase, question current users about how their autopilot reacts during a broaching situation, how long it takes to settle on a new tack, how it sets a course when activated, etc.

Fifth, no system will work perfectly right out of the box. It can take hours of testing and adjustment to refine the reactions of the autopilot to the boat and water conditions. All systems have a level of intelligence that "learn" the conditions, but significant changes must be dialed in by the skipper before the learning can occur.

Sixth, other electronics can impact the autopilot or vice versa. A single-sideband (SSB) radio uses a tremendous amount of power when transmitting, and even VHF radios use significant power. It is important that any radio wires be kept well away from autopilot wires. They should be run on opposite sides of the boat as much as possible. Interference can occur in both directions: with the autopilot disturbing the radio, or the radio disturbing the autopilot. I have even seen instances where the autopilot interfered with the radio on only one frequency band.

Seventh, sail trim, sail trim, sail trim. Nothing is more important. No autopilot can override poor sail trim. Even a small adjustment to trim has a significant impact on pilot operation, especially with the spinnaker where things can go bad very quickly.

Tacking and Gybing Using an Autopilot

Personally, I find that tacking with the autopilot is much slower and less accurate than tacking manually, controlling the tiller with my knees while I sheet in. Also, I pause halfway through a tack to pull the jibsheet back in (as described in Chapter 9, Sail Handling and Sailing Techniques). I also find that the autopilot does not settle on the new tack as quickly as I would like. During a tack the autopilot swings the boat over 90 degrees, but not as accurately as I would like. For these reasons, I do not use the autopilot to tack. I can do it much better myself. However, I know several singlehanders who do use their autopilots to tack very successfully. Skippers need to make their own decision on this.

This autopilot remote control from Madman Marine clips to my harness for immediate use wherever I am on the boat. I find the remote especially useful to make minute-to-minute tiny adjustments to my heading in puffs and lulls, keeping maximum speed without leaving my position on the rail.

I do use the autopilot to gybe. In this case the boat swing is only 30–40 degrees and the pilot has no trouble handling this change. (The gybing process is also described in Chapter 9, Sail Handling and Sailing Techniques.)

Autopilot Remote Controls

A remote control is invaluable on long voyages. It lets the skipper move about the boat, enjoy the sunshine at the bow, or sleep below while retaining control of the autopilot. It also helps manage the annoyance that comes with sleeping during shifty winds. The wind-shift alarm will sound every time the wind changes by 15 degrees. The remote control allows the skipper to react easily without having to get out of the bunk.

The remote also has a safety aspect. Most autopilot systems will turn the boat into the wind or through the wind if the skipper falls overboard while wearing the remote. Of course, it would be incredibly stupid to rely on this instead of wearing a harness. In a heavy sea, a boat that heaves-to 30 meters away might as well be 30 miles away.

Remotes also have significant drawbacks, however, and must be researched. Two problems commonly arise. First, is the radio range longer than the boat, or might a walk to the bow trigger the man-overboard safety protocol? Second, will weak batteries or turning the remote off to replace batteries also trigger the safety man-overboard protocol? The wireless receiver for the remote must be mounted near the center of the boat and away from significant metal objects like the engine. Third, remotes don't like to be immersed in water. If one is drenched and becomes inoperable, it may be possible to take it apart, rinse it in fresh water, and dry it with the heat of the engine. This method worked when the remote on *Rain Drop* was submerged in a cockpit full of water for 2 minutes.

There is much debate about who makes the "best" autopilot. Based on my observations, there is no clear-cut winner. Every system has received wonderful accolades and bitter complaints. The skipper is best to see what other, similar boats are using and make a decision only after speaking with other singlehanders.

CHAPTER 7 **POWER SYSTEMS**

Electricity is the greatest cause of frustration of every singlehanded sailor. Electrical problems lead to more voyage cancellations than any other issue, and electrical problems cause the skipper to spend more time in uncomfortable twisted positions below chart tables than anything else. Highly experienced singlehander Jeanne Socrates captures the essence of these frustrations during the course of just eight days:

- Managed to short across circuit while testing AP drive motor . . . 40A fuse blown— no spare. . . !
- Went to use multimeter to check fuse—"dead as a Dodo". . . ! Battery gone—no spare
- Used heatshrink butt joint to bypass fuse and join wires together—there's another 40A fuse in same circuit so protected still. . . Discovered instruments now permanently on—despite switch at chart table—seems I damaged relay in blowing circuit
- About to see if I can find out what the problem is with my ship's VHF radio—confirmed yesterday as not transmitting. Means getting (with difficulty!) to behind the instrument panel yet again . . . grrr! Maybe I'll be able to see why my SSB radio has lost its GPS input while I'm back there . . . and have another go at fixing the lost connection between the same VHF radio and the AIS unit . . .
- "In for a penny, in for a pound" . . . I delved deeper and removed the Pactor modem and HF/SSB radio front to see if I could restore the missing GPS input to the radio—another

loose connection dealt with . . . YES—success! Lat/long/UTC—all displayed again . . . I felt I deserved the dark chocolate I rewarded myself with later, after my meal!!

In her 2012–13 voyage, during which she became the oldest woman to circumnavigate nonstop without assistance, Socrates lost the use of two laptop computers and a sat phone. She was down to an old-style printing weather fax as her only source of weather information.

Socrates has circumnavigated three times singlehanded. She has faced these problems with electronics since I met her seven years ago. The specific problems listed above were encountered on a two-year-old boat with completely new electronics.

Jeanne Socrates adjusts her mast-mounted wind instrument. Working with electronics on a boat is never easy, either up the mast or below at the chart table. *(Courtesy Jeanne Socrates)*

She has had numerous professionals working on her boat and has become nothing less than an expert herself.

From Glenn Wakefield on *West Wind II*, as he enters the Southern Ocean on his second westward round-the-world attempt:

There's no juice coming from the wind generator and after talking to a service rep it appears the problem is inside the motor and may be diodes or the rectifier. This means that I'm now on solar power only and will have to seriously rethink my consumption.

There is only one answer. If a boat contains electronics, they will go wrong—without question. So the singlehander has two options: to attend university for four years to receive a degree in electronic engineering, or to drastically reduce the reliance on electronics. I prefer the second option.

> I am a sailboat.
> I need only wind to move my master safely and comfortably to any port in the world.

This should be engraved on a bronze plaque mounted inside every singlehander's boat. I love sailing. I want to spend my weekends sailing, not searching out fuses or looking for loose wires. And when I undertake a long offshore voyage, I do not want to be stopped by something that takes four years of university to understand.

With that statement I am not saying I don't use electronics. Skippers are welcome to load up their boat with as many gadgets as they like. I myself use a complex electronic autopilot. What I am saying is to reduce the reliance on electronics. The failure of electronics must never be an excuse to stop sailing . . . period. In 2013 my autopilot quit working for nine months. During this time I did not miss one race, one Saturday afternoon cruise, or one 25-knot-spinnaker launch. I see electronics as a convenience: nice to have but certainly not necessary to my enjoyment on the boat.

Before leaving the dock, a singlehander must ensure that the boat can be sailed safely to its destination even with a complete power failure. Singlehanded racers must be even more demanding. They must know that they can keep racing with a complete power failure. A power failure that will occur—depend on it. And yet this simple concept is beyond the belief of most sailors. I asked Class 40 skipper Joe Harris what would happen if his batteries shorted out two weeks from Cape Town during the upcoming Global Ocean Challenge. His answer: "I'm screwed." And yet this is exactly what happened to Derek Hatfield. His brand-new batteries shorted with a complete shutdown of the power system.

Modern civilization teaches us to look to electronics for all safety, comfort, and happiness. By "modern" I mean just the last ten years. Two decades ago no sailor would leave port without knowing how to use a compass and sextant. Today a GPS chartplotter tells us where we are, heading to the nearest port, and the location of every rock in between. Just four decades ago, the famous singlehander Bernard Moitessier undertook the Golden Globe Race without even a radio. He communicated through passing ships to the race headquarters using signal flags. Today, how many skippers would even notice if they passed a boat signaling with a distress flag?

I have rambled on about this here to make one point: electronics are bad—some parts of every system *will* fail. However, an electrical system failure need not be a disaster for a properly prepared singlehander. Chapter 9 on sailing techniques explains how to sail without an autopilot or windvane. Singlehanders are not prepared to leave the dock until they understand these techniques.

However, I am not so naive as to think that we can't use electronics to make our lives easier. The first thing a singlehander should do is reduce dependence on the boat's electronics so that disaster is limited in the event of a complete power failure.

The second step is to cut the power consumption of necessary items simply by turning them off. In her famous Vendée Globe race, Ellen MacArthur commented that she was spending 8 hours a day using a computer and Internet connection to research the weather. I was studying weather forecasting at the time and asked her what she was researching in 8 hours that could not be done in a half hour. She answered, "Nothing." The simple reason was that her boat was sailing itself perfectly without her constant input. She was just spending time. But she was also wasting power.

The singlehander should use a computer as necessary, but no more so. If it takes a half hour, then don't spend 1 hour or 8 hours. Turn the computer off and read a book.

Sailors have a bad habit of leaving their instruments running for the entire voyage, such as leaving the chartplotter running 24 hours a day in open water. Why? Every boat has a mechanical compass. The GPS can be activated for a few minutes every 4 hours just to check the course. After that, it should be turned off again and the mechanical compass used. Another good example is collision-avoidance equipment. The radar, AIS, Sea-Me active radar, or Collision-Avoidance Radar Detector (CARD) should be used only when the skipper is belowdeck (for more about these technologies see Chapter 10, See and Be Seen). They should not be used when the skipper is on deck day or night, except in thick fog. The skipper has eyes and should use them and not waste more valuable power.

In particular, the display screens of electronic devices can burn an inordinate amount of power. At the very least, put display screens in sleep mode when not in active use.

As a third step, use only DC power. Nearly all the electronics in the world are designed to function with DC power. Those intended for home use have a built-in AC adapter that converts home power from AC to DC before it enters the unit (that's the small black box commonly found on the end of a power cord). There is a very significant power loss in moving from AC to DC. So all electronics should be run directly from the boat battery using a DC to DC converter that converts the standard 12-volt current to whatever voltage is required for the instrument—not by using an inverter that changes your battery's 12-volt DC current up to 110-volt AC so that you

can plug in your adapter and have the current converted back down to DC, with huge losses along the way!

POWER BUDGET

Planning a power budget is tricky because there are several uncontrollable variables. The starting point is calculating all the power requirements for the boat. A simple spreadsheet is the best way to tackle this issue. The illustration (next page) is a worksheet adapted from the Pacific Cup.

Virtually all power usage figures can be found in the user's manual or on the website of the equipment manufacturer. For example, a quick look at the Raymarine website indicates that the model AIS 250 has a power requirement of 200 mA. When building a spreadsheet, however, the skipper must remember that some equipment works only in conjunction with other equipment. For example, the AIS 250 is designed to work with a multifunction display, which consumes another 250 mA.

The greatest risk for error in power consumption calculations is with the autopilot because this is by far the leading user of power. The consequences of an error here are a hundred times worse than the consequences of an error in the running lights. The problem is that the autopilot's consumption is directly related to weather conditions, which are difficult to predict or average out when building the system. For example, the B&G T2 hydraulic pump has a power consumption range from 5 to 22.5 amps. Actual power consumption within this range depends on the pilot's responsiveness required for the direction of sail (running downwind requires greater power) and the wind/wave conditions. (A choppy sea requires much more power than flat water.)

Power Generation

Given everything mentioned above, the single best approach to meeting power requirements is to cut power requirements. Reducing power requirements reduces cost, reduces problems, and reduces the risk of abandoning a voyage. Reduce, reduce, reduce, reduce. It's easy to remember, and it works. After eliminating a large part of the boat's power

Electrical Budget Worksheet (adapted from Pacific Cup)

Calculate your DC Loads:

Lighting	Amps	Hours	AH/Day
Running Lights			0.0
Masthead Tricolor Light			0.0
Anchor Light			0.0
Strobe Light			0.0
Spreader Lights			0.0
Cabin Light (small)			0.0
Cabin Light (big incandescent)			0.0
Cabin Light (flourescent)			0.0
Instrument Lights			0.0
Handheld Spot Light			0.0
Other			0.0
Lighting AH			**0.0**

Galley	Amps	Hours	AH/Day
Refrigeration			0.0
Prop Solenoid			0.0
Other			0.0
Galley AH			**0.0**

Electronics	Amps	Hours	AH/Day
Autopilot			0.0
VHF (receive)			0.0
VHF (transmit)			0.0
SSB (receive)			0.0
SSB (transmit)			0.0
SSB Digital controller			0.0
GPS			0.0
Instruments			0.0
Weather fax receiver			0.0
Radar (standby)			0.0
Radar (transmit)			0.0
AIS			0.0
Energy Monitors			0.0
Stereo			0.0
Computer (screen off)			0.0
Computer (screen on)			0.0
Computer (serial adapter)			0.0
Other			0.0
Electronics AH			**0.0**

Plumbing	Amps	Hours	AH/Day
Fresh Water Pump			0.0
Calculate using average water consumption.			
Bilge Pump(s)			0.0
This should be zero unless the boat leaks.			
Other			0.0
Plumbing AH			**0.0**

Take a thorough look at your boat and the electrical consumption aboard. *(Courtesy Pacific Cup)* requirements, the skipper can take the next step and determine which method of power generation is best for his boat and his sailing.

Watts, Kilowatts, Hours

Power is often discussed in terms of watts (W), kilowatts (kW), or kilowatt hours (kWh); current is measured in amps (A) or milliamps (mA). Power (in watts) is equal to volts times amps. Since smaller boat systems usually are 12 volts, most power discussions focus on watts. We can often ignore the aspect of amps and just work directly with Power.

The watt measures what is happening at any moment. For example, a solar panel producing a 40 W output can power a 40 W light bulb (assuming no losses). A kilowatt is equal to 1,000 watts. A kilowatt-hour is the total power from a constant stream of power (either produced or consumed) of 1 kW for 1 hour. A solar panel with a 40 W output, for example, would require 25 hours of direct sunshine to generate 1 kWh of power. But, note that the solar panel output only occasionally reaches its "rated" power in watts. The rated power of a solar panel represents the output at ideal solar conditions, which may not occur all that often. Typically a horizontal panel might *average* around 50% to 60% of its rated output over the sunny hours of the day. This also depends on location. On the way to Hawaii in June, the sun is directly overhead. On the same day in Australia, the sun is very low on the horizon, providing only a fraction of the power.

A battery that stores 1 kWh of usable power would light ten 100 W lightbulbs for 1 hour. With most batteries, however, only about 50% of listed capacity is actually "usable" if one expects a reasonable battery life. It is vital to examine the characteristics of the batteries closely to understand their exact usable capacity. Different battery types have different usable capacities.

Some examples of power production and consumption:

- My boat has a total of 130 W solar panels. During a sunny day at sea I can plan that they will receive usable sunlight for 9 hours. 130 x 9 = 1,170 or approximately 1.2 kWh.

- My autopilot consumes 5 W in easy conditions and 22 W in difficult conditions. I might assume an average of 8 W during my voyage. Over a day this is 24 x 8 = 192 or approximately 0.2 kWh. However, this could be as high as 22 x 24 = 528 or over 0.5 kWh over an entire day of rough seas.

- My Sea-Me radar reflector is listed as using 150 mA. (Convert amps to watts by multiplying by volts: 0.15 A x 12 V = 1.8 W.) Running the Sea-Me for 6 hours while sleeping will require 1.8 x 6 = 10.8 or approximately 0.02 kWh.

What does all this mean for my power budget? For just these two items, I need between 0.22 and 0.52 kWh a day. On a good sunny day my solar panels produce 1.2 kWh so I would be fine with lots of power to spare. This is the typical condition during the second half of the Singlehanded Transpac. The problem is on a cloudy, rough day at sea. This is exactly what happened to expert skipper Ronnie Simpson during the first third of the 2012 Singlehanded Transpac. His solar power could not keep up with the choppy water and low sunlight conditions that are typical off the California coast.

The question becomes, does the singlehander design his power system for ideal conditions (lots of sunlight and long rolling seas), horrendous conditions (cloudy and choppy seas), or average conditions somewhere between the two? It is easy to say that he wants a system for the worst possible conditions, but this has a significant cost in power generation and battery size. My solution is to design a system for the top half of the range, but not necessarily the worst imaginable conditions. After this, the skipper must be prepared to manage the boat using other techniques.

Batteries

First, it is impossible to "force" power into a battery. A battery draws power in, just like sucking it up a straw. Power cannot be forced in any faster than the battery wants to draw. A deeply drained battery will draw power in quickly. A battery that is nearing capacity will draw power in slowly.

Power will flow in any direction, from the highest to the lowest levels. So the only way to charge a battery is to supply power at a higher voltage than what the battery contains. So, for example, a solar panel may be called "12 volt," but this is a nominal value. In fact, it will supply more than 12 V. This is necessary because in order to charge a 12-volt battery, the solar panel must supply a greater voltage.

Because a drained battery draws power much more quickly than a battery near capacity, it is rarely worthwhile attempting to fill a lead-acid, gel, or AGM (absorbed glass matt) battery all the way to capacity while at sea. The battery will fill from 50% to 80% much more quickly than it will fill from 80% to 90%, or 90% to 95%. That is, it will take much longer with a solar panel, even in the same sunshine, to get the battery from 80% to 90%, than it will take to get it from 50% to 80%. Many skippers plug into shore power over extended periods to get their batteries up to 100%, but only charge to 80% while at sea. It is a more efficient approach. As discussed later, lithium batteries operate differently.

Much of the following information is sourced from: http://www.windsun.com/Batteries/Battery_FAQ.htm

Internal resistance is a primary issue with batteries. Slower charging and discharging rates are more efficient. A battery rated at 180 amp-hours (Ah) over 6 hours might be rated at 220 Ah at the 20-hour rate, and 260 Ah at the 48-hour rate. Much of this loss of efficiency is due to higher internal resistance at higher flow rates. Internal resistance is not a constant—it's a situation of "the more you push, the more it pushes back."

Starting batteries are commonly used to start an engine that needs a very large current for a very short time to start. They have a large number of thin plates for maximum surface area. The plates are composed of a lead "sponge," similar in appearance to a very fine foam sponge. This gives a large surface area, but if the battery is used like a deep-cycle battery, heavily discharged before charging, this sponge will be consumed and fall to the bottom of the cells. Automotive batteries generally fail after 30–150 deep cycles if used this way, while they may

last for thousands of cycles in normal starting use (2% to 5% discharge before recharging).

Deep-cycle batteries are designed to be discharged down as much as 80% time after time, and have much thicker plates. The major difference between a true deep-cycle battery and others is that the plates are solid lead plates—not sponge. This gives less surface area, thus less "instant" power like that from starting batteries. Although these can be discharged down to a 20% charge, the best life span results from keeping the average cycle at about 50% discharge.

Marine batteries are usually a hybrid between the starting and deep-cycle types. In the hybrid, the plates may be composed of lead sponge, but it is coarser and heavier than that used in starting batteries. It is often hard to tell what is in a "marine" battery, but most are a hybrid. Starting batteries are usually rated in CCA, or cold cranking amps, or MCA, marine cranking amps—similar to CCA. Any battery with its capacity shown in CCA or MCA may or may not be a true deep-cycle battery.

Plate thickness (of the positive plate) matters because of a factor called positive grid corrosion. This ranks among the top reasons for battery failure. The positive plate gets eaten away over time, so eventually there is nothing left—it all falls to the bottom as sediment. Thicker plates are directly related to longer life, so other things being equal, the battery with the thickest plates will last the longest.

Automotive batteries typically have plates about 0.04 inches thick. A typical golf cart battery has plates that are around 0.07 to 0.11 inches thick. While plate thickness is not the only factor in how many deep cycles a battery can take before it dies, it is the most important one.

Types of Batteries

There are several types and technologies for batteries: the major construction types are flooded (wet), gel, and AGM. AGM batteries are also sometimes called "starved electrolyte" or "dry," because the fiberglass mat is only 95% saturated with sulfuric acid and there is no excess liquid.

Flooded batteries may be standard batteries, with removable caps for monitoring and adding fluid, or so-called "maintenance free" batteries (that means they are designed to die one week after the warranty runs out). All gel batteries are sealed and are "valve regulated," which means that a tiny valve keeps a slight positive pressure. Nearly all AGM batteries are sealed and valve regulated (commonly referred to as VRLA, for valve regulated lead acid).

Flooded batteries include 6-volt golf cart batteries. What? Golf cart batteries on a boat? Yes, this is what I use. I have a pair of Trojan 240 Ah 6-volt golf cart batteries installed in series to produce 12 V. These are standard flooded lead acid batteries that must be checked and refilled periodically. I use these for a few reasons. First, they have a very deep cycle, meaning that they provide a steady stream of power for a long time, exactly what I need to run an autopilot for hours or days on end. And they have a high cycle life, i.e., they can be deeply discharged many times before replacement. Think about what they were built for: to run a golf cart through 18 holes several times in succession before being recharged overnight. The golf course does not want to replace these batteries every three months. Second, they are the least expensive of any type of battery for the amount of power they supply, and they are readily available from any battery shop. Golf cart batteries are not optimized to provide the cranking power required to start an engine, but they will not be damaged when used for this. These batteries can spill very dangerous acid so must be properly secured in the boat to survive even a complete knockdown.

My own experience has shown that they are a good choice: on the return trip to Hawaii, they twice ran my autopilot and electronics through several days of completely overcast conditions without a blip. I have recently replaced my batteries after constant use over five years. The cost of replacing the pair was just over $300. Their value for the cost is why I would recommend golf cart batteries over any other type of standard lead acid battery.

Gel batteries have added a silica gel to the liquid to stop it from sloshing around or spilling. They are sealed and never need refilling. However, there are several disadvantages. One is that they must be charged at a lower voltage to prevent excess

gas from damaging the cells. They cannot be fast-charged with a conventional automotive charger or they may be permanently damaged. This is not usually a problem with solar panels, but if an auxiliary generator or inverter bulk charger is used, current *must be limited* to the manufacturer's specifications. Bruce Schwab used gel batteries during both of his Open 60 circumnavigations and says: "They were a 360 Ah x 24 V bank made up from 8 x 180 Ah 6 V "golf cart" Gel-Techs. The configuration was two 180 Ah x 12 V banks in series. They were charged with a 130 A x 24 V alternator with a smart alternator regulator. When they were roughly 50% discharged (and properly conditioned) they could absorb 90-110 A for a good 30 min. or more. The key thing with gel is to have a smart regulator with external temperature and voltage sensing."

AGM batteries infuse the electrolyte into a fiber mat between the plates. These have the sealed benefit of a gel battery, without the limitations on charging. However, AGMs cost two to three times as much as a flooded battery with the same capacity.

Charging Batteries

A battery cycle is one complete discharge and recharge. It is usually considered to be discharging from 100% to 20%, and then charging back to 100%. However, you may also see ratings for cycles at other depths of discharge, most commonly 10%, 20%, and 50%. Be careful when looking at a rating for how many cycles can be expected from a battery unless the rating also states how far down the battery is being discharged. For example, most golf cart batteries are rated for about 550 cycles to 50% discharge—which equates to about 2 years of frequent use as would be faced on a golf course. On my boat, a five year replacement schedule seems appropriate.

Battery life is directly related to how deep the battery is discharged each time. If a battery is discharged to 50% every day, it will last about twice as long as if it is 80% discharged. If discharged only 10%, it will last about five times as long as one discharged 50%. This does not mean it cannot be discharged 80% once in a while. It's just that for planning a system for a boat's power usage, an

BRUCE SCHWAB ON LITHIUM BATTERIES

Bruce Schwab, who has sailed his Open 60 around the world twice, has studied all aspects of boat power extensively and is one of the world's top experts in this field. His company, Bruce Schwab Energy Systems, can meet the highest performance requirements of racers. Schwab made the following comments about the new lithium batteries. A full discussion is available on his website: www.bruceschwab.com.

No, they're not for everyone . . . but that's mostly because they cost a lot up front. However, here is a big point: over the life of the batteries they may actually cost LESS per kWh used than lead/gel/AGM. How can that be? This is because lithium batteries can be used for 2000–3000 cycles at 80% depth of discharge (DOD) levels. Compare that to the typical less than 400 cycles of an AGM battery at only 50% DOD.

Furthermore, the top 20% or so of the lead/gel/AGM capacity is rarely available while sailing, because it simply takes too long to charge them all the way up. With a good lithium system they can absorb charge at a fast rate, until nearly fully charged.

So, at typical fast-charging rates, you can charge back to about 95% or more of capacity before the current is reduced by the alternator regulator (or other charger). What does this mean? It means that a full 75%+ of the lithium capacity is "usable" and in the fast recharging range, compared to only 30-35% of lead/gel/AGM.

Ok, so you've done your power budget and you came up with an average consumption of 10

Ah (at 12 V). So you'd like 240 Ah at 12 V of usable power for 24 hrs, so that you only have to charge once per day. If you have a lead/gel/AGM you would need a roughly 720 Ah bank to get 252 Ah (35%) of usable capacity to reach your 24-hr target. That size of lead battery would weigh as much as 500 lbs., and the expected life would be 250–500 cycles at 50% DOD.

With a good lithium system of 360 Ah capacity (½ of the lead), you would have 270 Ah of usable capacity at the very conservative 75% capacity use. The system would weigh about 123 lbs. and have a cycle life of 2000–3000 cycles at 75-80% DOD. That is about one quarter of the weight, and 4 to 6 times the cycle life.

Using a Telecom 180 Ah AGM as an example, four of them (for the 720 Ah) would cost roughly $2,350. A Genasun LiFePO4 (Lithium Iron Phosphate) 360 Ah x 12 V system retails for $7,700. So that's 4 to 6 times the cycle life and one quarter of the weight for a little over 3 times

A lithium battery can be used for 2000–3000 cycles at 80% depth of discharge. *(Courtesy Bruce Schwab)*

the price. And we haven't mentioned the fuel savings from faster and more efficient recharging. More "efficient"? Yes, lithium has a CEF (Charge Efficiency Factor) of 99–100%, whereas lead/gel/AGM is typically around 85%. So that can be a gain of another 15% of effective capacity.

ABOUT BATTERY MANAGEMENT SYSTEMS (BMS)

The BMS modules (circuitry on top of the battery) do several things: they measure the voltage and temperature of the cells and send the info to the BMS master. The BMS master then tells the modules when/if to shunt off a little energy to balance the cells with each other. Once a bank is in balance the corrections are very small, so very little energy is lost.

Note that the better BMSs balance whenever there is a voltage difference between cells while charging. Many simpler BMS systems on the mar-

A battery management system like the one shown here monitors voltage and temperature of cells and directs energy to balance the cells. (*Courtesy Bruce Schwab*)

ket only balance at a set voltage point. Choose your system carefully.

Oh, that reminds me . . . did I mention the reduced voltage drop and the greater amps in/out efficiency? Or the lack of "Peukert's Effect" (the loss of capacity under high loads exhibited with lead)" with lithium?

average depth of discharge of around 50% should be considered optimum. Also, there is an upper limit: a battery that is continually discharged only 5% or less will usually not last as long as one discharged 10%. This happens because at very shallow cycles, the lead dioxide tends to build up in clumps on the positive plates rather than in an even film.

CREATING POWER

Solar Panels

Here is a bold statement: solar panels are the best method of generating power—no question. Any other method should be used only if solar panels will not work. Solar panels are the first choice because they are the simplest possible solution. No moving parts, nothing to break, nothing to wear

out, nothing to fix—ever. I've used my solar panels for ten years without giving a thought to even the slightest bit of maintenance. They just keep working. About the only thing that should be done is an annual current test to ensure none of the connections are broken and the panels are still providing maximum power.

A solar panel system only has three components: the panels, a charge controller, and the batteries. That's it.

Solar panels can be added as required for particular voyages. I have panels totaling 40 watts permanently mounted on the boat to meet all of my normal requirements fifty weeks a year. I add another 50 watts on a rubber mat for my annual offshore trip, and another 40 watts hanging off the transom for longer voyages. With 130 watts *Foolish Muse* had no problem sailing to Hawaii and back.

Foolish Muse passing under the Golden Gate Bridge at the start of the 2006 Singlehanded Transpac. I sent this photo to the solar panel company as an interesting example of their product, and they put me in their calendar.

This radar will cast a shadow over one panel most of the day.

Quieter and more robust, modern wind generators still have drawbacks. Research them carefully. *(Courtesy havebluepower.com)*

I believe that for simplicity, the best option is to have the panels mounted flat on the boat. Some systems mount on a moveable frame that allows the panels to be aimed more directly at the sun. This will generate more power, particularly in the morning and evening, but it moves away from my concept of maximum simplicity. If the boat has sufficient solar panels, aiming them at the sun would add only a small amount of extra charging. Keep in mind that we are only trying to get the batteries to 80%, so the extra effort to get to 100% is rarely worth the effort. Newer flexible panels now have outputs similar to those of rigid panels, but they are more expensive. It is certainly possible to use several panels to adjust to the contours of the boat deck. I use a series of panels, each measuring 13 by 5 inches, across the stern of the boat. This fits the curve very closely.

Solar panels must be mounted where they have a clear view of the sky. A shadow covering a third of the panel reduces its output to zero. Even a small shadow reduces output significantly. For this reason the best mounting location is on the stern or transom of the boat, behind any shadow from the mainsail or mast. A panel on the cabin top will be partially shaded all of the time.

With a solar panel system, a charge controller is required. A charge controller limits the rate at which current is added to batteries to increase the longevity of the batteries. A maximum power point tracker (MPPT) controller further optimizes the charging to provide the optimum voltage when the batteries are drained, such as after a long night of use.

Wind Generators

Wind generators have risen in popularity over the past decade, having become more robust and much quieter. Noise has long been a complaint against wind generators, and noise reduction has been an area of significant research. This in itself is a reason to closely examine newer models. Prices for typical units run from $800 to $1,200.

Of course, the wind generator must be in an apparent wind to function. All else being equal, they will generate much more power sailing upwind than downwind. For example, if sailing upwind in 5 knots of true wind produces 10 knots of apparent wind, the generator may output about 40 W power. However, if sailing downwind in the same 5 knots true with 2 knots of apparent wind, the generator will not produce any power at all. Most have a start-up requirement of 5 knots. In researching wind generators I've found a huge range of power output. In 10 knots of wind, rated power outputs range from 10 to 50 W. Skippers should research this carefully if thinking of using wind power. It appears that the modern designs produce significantly more power than older models.

A key consideration is to mount the unit well away from any operational area on the boat. I have seen a photo of an offshore sailor who was seriously cut by a wind generator blade while reaching over the transom. The "wingspan" of a typical generator is up to 46 inches (about 120 cm) across. They take up a significant amount of room and must be mounted high above the transom of the boat. Of course, the higher it is mounted, the higher the weight and resistance on the boat. In a broach, the wind generator will be the very first piece of equipment to break. They are built for air, not water.

Water Generators

There are three types of water generators (hydro generators): fixed, towed, and hybrid. The fixed units are bolted directly to the transom and hang below. The towed units are mounted on the stern rail and towed behind the boat on a long line. The hybrid units are towed on a short shaft. The significance of all water generators, compared to wind generators, is that they depend only on boat speed, and not on relative wind speed. They are just as efficient when sailing upwind or downwind. This is very important for extended downwind voyages—our greatest wish. Any type of water generator will create drag. This is not as important for cruisers but obviously is significant for racers. The effect of the drag is greater on smaller boats: a 20-footer will notice much more drag than a 40-footer. Of course,

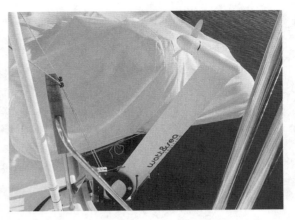

A fixed hydro generator in the up position. *(Courtesy Bruce Schwab)*

as described above, these should be left in the water only for the time necessary to bring the batteries up to an 80% charge—the most efficient charging period.

Fixed Water Generators

Fixed generators have recently appeared on the market. They bolt directly to the transom of the boat and extend into the water below. They can be swung up when not in use. These are being used in the big IMOCA 60 and Class 40 singlehanded races. The Watt & Sea model specifications indicate that it can produce an astounding 500 watts of power when traveling at just 8 knots. It produces some drag that slows the boat, but the rationale is that it is less than the drag of carrying 300 liters (about 80 gal.) of fuel required to produce the same power with a generator on a very long voyage. This unit sells for the equally astounding price of $4,995 for the basic unit, higher for the racing version. Obviously it is aimed at the serious market.

Towed Water Generators

For a true towed generator, there is nothing but a propeller and shaft at the end of a rope line. The line is connected to a generator on the stern rail. Thus the propeller and line both rotate all the way up to the rail. This type of unit generates about 12 W of power for every 1 knot of boat speed. However, to me it seems that towing a rope behind the boat is a lot like towing a drogue, designed to slow the boat.

MIKE HENNESSEY ON FIXED WATER GENERATORS

Here are some comments Mike Hennessey made about Watt & Sea water generators on the Sailing Anarchy forum:

The difference between the cruising and racing versions is that the racing has variable pitch blades that feather the blades based on boat speed (e.g., drag minimization) while the cruising version has fixed blades. The race version is also 1 kilo lighter than the cruising version.

A good number of Class 40s have either installed or are going to install the units. Several installed them for the Route du Rhum. In the U.S., the Atlantic Cup organizers are encouraging participants to install the units, in keeping with their goal for a green regatta. The Class 40s have all been going with the cruising version since the drag that is dealt with by the variable pitch control starts to become a real issue at over 12 knots of boat speed, and in a Class 40 the best way to deal with that is to simply pivot the generator out of the water and wait for slower boat speeds to charge. The Class 40s tend to average 9 knots or so, which makes this a viable choice for Class 40s.

The amp budget for my boat is in the range of 200 amp hours a day. For an IMOCA 60 it is not going to be that much more, just what is used to cant the keel. The problem with a 5-amp device is that it just is not going to make that much difference for the drag penalty you pay. And I am still going to need to haul heavy diesel fuel around, or a genset, or a fuel cell. I frankly have a similar issue with solar panels—I just don't have enough space on the deck to have enough panels to produce enough power that would make me fossil fuel independent.

The Watt & Sea unit can do that. 4 to 5 hours of deployment a day and I pay for my entire amp budget. Sunny days or shady. And while it won't help in really light conditions, I can basically count on it anytime the boat is going more than 4 to 5 knots.

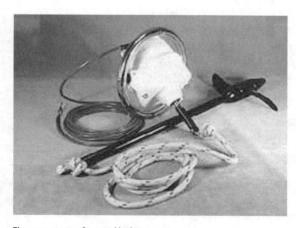

The components of a towed hydro generator.

There have also been instances of towed units being eaten by sharks, and the rope is prone to foul in bouncing seas.

Hybrid Water Generators

The hybrid water generator is made up of a ridged shaft and propeller, approximately 8 feet long, fixed to a generator on the rail. The shaft is gimbaled to move with the water. The propeller has a "diving plane" or wing to keep the propeller in the water. The unit I looked at was rated for 72 W of power at 5 knots of boat speed. These units claim 30% less drag than the towed line generators.

Some water generator units are advertised to have the capacity to function also as a wind

A hybrid hydro generator.

generator when mounted vertically with a larger propeller. The specifications show, however, that these have poor generating performance compared to a dedicated wind generator.

Power Cells (Fuel Cells)

Power cells are a new technology in the sailing world. Just a few years ago they shut off when tilted, such as when sailing to windward, making them unusable. However this problem has been corrected. Power cells are now being used by top racers in transatlantic and round-the-world voyages. In particular the Mini 6.50 racers find them most convenient.

Power cells use a simple chemical reaction to produce electricity. Methanol mixes with oxygen passing through a membrane to release electrons—thus electricity. A simple, quiet pump is the only mechanical aspect of the device. The methanol is used up in the process. The only byproducts are water and carbon dioxide (the same amount of carbon dioxide as a person breathing) so the unit can be used in the cabin.

A typical power cell produces about 1.1 kWh per liter of fuel, making it about 24% less efficient per unit of fuel than a gas generator. Many power cells have automatic on/off functions to ensure the batteries are always charged. This can lead to problems if used in conjunction with a solar panel system, so it is recommended that they be operated manually. Craig Horsfield used a power cell in the 2013 Mini Transat. He commented that 30 liters (about 8 gal.) of fuel would have been sufficient to meet his needs.

Power cells are also considerably more expensive and use more expensive fuel than a generator. However, the mechanical simplicity, reliability, and low noise make them a good choice for sailing in well-developed areas where the fuel is readily available. They would not be advised for cruising to the far-flung tropical islands of the world.

Generators

Small, portable gasoline or diesel generators have a longer history in sailing. They are more efficient than a fuel cell, producing 1.5 kWh per liter of fuel in a small model, and gasoline and diesel are readily available worldwide. With a full working engine, generators are mechanically complex with *(continued page 105)*

An Efoy power cell. *(Courtesy Efoy)*

ONE SAILOR'S EXPERIENCE OF USING THE ENGINE TO GENERATE POWER

Using the boat's engine is a common method of generating power. Racers using generators or the yacht engine speak of running the motor for 1 hour every 8 hours of sailing. Personally, I find this concept unappealing. If I had wanted a motor running, I'd have bought a cigarette boat and forgotten all about the canvas overhead.

However, those who do use the yacht engine have worked out methods for increasing the efficiency of the charging process. Richard Lett, sailing *Velocity Girl*, made the following comments (interspaced with notes from two-time circumnavigator Bruce Schwab).

Most, almost all stock alternators are sourced from the automotive industry. They are designed to recharge a starter battery after starting and to run lights etc. whilst the engine is running. All easy stuff requiring no great charging abilities, just a low constant power drain—almost the opposite of what a yacht needs, having run batteries to 50% and requiring as quick a recharge as possible.

In a car, the engine and batteries work together. On a yacht they work separately. This is where the voltage comes in; car alternators don't need high voltage to push in a charge, because batteries are always being charged as the engine is running. A car battery will only ever be at around 80% charge MAXIMUM, because it doesn't matter and the car alternator doesn't have the high voltage output to fill them any further. It just doesn't matter to a car.

Now on a yacht what we want are batteries as near their potential capacity as possible. When a battery is flat any alternator will do because the resistance to charge in the battery is low; as the battery fills, the resistance to filling increases (your 6th pint never goes down as quick as the first!). It is the voltage that provides the push. That is why overhead power cables run at really high voltages because the power (amps) has to be pushed for many miles around a country or across a continent.

So car alternators do not have the voltage to charge batteries once they get to around 70%. Why would a car alternator manufacturer go to the expense of building a high voltage alternator when it is not required by the industry?

Resistance gets really high as batteries get above 70% or so. Dedicated charging alternators for boats, such as Balmar, are built with high voltage regulators to keep pushing the amps into the batteries, or you can buy an after-market regulator to improve the performance of your basic car type alternator. These still will not fully charge your batteries—they will get them to 80% and will charge at a higher rate for a lot longer than the car type.

[Note from Bruce Schwab: the common "stock" alternator is small and has a single-stage internal regulator. They may not be suitable for fast charging and long use. Consider upgrading to the most powerful unit you can fit and afford with a programmable external regulator. For charging large [or lithium] battery banks it's often a good idea to slightly "de-tune" the alternator using the programmable regulator. This helps minimize overheating and adds life to the alternator.]

When you read about multistage chargers all they are doing is varying the charging voltage of the alternator. They do this when you have the time and luxury to charge batteries over many hours, like leaving on charge in the garage overnight. They cycle between high and low voltage to deal with bulk, trickle, and maintenance phases. When at sea racing, you don't have time for all that. What you do is leave batteries to run all the way down, whack charge as quick as you can until batteries get to around 80% charge, when you will see charge rate drop from around 80 amps to around 20 amps, because even a high-volt alternator cannot pack charge in quickly to a nearly full battery that is seriously resisting being charged. Quit trying to charge once the charge rate drops and turn the engine off; stop wasting fuel and making a noise—you are wasting your efforts.

Use the battery monitor to tell when battery state of charge has dropped to near 50%. Start charging. Watch the charging current on the battery (or ammeter), you will see the charge rate start high (the most your alternator can do) and slowly drop as the battery fills, then decide when to stop. For me charging starts around 90 amps; once I see the charge rate drop to around 25 amps, I stop. I don't even need to check, I just know the battery is around 80% full.

[Note from Bruce Schwab: If you use your engine as the generator, the more you can load it up the more fuel efficient it will be. On the Open 60 *OceanPlanet* the 29 hp engine had a 130 A x 24 V alternator (the same as 260 A x 12 V!). The battery bank was 360 Ah x 24 V (same as 720 Ah x 12 V) of Gel-Tech batteries. With this system even if there was no sun for the solar panels, I could get by on one hour of charging per day. On good sun days in the South Atlantic I sometimes went 3 days before needing to charge with the engine. Having a cutoff switch for the alternator regulator (or a "low power" mode) is essential with such a big alternator on a small engine.]

When in marina I leave the boat charging on a shore powered multi stage charger, so I start every voyage with 100% full batteries. They will never get above 80% again until back on the shore charger. Once you know this, live with it, charge when necessary, sail for the rest of the time, and enjoy the peace of knowing you are doing all that is possible whilst afloat.

Good quality batteries matter. AGM batteries, for example, can take most if not all the charge an alternator can provide. Cheaper lead acid types can be damaged if too many amps are thrown at them, so a powerful alternator and efficient charging systems are wasted. So if you want to keep charge time to a minimum, a combination of high amp output and full charge acceptance is what you want.

Batteries are one part of the equation. For offshore I suggest around 300 amps worth—once unplugged from shore power and charging from the engine you will only recharge to around 80% (technical reasons for this, but true whatever claims are made unless you want to run the engine for long periods of time). This means that you are running between 50% and 80% of charge which is @100 amps (on a 300 amp bank) at 5 amp per hour this gives you up to 20 hrs between charges, or two 60 amp top ups   *(continued)* per 24 hrs, which is a fairly relaxed and stress free schedule.

The alternator needs to deliver its amps at high voltage to push all that power into the battery. This is where most factory fitted alternators come up short. They only deliver their amps at around 13.7 or so V, so when they sense resistance from the battery as it fills up they start to reduce output, significantly. You can be running the engine (at whatever revs) and the alternator is only giving you less than 10 amps, you may as well not bother, unless you like the sound of the engine. The solution is either one of the Adverc systems that regulate the output of your existing alternator to more than 14 V or you buy a marine specific alternator like the Balmar that is designed to charge at higher volts. The higher the voltage of the alternator the more charge you get in before the alternator is defeated by the resistance.

Next, like many I have a clever battery monitor (only they are not as clever as they think). It is meant to count all the amps in and out. But after a few days it is wrong and not so helpful. However, the good news is the volt meter and amp meter work very well and can be used as follows. Run all systems until your volt reading is close to 12 V, which means the batteries are low, then run the engine. The alternator will push out nearly its whole potential and drop to below 20 amps when the battery reaches close to 80% charge—then you should stop. You may have added around 60 amps in that first hour; quit, enjoy the peace. Extra hours waste fuel, don't provide much extra amps, and charging twice a day for an hour

on a low battery is very economical and will provide you with around 120 amps per day or an average of 5 amps per hour. For one more hour of charging you can get up to 8 amps per hour, or you can shut something down. Regarding the amp reading on the battery monitor, you can use it to see when your alternator performance has fallen off a cliff and shut the engine down—this means the battery is up to 80% charge and the last 20% could take all day, and isn't worth the effort. It is because of the last 20% that shore-based chargers (however clever and however many stages) take all night to complete the charge.

Regarding engine speed—most pulleys are about 2 to 1 ratio, so double engine speed to know what alternator is running at. Between 1000–1400 should be optimal for most.

Regarding belts, any alternator over 100 amps needs 2 V belts or one of the newer serpentine belts. Two belts are never quite the same length and can be a real problem to set up. The new serpentine belts don't slip and can handle huge outputs. I had new pulleys made for the engine and alternator at J Class Marine (Shamrock) for £80. And they work a treat.

[Roy Hadland made this comment: As a marine engineer I often use pulleys with two, three, or even four belts. We specify that they must be matched when we place the order. The company will ship matched belts that are exactly the same length. Any local store should be able to do the same if asked.]

Regarding smart chargers for the engine—don't waste your money—OK if you are cruising and only have the engine to charge the batteries, you can leave the engine on all evening, night, or day to handle the full battery charge; if racing— just go for the hour charge on a low battery, accept you are running on 80% until you get back home— to charge quickly you only need good batteries, a high voltage alternator and patience to wait until the batteries are low to run the engine.

I run a Balmar 120 alternator, which still only provides 95 amps to a flat battery in the real world, but it does top it up very quick—as an aside, at that output it gets very hot—to keep everything happy make sure the engine bay is well ventilated to dissipate heat—also you need to start the engine at 1400 or so revs, as when the alternator kicks in after a minute or so of starting, if you are on tick over it may stall your engine! I have fitted a switch to disable the alternator if I need full engine power at any time, the 120 amp can draw up to 20% from my 20 hp Lombardini.

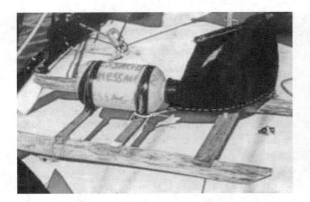

Two methods Bernard Moitessier used to communicate while singlehanding around the world in the 1968 Golden Globe Race. He didn't even carry a radio, let alone radar, AIS, or sat phone. *(Courtesy Bernard Moitessier)*

(continued from page 101)
many parts that can wear or break. Generators also produce dangerous carbon monoxide and thus must not be used inside the cabin. Their manufacturers claim generators are quiet, but I would not want to sleep near a running unit. Generators are known to have problems when tilted or in very rough seas when the oil system may not able to maintain pressure, causing a shutdown.

My initial premise in this chapter was that the best method of managing power is to reduce power requirements. After that, solar panels should be the primary method of generating power because of their simplicity and reliability. They offer the greatest benefit with none of the disadvantages of mechanical systems. I will stick with these ideas and leave it to the skipper to select a secondary source of power, if one is necessary at all.

CHAPTER 8

BOAT HANDLING AND GOING ALOFT

LEAVING THE DOCK AND RETURNING

Leaving the dock singlehanded is one of the trickier maneuvers because of tight quarters with other boats, low motoring speeds that limit turning ability, and wind that wants to push the boat in the wrong direction.

As a first step, the skipper should determine the prevailing wind direction at the dock and trade slips with someone else to get the best possible slip location for a singlehander. Considerable time passes between letting go of the final dockline and the boat starting to move. During that time the boat is at the mercy of the wind. If the wind is strong, the singlehander does not want to be pushed into another boat docked just a few feet away. It is best if the prevailing winds push his boat into the dock itself. The skipper can set up fenders to prevent damage on the dock, but he can't protect a neighbor's boat if pushed into it. For those rare instances when the wind is coming from another direction and is so strong that there is not sufficient time to motor out of the slip, just ask another boater to hold the bow until underway. Don't worry about asking—boaters offer their help much more often than we ever need it. This is probably the most social time of being a singlehander.

Once the boat is moving, a singlehander does not have any help fending off other boats, so this must be done right. When leaving the dock a boat moves at very low speed for the first 15 seconds, so the skipper needs to figure out how well the boat maneuvers at low speed. With an outboard motor, the boat can probably make a very sharp turn when backing out but not when moving forward. With an inboard motor the opposite might be true. The whole concept of prop walk, the tendency of the boat's stern to move one direction or the other in reverse gear, must be considered. The difference is determined by the way the water rushes past the rudder. The best choice is to tie up the boat (bow in or stern in) so that the greatest low-speed maneuverability is available when pulling out, because this is the time when the boat is at its lowest speed. You generally have higher speed when pulling back into the slip, because there is more room between rows of boats than between individual boats in slips.

Like most sailors, a singlehander usually returns to the same slip on the same dock every day. Perhaps only a few times a year does he use a different dock. So it makes sense to set up the slip perfectly for his boat. He will be using that slip at least 95% of the time, so he can take the time to make it really perfect.

Most sailors hang fenders on the side of the boat, stow them when they clear the dock, and hang them out again as they return. It makes more sense to hang the fenders permanently on the dock. With the fenders positioned for the worst possible conditions, the skipper can have confidence and less trouble sleeping. He should also consider if coming into the slip with a strong wind blowing will he be forced to slam into the dock faster than he would prefer? With advance thought, it is easy to position the fenders for greatest protection.

Similarly, most sailors keep their docking lines

on the boat, untie them from the dock cleat when they leave and jump off the boat to tie up again on returning. It is better to tie the lines permanently to the dock and drop them off the boat when departing. The key benefit of this is that the skipper can have them fitted exactly to hold the boat in the best position. He will never need to adjust the length of the line and will know that they are perfectly set.

As well, he doesn't need to worry about spring lines. He just needs one line at the bow set in a V, and another at the stern (see photo). The top ends of the V are tied to two points on the dock about 10 feet apart. At the point of the V form a loop just big enough to slip over the cleat on the boat—usually a loop about 6 inches across. When setting up the V lines, make sure they hold the boat in the correct position, where it won't bash the dock in front and won't hit the neighbor's boat. Adjust the length of the stern V line so that it will stop the boat before it hits the dock. The skipper will be grabbing the stern V line as he returns to dock. Next, set the length of the bow V line such that if the wind pushes the boat forward or backward, the tension on both V lines is the same. We don't want only one V line holding the boat. I know for a fact that this method will hold a boat very securely in all but the very worst conditions. Our docks have seen 40 knots of wind and my boat has not slipped its lines.

To leave the dock, remove the loop from the bow cleat first and toss the line neatly on the dock. Then walk back to the stern cleat and remove the loop, pulling strongly on the stern V line to start moving. Then toss that line on the dock and put the boat in gear. This is the easiest way to get the boat moving up to maneuverable speed.

When returning to the dock, use a boathook to snag the stern line off the dock as you pass by and slip it over the stern cleat. The line should be just the right length that when secure on the stern cleat, the boat will stop exactly where you want it. You want to be able to slip it on and forget it because now you will be busy at the bow cleat. Once again, use the boathook to grab the line and slip the loop over the bow cleat.

Another singlehander I know has installed a hook on a piling at the entrance to his slip. He

Use one docking line set in a V for the bow, and another set in the stern. If you have a permanent slip, you can leave the docklines tied at the dock and your fenders permanently hung on the dock too.

drapes the docklines over the hook when pulling out, to make it convenient to pick them up when returning.

Sails On and Ready to Go—Never Trust Your Motor

An important consideration in singlehanding is that the skipper must always be prepared with an instant backup plan for operating the boat. He must never leave the dock under motor power without at least one sail hanked on and ready to raise at a moment's notice. This could be the main or jib, it does not matter which, so long as he can raise that sail in less than 15 seconds. Likewise, when returning to the slip he should never pack away all of the sails until he is tied up at the dock.

Experience has proven, time and time again, that the boat's motor is an incredibly unreliable piece of equipment. I can guarantee that the motor will quit at absolutely the worst possible moment. The skipper must be prepared for this. Think about it now, what would be the worst possible moment for the motor to quit? My motor once quit when I was returning to the dock in 20 knots of wind and was less than 50 feet from the rock breakwater. The list of things that can go wrong with the motor is endless, but here are a few of the reasons my two-stroke outboard has quit at terrible moments: a dirty spark plug, a bad oil/gas mixture, a small hole in the rubber fuel line allowing air in, a rope caught in the propeller, running out of gas, the gas tank tilting on its side, and a cracked fuel line connector. One time, I was leaving the harbor in 15 knots of wind. When I shifted from reverse to forward, the motor bracket broke off the transom, dropping my 5 hp outboard into the water. Luckily I had a safety line in place. I immediately raised my jib and sailed out of the harbor, dragging the motor behind.

First rule: when the motor quits, *do not* attempt to restart it. There is a reason that it quit, and it will take more than 30 seconds to figure it out. When the motor quits, if outside the docks, the first thought must be to raise a sail immediately, and regain control of the boat. Once there is a sail up and drawing, the skipper can take all the time in the world to work on the motor. This is why a singlehander must never leave the slip or return to the slip without a sail hanked on and ready to hoist. I have watched inexperienced sailors pulling frantically on their starter cord as they drift into rocks—they would have done much better to raise a sail to regain control.

When the motor quits inside the docks, the skipper might not have the room needed to raise sail, and gain speed. This is where he will gain a new understanding of how boat hulls are built. A boat hull is a lot stronger than most believe. Most sailors think of fiberglass boats the same way they think of metal cars. But this is wrong. A car has a permanent dent from every small contact. Fiberglass is much stronger and much more forgiving than metal. A few years ago I motored into a dock far too fast, pushed by a strong tailwind. I chose the lesser of two evils and deliberately ran my boat into the

dock rather than hit another boat. My bow broke a wooden 4 x 4 in half, but there was nothing more than a scratch in my gelcoat. So when the motor quits and the skipper can't raise sail, he shouldn't be afraid to run the boat into a wooden dock, on either the bow or the side. I've done both several times and do not have any lasting scars. It is emotionally difficult the first time, but after a while I've learned to shrug it off.

Running a boat into other boats takes a lot more nerve, but that too may happen, so be prepared. First, what can the skipper do to slow down? He is probably going very slowly in any case. Can he turn into the wind until the boat almost stops? When one boat hits another, it is not the initial contact that causes most damage. More damage occurs as one boat slides along another and the lifelines, pushpits, and pulpits get caught or the masts and shrouds get tangled. The key is to stop the boat from moving after the initial contact. Grab the rails or lifelines of the other boat and hang on until things settle down. Tie the boats together to prevent movement. Only after you stop the motion can you make a better decision about how to solve the initial problem. I have to warn, however, that although you may know fiberglass is strong and forgiving, the owner of the other boat likely does not. That sailor may still think of boats like cars and so might get excited over what we consider a run-of-the-mill minor incident.

If the boat is moving toward a collision, the skipper should not try to stop it using his own brute strength. I'm not saying this because I'm worried about his safety. I'm saying this because I know that it won't work. A 10,000 pound (over 4,500 kg) boat at 4 knots has a lot of inertia. No one has the strength to stop it from going where it wants to go. I've proven that even a wooden 4 x 4 doesn't have the strength. Fortunately, an entire wooden dock does have the strength, so that is really the only choice.

With a full crew on board, a skipper has other sailors who can fend a boat off rocks or other boats. But singlehanders do not have this ability, so don't try to do what you can't do. Just live with what you can do, and be thankful for insurance.

FOLDING THE HEADSAIL AFTER DOCKING

When using hanks, it is easy to fold the jib or genoa for storage after a sail. Leave the sail hanked onto the forestay. Starting from the clew (back corner) of the sail, flake it back and forth while moving forward until the sail is laid out in a neat, narrow line. Starting from the back again, fold the sail over three or four times until it is in a neat pack. (Do not attempt to flake the sail with the exact same folds every time because this would cause wear creases.) Remove the hanks from the forestay and insert the sail into a bag from the back first. With this approach, you know that next time you can dump the sail on deck and the hanks will be neatly ready to clip onto the forestay again. In high winds, most of the sail can be kept in the bag until it is completely hanked on.

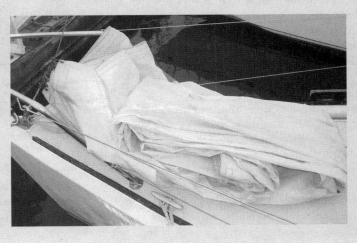

Stowing and folding a jib is easiest if you keep the sail hanked on and start flaking it from the clew, moving forward; once flaked, again starting aft, fold the sail up toward the bow, then stow into the sailbag.

ANCHORING

When anchoring, the idea is to do as much as possible from the cockpit, where the skipper has full control of the boat, only moving to the bow at the last possible moment. Under sail in a light wind, or if using a motor, the skipper should turn the boat into the wind and release the halyard to drop the foresail or put the motor into neutral, then walk to the bow and release the anchor while the boat drifts backward. In stronger wind conditions, it is better to heave-to. When the boat has nearly stopped, the anchor can be dropped. This means sailing past the desired anchor position and turning back to heave-to. After the anchor is dropped, the boat will swing around into the wind.

Another method is to bring the anchor and chain back to the cockpit to drop over the side. This can get messy with a dirty or rusty anchor. It is necessary to bring the anchor and all the chain back, or else the chain will scrape along the boat rail and topsides.

Remember to keep the boat under control at all times, especially in a tight anchorage. The best way to keep the boat under control is to keep the sails actively working, even if hove-to. A sailor has no control over a boat that is drifting. Only with wind in the sails can the boat be maneuvered.

MOORING BUOY PICKUP

Attach a 10-foot line to the mooring buoy with a 4-inch ring and pickup float on the end. A mooring line from the bow should be run outside the lifelines all the way back to the cockpit, with a carabiner attached at its end. Use a boathook to grab the pickup line from the cockpit as the boat passes by, and simply clip the carabiner to the ring. Once the boat has settled, haul in the mooring line at the bow and replace the carabiner with a strong line.

When anchoring or mooring under sail, it is vitally important to understand exactly how your boat will sit when hove-to. This topic is discussed in Chapter 9, but I want to point out now how precisely this can be done. You should know what point of wind at which to heave-to, what point of wind at which to exit the hove-to position, and exactly how the boat will settle on the water. There is no reason why an experienced skipper cannot pull up to an anchoring spot or mooring buoy in a perfectly hove-to position with the boat at a near standstill.

CLIMBING THE MAST

There are myriad ways for a singlehander to climb the mast, but three have proven more successful than any others: using a Mastclimber, ascender and Grigri (mountain-climbing hardware), or mast steps.

Mastclimber

Manufactured by ATN, the Mastclimber is a combination of bosun's chair and climbing system that allows a user to climb up on a single halyard. Using a foot strap system, the skipper pushes up with both legs to advance up the halyard about one foot per push. The bosun's chair is then raised, the skipper sits and raises the foot straps, then pushes up again. A one-way jammer on the bosun's chair and another jammer on the foot strap are used in alternating steps to advance securely up the mast. A complete description and video are available at atninc.com.

The user should not allow the two jammers to come together as they literally can jam and need to be pushed apart. They should be kept separated. This can become an issue when descending quickly. It might be better to use two halyards—one for each jammer. A second problem when descending is in dropping the foot straps too far, making it difficult to stand up high enough to release the bosun's chair jammer to proceed; in this case the user must

ATN's Mastclimber allows the singlehander the comfort of going aloft while sitting in a bosun's chair. *(Courtesy ATN)*

raise the foot straps back up a few inches. The best aspects of the Mastclimber are the comfort of sitting in a bosun's chair and the ability to work well above the masthead.

Ascender and Grigri

The ascender and Grigri along with a climbing harness and foot strap combination are standard mountain climbing equipment. The skipper should visit a reputable mountain climbing shop to purchase these and learn how to use them properly. To climb, the sailor stands in the foot straps while pulling the Grigri up on one halyard. Then he sits in the harness and pulls the ascender and feet up the other halyard, then repeats the sequence over and over. This method allows the sailor to climb the mast at about one foot per sequence.

The beauty of this system is that it allows for a rapid descent. Ascending is just as fast as with the Mastclimber, but descending is much faster than with the two jammers.

I prefer to use two halyards (one for the ascender and one for the Grigri), but it is possible using only one if necessary. In this case the climber must

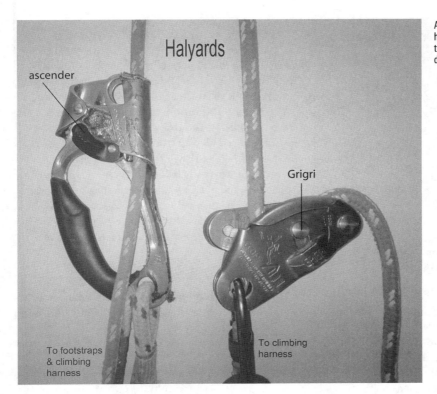

Halyards

ascender

Grigri

To footstraps
& climbing
harness

To climbing
harness

A combination of ascender (on left halyard) and Grigri (on right halyard) is the most efficient method to ascend and descend the mast.

Wrap your arms around the mast during the climb and your legs around the mast at the top to give the greatest stability, even on a moving boat.

keep the ascender and Grigri from connecting and becoming bound up. Of course, the halyards must be very well secured. I use both the halyard clutches and winches. When climbing, the feet can be spread around the mast for stability.

To descend, the skipper can slide the ascender well down its halyard, step out of the foot straps, pull the Grigri handle, and rappel to the deck quickly and under control.

Both the Mastclimber and ascender with Grigri methods can be used at the dock or underway. The halyard (for the ascender) must be kept very tight, but when underway the user will still tend to swing away from the mast. I find it better to drop the main and sail with only a jib. This allows me to wrap a safety line and my arms around the mast. I wear my normal harness with a much shorter tether strung around the mast. This extra tether keeps me from swinging wildly in a gust of wind. It is necessary to disconnect the tether line to pass the spreaders. This adds the benefit of stopping me from falling past the spreaders if the climbing gear fails. I find

A pair of lines tied using the Blake's hitch can be used to climb a pair of halyards.

it necessary to wrap one arm around the mast for leverage when pulling up on the Grigri.

Blake's Hitch—The Knot for Climbing Aloft

Several knots can be used in the place of mechanical climbing devices. The best known is the prusik loop, but I find that it binds when holding my weight. A better knot is Blake's hitch, which does not bind or roll over on itself under weight. A pair of lines tied in this way can be used to climb a pair of halyards. One is tied to the climbing harness and the other to the foot straps. See a full animation of tying this knot at http://www.animatedknots.com/blakes.

During the 2002 Around Alone, UK skipper Emma Richards had an extreme adventure at the top of her 80-foot mast after her main halyard parted at the masthead. Here is an excerpt from thedailysail.com, November 8, 2002:

She set off up the mast at 8:30 am GMT in 10 knots of wind. But by the time she was at the mast head, the wind had built to 25 knots and the mast was swinging back and forth, 20 feet either way. Making the repair became a seemingly impossible task in these conditions. Emma, however, showed her true mettle by completing the repair successfully and after four and a half hours, set foot back on the deck of *Pindar* at 12:52 pm GMT.

Commenting on the trip up the rig Emma commented: "It was horrible, just horrible—the most terrifying experience of my life. I went up the mast with a fairly steady breeze of 10 knots, but by the time I'd reached the top, this has built to 25 knots, with the wind constantly shifting direction. The mast was swinging back and forth, as much as 20 feet either side. I was blown upside down in my climbing harness, back to front, and thrown all over the place. I am bruised all over from being pounded against the mast—all up my arms, all along my ribs, and my legs are totally battered. My head smashed against the mast a few times, so thank god I was wearing a crash helmet. I was so scared, it is definitely the hardest thing I've ever had to do in my life, let alone my sailing career. It was a total horror-show."

Mast Steps

Mast steps are common on cruising boats, but racers consider them unacceptable weight and wind resistance aloft. Steps are undoubtedly the fastest way up and down the mast. Of course, a safety harness is a must.

Fixed, folding, and removable mast steps are available. The newest folding models are manufactured from a nylon/glass fiber. On *Nereida* Jeanne Socrates uses folding steps near the working areas at the base of the mast, and fixed steps farther up.

Simplicity and ease of use are the greatest benefits of mast steps. Going up the mast with mounting-climbing gear is not something I would do for fun. Following is an excerpt from Dave Abbott, referencing his adventures on his Privilege 39-foot catamaran, *Exit Only*, chronicled at maxingout.com:

Why do I consider mast steps to be essential cruising gear on our cat?

1. Mast steps keep me honest: Sailing offshore isn't a place where you should ever live in denial. When you don't pay attention to what is happening on your yacht and around your yacht, you have set your course for denial, and denial comes before disaster.

Mast steps keep me honest about what is happening to my rigging. Every time that I prepare to sail offshore, I climb the mast and inspect every piece of rigging. Because of my

In Ushuaia, at the very tip of South America, Jeanne Socrates uses mast steps and a climbing harness to install a new forestay and foil after a severe knockdown during her second round-the-world voyage. *(Courtesy Jeanne Socrates)*

Wash day—the one time when a crew would be handy. *(Courtesy David Bleakney)*

due diligence in making rigging inspections, I made it all the way around the world without any rigging disasters.

When I reached Bora Bora, I climbed my mast and found two diamond stays that had broken wire strands and needed replacement. During our five-year sojourn in the South Pacific, New Zealand, and Australia, I discovered and replaced diamond stays that had one or two broken strands of wire. In Turkey, I climbed the mast and discovered a broken wire strand on an upper diamond stay. When I reached Gibraltar, I discovered that my head stay had several broken wire strands, and I replaced my head stay. The only pieces of rigging that I didn't replace during our eleven year circumnavigation was our cap shrouds. They are still alive and well fourteen years later.

My mast steps made it easy to inspect the rig before every offshore passage. Every time I looked at those mast steps, I felt guilty of

neglecting my rig until I climbed to the top of the mast and verified that everything was in order. There's no doubt about it. My mast steps kept me honest.

2. My mast steps kept me safe: I always wanted to have a crow's nest on board *Exit Only*. But it was too expensive, and the diamond stays made designing one a real challenge. On the other hand, my lower spreaders were at an excellent height and functioned nicely as a makeshift crow's nest. My son would zip up those mast steps and have a look all around as we sailed through passes, into atolls, and among the coral heads of Fiji, the Tuamotus, Suvarov, the Bahamas, the Caribbean, the Great Barrier Reef, and many other destinations around the world.

Having someone up the mast pushes the odds in your favor when you are sailing into coral destinations. Mast steps make it easy to do what you should do—go aloft and have a look around.

CHAPTER 9 **SAIL HANDLING AND SAILING TECHNIQUES**

With this book I'm assuming that the reader has a basic understanding of how to sail a boat and the terminology used in sailing. I will concentrate on those sailing skills particular to singlehanding. I have developed these techniques through trial and error (many, many errors), through years on the water and a thousand sailing trips. I have always looked for two criteria in these techniques: the least chance of an error and the most efficient means of achieving the goal. I am often asked if I have considered "this" method or "that" method of performing a task. I have only two questions: is it as fast and is it as reliable as what I have done? If another skipper arrives at a method that is faster and more reliable, I am more than happy to accept a better idea.

UNDERSTANDING SAIL TRIM

The first premise is that the sails and the rudder of a boat, when working in combination, are highly effective brakes that can slow the boat down or stop it completely. Only when the sails and rudder are perfectly trimmed does the boat sail as it is designed. The vast majority of recreational skippers sail with one foot on the brake, but an educated skipper learns how to take the foot off the brake. Doing so increases sailing speed, reduces work effort, and increases overall enjoyment.

The most obvious brake is the rudder. This brake is applied every time the rudder is turned, even a little. A professional racer once told me that he preferred 2 degrees of weather helm. I smiled when replying that 2 is far too much, that 1.5 degrees is better. "Weather helm" is pressure that pulls the

tiller downward and attempts to point the boat upward. "Lee helm" is pressure that pulls the tiller upward and attempts to point the boat down.

The hand on the tiller should be as light as the hand of a lover during Chopin's finest waltz. It is used to guide with mere thought. Any pressure should be nothing more than the blush that arises from whispered sweet nothings. Like the lover's hand, the tiller should be little more than floating.

Pressure on the tiller should be the absolute minimum required to sail in the desired direction. The skipper must be always conscious of the amount of pressure on the tiller. The only way to sail with speed is to eliminate this pressure. When hand steering, it is very easy to feel the amount of pressure. A celebrity sailor once commented that she preferred a wheel because she was not strong enough to sail with a tiller. My immediate reaction is that if steering with a tiller takes more strength than a middle-aged woman can easily manage, then she is doing it wrong. Using a tiller takes no strength at all. If done properly, a two-year-old child would have enough strength—I can't make it any clearer.

When sailing with an autopilot, the singlehander should stand forward and actually look at the tiller. Just how far from center is it? An autopilot makes it very easy to expend effort untenable with manual sailing. I have often thought that autopilots should have pressure sensors and alarms for just this reason. However, by watching the tiller, the skipper can quickly judge the amount of pressure. The tiller should not be more than a few degrees off center.

Sail trim is more important for a singlehander than for a crewed boat because poor sail trim creates extra work (and excess wear and power consumption) on any autopilot or may simply overwhelm any windvane or storm jib steering system.

The only way for the singlehander to control pressure on the tiller is with proper sail trim. Sails that are trimmed too tightly are incredibly slow. Weather helm comes from too much pressure on the mainsail or on the trailing edge of a large genoa. Lee helm comes commonly from too much spinnaker, or more rarely from too much genoa.

To reduce weather helm, the singlehander should reduce sail behind the mast or increase sail in front of the mast. Proper sail balance is the key. Most commonly, weather helm is reduced by easing the mainsheet. As the wind builds, this may mean easing the mainsheet until the mainsail is just short of flogging. It is normal to sail with a reverse bulge in the front third of the mainsail, caused by the wind from the genoa through the slot between the genoa and the main. The trailing edge of the genoa can also cause weather helm. Easing the genoa sheet will reduce this problem. Weather helm would also exist in the ridiculous situation of using a large main with a storm jib or no jib at all in moderate wind conditions. As mentioned previously, sail balance is the key.

Lee helm can occur on a deep run, with the spinnaker pole pulled well back and perpendicular to the wind. To reduce lee helm the singlehander should reduce sail at the front of the boat or increase sail at the rear of the boat. If possible, easing the spinnaker sheet will reduce lee helm. If winds are strong, it may not be possible to ease the sheet enough without flogging the spinnaker. To retain maximum speed, a better solution may be to tighten the mainsheet and pull the main in a few feet, i.e., tightening the mainsheet to increase weather helm will counteract the lee helm caused by too much spinnaker.

The best reference book on sail trim that I've found is *Performance Racing Trim* published by North Sails (North University), specifically designed for racers. The advice it gives is a must for any sailor and particularly for a singlehander. But a skipper should not just blindly follow the book's directions. Rather, use it as a starting point for your own experiments.

Even today, after years of sailing and many trips, I still experiment with sail trim. Just yesterday I learned the effect of pulling the spinnaker pole down 6 inches (15 cm) on a beam reach in 12 knots of wind. What did it do to my sail shape, and most importantly, what did it do to boat speed?

A skipper should try new things every time out. What happens if the backstay is tightened by 2 inches (5 cm) in 10 knots of wind? What happens if it is tightened 2 more inches? While the North University book is excellent, it can only provide the general advice that applies to all boats. It cannot provide the specific advice needed for one specific 24-year-old boat with 8-year-old sails. That can only be discovered by experimentation. I'll give a hint right now: tightening the backstay by the first 2 inches increases my speed, but tightening it by 2 more inches reduces speed! (At least on my boat.)

The skipper should always keep one eye on the knotmeter. I consider the knotmeter the most important piece of electronic equipment on the boat, because it is the only thing that indicates if the boat is being well sailed. A skipper who is new to this concept will be amazed by the change in boat speed just from easing the mainsheet an inch, or by what happens to boat speed if the outhaul is pulled slightly tighter.

When watching boat speed, it is better to think in terms of percentages rather than absolute values. A half-knot speed increase may seem insignificant until one understands that represents 8% for a boat traveling at 6 knots. Think about cars on a highway. One car traveling at 100 kph would seem darned slow to another car traveling at 108 kph. Even better, think about NASCAR racing. In a typical 300-mile race, the first two cars finish less than a half-second apart. That may be just 0.02%, but it's a difference of $35,000 in winnings! A typical sailor isn't concerned with 0.02%, but 8% is huge. Keep one eye on the knotmeter and constantly experiment with sail trim.

SAILING UPWIND

As mentioned earlier, upwind sailing is where a racing singlehander faces the greatest disadvantage

Twist, evenly spread between the main and jib.

for the simple reason of a lack of crew weight on the rail. Most club racing boats are designed to have a thousand pounds of crew on the rail. Weight on the rail helps keep the boat level, which shows more sail to the wind. But more importantly, a level boat means the keel is pointing straight down, so the "wing effect" of the keel is at its maximum. The keel helps to keep the boat pointing upwind. The impact of this is dramatic. In races with a 20-knot breeze, I fall well off to leeward compared to crewed boats. It's bloody depressing. (For more on this, see Chapter 5, Keeping the Boat Upright.)

While the boat design features that help alleviate leeward drift are described in detail elsewhere in this book, in the short term, sail twist is the single-hander's best friend to reduce heel. Mainsail twist is added by keeping the traveler high while easing the mainsheet. Thus the top of the sail twists away, spilling a large amount of wind. In the same manner, jib twist is added by keeping the jib lead forward while easing the jibsheet. For best sail balance, both the main and jib should be twisted the same amount. Twisting one without the other would add pressure on the helm. Twisting the sails is the fastest way to reduce boat heel.

Tension on the luff and foot of the mainsail and jib performs the same function as the gears on a car. First gear (more power but less speed) is attained with a loose sail luff and foot with a large bulge in the sail. This shape is useful when accelerating after a tack or in choppy water conditions where the boat is constantly attempting to regain speed off of each wave.

Fourth gear (more speed but less power) is attained with very tight luff and foot on the sail. This is appropriate after full boat speed has been reached in smooth water. A tight luff and foot are also used to shed excess wind, once again to reduce boat heel. In high winds it is normal to keep the foot of the sail very tight, even if the sail is reefed. To do this, I remove the mainsail outhaul from the bottom clew and connect it to the reef point clew and pull hard to flatten the sail as much as possible.

Second and third gears are the sail positions in between first and fourth. I find it useful to think of my sail settings in terms of gears. If I say to myself "first gear," I know exactly where my settings should be.

With a highly skilled crew it is common for the sail luff tension—adjusted with the backstay—and

Two reefs and a storm jib keep the boat level in gale-force winds. *(Courtesy Andrew Madding)*

foot tension—adjusted with the outhaul on the main and the jib car—to be worked constantly while sailing. But a singlehander is unlikely to be constantly making adjustments to luff and foot tension after each tack or between waves. A singlehander is more likely to look at the general water conditions over the next half hour and adjust the luff and foot tension accordingly. It would also be extremely taxing and nearly impossible for a singlehander to adjust the backstay tension before and after each tack, as is commonly done on crewed boats.

In the long run, the negative effect of too much heel is so great as to override the impact of shortening sail. So a singlehander will shorten from a genoa to a jib or reef the main much earlier than a crewed boat. Without other boats to compare to, a singlehander may think that the boat is moving as fast as possible. But in a group, the skipper will quickly realize how much leeway the boat is suffering without crew on the rail. In typical races, the only step to take is reducing sail and bringing the boat back upright. Reducing sail often increases the velocity made good to the next waypoint.

In high, gusting winds, reducing sail will not reduce speed at all. This situation arises if the boat is sailing on the edge of control, where it is swinging back and forth with varying amounts of heel. It is just as fast and certainly more controllable to reduce sail to the point where the amount of heel is stable, rather than varying wildly.

In upwind sailing there are only two indicators that the skipper must monitor: the heel of the boat and the amount of weather helm on the tiller. If both of these are under control, the boat is likely sailing as fast as possible.

CHANGING HEADSAILS

Whether swapping a genoa for a jib or vice versa, the key is preplanning. Changing sails will require at least 5 minutes of clear water on the new tack. The single most important consideration is to reduce the amount of time with no foresail flying to an absolute minimum. These are the steps to follow:

1. On the existing course, lower the foresail just an inch to relieve pressure on the tack shackle.
2. Unroll the new sail on the windward side of the foredeck.
3. Disconnect the lazy sheet (the sheet not under pressure) from the clew of the existing foresail and connect it to the new foresail.
4. Hank on the new foresail below the bottom hank of the existing foresail.
5. Remove the tack of the existing foresail from the shackle and insert the tack of the new foresail. (The existing foresail may ride up a bit.)
6. Return to the cockpit and pull in the lazy sheet so the new headsail is about three quarters back on the windward side of the boat. Don't make it so tight that the sail can't be raised easily.
7. Clip your tether to the leeward side of the boat. This will be the windward side after the tack.
8. Press the buttons on the autopilot to initiate an auto-tack. Make sure the auto-tack will take the boat at least 10 degrees beyond the new close-hauled position.
9. As soon as the auto-tack starts, pop the jib halyard clutch and move to the foredeck.

The sail will fall to the deck as the boat swings through the wind. Pull it down quickly.

10. Immediately unhank the existing sail, disconnect the halyard, and connect it to the new sail. Leave the old sail on the (now) windward side of the deck so that it doesn't fall off the boat.

11. Move back to the cockpit and raise the new headsail.

12. Winch in the new headsail sheet, and bring the boat back up to top speed. Have a drink of water and relax. This is exhausting work.

13. Only after the boat is sailing at full speed with the new headsail on the new tack, retrieve old headsail.

14. Don't forget to connect the (new) lazy sheet to the new headsail, or you'll get quite a surprise 10 minutes later during the next tack.

Using this procedure, the boat should be without a foresail for less than 45 seconds. In most races, 45 seconds is an eternity. The singlehander should practice with a timer. I do!

REEFING THE MAINSAIL

As with changing headsails, the key consideration in reefing is to shorten the duration of the maneuver as much as possible to reduce the time that the mainsail is not drawing.

I do not use any type of jiffy reefing system on my 30-foot boat. It is simply not necessary and would slow the reefing process considerably. I also have reef lines only on the leech, not the luff of the sail. The steps I follow in reefing are these:

1. Release the mainsheet completely, allowing the main to flog.

2. At the mast, lower the main halyard sufficiently to connect the reef luff cringle to the hook, and pull the halyard tight again.

3. Still at the mast, pull the reef line hard to bring the back of the boom up to the sail at the reef point.

4. Back in the cockpit, trim the mainsheet to bring the sail back in. (The first four steps of this process should be completed in less

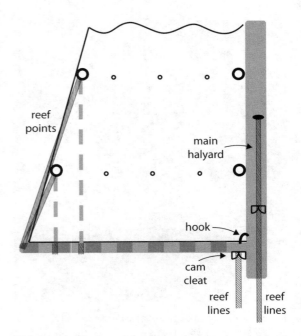

With this mainsail reefing setup, at the mast I can drop the main halyard, hook the luff reef cringle, tighten the halyard, and pull the reef line to bring the boom up to the sail at the reef point, all within 30 seconds. Only after trimming the mainsheet do I tie the intermediate reef points.

than 30 seconds; thus the mainsail is not working for only 30 seconds.)

5. If the reef line does not apply sufficient tension on the foot of the main, the outhaul can be used to flatten the sail farther.

6. Only after the boat is sailing back up to speed should the intermediate reef lines be connected at the reef points and tie them under the boom. These do not give any strength to the reefed sail—they simply help keep the sail in a bundle.

Jiffy Reefing Systems

Very few sailors are satisfied with a single-line jiffy reefing system in which a single line pulls both the reef tack and the reef clew down to the boom. It appears that this is too much work for a single line and is difficult to tighten completely, even with a winch.

However, dual-line systems have been successful. With this type of system, a reef line at the end of the boom runs up through the reef clew, back down to the end of the boom, forward along the boom exiting at the gooseneck, down the to the deck, and back to the cockpit. A second line at the front of the boom runs up through the reef tack, back down to the deck, and back to the cockpit. A boat with three reef points would have six lines running back over the deck, each with its own rope clutch. This is what is used on a Class 40 racer. The main halyard must also be controlled from this point, requiring a seventh rope clutch. Because all these lines run back to the cockpit, it is likely that they must be winched tight, rather than pulled by hand. Since this involves a lot of extra effort and time, it's wrong to call this system "jiffy." It is significantly faster to perform these jobs at the mast by hand.

I find that crewed boats rarely reef and never practice the reefing process. So a singlehander who regularly reefs the mainsail should be able to do so much faster than a crewed boat.

Reefing a Headsail

As with changing a headsail, the reefing process is easiest to do while tacking. The steps are:

1. Move the lazy sheet up to the reefed clew position on the sail.

Reefed jib on a Mini. (*Courtesy Eliza Chohadzhieva*)

2. Press the auto-tack button on the helm.
3. Release the active sheet.
4. As the boat swings through the tack, drop the halyard just past the reefed position.
5. On the new course, walk to the bow and pull the sail down to the reefed position.
6. Back in the cockpit, raise the halyard tight.
7. Sheet in the shortened headsail.
8. Once sailing on course, walk to the foredeck to move the remaining sheet and bundle the foot of the headsail with reef lines.

TACKING

The easiest way to tack is with a self-tacking jib. However, if the boat is not equipped with this convenience, it takes quite a bit of practice to become proficient at tacking a standard jib or genoa.

With a crewed boat, tacking through the wind usually consists of turning past close-hauled and allowing the jib to fly out past the lifelines, then winching hard to bring the jib back in as the boat is steered up to close-hauled. This is the best way to bring the boat back up to speed as quickly as possible. The exact opposite approach is taken when singlehanding, because of the difficulty of winching in the sail with one hand while steering a proper course with the other.

As previously mentioned, I prefer not to use the auto-tack setting on the autopilot. I find that it performs the maneuver very slowly and that it does not settle down to the new close-hauled course for an extended period. I am able to perform the tack much more quickly and more accurately, usually with my knees on the tiller.

Keeping in mind that we are sheeting to the high side of the boat (see Chapter 3, Sailboat Design and Setup), the steps to a perfect singlehanded tack follow.

1. Ensure that the lazy sheet has a half wrap around the unused winch.
2. Remove the active sheet from the cleat of the self-tailing winch, but leave two wraps on the winch.
3. Start the turn.
4. Just as the jib is backwinded, remove the wraps from the winch and release the sail.

5. Pause the turn just 20 degrees past head to wind, controlling the tiller with your knee. This pause should only last a few seconds and not long enough to lose speed.
6. Moving across the cockpit, grab the lazy sheet, pulling fast and hard. The plan is to keep the sail inside the lifelines. That is the only measurement of success: the sail being completely inside the lifelines.
7. Using the knee, control the tiller to drop the boat down to close hauled.
8. Sit down on the new windward side with the tiller in the leeward hand.
9. With the winch handle in the windward hand, winch the remainder of the sheet. It may be necessary to steer with the tiller under the knee and use both arms to drive the winch.
10. Trim the mainsail using the sheet and traveler as necessary.
11. Get the boat under control and at best possible speed on the new tack.
12. If unsuccessful at keeping the sail inside the lifelines, there are two possible approaches:
    - If racing, activate the autopilot and walk to the foredeck to skirt the sail.
    - If cruising, ease the jibsheet and turn head to wind. Winch in the sail as it flops inside the lifeline, then bear away to fill the sail.

Ken, who has singlehanded a J/80 for many years and has just moved to a much larger J/105, notes that he does not need to use his knees to steer through the tack process. He just releases the helm (a tiller on his J/80 and a wheel on his J/105), allowing the normal weather helm to pull the boat up through the wind. Only after moving the jib across the boat does he need to manually adjust the helm onto the new course.

Ken has a small block on the clew of the jib on his J/80. The jibsheet runs from the forward end of the jib car, through the block and back down to the jib car, and then back to the cockpit. With this 2-to-1 purchase Ken rarely needs to winch in his jib—pulling is enough to sheet in all the way.

The steps above are far easier with a small jib than with a large genoa, but the steps are the same for both. With a genoa, the pause at the top of the turn will last longer as more sail must be pulled backward.

Singlehanded tacking requires extensive practice to master. Each boat has its own required timing for each step, changing with each wind level. Only with hundreds or thousands of practice tacks will it become second nature.

THE SYMMETRICAL SPINNAKER

There is absolutely no reason why a singlehander should not use a spinnaker as aggressively as a fully crewed boat. One of the greatest compliments I've ever received came after a very-high-wind race. The skipper of another boat said, "We weren't going to raise the chute until one of the crew pointed out that you had." I've been asked under what conditions I'll raise a chute, and I answered, "If I'd do it with a crew, I'll do it alone."

I also know that a singlehander can raise or douse a spinnaker every bit as fast as a full crew. A singlehander should raise the chute just seconds after rounding a windward mark, and should douse just seconds before the leeward mark. This is why I advise against spinnaker socks: they are unnecessary and cause delays. Likewise I advise against a singlehander raising or dousing into the forward hatch, which works with a crewed boat because there is someone up there to do it. A singlehander would have to run to the foredeck, douse, then run back to the cockpit to turn the boat. Any steps that cause a delay should be eliminated. I have worked out a process that is failure proof in all conditions and extremely fast, and that gives me total control of the sail and the boat at all times.

I also recommend tying the spinnaker sheets to the clews with a simple bowline knot. Quick-release shackles are common on large crewed boats, allowing the guy to be released from the foredeck, but a singlehander will not be on the foredeck. Any other type of clip is prone to releasing on its own. A bowline has never failed me.

Using the method described below does not put undue strain on the auto-steering system. It is more important that the skipper concentrate on raising and trimming the chute than worry about the tiller. However, if he doesn't follow these steps the auto steering system will be challenged beyond its limits. Activate the autopilot with three quarters of maximum responsiveness.

1. Packing the chute is vital. This is the leading cause of later problems. Start at the head and run the right hand down the green tape on the starboard side of the sail. It is important to use the right hand on the green tape.

2. Start at the head again and run the left hand down the red tape on the port side of the sail. Now the skipper knows that there are no twists in the sail.

3. Push the sail into the sail bag with the green tape on the right and red tape on the left, and leave the three corners on top of the pile.

4. The best launching position is from the lifelines, just at the forward end of the cockpit on the leeward side of the boat. The skipper wants to be able to work with the sail while standing in the cockpit. Clip the sail bag to the lifelines, making sure that the red and green corners are facing the correct direction, depending on whether it is being launched from the port or starboard side of the boat. (I keep harping on the red and green sides, and the left hand or right hand, and the port and starboard side of the boat because these concepts are vital to success. If a singlehander follows these directions consistently, he will never worry about lines crossing each other as the sail is raised, creating an hourglass. If he blindly grabs one color in one hand and the other color in the other hand, then 50% of the time he will be causing a bad twist by trying to pull up the wrong corners of the sail. Red in the left hand, green in the right!)

5. It is important that the spinnaker be very secure inside the bag until needed. If not, the clews, more likely the head, will pull out and catch the wind. It is not amusing trying to control 10 feet of spinnaker flying out on the leeward side of the boat in high winds.

6. Run the spinnaker sheet through the leeward block to the aft clew of the spinnaker. Wrap the sheet around the winch, but leave at least 10 feet of slack. *Do not* tighten the sheet. Some may think that this would give better control of the chute, but in fact, all it does is drive the boat up into a broach as soon as the chute is raised—a very bad thing. Leave at least 10 feet of slack in the sheet.

7. Run the guy around the bow, through the pole, and to the forward clew of the spinnaker. Raise the pole uphaul to the appropriate height. In moderate or strong winds, snug the downhaul, and pull the pole about 3–6 feet back from the forestay.

8. Clip the tweaker lines onto the sheets, or at least the windward (guy) side sheet. This will be needed for control.

9. Tie a slip knot about 3 feet from the end of the sheet and guy. This will stop the sheets from running out when they are released—a common occurrence.

10. Clip the halyard to the head of the spinnaker.

11. Sail down to about 145 degrees off the wind. Set the autopilot to this wind direction.

12. Slacken the jibsheet so that the jib is properly trimmed for this sailing angle. A tight jib may backwind the spinnaker and lead to a twist. Slacken the mainsheet but do not ease the main onto the spreaders or shrouds or the spinnaker halyard would get caught between the main and the spreaders.

13. Pull the guy so that the forward corner of the chute is three quarters of the way to the bow. It may be necessary to pull the sail out of the bag by hand—this is the reason to have the sailbag next to the cockpit.

14. Raise the halyard quickly, without letting the sail drop into the water. At some point it may be necessary to pull the jibsheet in by hand to clear the chute out from under the jibsheet.

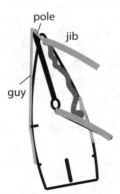
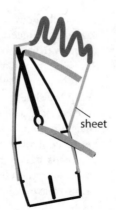
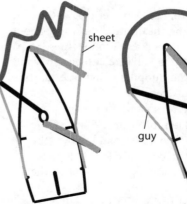
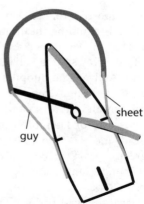

Pull the guy to lay out the spinnaker ¾ to the bow inside the lifelines.

Raise the spinnaker halyard; the sheet is loose.

Pull the pole back; the sheet remains loose.

Turn the autopilot off and take the tiller in hand; trim the spinnaker sheet; drop the jib on deck.

Raising a symmetrical spinnaker.

15. Immediately pull the guy to bring the chute out around the bow so that 3–6 feet of the chute is showing. However, because the sheet is very lose, the spinnaker will not fill but will simply flog in front of the boat.

16. In moderate or high winds, disconnect the autopilot and hold the tiller under your knee. The autopilot would not be able to handle the boat with the spinnaker suddenly filling.

17. Pull the sheet so that the sail fills completely. At this point the chute is up and under control, sailing at 145 degrees off the wind. If this is the intended direction, ease the downhaul, pull the guy, and ease the sheet until the pole is hauled back aft to the proper position.

18. Reset the autopilot to control the boat. It is not necessary to rush to drop the jib to the deck, but ease the jib halyard a few feet to allow the top of the spinnaker to fill. Only when everything is completely settled should the skipper worry about dropping the jib altogether.

19. Grab the jib halyard and release the jib halyard clutch. Holding onto the jib halyard, move to the foredeck and pull the jib down to the deck.

The entire process of raising the chute should take less than a minute. There is no reason that it should be any slower than on an average crewed boat, the only difference being that the single-hander has to sail deeper than may be desired to get it done. Back in the cockpit, now turn to the desired sailing course, and trim the chute accordingly. The autopilot may be overstressed if sailing a high angle into strong winds. It is better to take the tiller in hand (or under leg) while trimming the sheet and guy if heading up.

Trimming the Spinnaker

Spinnaker trim is a matter of both speed and safety. An improperly trimmed spinnaker is both slow and dangerous. Dangerous? Yes, an improperly trimmed spinnaker wants to drive the boat either up or down. The process is very different from that on a crewed boat.

The first step is to ease the sheet until the forward edge of the chute starts to curl, then pull back on the sheet just a few inches. Then leave the sheet in place. On a crewed boat, the "sheet trimmer" constantly adjusts the sheet to keep it slightly tight, on the assumption that the helmsman is working independently of the spinnaker to keep the boat on course. The complete opposite is true for the singlehander. The autopilot has limits in steering.

WATCH FOR ROCKS!

As said elsewhere, most of the advice in this book comes from my own experience; here is another bit of hard-won wisdom. Raising the spinnaker and dropping the jib is the one activity where the skipper is concentrating solely on the lines and sails for an extended period. I tend to ignore anything going on outside the lifelines for the entire process. This is a bad idea on the open water and, as I realized yesterday afternoon, even worse in close quarters of a race course. The problem is that telling a singlehander to watch for rocks is not sufficiently specific to change behavior. "Of course I'll watch for rocks—right after I finish here."

So I am going to prescribe two precise moments when the skipper must stop the spinnaker launching process for just 3 seconds and take a deliberate look ahead. The first moment is immediately after engaging the autopilot on the new course but before pulling the spinnaker guy forward (step 11, raising the chute). *Press the button, stop everything else, and look forward.*

The second moment is immediately after the spinnaker is up and trimmed, but before releasing the jib halyard (step 19, raising the chute). *Put one hand on the halyard clutch, stop everything else, and look forward.*

I'm only asking for 3 seconds in each case, not enough to impact the launch, but certainly enough to spot danger ahead. Learn from my experience.

If the boat rounds up by 10 degrees over a normal wave and the sheet is tightened, this will drive the boat up farther—very quickly. The spinnaker sheet should be loose enough that it will curl over on itself if the boat rounds up and then uncurl as the boat comes down again. This is an automatic method for dumping wind. Under good conditions, even with a high wind, the boat will sail itself while the skipper enjoys dinner and a coffee.

It is often thought that in high winds, it is safer to hide much of the spinnaker behind the mainsail by moving the pole forward. This is a mistake that can lead to serious broaches. We must always go back to the initial concept that sail trim is vital. If the spinnaker pole is well forward, the sail trim assumes that the boat is on a reach rather than a run, and the spinnaker will pull the boat up into a broach. An autopilot or windvane cannot overcome this pressure. A much safer approach is to switch down to a smaller spinnaker and pull the pole back to its proper position, perpendicular to the wind. In this position the spinnaker is properly trimmed for the wind direction.

It is important that the skipper have control over the sheet, guy, and downhaul from the standard helm position. This requires leading the spinnaker sheet across the cockpit to the windward jib winch. I usually do this after the chute is up and the jib is down, when I'm moving onto the correct course.

Gybing the Spinnaker

I contacted the Artemis Offshore Academy with the simple question: "How do you gybe in 30 knots of wind?" The answer I received was a complete surprise. I call it the "main-first method."

Crewed boats gybe the spinnaker and mainsail simultaneously. Obviously a singlehander cannot do so. For the previous seven years I had always moved to the foredeck and gybed the spinnaker before hurrying back to the cockpit to gybe the main. It is during this in-between period that the boat is in its most precarious position. The main-first method was taught to me by Charles Darbyshire and Nigel King, both of the Artemis Offshore Academy.

As a first step, the singlehander must learn how his boat handles without a spinnaker pole. This is best done in moderate, 10- to 15-knot winds. Launch the chute as normal with the pole and steer down to 150 degrees apparent. Make sure both tweaker lines are attached to the sheets; they are very important. Then move to the foredeck and disconnect the pole and allow it to drop away from the guy. The boat should then be gybed back and forth, numerous times, without allowing the spinnaker to collapse or wrap itself around the forestay. If the boat is sailed too high, the spinnaker will fold over on itself. If the boat is sailed too low, the spinnaker will wrap. King said that the key is to "learn to keep the boat underneath the spinnaker."

During this pole-less practice, the skipper will learn that the windward sheet should be eased, such that the clew of the spinnaker is just a few feet back from the forestay and allowing the boat to sail higher. Likewise, the leeward sheet should be pulled in, bringing the leeward clew back about halfway. The skipper should practice using both tweaker lines to control the chute. What happens if one is pulled tight? If both are pulled tight? During this stage the skipper will also learn that if the boat is sailed at 180 degrees apparent, the spinnaker will wrap around the forestay—to be avoided.

Luckily, without the work of gybing the pole, it is very easy to practice a few dozen gybes simply by changing direction and swinging the main back and forth. The key is to learn the positioning of the spinnaker that allows it to fly without wrapping.

In the main-first gybing method, the mainsail is gybed before the spinnaker. (See diagrams, next page.) With practice, as described above, the singlehander will be confident in his ability to sail the boat without the traditional pole on the windward side. Following are the exact steps for moderate winds.

1. Clip the safety harness tether on the current leeward side of the boat.
2. Sail fairly deep, down to 160 degrees apparent.
3. Pull both tweaker lines down as far as the lifelines.
4. Release the spinnaker pole downhaul.
5. Pull the guy to bring the pole back about two thirds.

6. Ease the sheet so that the clew of the spinnaker is about 2 feet from the forestay.
7. Push the buttons on the autopilot to steer down to 180 degrees, and gybe the mainsail by hand. (With the spinnaker up, the boat should be sailing sufficiently fast that there is only light pressure on the main.)
8. Immediately reset the autopilot again to steer the boat up to 160 degrees on the new heading. When the boat has settled on the new heading, move farther up to 145 degrees apparent. (My autopilot has a tendency to overshoot, which is why I use a two-stage process to get to 145 degrees.)
9. The spinnaker should still be full, with the tweaker line holding the new guy stable and the pole on the new leeward side of the boat.
10. Move to the foredeck on the new windward side of the boat.
11. Facing forward, grab the sheet in the windward hand.
12. Use the mast-side hand to remove the pole from the mast.
13. Connect the sheet to the pole and disconnect the old guy from the pole.
14. Slide the pole up the new guy to the clew.
15. Attach the pole to the mast.
16. Return to the cockpit, tighten the pole downhaul, and trim the chute as appropriate.

The main has been gybed, but not the pole. The tweaker lines are tight. It is possible to sail in this position for an extended time to round a buoy or an island or if pushed up by another racer, rather than perform two gybes.

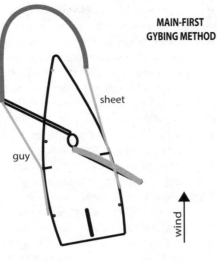

**MAIN-FIRST
GYBING METHOD**

sheet

guy

wind

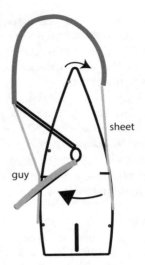

sheet

guy

Step 1.
Steer down to 160 apparent.
Pull the tweaker lines tight;
pull the pole back 2/3; ease
the sheet 2 feet from the forestay.

Step 2.
Steer down to 180. Gybe
the mainsail by hand;
immediately steer up to
160 on the new heading.

wind

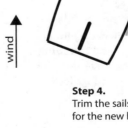

Step 3.
Move to the mast. Grab
the sheet in windward hand and
the pole in the leeward hand.
Move the pole to the windward
side up at the clew.

The process for gybing the main first.

Step 4.
Trim the sails as appropriate
for the new heading.

It is important to remember that if the boat is sailed too high without the pole, the spinnaker will fold over on itself. If the boat is sailed too low, the spinnaker will wrap. (I speak from experience on this, and King confirmed it.)

Although the description of the steps above has a large number of instructions, the entire process should take only about 30 seconds. The only way to get good at this is to practice, practice, practice. A keen singlehander should just sail out and gybe ten times—just for fun! I have done just that since learning the new main-first method.

Gybing without the Pole

Once the skipper has learned to gybe using the main-first method, it becomes obvious that gybing the pole is not necessary at all in short-term situations. I use this technique often when I need to get around a mark or around a small island. Simply ease the sheet until the clew is 2–3 feet from the forestay. Then harden down on the sheet-side tweaker line. Swing the boat and gybe the main and continue to sail in the new direction. It does take a little more attention to keep the chute from collapsing on itself, but I have sailed for as long as 15 minutes with 25-knot winds up to 135 degrees apparent. There is no loss of speed and it is much easier than gybing the chute twice in short order to round a mark.

Gybing in Higher Winds

The excitement of this maneuver builds as the winds grow. In 20-knot winds, the tweaker lines must be pulled right down to the deck before releasing the downhaul. The pole should be allowed to float, hanging only from the uphaul.

King commented that in 30-knot winds he steers by hand during the gybe because his autopilot cannot reliably change course without rounding up. Only after settling on the new course does he reactivate the autopilot and move to the foredeck.

Gybing the Spinnaker without an Autopilot

I singlehanded my Tanzer 22 for five years with nothing but a bungee cord for self-steering. I searched and searched for a foolproof method of gybing a spinnaker but could never find it. The boat would always round up or down.

Last year the autopilot on my Olson 30 died. Rather than getting an immediate repair, I took it as a very good opportunity to get back to basics and relearn how to properly handle the boat. I have been using a bungee cord alone for the past nine months, including many races and numerous spinnaker launches and douses in 25–30 knots of wind. (Even Tiger Woods, perhaps the greatest golfer of all time, gets back to basics. During one bad tournament he spent hours practicing his swing in a hotel room. The next day he came from behind to win! This is what it means to get back to the basics.) Only later did I finally decide it was time to get the autopilot repaired.

Last summer, in the middle of the nine months without an autopilot, I finally figured out how to gybe the chute. I have since tried this method in up to 20 knots of wind, and it works without fail. (In fact I was out sailing today and used this method in 15 knots of breeze.) Since I posted it on a forum, other singlehanders have also used it with success. The method is shown in the diagrams. Here are the steps:

1. Clip your tether on the leeward side jackline.
2. Steer down to 160 degrees apparent. Pull the tweaker lines tight and pull the pole back two thirds.
3. Ease the sheet 2 feet from the headstay.
4. Steer down to 180 degrees and gybe the main by hand. Immediately steer up to 160 degrees on the new heading. It is possible to sail in this direction for an extended time with the spinnaker full.
5. Release the old guy so that the spinnaker streams out in front of the boat. Secure the tiller with the bungee cord. Make sure that the position of the tiller will keep the boat on its current heading for at least 30 seconds—that is all you need.
6. Move to the mast. Facing forward, grab the new guy in your windward hand and remove the pole from the mast in your leeward hand. Clip the pole to the new guy and slide it up to the clew. Reconnect the pole to the mast.
7. Return to the cockpit and remove the bungee cord. Pull in on the new sheet until the spinnaker catches.

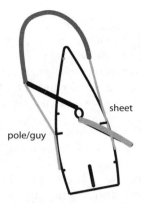

sheet

pole/guy

wind

Step 1. Steer down to 160 apparent. Pull the tweaker lines tight; pull the pole back 2/3; ease the sheet 2 feet from the forestay.

Step 2. Steer down to 180. Gybe the mainsail by hand; immediately steer up to 160 on the new heading. It is possible to sail in this position for an extended period waiting for smooth conditions.

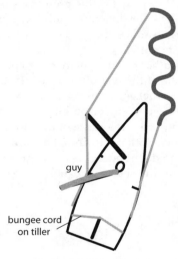

guy

bungee cord on tiller

Step 3. Release the old guy so that the spinnaker flogs in front of the boat. Wrap the bungee cord around the tiller and make sure the boat is sailing in a constant direction.

Step 4. Move to the mast. Grab the new guy in the windward hand and the pole in the leeward hand. Move the pole to the windward side up at the clew.

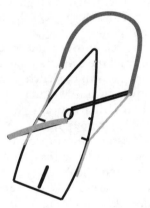

Step 5. Return to the tiller and remove the bungee cord. Trim the sheet until the spinnaker catches.

All that is required to gybe the spinnaker without an autopilot is a bungee cord to hold the tiller briefly while you switch pole ends.

Dousing the Chute

Dousing rarely leads to problems if done properly.

1. Before taking any steps, examine the three corners of the sail to ensure none of the lines are caught or tangled and may prevent the douse.

2. In moderate or heavy winds, sail down to 145 degrees. In light winds it is possible to sail higher.

3. Raise the jib, leaving the jibsheet moderately slack.

4. Make sure that the guy and halyard are free to run—they will run very quickly. Tie a slipknot at the end of the guy.

5. Stand at the front of the cockpit facing forward.

6. Release the tweaker line on the sheet side, but not the guy side.

7. Uncleat the guy, but leave it wrapped on the winch.

8. Reach under the boom and over the lifelines and grab the sheet in your leeward hand.

9. Flip the guy off the winch and let it go. It will run out extremely fast.

10. Pull in on the sheet, beneath the boom. Grab as much of the foot of the spinnaker as possible in just a few seconds. It is not necessary to grab the entire foot. Even just the corner will do in high winds.

11. Release the halyard clutch and let the halyard fly.

12. With a hand-over-hand motion, immediately pull the entire sail into the cockpit or dump it down the hatch. If pulled quickly enough, the sail will not get wet. It is best not to pull frantically, just quickly and steadily. There is time.

13. If necessary, you can control the halyard under one foot so that the spinnaker does not drop in the water.

14. Turn to the desired course and trim the jib.

15. Only after attaining speed on the new course should you store the pole.

At some point, it becomes uncomfortable for a singlehander to gybe the chute. The wind level and sea state at which discomfort begins will increase with experience. However, the wind level at which a spinnaker is flown will also increase with experience. When conditions exceed your level of comfort, the best approach to gybing is to douse the spinnaker, tie the sheets and halyard together and pull them around the boat, reattach them to the spinnaker (or preferably to another spinnaker that is properly packed), and raise the spinnaker on the other side.

When Spinnaker Things Go Bad

The challenge of flying a spinnaker is that things can and will go bad very quickly. Fortunately there is a remedy for every situation, and nothing has proven to be fatal to this skipper or boat. One overriding principle is *Do not release the guy until the spinnaker is to come down*. Releasing the guy almost always causes greater problems. Think of the spinnaker exactly the same as any other sail. If a gust of wind hits the main, the first reaction is to release the sheet. Likewise, if a gust hits the spinnaker, release the sheet. Think of the guy as a permanent attachment, just like the tack on the main or jib.

Problem: Spinnaker Hoist with an Hourglass

The only real remedy for this problem is to lower the halyard by 4 feet. Often this solves the problem because the halyard itself caused the twist, and now will allow it to untwist.

The only other possible solution is to pull down on the middle of the foot of the chute. If this does not solve the problem, nothing else will work. Pulling on the sheet or guy or pulling on the corners will not do it, and it is a waste of time to keep trying. The faster solution is to drop the spinnaker into the cockpit, undo the hourglass even if this requires disconnecting the sheets, and raise it again from

When a spinnaker hoist leads to an hourglass, the first remedy to try is dropping the halyard by 4 feet or so. *(Courtesy Andrew Madding)*

the cockpit. If the spinnaker was properly packed and raised as described earlier, it will not go up with an hourglass. Two minutes of preparation during the beat to windward is worth 10 minutes of struggle while watching the fleet sail away.

Problem: Boat Rounds up Immediately on Raising the Chute

This problem is caused by having the sheet too tight. The solution is to immediately release the sheet by 10–20 feet. Do not release the guy in this situation. If the correct procedure is followed for launching the chute, this problem should not happen. But some skippers continue to believe that they have more control over the spinnaker if the sheet is tight. As with a teenager, it is impossible to gain control by holding too tight. Only by letting go can one hope to have some influence over its behavior.

Problem: Gust of Wind Causes the Boat to Heel

Once again, simply release the sheet by 10 feet. There is no problem with having the spinnaker flapping in the wind for a few seconds.

[Below] Royal Victoria Yacht Club photographer Andrew Madding deftly captured author Andrew Evans's spinnaker handling on his Olson 30 *Foolish Muse. (Courtesy Andrew Madding)*

Spinnaker sheet too tight.

Too much wind is causing excessive heel.

The spinnaker sheet has been released, relieving the heeling and allowing the boat to get back on course.

Problem: Spinnaker Wraps around the Forestay and Jib Halyard

This is a major problem that cannot be solved quickly. Do not release the sheet or guy. But before leaving the cockpit, ensure that the sheets will not fall off the boat and sink if they are untied from the chute. I speak from experience.

Sail downwind at about 145 degrees. Grab two sail ties in hand—they will be needed at the bow. Release the spinnaker halyard and move to the bow to pull the chute and sheets down to the deck. It may be possible and necessary to unwrap it once or twice by hand enough to pull it down.

However, do *not* attempt to unwrap it completely while it is still up. It is *really, really bad* to have the spinnaker suddenly fill when you're standing at the bow, a long way from the boat controls and with the halyard out 30 feet from the mast head. Climbing back to the cockpit when the boat is heeled 65 degrees is more fun than most skippers want.

On the other hand, a few years ago I put a 50-foot rip (top to bottom and side to side) in my best spinnaker after it fell in the water when I unwrapped it in 25 knots of wind. The boat sure stopped quick! A much better idea is to use the sail ties that I mentioned earlier and tie the spinnaker to the pulpit. Bundle it up, bring it back to the cockpit and start again. I'll repeat this again because it is the only proper solution. Bring sail ties to the bow and tie the spinnaker into a bundle as you bring it down. Do not, under any circumstances, let the spinnaker fill with air.

Problem: On Dousing, the Spinnaker Comes in behind the Mainsail and above the Boom

This problem will occur when attempting to douse the chute in higher winds at a high angle. When the guy is released, the spinnaker drives back behind the mainsail. No one is strong enough to hold the sheet in front of the boom. It will not be possible to clear the mess before dousing. Simply continue to douse from behind the main. Afterward, disconnect all the lines. This problem could have been prevented by sailing down to 145 degrees before dousing, but sometimes this is not possible. In a race it is more important to continue sailing towards the next mark.

Problem: In High Winds the Spinnaker Simply Gets Away

Sometimes the pressure on the guy is so strong that it runs out from the skipper's hands, even causing a rope burn. This is why it is very important to have slip knots at the end of the sheet and guy. Let the guy run out all the way to the slipknot. Grab the sheet and release the halyard to douse the chute as much as normal. (Have a knife mounted in the cockpit to cut the sheet, as a last resort.)

Problem: No Slipknot on the Sheet and the Spinnaker Is Attached Only at the Top of the Mast by the Halyard, with the Sheet and Guy Flapping Wildly a Hundred Feet away from the Boat

Again, I speak from experience. Do not release the halyard until this situation is under control. If the halyard is released, the chute will fall in the water well behind the boat. This is a major cause of mast breakage. Even if the mast does not break, it will take 10 minutes to drag the spinnaker back on board—I've done it. The only possible strategy is to sail down in an attempt to cover the chute behind the main. Use any means possible (such as a boathook) to snag the flapping sheet or guy and pull it into the cockpit. Then release the halyard and douse the chute. With enough flapping in the wind, I once had a 60-foot sheet tie itself into a single knot measuring a cubic foot.

All of the problems above become especially interesting if sailing directly toward a rocky shoreline with just 2 minutes until impact. The key to singlehanding is the ability to very thoughtfully, but very quickly, consider all the options and arrive at the best possible solution. But this is why we took up singlehanding in the first place. We have more fun and face more challenges flying a spinnaker than in any other aspect of singlehanding. The only important thing is to laugh at the problems and at ourselves. It we can't do this, we should take up basket weaving. As mentioned elsewhere, I know—absolutely—that something will go wrong every time I go sailing. But I have never once had a bad day sailing.

Tweakers—Use them Properly

Tweaker lines are invaluable for spinnaker control. In high winds on a beam reach or broad reach, the spinnaker pole should be tightened down hard to flatten the luff, and the sheet-side tweaker must be kept lose. This allows the spinnaker leech to twist off, dumping excess wind. Think of the spinnaker just like the jib or main: in high winds let the sail twist.

However, in high winds on a deep run, the opposite may be true. Some have suggested that both tweaker lines be pulled tight. If the sheet tweaker is slack, the boat will start rocking and rolling—a very bad situation. (See Chapter 3 for more on tweaker lines.)

ASYMMETRICAL SPINNAKERS

Earlier I introduced Ken, who singlehanded a J/80 for many years before recently buying a J/105. He perfected raising an asymmetrical spinnaker after being taught by past J/80 World Champion Kerry Klingler. The key is to *not* pull the tack forward until the halyard is completely raised. There are two reasons for this. First, the tack is very likely to catch on fittings as it is pulled forward. Second, we don't want the sail to fill until the halyard is raised completely and the boat is under control. Here are the steps:

1. Extend the pole.
2. Ensure that the sheet is sufficiently loose such that the spinnaker will not fill—even when the tack is pulled forward.
3. Raise the halyard completely. The chute will be in a long column shielded by the main.
4. Pull the tack line to bring the tack completely forward.
5. Trim the sheet to fill the sail.

Dousing an Asymmetrical

1. Release the tack.
2. Gather the entire foot of the chute.
3. Release the halyard and pull the chute into the bag in the companionway.

Ken commented that by gathering the entire foot of the sail, he kept everything in good order and the sail did not require sorting for the next launch.

Ken's J/80 came with a spinnaker sock, but it was difficult to use. The sock was hauled down from the mast, while the resistance was well forward from the end of the pole. The difference in angle made it difficult to pull down. On his new J/105, the sock pulls down to the end of the pole, so the effort is directly in line with the sail, making it much easier to douse.

EXTREME WIND GYBING—MAIN AND JIB ONLY

When the wind is too high to fly a spinnaker at all, and just a mainsail and jib are being used, gybing is a special challenge. If the main is not sheeted in properly, it will swing across and break the boom or gooseneck. If the main is sheeted but the gybe is not completed immediately, the wind may catch the main and drive the boat upward into the path of an oncoming freighter at midnight. (Yes, that happened to me.) In very high winds the singlehander has just seconds to pull in the main, complete the gybe, and release the main.

When gybing the main and jib, completely ignore the jib at first and concentrate solely on the main. When heading downwind, the jib will not cause any problems if it is backwinded. Here are the steps for gybing in an extreme wind:

1. The overriding priority is to complete these steps within a matter of seconds. Any delay will have dire consequences.
2. Head down as far as possible.
3. Sheet in the main as far as possible. It must be within 20 degrees of center.
4. Immediately gybe to 170 degrees on the new course.
5. Immediately release the mainsheet and let it ease out slowly while controlling it by hand. Do not let it slam back against the spreaders. This is the fun part.
6. Wrap a few turns of the jibsheet around the lazy winch.
7. Release the jibsheet of the backwinded jib and pull on the newly active jibsheet. The jib will easily fall into place in front of the mainsail.
8. Steer to the proper course and trim the sails.

DOWNWIND AT NIGHT—POLED-OUT HEADSAILS

Once the wind gets up over 15–20 knots, a singlehanded skipper might not be comfortable leaving the spinnaker flying while sleeping below. This is

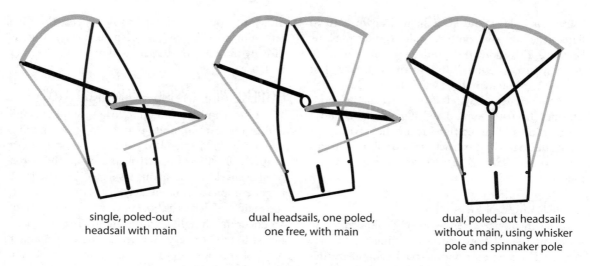

single, poled-out
headsail with main

dual headsails, one poled,
one free, with main

dual, poled-out headsails
without main, using whisker
pole and spinnaker pole

Three methods of poling out dual headsails. If using the method shown in the illustration on the right, the boat needs both a spinnaker pole and a whisker pole.

particularly important in the trade winds to Hawaii where persistent squalls can suddenly jump the wind up over 30 knots. In this situation, a poled-out headsail is an excellent alternative.

While this will reduce the sail area somewhat and be a little slower, the benefit is that the configuration is incredibly stable. With a spinnaker, the bulk of the sail area is at the top half of the mast. Thus there is a significant tendency for the boat to rock from side to side and end up broaching if not managed. With a triangular genoa or jib, less than a third of the sail area is at the top half of the mast, and when the sail is poled out, even this small portion is twisted away, so virtually all of the sail area is on the bottom half, or even bottom third of the mast. The result is that the boat does not rock from side to side at all—even in high winds.

Three configurations are often used:

1. For most boats carrying a spinnaker pole, the easiest solution is a single poled-out jib on the windward side and mainsail on the leeward side. I used this method at night during the Singlehanded Transpac. I flew my big genoa even in 20- to 25-knot winds. With the boat moving at 8 knots, the apparent wind on the sail was only 12 knots. The

boat was perfectly stable. During the 30- to 35-knot squalls, I simply gybed the genoa over to the leeward side where it was slightly protected behind the mainsail. I never once felt that the sails were overpowered (although I was moving at a good clip).

2. Other skippers in the Transpac add a second headsail without pole, on the leeward

Tony Gooch used twin poled-out headsails in the Southern Ocean during his solo circumnavigation. *Taonui* has twin roller-furling headsails (see inset photo), so it was an easy matter to reduce sail area in higher winds. He used strong sheets with a block on the jib clew to provide even greater leverage and control over the pole position. *(Courtesy Tony Gooch)*

side of the boat. On a typical boat with one forestay, the hanks of the two sails are interlaced.

3. For very deep running, the mainsail can be dropped altogether and two poled-out headsails mounted. Of course, the skipper would need both a spinnaker pole and a whisker pole for this configuration.

HEAVING-TO

Heaving-to is a vital skill for singlehanders but is shockingly little known and little used. During a discussion with the singlehanded skipper of an Open 40 who had faced an extremely dangerous storm, I asked if he had considered heaving-to and allowing the storm to pass. He replied that he had never practiced heaving-to and did not know if it could be done with his boat. I was fairly amazed by his response that he did not know how to perform this most basic and possibly most crucial of sailing skills.

On the other hand, my friend Jeanne Socrates has sailed around the world three times. She makes it a practice to heave-to whenever the winds reach storm conditions. She finds this a very comfortable way to wait for better weather.

Heaving-to is vital in many instances:

- When nearing the dock without an autopilot, heaving-to allows the skipper to calmly and safely drop the sails, mount fenders, start the motor, etc. (It is especially impressive to stop the boat just 20 yards from the harbor, calmly ready the boat to dock, and then motor in.) I used this method every single time I returned to dock through the years that I singlehanded before having an autopilot.
- In cases when the motor fails at a crucial moment, heaving-to gives the singlehander all the time necessary to check the fuel tank and fuel lines, or even remove and check spark plugs. I have done all of these just outside the harbor entrance.
- Without an autopilot, heaving-to is the best way to put reefs in the mainsail, which is flopping in the wind anyway.
- Heaving-to is an excellent way to drop the

jib and have it fall on the deck rather than in the water even if the singlehander has an autopilot. It drops well because it is sitting, backwinded, directly above the foredeck.

- Heaving-to is a great way to take a nice break on a very windy day, especially for the rookie singlehander. After a long period of exertion, you can heave-to just to sip a coffee or have a sandwich. In open waters, you can even safely have a sleep.
- Heaving-to works better in higher wind conditions. It does not work if there is no wind, but then the boat can just drift.

Each type of boat behaves differently when heaving-to. For example, some boats require a slight pressure on the mainsail, while others heave-to with the main completely loose or dropped. And each boat behaves differently with different sail combinations. For example, my boat holds its position better with the genoa than with the jib.

Heaving-to is very simple. On a typical modern sloop it can be done with just a short line tying the tiller or using the autopilot. In a hove-to position, the foresail is tight but backwinded, the mainsail is loose to flogging, and the tiller is tied to the leeward rail.

Here are the steps to heave-to from a beat or close reach:

1. Sail as usual on a tight beat with the jib and main sheeted in completely. The boat should be heading directly opposite to the heading desired in the hove-to position; i.e., if the skipper wants to be hove-to pointing due west, he should be sailing due east.
2. Tack the boat through the wind, but *do not* release the jibsheet. This will backwind the jib against the mast and shrouds.
3. Immediately after the boat has passed head to wind, release the mainsheet completely. The mainsail will fall against the new leeward shroud. Even in high winds the main will only flog gently. The boat will fall off the wind past the close-hauled heading.
4. Push the tiller to the newly leeward rail and tie it in place.

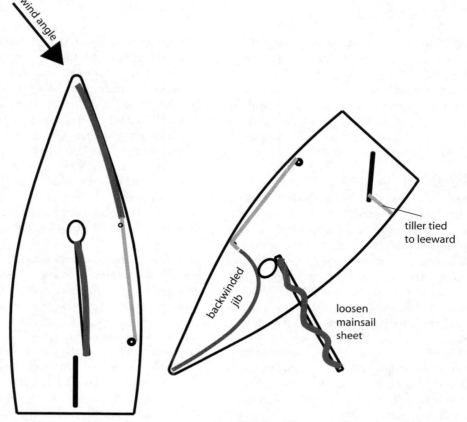

When heaving-to from a beat, after you have tacked, don't release the jibsheet; let the mainsheet out and tie the tiller to leeward.

5. The boat will settle in a heading directly opposite the original heading, on a beam reach.
6. If desired for an extended stay, the mainsail can be dropped to the deck.

Here are the steps to heave-to from a broad reach or run:

1. Drop the spinnaker and raise the jib or genoa.
2. Sail down to 160 degrees off the wind so the jib is shielded by the main.
3. Sheet the jib in until it is tight.
4. Gybe the boat but do not release the jibsheet.
5. Remember when gybing to sheet the main all the way in, turn the boat, and then release the mainsheet on the leeward side.
6. Allow the boat to head up to a beam reach

with the backwinded jib on the windward side.
7. Push the tiller to the leeward rail and tie it in place.

The action of the boat when hove-to is that the backwinded jib is trying to push the boat down while the rudder is trying to steer the boat up. They will counteract each other perfectly as the boat continues to move at a very slow speed, perhaps a half knot. Different foresails have different results. For example, my boat is nearly dead in the water when hove-to with my 155% genoa, but it moves at about a half-knot when hove-to with my 100% jib.

Note that the mainsail and tiller can be used to adjust the boat heading when hove-to. Pulling in the mainsheet to put some pressure on the mainsail will aim the boat more upwind to a close reach, suitable

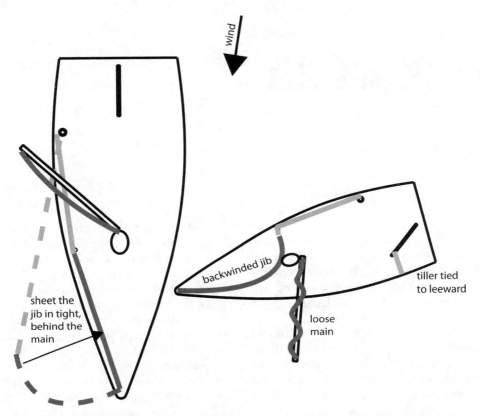

To heave-to from a run, sheet in the jib tightly, gybe the main, do not release the jibsheet, release the mainsheet, and tie the tiller to the new leeward.

in large waves. Moving the tiller a little toward the center will drop the boat to a broader reach. The skipper should choose the most comfortable boat direction and make adjustments accordingly.

Practice heaving-to to determine how your boat will react with different foresails and in different conditions. Stopping the boat may require easing the jibsheet or changing the tiller position slightly.

Follow these steps to start sailing again:

1. Untie the tiller and take it in hand, or activate the autopilot.
2. Release the tight jibsheet.
3. Trim the newly active jibsheet.
4. Trim the mainsheet.

The boat will start sailing again on a beam reach with perfect control.

DROPPING SAILS

When dropping sails to enter a harbor, follow these steps. They can be done calmly and slowly regardless of wind conditions:

1. Heave-to.
2. Drop the mainsail and secure it to the deck or boom.
3. Tie the fenders to the boat rails.
4. Start the motor, but keep it out of gear.
5. Release the jib halyard. The jib will fall neatly on the foredeck. It may require some pulling to get the jib completely down.
6. Release the tiller.
7. Put the motor in gear and enter the harbor with a smile.

CHAPTER 10 SEE AND BE SEEN

NAVIGATION

Numerous reference books are available on navigation. Here I will concentrate on the only aspect of navigation that is a particular challenge to the singlehander: navigating in tight quarters. The singlehanded sailor should own a handheld GPS chartplotter.

Experience has shown that it is very difficult for a singlehander to refer to paper charts when sailing, or even motoring, in tight channels or shoal-littered waters. It is extremely difficult to follow a position with one finger on the chart and the other hand on the tiller, especially during tacks. These tasks are

Even the chartplotter app on my BlackBerry is handy for avoiding rocks.

easy on a crewed boat but nearly impossible for the singlehander. And if it's raining, then the chart will be belowdeck where the skipper can't see it at all.

A mounted chartplotter is suitable only if it is clearly visible from all tiller positions.

A handheld chartplotting GPS is the best solution. It allows the skipper to follow his position precisely relative to any navigation hazards. The skipper can hold it in his hand and closely examine the location of buoys or rocks ahead. With the advent of smart phone apps, chartplotting has become less expensive and more readily available.

The major caveat is that the screen should be zoomed in to clearly show all hazards. Some units or apps do not show all hazards when they are zoomed out. I know of one boat that ran on a rock that was not shown in the macro view on the skippers' GPS. After hitting the rock he zoomed in and saw the rock clearly marked.

Maintaining a Lookout

The International Regulations for Preventing Collisions at Sea (COLREGs) Rule 5 states:

> Every vessel shall at all times maintain a proper look-out by sight and hearing as well as by all available means appropriate in the prevailing circumstances and conditions so as to make a full appraisal of the situation and of the risk of collision.

Obviously, it is impossible for a singlehander to abide by the letter of this rule. This is a significant controversy in the sailing community. As Bernard

Hayman writes in "Troubled Waters":

For 19 of the 35 years that I worked for the magazine *Yachting World*, I was a member of the UK Safety of Navigation Committee. During those 19 years I never met a single professional mariner be he a shipmaster; a pilot; member of the Nautical Institute; of Trinity House; the RNLI; or what is now the Marine Safety Agency who did not consider that long distance singlehanded sailing was unlawful. Thus I am dismayed to see a singlehanded transatlantic event promoted by the RIN. Of course I am aware that single-handed events exist but by what right do these 'adventurers' claim that Rule 5, the requirement to keep a proper lookout, need not apply to them. If anyone can offer a valid reason why Rule 5 should be rewritten, I should be interested to hear it. Until it is rewritten it is like any other rule in COLREG and should be obeyed. The RYA summed up the situation in its comment: 'This is the most important Rule. If it is not observed, the rest of the Rules might as well not exist.'

Even if we recognize that a singlehander cannot live within the letter of the rule, is it possible to live within the spirit? Here's a reply by Michael Richey:

My good friend Bernard Hayman's memory on this occasion seems a bit selective. I too served on that Committee for many years and was far from aware of being isolated in holding that single-handed sailing could be compatible with the Collision Regulations. Rule 5 ("Every vessel shall at all times maintain a proper look-out . . . ") is entirely concerned with the risk of collision so that in the (hypothetical) situation where no such risk exists, it can have no application. From this it is not a long way to saying that where the risk of collision is small, some relaxation of vigilance can be accepted. As one of the authors (Cockcroft) of *A Guide to the Collision Regulations* put it, no one would admonish a ship's master experiencing continuous fog in the North Pacific Ocean over several days for failing to sound his whistle every two minutes throughout the 24 hours.

In other words safety at sea is the criterion and the Regulations should be applied with common sense. The views of the International Association of Institutes of Navigation, incidentally, as submitted to the International Maritime Organisation on this matter and IMO's comments on them are printed in the Journal for January 1979.

Whether we live within the spirit or the letter of the law, we are the only ones who will suffer in any case. The following comes from Dag Pike ("On the Lookout"):

Bernard Hayman in his letter [above] is concerned about singlehanders flouting the Colregs by not keeping a lookout all the time. The Colregs are flouted by virtually every vessel at sea, particularly small craft. It may be navigation lights not meeting requirements, not sounding fog signals, simply keeping out of the way of larger ships, etc. In this radar-governed world, when did you last hear a ship sounding fog signals? Most people including single handers get away with it and I could be cynical in saying that the Colregs are not there to govern our behavior at sea but are only so that there is someone to blame when things do go wrong. In the current lawyer's paradise where we need to sue someone when an accident happens, the Colregs perform a vital role. In the practical world, I see no problem with singlehanders keeping the level of lookout they feel comfortable with. After all, they will be the ones to suffer if a collision occurs.

Obviously a sailor must sleep, even if for 20 minutes at a time. Most singlehanders also spend a significant amount of time belowdeck navigating, studying weather charts, cooking, reading, and even just staying out of bad weather. The more comfortable that the boat is below, the longer the singlehander will stay below.

In the open ocean, away from major shipping channels, the chances of collision with another vessel are extremely slim. Unfortunately, most voyages do not cross the open ocean. As I've said elsewhere, while we all dream of crossing the great oceans, 95% of our trips are within a few hours or a few days of our home port. This means that 95% of singlehanding is done in the middle of shipping lanes, mixed in with freighters, cruise ships, tugboats with barges on a quarter mile of cable, and fishing boats dragging miles of net. Although we would love to remain purists with only the wind at our backs, the desire to continue living means that we must take precautions.

TECHNOLOGY FOR COLLISION AVOIDANCE

Technology has leapt ahead in the past decade with a number of user-friendly mechanisms enabling singlehanders to keep a good watch while belowdecks and even while sleeping. There are skeptics of every one of the solutions offered below, however, and their skepticism is valid. But if used in combination, these solutions provide as close to perfect protection as is technically possible.

Radar

Radar offers the ultimate protection at the greatest cost and complexity. The least expensive radar systems start at $1,000, not including the many accessories needed to mount the unit and the screen to view the output. Most systems offer collision avoidance and guard zone alarms that ignore ships passing in the distance. Here are excerpts from a 2009 write-up on radar from Chuck Husick from the BoatUS.com website:

> Put a radar on your boat and you will be able to "see" through fog, rain and darkness. In the hands of a competent operator radar is a remarkable aid to safe navigation. It can confirm your position relative to landmarks and navigation aids such as buoys and by detecting other waterborne traffic make a great contribution to collision avoidance. Once reserved for large yachts and ships, today's radar products are available at prices and sizes suitable for use on boats as small as 18 feet. Even the least costly radars provide quite complete operational capabilities, including on screen display of the range and bearing of targets. Electrical power consumption is modest and well within the capability of virtually any boat

This cool little multifunction display unit toggles between radar, AIS, chartplotter, and depthsounder.

equipped with an engine. The ultimate value of a radar rests with the user's ability to understand and properly use the information on the screen.

Choosing radar requires evaluation of a number of performance specifications. The maximum range specification and transmitter power rating are often quoted as meaningful measures of the suitability of radar for a particular boat. Although of interest, they are not particularly appropriate measures on which to base a selection.

Radar energy, like the energy emitted from the VHF transceiver, travels in a generally straight line. Horizontally directed radar energy is soon well above the curved surface of the earth and can illuminate only those objects tall enough to protrude above the radar horizon. Regardless of the size of the vessel it is most often used to scan for targets not more than about 6 miles distant and will frequently be operated at ranges of less than 2 miles. Choosing a radar on the basis of maximum range is not a good idea.

Radar transmitter power is defined as Peak Pulse Power. Although manufacturers typically provide increasing power levels in their longer range and most costly sets, a modest amount of power is usually sufficient for the relatively short ranges most often used. Two kW transmitters can provide excellent results. For most recreational boats, transmitter power becomes important only in very heavy rain conditions. Rain reflects and absorbs radar energy. The reflection is useful in showing us the location and shape of rain showers. The absorption of radar energy can prevent a radar from portraying targets it would normally detect. Higher transmitter power can be valuable in such cases, however there are some tropical downpour conditions that can absorb all of the energy of even the most powerful ship radar sets.

The size of the radar antenna plays a key role in determining the overall performance of radar. Marine radars use the same antenna for both transmission and reception. The transmitter energy is carefully focused, much like the light from a well designed searchlight. However, unlike a searchlight, where the desired pattern of projected light is usually circular, the energy from the radar must illuminate a relatively wide vertical swath to ensure that the target area is well covered as the boat rolls and pitches in the sea. At the same time, a narrow horizontal beam is needed to allow objects close to one another in azimuth to be seen as separate targets and not as a single blob. Typical vertical beam angles are ±12.5 degrees. Horizontal beam angles, which are largely determined by the length of the antenna, range from about 2.4 degrees for the smallest antennas to 0.75 degree for antennas about 10 feet in length. Even the smallest antennas will provide useful target information at the relatively short ranges most often used by small craft.

The radar antenna, transmitter, and receiver are usually packaged as a single unit, enclosed in either a radome or in a housing with a rotating, bar-like antenna mounted on its top surface. The smallest radome housed units are less than 12 inches in diameter and weigh less than 10 pounds, making them practical for installation on even quite small boats. The antenna should be mounted at a height that places it at least two feet above and four to five feet from the head of anyone on board and in a position where crew members will usually be at least five feet from the antenna. Mounting the antenna more than about 22 feet above the water will not make a worthwhile contribution to maximum range operation and can degrade the radar's ability to show important close-in targets. A radar mounting pole that places the radar about eight feet above the deck works well.

Broadband Radar

Broadband radar is the trademark of a new technology developed by Navico and sold under the Simrad, Lowrance, and Northstar brand names. Here is a summary of information presented on the Lowrance company website:

Conventional pulse radar uses a magnetron to generate a pulsed microwave signal that is transmitted from the rotating radar antenna. This burst of microwave energy is reflected off any target that it hits and returns to the radar, with the time it takes determining the range and bearing. This type of radar transmission is, in layman's terms, like shouting loudly in one direction and then listening to see if you hear an echo, turning, and then repeating.

Broadband radar uses a different type of technology that allows the radar to send out a continuous radar signal, with a changing tone or frequency, at a very much lower power and at the same time listen for the change in that signal. This is like continuously whispering and listening at the same time for the echo and is made possible by the radar using two antennas, one to transmit and another to receive.

The change in the tone of the transmitted radar signal determines the time taken for the signal to reach the target and return. This time determines the range and the bearing.

There is a distinct advantage in sending out a much lower-power signal. The distortion in a normal radar transmission, which can be likened to a shout, gets distorted at very close ranges. This is often referred to as "main bang" interference and appears on the screen as a sunburst in the centre of the display. At very short ranges this noise covers up any close-in

Two methods of mounting radar. The radar unit up the mast adds significantly to weight and windage where we do not want it. The radar mounted on pole aft is in a better position, just above head level.

targets, making the radar ineffective at short distances. Many types of conventional radar suppress this pulse and hide the noise; but this again hides any short-range targets, thereby effectively blinding the radar to nearby targets.

With the Broadband Radar emitting only low levels of energy the noise and distortion is just not there, with the result that there is no distortion in the centre of the screen and therefore no need for any suppression. The benefit of this is that close-up targets are not lost or hidden, and the radar is able to show approaching targets until they are just a few feet from the transmitter. This short-range performance has never before been seen in leisure marine radar.

Conventional radars emit a pulse, and this pulse varies in length depending on the range. The length of the pulse determines the ability of conventional radar to distinguish between close targets on a similar bearing, and generally this can be down to 90 ft at short ranges and up to 500 ft at longer ranges. However, the Broadband Radar, using its continuously transmitted signal, is not only able to see targets as close as 6 ft from the dome on the shortest scale but can also separate targets just 30 ft apart on the scales used for general navigation.

Further evidence of this short-range performance can be seen from the ability of broadband radar to go beyond the conventional minimum range of 1/8th to 1/32nd of a mile.

Broadband radar allows the user to display at just 400 ft, 300 ft and 200 ft, with range rings of only 100 ft, for superb target resolution and differentiation.

According to manufacturers' websites, broadband radar uses significantly less power than traditional systems, 17 W in active mode and 1.6 W in standby. As well, "instant on" means that the user need not wait 2–3 minutes of warm-up time as in other systems.

The usual practice with radar is to set an alarm with a guard zone. The skipper should learn the lesson from Jessica Watson discussed later in this chapter, where the ship was already inside the guard zone when the radar was activated.

It is common practice to mount a radar dome two thirds of the way up the mast where it will not be caught by the jib during a tack. Of course, this contradicts the goal of keeping the weight and windage low, as discussed in Chapter 5. A much better solution is mounting the radar on a separate pole on the stern, just above head height. I have never seen it done, but a simple means to lower the radar dome all the way down to the pushpit when not in use would be even better.

Radar Reflectors

Active Radar Reflectors

The Sea-Me (www.sea-me.co.uk) is the most popular active radar reflector system. Another brand is the Echomax Active-XS (www.echomax.co.uk). (Note that several other brands have disappeared from this market: Ocean Sentry, Sea-Hawk, Activ'Echo, Tron ARR, and Rasmus.) These units perform two functions. First, they "actively" reflect back a radar signal to the passing ship that sent it, i.e., they electronically amplify the radar signal, making a small sailboat look much bigger to the ship. Second, they beep to alert the sailboat that it has been hit by a radar signal.

Here is a brief excerpt from Capt. Phil Gallman, Ph.D. on his website theradarreflectorsite.org. Gallman has done extensive research on radar reflectors for sailors and has published a book on the subject, available at his website.

Echomax's active radar reflector.
(Courtesy Echomax)

Q. What should I look for in an RTE (radar target enhancer)?

First, you want adequate RCS (radar cross section). The IMO recommends 7.5 m^2. Much larger than this becomes impractical for smaller vessels. I suggest in my book that if your sailing is restricted to benign conditions in protected waters a smaller RCS may be adequate. Equally important to magnitude of RCS is how RCS varies with aspect, or orientation of the unit relative to the radar. First, the RTE must provide a good response at large enough elevation angle so that you are visible when heeled at the maximum angle of heel you expect to encounter (depending on your vessel type and sailing environment). Second, there should be no gaps in coverage, i.e., regions in azimuth and elevation where the RCS is extremely small, so that you will never encounter the situation in which you are invisible right up to point of collision. Finally, even though the RCS can vary as the orientation changes as your vessel rolls, yaws, and pitches in a seaway, the variation is not so severe that detection becomes intermittent. Intermittent detection is hard for a human operator to handle and may keep your vessel from being detected at all.

Active radar reflectors are very popular with singlehanded offshore racers, mainly because of the low power draw. Several blogs reference their use. When being struck by radar, they use up to 350 mA of power. In standby mode they use as low as 35 mA. I use the Sea-Me unit when sailing. My only testimony is that I'm still alive, so I assume it works.

Important: Note that active radar reflectors, like the Sea-Me and the C.A.R.D. (Collision Avoidance Radar Detector) do not work with broadband radar. They do not reflect any signal back to the originating radar station. This is important as use of broadband systems increases.

The C.A.R.D. and MER-VEILLE brands of radar receiver have fallen out of favor of late (and C.A.R.D. is no longer on the market). These notify the skipper that the boat has been hit by a radar signal but do not reflect back to the passing ship. With the advances in active reflectors and AIS, we are seeing less of these methods. John Hayward on the Valiant 40 *Dream Chaser* made this comment about the C.A.R.D.:

> I have a CARD system on *Dream Chaser.* In the 2008 Transpac I ran it a lot and it never once went off even when large ships that the AIS picked up were visible. In the 2010 Transpac I turned it on several times when I picked up traffic on the radar or the AIS and still nothing. I have picked up signals in the harbor with it but I don't think it's worth the power consumption (low as it is) while singlehanding.

Passive Radar Reflectors

Capt. Gallman has also done a detailed comparison of passive radar reflectors. The entire study is available in his book and excerpted on his website.

Many designs are available. In brief, the popular tubular shape, such as the Mobri S-4, provides a strong cross section when vertical, but there is virtually no response when tilted past a few degrees, as is normal on a sailboat. The least expensive octahedral reflectors, such as the Davis Echomaster (www.davisnet.com) provide a strong response at some ranges, particularly at large elevation angles. Gallman recommends that these units be rigidly mounted because the common practice of hanging them from the spreaders with a line allows them to flop around, producing an intermittent

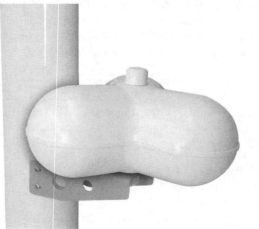

Two examples of passive radar reflectors. The octahedral reflector is popular; the Tri-Lens reflector achieves good results even when the vessel is heeled.

response. One of the most expensive units, the Tri-Lens (www.tri-lens.com), produces the best overall reflection in all directions and at heel angles up to 50 degrees.

AIS

AIS, the Automatic Identification System, has become very popular with singlehanders. A full AIS unit transmits the vessel's name, position, course,

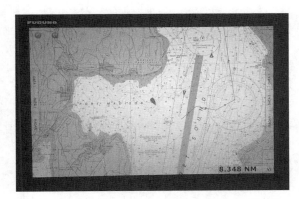

AIS display showing nearby vessels (blue triangles). The software can be configured to show various amounts of vessel information, including name, hailing port, distance from your own boat, etc.

and speed. It allows a skipper to identify nearby ships and then to hail them by name if necessary. Systems can be configured to detect potential collisions.

Jeanne Socrates used her AIS extensively on three circumnavigations. She often uses her VHF radio to hail ships entering her comfort zone and has been known to yell into the radio if they do not change course appropriately.

The ISAF Offshore Racing Rules now require that an AIS transponder must be carried for Category 2 races and above. The International Maritime Organization's International Convention for the Safety of Life at Sea (SOLAS) requires AIS to be fitted aboard international voyaging ships with gross tonnage of 300 or more tons and all passenger ships regardless of size. It is estimated that more than 40,000 ships currently carry AIS Class A equipment. In 2007, the new Class B AIS standard was introduced, which enabled a new generation of low-cost AIS transceivers. This has triggered multiple additional national mandates affecting hundreds of thousands of vessels.

Craig Horsfield has sailed twice across the busy Atlantic in his Mini 6.50. He said that in the open ocean, "all of the ships are using AIS," but in the busy fishing zones, the fishermen turn the AIS off so they don't let competitors know where the fish are congregating.

Class B AIS systems are most appropriate for sailboats. They transmit at 2 W and are not required

to have an integrated display—they can be connected to most display systems, on which received messages are displayed in lists or overlaid on charts. The Class B type standard requires integrated GPS and certain LED indicators. Class B equipment receives all types of AIS messages.

AIS systems are available with either receive-only or transmit/receive functions. Receive-only systems receive data from other vessels nearby. Transmit/receive systems also transmit the sailor's information to other vessels every 30 seconds. Typical power usage is about 2 A during the receive phase and up to 6 A during transmission. The receive-only systems are considerably less expensive, in the $600 range.

I posed a question about the usefulness of AIS on the Singlehanded Transpac website. Here are some of the replies:

I was personally far less than impressed. I used it during my sea-trials and qualifier, and some of the delivery home, but I don't even think I used it during my Transpac at all. There are so many vessels out there that don't even transmit that it's not even funny. It gives you a false sense of security. It seemed like when I did use it in a place with lots of traffic (like SF Bay, or just offshore near the shipping lanes), it picked up a majority of freight ships, but nowhere near all of them. This is strictly my opinion.

From my experience using both [radar and AIS], AIS works well offshore and alerts you to shipping traffic beyond the range of the radar, including localized stuff the radar does not see due to squalls. The radar works well for picking up things that aren't running AIS—other small boats and warships, for example. I really like running both, the AIS continuously and the radar on a 5 minute guard zone mode—the radar wakes up every 5 minutes, scans for a minute, and if nothing is found it goes back to sleep.

I loved my AIS! In fact, it worked too well. I used a splitter which shared the whip on the masthead with the VHF. This configuration gave me targets 80 miles out! I would spot them, want to talk, but our CPA was three hours.

I loved my AIS! And it seemed that my little 25-foot Folkboat was a freighter magnet during the Transpac . . . compared with others in the fleet . . . we saw a ton of shipping and my little standalone Nasa Marine AIS unit was spot on . . . a false sense of security or not—it helped me sleep better at night.

But even if just one ship in 2200 miles happens to find your boat while you're sleeping, wouldn't you want to know about it, and better yet, wouldn't you want the ship to "see" you? You can forget about them seeing your radar reflector until it's too late, if at all.

AIS came in handy for one ship that was insisting on running us over until I called them by name. They then said "yeah, we see you and have you on radar. clear astern.

Nigel Sly from Manchester made this comment: Most sail boats use a Class B transceiver. Many commercial vessels using Class A filter out Class B signals when in harbours to cut down on the number of targets, but then forget to reset the filters when back at sea.

I'm in the habit of calling up commercial vessels and ask if they have my AIS signal. If not, I ask them to check if they have filtered out Class B, many have.

Something to bear in mind. I am a skipper on Maersk Anchor handling tugs and know that this can happen.

Flashlight

Every singlehander should carry a really big flashlight in the cockpit. A sailboat is nearly invisible at night. A sailboat with a spotlight shining on the sails is impossible to miss. I find this method very effective when sailing in congested waters, surrounded by tugboats and fishing boats. Their radar systems are designed to hit targets in the distance,

not two boat lengths away. A flashlight on the sails is the best approach in a crowded channel.

CASE STUDY ON COLLISION AVOIDANCE: JESSICA WATSON'S COLLISION WITH A BULK CARRIER

A recent encounter between a singlehanded boat and ship provides a worthy case study of collision avoidance.

In the 2009 run-up to her round-the-world voyage aboard the 34-foot sloop *Ella's Pink Lady*, Jessica Watson, an Australian 16-year-old, laid her head down for a moment and struck the 225-meter bulk carrier *Silver Yang*. The mast was destroyed, and Watson motored back to port. The Australian Transportation Safety Bureau (ATSB) completed perhaps the most comprehensive incident report ever done on a yacht-ship collision. The entire report is available at http://www.atsb.gov.au. It goes into detail on the failings of both Watson and the *Silver Yang*'s crew. From our point of view, the only important thing is to learn from what Jessica could have done differently. It does us no good to blame the ship's crew as your boat sinks away below us.

Following are excerpts from the report:

At about 0146 (4 minutes before the collision) *Ella's Pink Lady*'s skipper prepared for another catnap. The yacht was making course 144°T at 6.8 knots. The skipper checked the radar and noted that there was a vessel about 6 miles off the starboard quarter. She could not see it visually but monitored its progress on radar for about 1 minute. Once she had determined that it did not present a collision risk, she again set the radar guard rings and alarm clocks before going to bed. By this time, *Silver Yang* was about 1 mile to the south-southeast of *Ella's Pink Lady*'s position. However the yacht's skipper had not detected the ship's presence.

The ATSB report makes several comments and recommendations.

The yacht's skipper, like many solo sailors, considered that because hers was a sailing vessel, and hence had the right of way over power driven vessels, that it was acceptable and safe for her to sleep from time to time.

During my years of sailing in the waters off Victoria, on Canada's West Coast, I have crossed tracks with more than a hundred ocean-going ships. I have never, not even one time, seen any of these ships make the slightest change to their course because of my boat. Even in races with a dozen or more sailboats in their path, the ships just keep moving straight ahead while the boats scatter. Rather than relying on the irrelevant notion that the powered vessel must give way, the singlehander should simply reverse the rule and make it a law that the sailboat must give way. A skipper who understands that this is the new law of the sea will never even consider the other possibility.

The skipper reported that she checked the radar and saw a ship that did not pose a collision risk. She then visually checked the horizon and saw nothing. However, had she scanned the horizon thoroughly in all directions, she would have seen *Silver Yang*, which was only about 1 mile away.

Human information processing is not infallible and, due to a wide range of factors, errors can occur. Research has shown that in road accidents, critical or important information may have been detectable but the motorist did not attend to, or notice, that information. These are often termed "looked but did not see" events and cover phenomena such as "change blindness" or "inattentional blindness."

To me, this seems like a perfect example of the "3:00 A.M. effect" discussed in Chapter 2. At this time of the night, a singlehander is incapable of making a conscious, intelligent decision. I don't care how rested the skipper feels. The brain simply does not function properly, if at all. I have done many nights of sailing and I know that at 3:00 A.M., I am a clumsy, stupid oaf. The only solution is to set up the boat so that it can take over the intelligence required for the task.

"Change blindness" occurs when a person does not notice something that is different about the visual environment compared to before the change.

"Inattentional blindness" occurs when one does not notice an object that is fully visible but unexpected, because the person's attention is engaged on another task. It is a failure to perceive what would appear to others as obvious—like a ship! A few years ago I was sailing late one night on a beautiful spinnaker run to Vancouver. Up ahead I clearly saw the Sand Heads Light off the wide shallows of Roberts Bank, near Vancouver Airport. I just had to skim past the western side of that light. I had no need to check my position, but I turned on the GPS just to alleviate boredom. Strangely, the GPS showed that I was a mile farther west than what I could see was my position from the light ahead. With about 1 mile to go, I suddenly realized that I was deliberately attempting to skim closely across the bow of a ship that was steaming at full speed in the opposite direction! I was looking at the solid red light on its starboard side, not at the blinking red Sand Heads Light.

In another instance I was well down the Juan de Fuca Strait and could see the red starboard light of a ship ahead as I tacked over to the south side. But it was no problem; it was clearly going to pass a long distance in front of me. It was quite a feeling to look up and see the light change to green. I had just crossed the ship's bow without even knowing.

Every sailor knows how different things look at night. It is impossible to perceive the distance to a light, and it is impossible to notice if a light is moving or stationary. I have no doubt that Jessica could have been subject to change blindness or inattentional blindness, or the 3:00 A.M. effect. It does not matter what we call it. It only matters that singlehanded sailors recognize that in the middle of the night, nothing works—not the eyes, rarely the muscles, and certainly not the brain.

The ATSB report goes on to discuss fatigue at length:

It is possible that she was feeling the detrimental effects of fatigue when she failed to see *Silver Yang*.

In the context of human performance, fatigue is a physical and psychological condition that is primarily caused by prolonged wakefulness and/or insufficient or disturbed sleep. Fatigue can be caused by a number of different sources, including time on task, time awake, acute and chronic sleep debt, and circadian disruption.

The Australian House of Representatives inquiry into managing fatigue in the transportation industry stated that an individual who is fatigued is unable to function at a normal level of alertness and efficiency, possibly leading to slowed reaction times, reduced vigilance, memory lapses, inattention to tasks, complacency, lack of awareness, lack of communication, mood changes, lack of judgment, decline of motivation, and falling asleep.

The skipper was using regular 5 minute catnaps as a fatigue counter measure. However, while using naps can be effective, most guidance suggests that a minimum 15 minute nap every 2–3 hours is required and that napping is not effective long term.

The skipper reported that she did not feel fatigued. However, studies have found that there is a discrepancy between self-reported fatigue and actual fatigue levels and that people generally underestimate their level of fatigue.

The skipper had been awake for approximately 17 hours without a proper sleep and, therefore, it is likely that she may have been experiencing an associated decrease in her level of performance.

The electronic aids: *Ella's Pink Lady* was fitted with radar and an AIS unit, both of which were operating at the time of the collision.

It was the skipper's habit to use the Simrad Navstation in split screen mode. In this mode half the screen displayed radar information and the other half displayed an electronic chart with an overlay of icons representing vessels identified by the AIS interface.

While it is possible the skipper looked at the radar and AIS displays and did not see *Silver Yang*, there are further reasons as to why these devices did not alert her to the ship's presence.

Radar. It was the skipper's routine to set the radar guard ring alarms to operate only when she was sleeping. She stated that this was probably because the alarms sometimes activated when a ghost echo crossed the guard ring, causing her unnecessary distraction. As a result, the guard rings were not set for activation in the period leading up to the collision. When the skipper set them prior to taking the catnap, *Silver Yang* was only about 1 mile away, a position that was already inside both guard rings. As a result the alarm never activated and the skipper was not alerted to the ship's presence.

AIS. The Simrad Navstation AIS would have displayed an icon indicating *Silver Yang*'s position well before the collision, but the skipper did not detect its presence on the AIS display. The skipper had not set the AIS alarm function. . . . The skipper demonstrated an understanding of the basic workings of the AIS unit, but had not been formally trained in its use. As a result it is possible that she was not aware of all its features and how to best utilize them.

These last two notes indicate to me that if we are to rely on technology, we had better understand the settings that we use. As a simple example, if Watson had understood that her radar alarm would not sound for objects closer than 2 miles, she might have made a better, more thorough visual scan around the boat. In her late-night mind, she was probably thinking, "The radar alarm is set, I'll make a quick look around and be fine." Had she consciously thought about the 2-mile radius, she might have been more thoughtful about looking around.

It was usual for the skipper to set the Nav-Station display in split-screen mode with the radar section displaying head-up information and the chart displaying north-up. In this situation, with the vessel heading southward, the two side-by-side displays were essentially upside down with respect to each other. The AIS chart would have shown *Silver Yang* below her position, but on the radar, the ship would have been displayed above the yacht's position. It is possible that the skipper may have been confused by the different ways in which the information was displayed. She may have detected *Silver Yang* and wrongly concluded that it did not pose a collision risk.

This method of using the split screen with different orientations was a mistake, even at the best of times, let alone in the middle of the night. I think that this would also be a great way of running into a shoreline in the fog. **It makes much more sense to have all screens set to a head-up orientation.** If I look up on the screen I see the same thing as when I look up on the boat. If I look left or right on the screen, I see the same thing as if I look left or right on the boat. And below me on the screen—I'm looking backward on the boat. It just makes sense.

From the point of view of *Silver Yang*, the ATSB found that *Ella's Pink Lady* was not fitted with a passive radar reflector: "The yacht was equipped with an Echomax X-Band radar transponder. However at the time of the collision the Echo-max was turned off. When interviewed, the yacht skipper was not able to offer an explanation as to why it was not turned on." On board *Silver Yang*, the ATSB reported: "It is possible that the second mate did observe the radar display from time to time and that he did not detect *Ella's Pink Lady* because the radar was not correctly tuned or the echo provided by the yacht was either faint or intermittent."

Not much can be said about this. A passive radar reflector is a standard part of every boat's equipment for nighttime sailing. I can't imagine leaving the dock without it. With the active reflector, it was probably that she just forgot. How many electronic devices did Jessica have on board? For a singlehander, simplicity is always better than complexity.

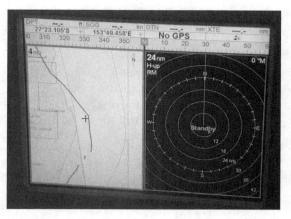

The display from Watson's sailboat—the displays were set for different orientations.

Ella's Pink Lady was fitted with a Class B AIS unit, which was operating at the time of the collision. While the operation of the unit was checked before departure, it was not transmitting the correct vessel type information. Hence it is likely that the vessel type information had not correctly been entered into the AIS unit prior to departure.

As a result, *Ella's Pink Lady* was visible to AIS units fitted on board other ships. However it was indicating the vessel type as "unassigned."

On board *Silver Yang*, the ATSB reported: The vessel was detected by the ship's AIS at least 38 minutes before the collision. The data indicate that the ship's AIS unit did not display the yacht's name or ship type, only its MMSI number and specific navigational data. While the ship's AIS would not have alerted the second mate to the presence of *Ella's Pink Lady* or a yacht, it would have indicated that there was a vessel in close proximity.

However, the second mate did not detect the yacht until he saw it visually 2½ minutes before the collision. This indicates that during the period of time leading up to the collision, (at least 38 minutes) he either did not check the AIS unit display or did not comprehend the information it was displaying.

Since we singlehanders cannot get every second mate on every ship to keep a better watch, the only thing to do is make sure that we take every possible step to keep out of the way of ships and make sure they see us and recognize what we are, even if we still can't depend on them turning.

Dag Pike's earlier comment appears to hold true: "After all, they [singlehanders] will be the ones to suffer if a collision occurs." This suffering might be physical, or it might be financial when the lawyers get involved. But I tend to agree that we are the ones who will suffer.

When Jeanne Socrates started on her second round-the-world attempt, I wished her a "great adventure." When she asked why I didn't wish her a "safe trip," I said that if her only goal was safety, she would not be doing it in the first place. Singlehanded sailing is a necessarily dangerous activity. We do it because the enjoyment we get outweighs the risks.

A TESTAMENT TO THE CENTERBOARD SONAR

From a letter I wrote to *48 North* magazine:

I can personally speak to the incredible technological advancement of the centerboard sonar. My Tanzer 22, *Foolish Laughter,* was equipped with this marvel of advanced engineering and I made use of it numerous times while sailing in Ottawa. In fact, on the very day of my boat launch, my wife and I used the CBS to discover that we were getting too close to the Quebec side of the river. (I think it could sense the maple syrup.) A simple gybe got us back into navigable waters with nary a scratch. Three months later, while singlehanding in the club's 50-mile race, I used the CBS on three occasions. (Refer to the poem "The Foolish 50 Miles" on page 20.)

But my greatest testament is when the CBS actually saved my life! I was returning to the club after a nice day sail when a massive thunder squall came up. As could be expected, my outboard chose this moment to die and I could not enter the harbor in such high winds. I dropped the genoa and aimed east above the rapids that sit between the club and the Quebec side. With only the mainsail up I was not able to tack into the wind, so I traveled much further than planned. I was halfway across the river when the CBS alarm sounded.

I raced to the bow and threw out my anchor and a full ten feet of rode. Thanks to my strong belief that Poseidon cares for foolish sailors, the anchor stuck fast under a rock. Under strong winds and even stronger current, the boat swung to sit a mere six feet above the start of a 100-yard stretch of rapids.

There were no tow facilities on the river, so I dialed 911, and a half hour later the fire department sent out their rescue RIB. But they were equipped only to rescue people, not boats, so my beloved was left in the most treacherous part of the river. I found a volunteer to tow my boat, but he would not go anywhere near the rapids. It was quite amusing to ask the fire department to put me back on board. They had to seek permission from several levels of command before they agreed. Once the boat was ashore, the local media showed up and asked if I'd be willing to take the boat out again, just for pictures.

It is based on this adventure that I started a Coast Guard Auxiliary at the club. We applied for a grant from provincial lottery funds for a rescue RIB, complete with twin 250 hp outboards and a launch ramp. So it may be said that the centerboard sonar saved both my life and perhaps many, many lives in the future.

CHAPTER 11 **MANAGING HEAVY WEATHER**

Excellent books have been written on managing heavy weather and I do not want to simply duplicate their information here. I refer the reader to *Heavy Weather Sailing* by Peter Bruce and Adlard Coles and *Surviving the Storm* by Steve and Linda Dashew as two excellent references (see Bibliography). However, it is important to adapt this information to be useful for the lone skipper.

In this chapter I want to present a few examples of situations that have been faced by typical off-shore singlehanded sailors on what would normally be considered safe voyages. Under some circumstances there will simply be too much weather, for too long, for the singlehander to manage. A boat need not be south of Cape Horn to face these conditions; they can be found on a simple return trip from Hawaii in the height of summer. Let us take a look at these situations with a critical eye and an attempt to learn something valuable, while we are safe in our living room onshore.

HEAVY WEATHER ACCOUNTS

Following is an excerpt from Skip Allen's narrative about his return to California aboard *Wildflower*, a Wylie Custom 27, just after winning the 2008 Single-handed Transpac. Allen's log is an incredibly well-written adventure story and can be enjoyed for that reason alone. But I am presenting this as a real opportunity for learning. The reader should pay specific attention to:

- Allen's long sailing experience.
- His positions on the chart, sailing direction, and wind direction.

- The long-range forecasts that he was working with.
- His physical and mental condition.
- The boat's condition—including the hatch-boards.
- Communications with friends and with the Coast Guard, in particular via single-side-band radio (SSB).

His words should be considered as a significant lesson for anyone taking up this sport:

On Saturday, 8/23, 10 days after leaving Hanalei, we were halfway home to Santa Cruz with 1190 miles to go. We had passed the Pacific High, and were running in the Westerlies at latitude 38–38 x longitude 147–17. So far, the passage had been going well, my sixth return passage from Hawaii aboard *Wildflower*. But an ominous note on the thrice daily weather fax charts was the notation "GALE" between our position and the Pacific Coast.

I began to plan for this possible gale by increasing latitude, slowing down, and closely monitoring projected GRIB files out to 144 hours. It appeared from all forecasts that we needed to slow down for at least 48 hours to let the gale ahead abate. However, it is against my instincts to slow a boat down, and so with difficulty I reefed the main and dropped the jib in 8 knots of wind, reducing speed to a sedate 3.5 knots in smooth seas.

On Wednesday, 8/27, the morning GRIB file showed the area of most wind ahead was between 124 and 128 degrees, with no weather abatement until at least Monday, 9/1 earliest. Dwight Odom on *Na Na*, 450 miles ahead, had reported gusts of 42.5 knots from the north between latitude 127–128 and having to run off under storm jib 80 miles. *Na Na* reported 20 foot seas the previous night near 37 x 124–30. I hoped that *Wildflower*, by being at the latitude 40 degrees, would allow us to run off 180 miles to the latitude of Santa Cruz, should conditions worsen.

On Friday, 8/29, at sunset near 40N x 130W, conditions began to rapidly deteriorate. I changed to the #4 (75% short hoist) and storm staysail, dropping the main completely.

The following day, Saturday, 8/30, with Santa Cruz 365 miles on a bearing of 095 T, we were having to run off due south (180 T) in winds 30–35 knots. By 15:30, the sail combination proved too much, and I dropped the #4, flying the storm staysail (39 sq. feet) and towing a 30" diameter metal hooped drogue. It was uncomfortable, windy, and rolly that night, with the cockpit filling about every five minutes, and the boat being knocked down to 70 degrees at least half a dozen times. *Wildflower*'s shallow cockpit and oversize drains allowed full drainage in about 90 seconds, and this was not a problem.

The electric Auto Helm 1000+ tiller pilot was doing an amazing job steering, as it was being continuously drenched, even submerged. The Sail-O-Mat windvane was useless preventing or correcting breaking wave induced broaches and I retracted its oar to avoid fouling the drogue rode.

On Sunday, 8/31, the wind was steady 30–35, with higher gusts and a confused wave train from the NW, N, and NE. At 09:15 I winched in the drogue to change from a hi-tech spinnaker sheet to stretchy nylon anchor line. Unfortunately, I found the drogue had split, and was no longer effective. I deployed my spare drogue, but without a metal hoop, it would periodically collapse astern in a breaking crest. I think a series drogue is the best available. But

really, anything will work as a drogue, including a tire, milk crates, or anchor and chain.

(With my drogue, I was still going 4–6 knots under bare poles. With no drogue, I was surfing faster, 6–10 knots. Taking off on a breaking wave with no one on deck is a recipe for a roll over as the boat could easily get sideways and broach. I believe my use of a drogue was justified in slowing the speed and keeping the stern aligned with the oncoming waves. The amount of water coming over the stern was manageable and not a significant problem. There was no water getting below, as my hatch boards were bullet proof. Had a breaking sea come over the side of the boat, things would have become more serious.)

At noon, it looked like the gale was lessening. I left the safety of the cabin, and with two safety harnesses affixed to the windward rail, began to hand steer eastward on a reach with the #4. It was mogul sailing at its best, having to radically bear away to avoid hissing 8–12 foot breaking crests on the top of 15–30 foot seas.

At sunset I again went below with the Auto Helm tiller pilot continuing to steer nicely under #4 jib. Not long after, the wind came on to blow from the NNW, and the seas began to build further. That night I stayed suited up below with full foulies, headlamp, and harness, ready to dash out the hatch and take the tiller if the autopilot failed and we subsequently rounded up. In addition, I dropped the storm staysail, as we were running too fast at 6–9 knots. Under bare poles DDW [dead downwind], the speed was better at 5–7 knots.

What followed ultimately played into the following day's events. During the long night, my third in this particular gale, breaking crests would poop the boat about every five minutes, filling the cockpit and surging against the companionway hatch boards. Even though I had gone to lengths for many years to insure fire hose watertight integrity of the companionway hatch, I found the power of the breaking wave crests slamming the boat would cause water to forcefully spray around the edges of the hatch boards and into the cabin.

During the long wait for daylight, I had more than enough time to ponder what might happen if the autopilot was damaged or was washed off its mount. I had two spare tiller pilots. But it would take several minutes, exposed in the cockpit, on my knees, to hook up a replacement in the cockpit, on a dark night, when the boat was being periodically knocked down and the cockpit swept.

In addition, I pondered the fate of the *Daisy* that had been lost in this spring's Lightship Race, presumably crushed and sunk by a large breaking wave. I also reminded myself I was responsible for not only my own life, but was also a family caregiver at home.

There was no doubt that if *Wildflower* tiller pilot was lost that we would round up and be at the mercy of these breaking waves, some of which I estimated to be in the vicinity of 25–35 feet, and as big as I hadn't seen since the '79 Fastnet Race storm on *IMP*.

The anxiety and stress of this night, with the whine of the wind in the rigging, the wave crests slamming into the hatch boards, and the 70-degree knockdowns that would launch me across the cabin, created serious doubts that we could continue this for another night, much less the 3–4 days the conditions were expected to continue.

The boat was fine, and had suffered no serious damage. My physical health was OK, but I could see with minimum sleep that my decision making could be beginning to be compromised

At 0715 the following morning, Monday, 9/1, I sat phoned my long-time sailing friend, ham radio contact, router, navigator and weatherman, Joe Buck, in Redondo Beach. Joe and I had maintained two per day ham radio schedule since leaving Hanalei, and he had instant Internet access to all forecast weather and wave charts. I explained the current situation to Joe: that I'd had a difficult night, and wasn't sure I could safely continue.

Joe's weather info had the highest wind and wave overhead on my current drift southward continuing for at least another three days, with continuing gale force winds and 18–22' significant wave height.

I asked Joe for help in some difficult decision making I had to do. First, would he phone San Francisco Coast Guard Search and Rescue (SAR), and query what the protocol was for asking for assistance, all the while making sure the Coast Guard understood I was not in trouble and was not asking for help at this time. (Coast Guard NMC Pt. Reyes, Kodiak, and Hono were not answering my radio calls on their published 4, 6, 8, and 12 mg frequencies, both simplex and duplex.)

Joe called back an hour later (0830) on ham radio 40 meters and said that Lt. Saxon at SAR reported no military assets within 200 miles or 20 hours, that *Wildflower* was 200 miles beyond helicopter range, but that there was an inbound container ship *Toronto* coming in my direction at an undetermined distance.

Joe helped me to understand if the boat were lost, I would likely be lost also. But if that I left *Wildflower* in advance, that only the boat would be lost. I told Joe of my hesitation of putting my life in the hands of a possibly foreign crew on a big commercial ship during a transfer off *Wildflower* in these conditions, especially at night. We agreed that a decision had to be arrived at soon, before 11:30, and before *Toronto* passed by.

I spent the next hour, sitting on the cabin sole on my life raft, debating whether to ask for assistance in leaving my beloved *Wildflower*. "Fleur" was my home, consort, and magic carpet that I had built 34 years ago. I cried, pounded my fist, looked out through the hatch numerous times at the passing wave mountains, remembered all the good times I had shared with *Wildflower*. And came to a decision.

I was three days/nights in the gale. Except for a few hours, I was below decks, much the safest place to be. "Sleep" was not possible given the conditions, though I dozed in a half awake state for many hours. Despite wearing earplugs, and a watch cap pulled over my eyes, the whine of the wind in the rigging, the hissing and crunching of the waves as they came aboard, the motion of the boat, and the worry, anticipation, and feeling of helplessness precluded any sound sleep: I was dressed and ready to immediately take the deck in the event of calamity or loss of steering if the autopilot was swept overboard.

This led to exhaustion, a state I was familiar with from my many miles of singlehanding. I knew that both intelligent decision making and physical stamina was compromised by exhaustion. It was important to me to monitor my mental and physical well being, knowing I was deteriorating because of exhaustion. I was likely to be called upon to perform some self rescue, and I wanted to be in the best possible condition to successfully pull that off if/when the time came.

At 11:15 I called Joe back and told him to again call Lt. Saxon at SAR and inform her that I was asking for assistance. Joe called back and informed me that *Toronto* was 5–6 hours away, and that SAR needed to hear from me directly as to my request.

At 12:00, like a gopher popping out of its hole, I slid the hatch open to get a clear sat phone signal, and called SAR. Lt. Saxon already knew my details and position, and only asked "What are you requesting?" I replied, "I am asking for assistance to be removed from my boat."

We kept the conversation short and to the point, due to my exposure topsides with the sat phone. She said the MSC *Toronto* would be requested to divert, that I was NOT to trigger the EPIRB, but that I was to take the EPIRB with me when I left *Wildflower*. Contrary to published reports, at no time did I call "PAN PAN," and no com schedule was kept with the Coast Guard, although I did check in with Joe every 30 minutes on ham radio.

Lt. Saxon also said that if I left my boat, she would be considered "derelict" and a hazard to navigation. I assured her I would not leave my boat floating or derelict.

An hour later, at 1300, *Wildflower*'s AIS alarm rang. MSC *Toronto* was showing 30 miles away, and closing at 23.4 knots from the south west. I had to do some fast planning.

But with no idea how the transfer would be made (jump, swim, climb, hoist?), I didn't know what I could pack into my bag, bags, or backpack. I decided on my documents, wallet, passport, laptop, camera, cell phone and sat phone, logbook, EPIRB, and a change of clothes and shoes. All this I bagged into waterproof bags. And in a moment of whimsy, decided to try and offload the two Single Handed Transpac perpetual trophies, as they had 30 year historical value to our Race.

At eight miles, the captain of the MSC *Toronto* rang on the VHF. He spoke perfect English, and as I had a visual, directed him to alter 20 degrees to starboard to intercept. He explained his ship was over 1,000 feet long, that he would lay her parallel to the waves and make a lee at a forward speed of Slow Ahead (6 knots).

The captain also explained that I would board his ship from a rope ladder that led to the pilot's door, on the aft starboard side.

I asked if he could slow to a speed between 3–4 knots, and he willingly agreed to try.

At five miles, a sharp eyed lookout on MSC *Toronto* sighted *Wildflower* ahead. But the ship's radar did not register my boat until 2.5 miles in these conditions.

At 1415, one of the world's biggest container ships was bearing down on *Wildflower*, less than five boat lengths (125 feet) dead ahead, the huge bulb bow extending 20 feet and making a five foot breaking wave. With my heart in my throat, I motored down the starboard side of a gigantic black wall, made a U turn, and pulled alongside the pilot's door and rope ladder.

The crew threw a heaving line, and in the next five minutes we transferred three bags, including the perpetual trophies. Knowing I was next, I jumped below decks, said a final quick goodbye, and pulled the already disconnected hose off the engine salt water intake thru hull.

Back on deck, I reached for the bottom rung of the Jacob's ladder, which was alternately at head height, or 10 feet out of reach, depending on the ship's roll. I grabbed hold, jumped, and did a pull up onto the ladder, and climbed up, wearing a 15-pound backpack with my most valuable possessions and EPIRB.

At 1429, on Monday, 9/1, at position 35–17 x 126–38, the MSC *Toronto* resumed its voyage to Long Beach, leaving *Wildflower* alone to bang and scrape her way down the aft quarter of the ship and disappear under the stern. I watched, but could barely see through my tears.

Four hours and 100 miles SE of where I left *Wildflower* I was on the bridge of MSC *Toronto* watching the anemometer True Wind Speed graph continuing to register 32–35 knots. From 140 feet off the water, the swells below still looked impressive, and the ship was rolling enough to send spray above the top containers on the forward part of the ship.

For the next 24 hours aboard MSC *Toronto* (1065' LOA, too wide for Panama) I was treated with the utmost kindness and compassion by Capt. Ivo Hruza and his crew of 24. We stood watch together, ate together, told stories, viewed family photo albums, discussed the world situation, toured the ship and engine room (12-cylinder, 93,360-horsepower diesel). By the time we came down the Santa Barbara Channel, ahead of schedule, and docked at Long Beach, I felt a part of this happy crew of 6 nationalities. I could not have been assisted by a better or more professionally manned ship.

On Tuesday afternoon, after clearing customs and immigration aboard, I shook hands with each and every crew member. And descended the gangway alone, to meet Joe, sister Marilee, and begin New Beginnings.

I will never forget *Wildflower*. She took a beating in this gale. She never let me down, and took me to amazing places, where we met wonderful people and made new friends.

In this time of loss, a most wonderful thing is happening: many loved ones, friends,

interested parties, and people I've never met are closing a circle of love around the mourning and celebration of *Wildflower*.

Treasure Each Day,
Skip Allen 9/3/08

After reading Allen's great adventure, we need to look at the other side—from the rescuer's point of view. Here is an incredible story from the 2013 Bermuda 1–2, as told by Dan Alonso, singlehanding the Hallberg-Rassy 49 *Halcyon,* and his rescue of Jan Steyn from the stricken Columbia 32C *Solid Air*:

The race was off. Day one the winds were enough to get *Halcyon* moving. The second day it shut down. Doldrums. Fortunately, it didn't last. When the wind returned, it would change direction and make this a reaching race.

The router shows the wind will be around 18 knots out of the south for days. I'm hoping it's enough but more would be better. I need it big enough to shut down the other boats. *Halcyon* can take it. Heading to the entry point in the Gulf Stream, the wind continues to build. *Halcyon* is starting to go.

Out in front of me are two boats, *Bent* (S2 9.1) and *Kontradiction* (C&C 110). *Bent* is in my class. They are far away but good targets. The wind is getting strong. I am nearly at full sail, just a small reef in the main. I can feel *Halcyon* pushing forward. The water is now a steady sound, a crushing wave being pushed off *Halcyon*'s bow. It is "go" time, and *Halcyon* is a raging bull just driving through the building sea. After a few years of trying to race this "north sea" cruiser and getting killed in light air, we finally have the race conditions *Halcyon* thrives in: big winds and nasty sea state.

Since entering the stream, *Halcyon* has not dropped below 11 knots over the bottom and often in the 12s. We had spent over $5,000 getting the auto pilot repaired just days before the race, but I'm now listening to the motor over working and I'm feeling sick. I've just sailed from Charleston to Bermuda and then Bermuda to Newport solo with a constantly failing auto pilot—1,400 miles of offshore sailing without a pilot. I just can't bear the emotional stress of a failing pilot again.

Halcyon is no longer keeping her course. It's happening again, no pilot.

The backup plan for this summer of racing was to use the Hydrovane, "Hydi," a wind driven autopilot that we installed just before the Charleston to Bermuda race. At the start of that race, and just a few hours before entering into the Gulf Stream, Hydi broke off the stern. I was barely able to wrestle it back aboard.

Hydi is now reinstalled but completely untested. I'm not sure if it's big enough to steer the boat or if the seas will tear it off the stern again. Fortunately in this whole mess, the wind is on the nose and likely to remain a close reach for the entire race. If both pilots fail, I take comfort knowing I can lock the wheel and at least balance the helm and get close enough to hand steer into Bermuda.

There's no stopping *Halcyon*. Pilot or not. She's crushing the ocean. I feel like I'm standing on a freight train and we're reeling in *Bent* and *Kontradiction* fast. I finally pass them and start looking for more. Who's next? A day later, I'm hearing VHF transmission. It's from boats in the first class. I thought they would be long gone. Am I doing that well? Maybe this could be my race. Neither pilot is able to steer the boat on their own so I'm using them together. Hydi takes the load off and the autopilot steers the rest. My pilots are a team. It's working and if I can hold it for a few days, I'll finally have my race.

Then the call comes. *Halcyon* being hailed. Someone's requesting assistance. He's got an accent. I think it's *Kontradiction*. Are you kidding me? This is my time, and the race I've been hoping for. I'm sick for getting beat in light winds. I've got no dependable auto pilot but it's working and I have to stop? I'm pretty sure I'm the only boat in my class doing 9+ knots in this crap.

I think, "Assistance? What does that mean?" We're 250 miles from Bermuda in the middle of the ocean. There is another boat on its way, but I'm

closer. The sun will set shortly. He wants to know if I can help. The other boat is at the back of his class. He can't win. Why stop my race? I'm thinking why me? I can win, *Halcyon*'s killing it. Why me? He's 17 miles away and I'm 5. What's the big deal?

And then it takes a moment, but it settles in. Assistance! This guy is leaving his boat! You don't give assistance in this crap. It's blowing and the seas are big. It's freaking bad out here. This is an abandon ship. He needs to leave his boat. Something bad has happened and he's leaving his boat. My race is done. This guy needs help.

I douse the genoa and put away the main. I hail Mike Schum from *Kontradiction*. He had a strong accent and sounded just like the guy asking for assistance. I was sure this assistance call was Mike. *Kontradiction* hails back saying he's fine. He doesn't know what I'm talking about.

I was just talking to this guy. He told me he's losing his keel and needs help, he's abandoning ship. I quit the race and he's fine? What the f#ck? Am I losing my mind? Did I imagine that? What's going on here? I hail back to the distressed boat. He responds. The vessel's name is *Solid Air*, it's not *Kontradiction*. It's real and this was a glimpse of my potentially fragile emotional state. I actually thought I may have imagined it. No kidding, questioning my mind.

Solid Air communicates his lat/lon. Just writing it down is a task. Every time I leave the helm to communicate or work the plotter, *Halcyon* breaches, leaning over a good 30–40 degrees. Without the pilot and in these seas, everything is crazy hard and now I'm breaching every fifth wave. I finally create a waypoint and get going. He's downwind and it looks like it will take about 45 minutes to get there. I've got to hand steer. I'm sailing with our small wheel and the steering is stiff, just turning the wheel is a workout. I've got the auxiliary on and just the storm sail up. The seas are about 8–12 feet. I'm running with the wind and seeing 30–35 mph.

Halcyon is surfing down each wave. It's hard to keep her straight. She wants to veer off. How the hell am I going to get this guy aboard? I know the life sling drill, but really? In this sh#t?

After about 20 minutes I hail the skipper to work out our plan. He's thinking of putting out a few fenders. Right! I hail back, "Skipper, you're going to get wet."

The tension is building. I know I've got to get him but I've got no pilot, can't steer the boat worth a crap, and it's really really awful out. I'm getting closer so I call to update his lat/lon. He now gives me coordinates that are different. I'm not talking drifting a half mile different. He's 8 miles upwind, where I just came from.

The sun's going down, 8 miles upwind, an hour and a half ride, and you're where? What the f#ck? Where are you? *Kontradiction* is listening and also takes the lat/lon. Mike, skipper of *Kontradiction*, is a comforting voice and another mind working on this feels good. I'm terrified of wasting more time motoring to new positions where he is not. Dousing the storm jib, I realize it's windy, really windy. The sail lifts me off the deck with ease.

The drive upwind was nuts. The waves were now pushing 15 feet. The bow was launching into the sky. Things that had never fallen in the cabin after years of storm sailing were now flying about. With no canvas and a big sea state, *Halcyon* is pitch poling, badly, in all directions. Steering is far beyond difficult, nearly impossible.

I start thinking it was beyond me. I can't do it. After years of being proud as "Mr. Bad-Ass-Ocean-Storm-Sailor," I can't do this. I just can't do this. It's too much. What do I do? I still don't know where he is. What if this new location is also wrong? The sun's on the horizon now and I'm an hour and a half downwind. Are you kidding me? I'm broken. This should be for helicopters, but we're too far offshore. What do I do? I can't do this.

As a wrestler, you could break my arm and I wouldn't quit, but this is too much. Just steering is a monumental task. It takes all my focus and energy. Mike had offered help and I had turned it down. How is that going to help? Two boats? More boats to crash into each other. I'm suddenly overwhelmed with the consideration

that I simply will not be able to find him. Here I am terrified of the pickup and I can't find him. I ask Mike to stick around. Two sets of eyes are better than one. I request a flare. I'm hoping for something visual. *Solid Air* feels we're too far apart to see the flare and wants to wait. It makes sense, so we wait.

In Mike's effort to join the rescue, he loses his jib while dousing and wraps a jib sheet in his prop. I'm already being pushed. Pushed beyond what I'm able to handle, and now I'm thinking, is this going to turn into two rescues? *Solid Air* hails. He's using AIS to try to get a heading. He tells me I need to head 135 degrees. This makes no sense. This is not in the right direction. It's a least 100 degrees off. Where is he? I'm just sick, getting my ass kicked heading upwind, the sun's down and I still don't know where he is.

While Mike is trying to recover, *Solid Air* fires a flare. I see it. Thank God, I see it. What a beautiful thing. A SOLAS rocket flare hanging in the sky. I look at the compass. It's about 180 degrees. I realize that I need to turn on the compass light for the next flare. It's too dark to read it. When I leave the helm, the boat falls off and is slammed by a wave. More crap flying around the cabin.

I'm cold, soaked and struggle to climb the companion way to get the boat back upwind. Another flare. This one is closer and now at 220 degrees. I request he put all lights on so he'd be easier to see. As I approach, I finally get visual contact. I need to get near enough to evaluate this carefully. This could be really bad if we collide.

I come around and approach from upwind. I didn't want him getting blown down on me and foul our rigs. I'm really close, 200 feet. Each wave is a pitch poling nightmare. All of a sudden he's gone. He was just right in front of me and now he's gone. Lost in the dark.

I climb out of the cockpit to try and see him. Having left the helm, *Halcyon* is veering out of control again. I'm about to hit him. He's right here somewhere and I can't see him. The seas are huge and *Halcyon* will crush him if we collide. I know I'm only seconds from impact. I can't see him. Maybe he turned down wind and his lights are faced away. I finally see him and climb back to the helm. With all my might, I'm straining to keep him in sight. I can't lose him now.

I later learned from Jan that he had put the boat away, turned off the lights and secured the cabin at my approach.

Solid Air is leaning funny. Her stern to the wind. And she's lurching strangely. *Halcyon* is wanting to surf each wave. It's just too much. Docking a 27 ton boat, heeling 35 degrees while surfing at 10 knots. This is just insane.

I had decided earlier to use the sling on a spin sheet. I wanted the heavier line for winching and more mass to throw. The line that comes with the sling floats and the spin sheet does not. I'm risking a prop wrap if I miss and that just CAN NOT happen. The line is now carefully coiled, short and sitting on the stern quarter. It's time.

I head to *Solid Air*. *Halcyon* is charging at her stern quarter. At about 40 feet from collision, I turn the helm to port. I know she would fall off like a breach and as she does, I run for the sling. I'm now about 20 feet away from him but heading away. I throw the sling and it hits him in the chest. I scurry back to the helm to back down on the auxiliary and ditch as much speed as I can. *Halcyon*'s breaching.

Jan, skipper of *Solid Air*, has his arm through the sling. I run the line to the winch and with a power drill begin hauling. *Halcyon*'s momentum launches him from his stern and he's skipping across the water.

I got him. Thank God I got him.

I knew this had to fly first shot. A second try would be in total darkness; he would be impossible to find. As he approaches the rail, the battery quits. I try to lift him but it is not going to happen. I go to the winch and start to crank by hand. It's taking too long. He is being slammed under the *Halcyon*'s hull with each wave. We can hear each other. He is being battered under the hull but is okay.

I suddenly think of the boarding ladder. I quickly dig it out and put it on the rail. It is still

too high. I continue to winch. Just a little higher. He is finally able to reach it. I lean over and together with a last effort, he is aboard.

Halcyon is still bare poled and out of control. I raise the storm jib and put out some mainsail. With *Halcyon*'s helm balanced, I can lock the wheel and get us under control. I am back under way but hardly a racing clip. I have no idea what had just happened. I am wet and miserable. Jan calls the race committee to update them while I shower. How nuts. Still in a storm, just completed a rescue and I want to be showered and dry. Needing to wash off this trauma.

Jan showers next. I give him dry clothes. We eat paella I had made the day before. I put him to bed and turn *Halcyon* back towards Bermuda. Pulling an email from the Sat phone, I discover that *Aggressive*, the leading boat, is in front of me. I want to race but I'm struggling. I'm struggling to find the drive, the courage to sail aggressively. I have smaller sails up.

Balancing the helm with bigger sail area and autopilot issues is too much; not now. I'm still freaked out and feeling timid. Before the rescue, *Halcyon* was cranking along at 9.5 knots in what was approaching gale conditions. We were now comfortable and going 6.5 so I set my alarms and sleep.

Waking, I find that *Bent* is in front of me and beatable. Jan explains to me that I would be given back the lost time from rescue. So once again, it's "go" time. I tell *Halcyon*, "*Bent*'s in front of you." Like an excited puppy, she lights up as we start chasing him down. I pop the Genoa, unfurl the main and she is powered up again. At 9.5 knots she is quickly closing the gap. I know the dream of winning first in class is not likely. I just want to cross the line ahead of *Bent*. I need to find the racer in me, something stronger than the broken rescuer.

It looks like I'm going to roll *Bent* again. The winds are blowing 28 and *Halcyon*'s loving it but there's a problem. Without a pilot I can't come off the wind. I need another 30 degrees to avoid hitting the reefs. It's still too far to hand steer. I'm catching up quickly but I'm going the wrong

HEAVY WEATHER READING

Singlehanding presents its own challenges in heavy weather because there is no one else to take watch. Every book written on the great singlehanded races contains long chapters about the fight against storms. They all tell the story of spending 24, 36, 48, or more hours at the helm. Here is an excerpt from Derek Lundy's famous book *Godforsaken Sea*, published in 1998, about the BOC Challenge:

The wryly laconic Australian David Adams, with his fifty-foot boat *True Blue*, was sailing right up with the big boats and leading class two as he sailed his boat like a big dingy.

"I'm absolutely stuffed," he reported to race headquarters. "Been twenty-four hours at the wheel in 40 to 60 knots. Had four knockdowns, with the mast in the water. Once we went down a wave like that, on our ears. It's just survival out here, not racing."

He later wrote: "In a huge storm when you're running on sheer adrenaline, it's enough to get through the next half hour alive and bugger the race." "People often asked how I managed to hand-steer for hours and even days through these storms," he wrote. "Fear is a great motivator. I thought if I stopped steering I would die. Simple as that. So I kept steering."

way. If I reef, I may be able to come off wind and get my heading but I'll lose boat speed. With only a few miles to go I reef. *Halcyon* loses speed, and I know it's done. With a few tacks the race is over. My battle with *Bent* is done and it's time to just stop.

Arriving in Customs, I am greeted by Jan's wife. She is crying, hysterical. Barely able to make words, crying "thank you," calling me a hero. "Thank you for saving my husband."

I don't even understand. I am so blown away by her. This moment is a powerful shift. It cracks open my emotions. This was more than picking up another racer. In the harbor, alone again, anchor finally down, I lie on the fore deck and just lose it. Just cry and cry.

Everything had gone fine, and I'm just emotionally destroyed. The guy just needed assistance. Right! What is assistance 500 miles offshore? It's not bringing a guy a fan belt. It's one scary thing that leaves you depleted, damaged and grateful to have pushed through when you thought you could not.

[On corrected time, Dan Alonso on *Halcyon* finished second in class and fourth in fleet . . . with a little detour.]

KEY HEAVY WEATHER CONSIDERATIONS

What are the key considerations for a singlehander in bad weather? The skipper should know that bad weather does not just mean a single gust of wind or one bad wave. The books tell heroic stories about how the skipper had to cut away the mast after the boat rolled, but the books never talk about the wave conditions after the first roll. We need to remember that after the boat rolled, the weather did not suddenly turn calm. The winds are still blowing at 60 knots and the waves are still 30 feet high. The immediate repairs must be done in these extreme conditions. So the following points are vital:

Hatchboards, downflooding. Carry a second hatchboard that is much stronger than the day-to-day set. Perhaps a piece of three-quarter-inch plywood tightly fitted with gaskets would be appropriate. Keep the hatchboards closed and locked, and the boat well sealed at all times. Although the main hatch might be only 4 square feet in actual size, envision a 25-foot wave crashing over the stern directly into the hatchway. How much force does this wave carry and how much force will the hatchboards withstand? As well, it is guaranteed that the boat will broach beyond anything the skipper has experienced.

If the boat fills with water, it will destroy all of the electronic systems on board, most likely including the autopilot computer and the radio system. It is not difficult to imagine what it would be like to have to bail out the boat with water up to the bunks, at the same moment that all of the lines are detached and dragging overboard, at the same moment that the boom has broken at the gooseneck and the mainsail is bashing around.

On a crewed boat, the skipper would yell, "Anna, you get a bandage on Sharon's head and get her in a bunk. Helen, go below and bail like hell. Kayla and Alecia, you grab the lines and pull the mast back on board before it smashes the hull. Anita, try to get the radio working and notify the Coast Guard of our position. I'll do everything I can to keep our stern to the waves." An awful (and I use that term deliberately) lot will happen in a severe knockdown. A crewed boat is pushed to its limits, and they will have barroom stories for years. It is impossible to quantify the impact of the same situation to a singlehander.

Securing the boat. Make sure *everything* below is well secured. Absolutely every book about a singlehander in a storm describes how supplies and tools flew around the cabin and were broken or lost during a knockdown. After pitchpoling and breaking his mast at Cape Horn, Derek Hatfield used a Leatherman pocket knife to detach all of the rigging and release the mast before it smashed a hole in the boat. This was because all his tools, including a bolt cutter, were lost somewhere inside the boat. Before a voyage, a singlehander should imagine what would happen if Poseidon picked up the boat by its keel and shook it. This is exactly what a storm can do. The boat should be equipped with internal straps to secure all tools and supplies in place, whether they're on the cabin floor or in a locker.

Here is an excerpt from Jeanne Socrates' log just after a knockdown while rounding Cape Horn (www.SVNereida.com):

We were well heeled, and there were plenty of big seas . . . and suddenly, near 2:30 pm, while I was fortunately leaning against a wall in the head, all hell let loose—and everything that could move was re-located to the starboard side of the cabin. . . . Water was pouring in from under the sliding hatch and there was chaos everywhere. Slowly we righted and soon after I looked to see what damage there was—clearly there was some—no instruments, for a start! . . . but I could not budge the hatch to open it—try as might. . . ! I had to climb out of the aft cabin hatch to access the cockpit—which I'd already seen enough of to realize the boom was broken in half and the canopy/dodger over the companionway was missing, along with its framework. . . . There was safety glass everywhere. I soon realized why the hatch wouldn't slide open—the halyard bag full of heavy wet lines, was lying on top and was soon removed along with several lines lying loose . . . Going down below, I noticed the perspex hatch was cracked in half—a worry if we should ever get pooped. Next, I got the instruments working—a connection in the aft cabin had been hit by flying/sliding objects . . . In brief, I didn't know where to start . . . Tried to clear up a

The interior chaos after *Nereida's* knockdown while rounding Cape Horn. *(Courtesy Jeanne Socrates)*

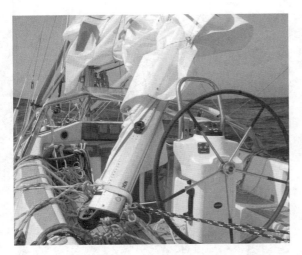

Nereida's broken boom pins the main hatchway closed after a knockdown rounding Cape Horn. *(Courtesy Jeanne Socrates)*

bit on deck—not much I could achieve there . . . down below—impossible to clear up wet things (all pillows and bedding were sopping wet at their end . . . still beam on to oncoming seas . . . not good).

Keeping fed, managing energy and sustenance. How difficult will it be to cook during a storm? A couple of thermoses of coffee and a thermos of hot stew cooked before the storm will be necessities. The skipper cannot send a designated cook below to whip up a hot meal. Many snacks and bottles of water should be kept in the cockpit within reach from the helm.

Heavy weather sails. The storm sails should be readily available. Most sailors never face a real blow. Many will not leave the dock with a wind above 25 knots. Their storm sails are neatly tucked in the bow of the boat, still in the bags. I know from experience that crawling to the bow in heavy weather is nigh on impossible. The storm sails should always be stored near the main hatch, and should be lashed on deck if bad weather is approaching. Of course, a storm is not the time when the skipper should be unpacking the storm jib stay sail, or be putting in a third reef for the first time in a year. I was recently out in a blow and discovered that three of the piston hanks on my storm jib were seized with salt. It was not pleasant sitting on the bow, in high winds, prying the hanks open with my multi-tool.

Self-steering preparations. What would happen in the highly likely circumstance of the self-steering system being destroyed? Skip Allen reported that his windvane was damaged beyond repair. He abandoned *Wildflower* partly because of his fear of losing the autopilot as well. Singlehanders should think about this before the voyage. What will he do if it occurs? This is not a reason to abandon a voyage, but it is a reason to think ahead. Is the skipper equipped, mentally and physically, to spend 24–48 hours at the helm?

Sleep. How will the singlehander sleep during the storm? As mentioned earlier, I have a "sitting hammock" in my cockpit with my back to the main hatch. I can sleep quite comfortably within reach of the autopilot, tiller, and sheets. Has the boat been set up to sleep on the floorboards, the lowest and most stable position on the boat?

The books about heavy weather were written for crewed boats. But in a crewed boat, all of the considerations above are not nearly as important. The crew can rotate at the helm and in their secure bunks. They have assigned tasks to cook, bail the boat, and work the lines. A singlehander does not have these luxuries.

DROGUES—SLOWING THE BOAT

Perhaps the greatest invention to assist the singlehander in storm conditions is the Jordan Series drogue. The Dashews have dedicated more than 50 pages of their book to the topic of drogues. It is clearly of importance during extreme situations.

If you cannot control your vessel in the existing conditions (whether due to wind and sea state or a steering-related mechanical problem), the use of a sea anchor or drogue may provide the only way to increase security. It is safe to say that in moderate storm conditions, where risks are low that a breaking sea will cause a capsize, slowing down is an excellent means of getting some rest.

If you are heading into the seas at speed, then the speed of the wave added to boat speed increases impact. On the other hand, when you are running with the sea, the speed of the boat is subtracted from wave speed. Consider that the impact energy of a wave is a function of its velocity squared, you can see how reducing this relative impact speed, even a modest amount, has a big effect on the energy absorbed. You can infer from this that the faster you go downwind, the less problem the waves will be. This is how it works in the real world.

While there are many variables, the one thing we can agree on is that being beam-on to the seas—or even at a 60 degree angle—is far more dangerous than having one or the other ends of the boat pointed into the waves.

However, we would like you to keep in mind that in many situations there comes a time when it is safer to have the boat moving—with the rudder under control so you can work the waves—than to be passively tied to some form of sea anchor or drogue.

Based on this, there is some agreement among sailors that it is better to use a drogue from the stern that slows but does not stop the boat.

The other method is to deploy a sea anchor from the bow of the boat. This is essentially a single large parachute. These were considered very useful for older-style, long-keel boats with attached rudders. These boats would maintain a steady position relative to the sea anchor, without swinging from side to side. Modern, fin keel boats will tend to yaw (swing back and forth), sometimes violently if held from the bow. This is because the wind pressure is on the bow of the boat, but the pivot point of the boat's swing is provided by the keel and rudder toward the stern.

A drogue from the stern performs two functions: first, it slows the boat, which is particularly important during wild surfs down a steep wave. As the Dashews intimate, a boat maintains control only if there is water flowing past the rudder. Thus the idea is not to stop the boat dead but just to slow it down to a manageable speed.

Skip Allen said that his drogue reduced boat speed by just 1–2 knots, but this was enough for him to wait out the storm below rather than at the helm. Skip's electronic autopilot was able to keep the boat on course under these conditions.

Second, the drogue keeps the stern of the boat

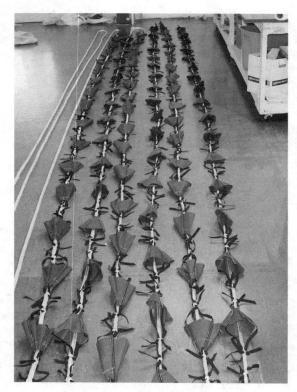

A Jordan Series drogue consists of fabric cones on a line deployed from the stern. *(Courtesy Dave Pelissier)*

A single cone of a series drogue. *(Courtesy Dave Pelissier)*

at right angles to the waves, particularly breaking waves. A boat that shifts from a right angle in a breaking wave will broach, or possibly roll or even pitchpole.

A Jordan Series drogue is made from 100–150 small fabric cones (each about 6 inches across) connected to a long line (300 feet of line would be appropriate). The drogue is dragged behind the boat, stretching well behind any breaking waves. These units are available complete in the range of $1,200–$2,000 or at lower prices for do-it-yourself kits. I have spoken to several singlehanders who have sewn their own drogues.

The drogue is attached to the boat with a V-shaped bridle off the transom. The legs of the V can be adjusted to swing the drogue toward one side of the boat if necessary when the waves are not running at right angles to the wind.

Extensive information is available at www.jordanseriesdrogue.com. The following was written by the inventor, Don Jordan, who passed away in 2008:

With the data from the 1979 Fastnet Race in hand, I started by making scale models of some of the boats in the race and testing these models in natural waves and man-made waves. It is a fortunate fact that small waves behave like large waves and small models behave like full scale yachts if some simple dynamic similarity rules are observed in the model design and testing. I had no preconceived ideas on what these tests would reveal.

At the same time, extensive tests were being conducted in the U.S. and Europe to determine whether the Fastnet tragedy was caused by the design features of modern yachts compared to traditional designs. "Killer Yachts" they were termed by some leading naval architects. After much effort, it was concluded that there was no significant difference in the capsize vulnerability of modern yachts or traditional designs. I repeated these tests and got the same results. The Fastnet disaster was caused by the severity of the storm, not the boat design or the tactics of the skippers.

I then undertook a program of basic research and development to understand and find a solution to the storm survival problem. In this effort I was greatly assisted by the U.S. Coast Guard, who made all their applicable facilities available for my use, and finally tested the series drogue in breaking waves at their motor lifeboat test site. The program, which continued for four years, led to the following general conclusions:

1. To protect a yacht in a hurricane, an outside force must be applied from a drag device. No design changes to the boat and no storm tactics on the part of the skipper can result in a significant reduction in risk.
2. The drag device must be a drogue, i.e., the boat must be tethered from the stern.
3. A sea anchor cannot be designed to protect the boat. When tethered from the bow, the boat will yaw and develop unacceptable loads. The reason for this is that all boats must be designed to be directionally stable when moving forward—or it would not be possible to steer the boat. Therefore, if moving backwards, the boat will be unstable and will yaw and turn broadside to the sea.
4. The drogue must consist of multiple drag elements strung out along the tow line. A single drag device of any size or shape will not provide protection.
5. The drogue must be designed so that a significant number of the drag elements are deeply submerged and do not lie on the surface. This is done with a heavy weight at the end of the drogue.
6. The design of the multiple design elements must be such that, in a "worst case" breaking wave strike, peak transient load will not exceed the design value for the drogue components or the boat attachments.
7. The strength of the drogue and the number of drag elements must be adjusted to be compatible with the displacement of the specific yacht.
8. With a proper drogue, a yacht and crew can survive a storm of the severity of the Fastnet or 1998 Sydney–Hobart storm with no serious storm damage or crew injuries.

A series drogue has significant advantages over a single large drogue model. First, there is no one single breaking point for the drogue cones. It would have no effect if a few of the cones ripped, and because the pressure on each cone is quite small, the chances of a rip are very low. Second, it is not necessary to deploy the entire drogue. A smaller section can be deployed in lesser conditions. (To do this, the cones could be connected in sections of 40 cones followed by 20 feet of clear line, then 40 more cones, etc.)

Drogue Launching and Retrieval

A series drogue is fairly simple to launch and extremely difficult to retrieve. To launch, flake the drogue down with the bridle end at the bottom of the bag with the bridle legs fastened securely to the corners of the transom. The weight at the end of the line, kept at the top of the bag, is dropped overboard and the drogue fed out slowly. The weight will pull the drogue down and away from the boat, preventing fouling. Eventually the drogue will catch the water and secure the boat.

Series Drogue Launching

A skipper might be reluctant to launch a series drogue while running fast in high winds, knowing that it will quickly catch the water and rip through his hands uncontrollably. The first option is to run the drogue line over a winch that can absorb the primary force. If this is impractical, there is good reason to heave-to, feed the drogue over the

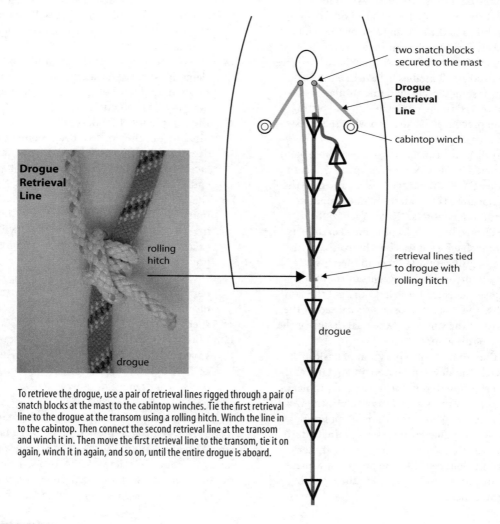

To retrieve the drogue, use a pair of retrieval lines rigged through a pair of snatch blocks at the mast to the cabintop winches. Tie the first retrieval line to the drogue at the transom using a rolling hitch. Winch the line in to the cabintop. Then connect the second retrieval line at the transom and winch it in. Then move the first retrieval line to the transom, tie it on again, winch it in again, and so on, until the entire drogue is aboard.

stern—weight first—and then resume sailing with the drogue pulling behind the boat.

Series Drogue Retrieval

Because of the significant resistance provided by 100–150 cones, it is very difficult to retrieve a series drogue. (Most large single-piece drogues have a collapse mechanism that eliminates their drag.) Some skippers have even been known to cut a series drogue loose and abandon it in frustration. At best it will take a half hour of significant effort to retrieve the drogue on a large winch.

To assist in retrieval, prior to launch the skipper should affix a single line to the apex of the bridle. This can later be winched in to bring the main drogue line up to the boat. All winching should be done not from the stern but from the cabintop. This brings the drogue up into the cockpit. A pair of drogue retrieval lines is used, of proper diameter for the winch. It creates a mechanical advantage to tie a pair of snatch blocks to the mast and run the retrieval lines from the winch, through the snatch blocks, and back to the drogue itself (see illustration). Once the drogue line is on board, the most efficient method is to attach the retrieval line to the drogue with a rolling hitch. This is easy to tie and remove. The drogue is then winched in toward the mast until the rolling hitch is up on the cabintop. At this point the second retrieval line, around the other winch, is tied to the drogue and winched in. The first retrieval line is then slack and can be moved and tied farther down the drogue, and so on. Depending on sea conditions, this can take about 20–30 minutes.

It should be noted that Jeanne Socrates does not use the method described above. She simply runs the entire drogue through the winch, cones and all. Others have found that the winch damages the cones.

Another method of drogue retrieval is to heave to and pull the drogue on board from a standstill.

Drogues and Singlehanders

From the book *Drag Device Data Base* by Victor Shane:

Swift Cloud, Brooke cutter, LOA 37' x 6 Tons. In June 2002 *Swift Cloud* left New Zealand for Rarotonga and ran into a Force 10 storm. Her singlehanded owner deployed a homemade series drogue consisting of 30 cones, each 10 inches in diameter. "At 45 knots the drogue held *Swift Cloud* stern to, but at an angle of about 20 degrees to the wind. At 60 knots she was taking wind and sea dead astern. "The ride was a little like being on a bungee—I could feel her accelerate as a sea approached, but as she went up the face of the sea the forward movement would slow and then reverse." The stern of the yacht took a beating, however, water coming in through the companionway "as though from a shower nozzle." The self-steering gear was carried away when a weld failed, "but the boat was kept well under control." *Swift Cloud* was tethered to the series drogue for 60 hours during which time she drifted in a circle of about 20 miles radius.

Jessica Watson, who completed her singlehanded circumnavigation at age 16, used a parachute drogue nearing the Bass Strait toward the end of her voyage in 2010. She proved that a drogue is not the answer to every problem and still requires vigilance. From the Jessica Watson website at www.JessicaWatson.com.au:

And last night things sure got interesting. I put the drogue (a parachute like thing that you trail behind the boat to slow you down in really big seas) out to stop us losing too much ground and to stop us being knocked down. The wind gusted at 55 knots and the sea was (and still is!) a total, gigantic mess, with 8–12 meter swells. Although the wind is easing now, the sea's still rising.

Riding out the weather with the drogue out was a lot like my first gale in *Ella's Pink Lady* because of the new motion and all the new noises. It didn't make for the most relaxing night as I played around with the bridle to try and get us sitting at the right angle to the waves. Then when I did put my head down for a bit of sleep we were knocked down again when the lashing came off the tiller and a big wave caught us on the side.

As a further example on this topic: Jeanne Socrates launched a series drogue to retain control after *Nereida*'s knockdown (described earlier in this chapter), suffering severe damage near Cape Horn. A local fishing boat arrived to take her in tow.

> When I retrieved my series drogue, my suspicions were confirmed . . . Looks as though the fishing vessel, when approaching and circling us in the night, cut the line with its prop—of 125 cones, only six are now there with a very reduced length of line . . . and no chain, of course . . . !

This only proves my continuing view that the singlehander must be prepared for the worst possible things to go wrong at the worst possible moment, even after having taken the best possible precautions.

Through all this discussion about drogues, it must be remembered that they only allow the boat to sail downwind. They cannot help skippers fight their way upwind. In 2007–08, Glenn Wakefield attempted a westward circumnavigation (the wrong way against the wind) on his Cheoy Lee–designed Offshore 40 *Kim Chow*. When sailing in the roaring 40s, Wakefield would reduce sail to a triple-reefed main and "hankee yankee" and then even further to just the hankee yankee as winds increased. This sail is just 8 square feet and is used only to hold the bow into the wind. By doing so he could keep the boat in a safe position to the waves, climbing up them at a 45 degree angle. During these conditions, Wakefield's forward progress was reduced to single-digit miles per day, even falling back some days.

CHAPTER 12   DEALING WITH DAMAGE

It is guaranteed that damage will occur during short sails on sunny afternoons and during long voyages with calms and storms. Things will break—important things. The key to being a successful singlehander, and perhaps the great joy in what we do, is in how we handle these situations. My great disappointment is singlehanders who are forced to abandon their voyage or call for help for something that should be repairable. My greatest respect goes to those who solve their problems and continue with their voyage.

CASE STUDIES: DISMASTINGS

Ruben Gabriel broke his mast during the 2008 Singlehanded Transpac. The situation was posted in the race logs. Excerpts follow (see also the section later in this chapter entitled Lessons on Jury Rigging from *Sparky*'s Dismasting).

July 27: Ruben Gabriel (sailing the Pearson Electra 22 *Sparky*) flies his spinnaker and hand steers from the am to the pm check-in, then puts up the twins at night. He's done this daily from the first day he was downwind. Today he decided to take a break and put up twin headsails during the day. In the early afternoon he hoisted and reefed his mainsail (in addition to the twins) to increase his speed. At about 11:45 am, Pacific Time, there was a gust of wind, he rounded up, and the mast broke 2 to 3 feet above the boom gooseneck. Fortunately there were no holes in the boat or in Ruben. It took him several hours to retrieve the mast and rigging from the water.

After spending time bobbing around, he's managed to use the bottom portion of the mast and the lower shrouds, forestay, and a halyard on the stern to jury rig a new mast. Using his jib, he's able to steer a steady course going between 1.8 and 3.5 knots.

He said the mess on his boat is unbelievable and is doing his best to clean it up. He's tired, but now with the new rig he's feeling better.

July 28: With the hope of increasing his speed, tomorrow he plans to replace the current jury rig with the larger portion of his mast, which is approximately 12 feet high. He's feeling better and his spirits are high.

July 29: Today was the launch of phase two of his new jury rig. He topped his current rig by opening up the mangled, squished portion of the piece of mast he was using for phase one, and inserting the twisted, crooked, piece of what's left of a spinnaker pole. He then ran a jib halyard up the pole.

The successful phase two is now 8 to 9 feet tall running twin headsails. While talking to him on the phone tonight, he hit the downside of a swell at 6.6 knots! His speed is ranging from 3.5 to 5.5 knots.

August 2: The last couple of days have been full of ups and downs. Thursday there was very little wind, which provided the opportunity to deploy Operation *Sparky* Phase 3. He began using the top portion of his mast, which was about 12 feet tall (much larger than Phase 2), and attempted with all of his strength and ingenuity to re-step it. After agonizing and struggling for hours in trying to get it up and secured, he realized that he needed to make it a little shorter. So he removed 2 feet from the bottom and, after blood, sweat, and tears he successfully secured it. Now he can use his existing lower shrouds, forestay, and a halyard for the backstay. In addition, he now has running halyards. The plan (once there is wind) is to continue using his twin headsails and fly an asymmetrical spinnaker. The rig is also much more stable.

August 8: *Spark*y finished SHTP 08 this morning at just after sunrise (6:34 HST). It was a beautiful morning with misty squalls inshore against Kauai's peaks, and a light offshore breeze. Ruben's jury rig is the top 9 feet of his mast stepped on deck with sails hanked to the shortened headstay. After anchoring in the Bay, Ruben was whisked ashore to a welcoming with Robbie and his family, who had flown in from New Mexico. Not a dry eye in the house. This evening at Tree Ruben will receive his SHTP 08 belt buckle.

My friend and yacht club mate Glenn Wakefield was on day 116 of his second westward round-the-world attempt (after rolling in the Atlantic on his first attempt) sailing 1,700 miles west of Australia when he faced rig failure:

The weather forecast was for calm. I had time on my hands, so decided to take advantage of it and do a thorough inspection of the rigging and sails. I started with the standing rigging upper and lower shrouds and mast head shrouds. First I removed the protective tape that stops chafe of the sails against the turnbuckle cotter pins. I had only done the port aft lower shroud when I noticed that one of the wire strands had separated from the swaging, commonly known as rigging failure. I was very taken aback and quickly removed the rest of the tape and inspected the remaining five shrouds. To my horror, I found one more wire strand had broken loose, this time on the port forward shroud.

My mind started to work on solutions. I came up with temporary ones that satisfied me and that I thought would work, but for how long I didn't know. I started to realize that this had to be repaired before I could go any farther. Lots of questions. Could I go on to Africa and make repairs there? How many more cyclones could I expect in getting there? Australia is 1,700 miles back to the east. Africa is a thousand miles further away than Australia. What would I do if I lost my mast? Could I still use the radio?

The more I thought about it, the more it made sense to go back to Australia and make repairs there. It should take about three weeks, 1775 nm.

I couldn't see myself making it to Cape Horn early enough to make a safe rounding this season. It means the end of my goal, my dream. I am not happy about it, but nor do I want to be caught out again and have to ask for help. I will go slowly and make my way back and then see from there.

As the days go by, I will see how it feels to let go of something I have worked hard towards for ten years.

There is no doubt that Wakefield made the most difficult but correct decision. A broken mast is perhaps the most common significant fear of singlehanders. Many of the most famous books about our heroes describe how they were able to jury-rig a mast and finish their voyage. The book that started me on the singlehanded journey, John Hughes's *The Sailing Spirit*, tells the story of the first man to round Cape Horn after a dismasting in the Southern Ocean:

Instantly awake, I lay still for a split second, my mind registering only noise, a terrible crash stretching into a drawn-out rumble. Underneath me, I could feel a change in the way *Joseph Young* was moving, sluggishly, as if a great weight was bearing down upon her.

For the first time I tasted real terror. "No. Oh, no." I whispered, over and over, as I slid back the hatch to confirm what I already knew—the mast had broken.

Sheared off flush with the deck, the butt

of the mast had jumped off to port and driven down through the cabintop, punching a jagged hole into the interior of the boat. Falling quickly, the spar had then bent in an almost perfect right angle as it jammed in the hole. In the cabin, the bottom four feet of the mast was grinding around above the chart table. On deck, the remaining fifty-five feet was lying over the starboard side, held almost on the surface of the water by the port shrouds. All the rigging was still intact, as were the spreaders. (The wind hadn't been overly strong and there seemed to be no obvious reason for this horrendous event to have occurred. Later examination of the lower part of the mast came up with metal fatigue as the most likely cause.)

Shaken badly, my mind numbed with shock and fear, I scrambled feverishly to collect the bolt cutters and my knife. A confusion of tangled ropes and rigging lay everywhere. All I knew for certain was that the biggest threat to my survival lay with the slowly sinking mast alongside. For the moment it was held quite firmly in place by the piece wedged through the deck and the straining shrouds. If it pulled clear and went completely overboard, it would become a deadly battering ram. With the multitude of lines holding it close to the boat, it could easily drive another hole in the hull, probably below the waterline. The consequences didn't bear thinking about. I knew that I had to cut the whole mess away before I found myself in real trouble.

DEALING WITH DISMASTING— AN ALTERNATE APPROACH

Hughes's reaction to this situation was standard. His thought that the mast must be cut clear and sent to Davy Jones' locker is repeated in every story I have read about sailors in a similar situation. Personally, I am led to wonder if this is the best approach. Just a month before writing this I lost my own mast. It happened in 25 knots of wind with my big spinnaker flying. A Spectra eye splice in the adjustable backstay broke and the mast fell forward. Having read all of the books, my immediate

While sailing under spinnaker in 25 knots of wind, a Spectra eye splice in the backstay of my Olson 30 parted and the mast fell forward.

reaction was the same—dump the mast. In hindsight, my thoughts have changed completely.

The situation was that my keel-stepped mast had sheared at the deck and fallen forward, extending some twenty feet over the pulpit. It was held at the base by a small remaining strip of aluminum, and was resting on the pulpit fairly comfortably. After 10–15 minutes, as I worked to bring the shredded spinnaker, jib, and main on board, the strip of aluminum at the base broke and the entire mast fell over the starboard side. Only after it fell overboard did the mast pose a threat to the boat.

I now firmly believe that a better approach would have been to immediately lash the mast in place in its broken position. Had I lashed it securely at the base and at the pulpit, it would not have fallen overboard when the strip of aluminum gave way. It would have remained secure, and I could more easily have retrieved the sails and then moved the mast to a better position later.

CIRCLING FREIGHTERS

Two freighters can be seen at the top of the photo of my broken mast. Before the dismasting, I had seen them heading west, out to the open ocean. After pulling the sails off, I noticed that they were still circling around and watching my situation. I used my handheld VHF to issue a message, "Pan-Pan, Pan-Pan, Pan-Pan. This is *Foolish Muse, Foolish Muse, Foolish Muse*. I'm the 30-foot sailboat with the mast down south of Victoria Harbour. I notice two ships circling me. Be advised that I do not need your assistance at this time. Thank you." Upon sending this message I was contacted by Victoria Coast Guard, who had heard my Pan-Pan. After some discussion and with night falling, the local volunteer search-and-rescue squad came out to tow me in.

Looking back at John Hughes's story, I note that he says, "For the moment it was held quite firmly in place by the piece wedged through the deck and the straining shrouds." With 25 years of hindsight and my own experience, I wonder if a better approach would have been to tie the rig securely in place where it rested, until a more reasoned approach could be taken. Hughes's story continues:

I was also aware that whatever I could salvage would prove useful in the days ahead. With this in mind I attacked the boom first, working frantically to cut the foot of the mainsail clear. Next I grabbed a wrench from the tool box and set about trying to unbolt the boom from the mast. I had been at it for a mere ten minutes when *Joseph Young* rolled off a swell, throwing the base of the mast back out of the hole. Scrambling clear as it swung dangerously across the deck, I knew that my time was now very limited. Bolt cutters in hand, I dashed aft and began chopping away the rigging according to a hastily conceived plan. First to go was the backstay, followed quickly by the runners and checkstays. Given the strength of the damned, I found it surprisingly easy to cut through the heavy wire. Next, the boom vang and the maze of running rigging clustered around the base of the mast. The starboard shrouds were not carrying any weight, so they were cut too. To try to get forward past the bucking mast would have been fatal, so the forestay would have to wait till last. All that remained now were the port

shrouds. Saying a silent prayer, I knelt down and sheared them all in rapid succession. Wide-eyed, I watched as the tangled mess bumped and scraped its way across the deck. With a final lurch it dropped overboard, carrying with it the port lifelines. From up on the bow there was a sudden bang, like a gunshot, as the forestay parted. Except for a couple of blocks and the boom-vang tackle, everything above deck level aboard *Joseph Young* was now sinking toward the ocean floor, some two miles below.

From the reports of various dismastings, it seems that the most damage, including damage to the hull, occurs at the actual moment that the mast falls. For example, in the 2011 Volvo Ocean Race, Abdu Dhabi Ocean Racing reported, "Boatbuilders were also having to repair the hull which was punctured by spreaders as the mast toppled over." Instances where the mast causes hull damage long after it falls appear to be more rare.

Of course it is easy to second guess Hughes's approach from behind my laptop. However, given my own experience just a few weeks ago, I would say that if a singlehander loses the mast, her first thought should not be cutting it away. Rather, her first thought should be to lash the mast in place so that the situation cannot get any worse, as happened to myself and to John Hughes. He notes that the mast was stuck in the deck for 10 minutes before it bounced loose, and my situation was much the same. It seems to me that enough could have been done during this period to save both of our rigs and significantly reduce later problems.

Of course, every situation is different, and the integrity of the hull is exponentially more important than saving the mast, but I'll just put out the statement that if the mast falls, the skipper should take 30 seconds to consider lashing it in place before making the decision to send it to the deep.

LESSONS ON JURY RIGGING FROM *SPARKY'S* DISMASTING

Lashing the fallen mast in place where it fell is exactly what Ruben Gabriel did when his mast fell on *Sparky* as introduced at the beginning of this chapter. I later had a long interview with Ruben.

The conditions during his dismasting were perhaps less than normal for that stretch of the Pacific. Blowing 15–17 knots and bumpy seas. This made it difficult to walk around the small boat with the mast and rigging covering the deck. Gabriel quickly understood that he needed to salvage as much as possible. Being 680 miles from Hawaii is significantly different from my dismasting a mile south of Victoria Harbour, where a tow was just a phone call away. Ruben was trailing the race pack and he did not want to request help.

An interesting part of the experience was his ability to focus on a difficult technical problem. A few hours earlier, Gabriel had called his father by sat phone and explained that he was going to take it easy and rest. He was exhausted after two weeks of sailing and felt a tremendous need to relax. This was the reason he was flying only twin jibs and a main, rather than a spinnaker. But immediately after the mast falling, his mind cleared and he was able to remain focused and sharp for the next several days until he created a permanent jury rig.

It took a few hours for Gabriel to clear the deck of the mess and remove the sails from the fallen structure. Only after that did he report his situation to the race committee. After talking with them he understood the need to look after the situation himself.

His first problem was stabilizing the boat. It was turning circles and rocking with every chop of the waves. This made it difficult to perform any tasks

and certainly did not get him any closer to Hawaii. Using the stump of existing mast, he had a short rig in place. This was moving the boat at only 2 knots, but at least the rocking stopped and he was pointed at Hawaii.

Ruben Gabriel's first mast fix. *(Courtesy Ruben Gabriel)*

Gabriel's second mast fix with the spinnaker pole pushed down into the broken mast. *(Courtesy Ruben Gabriel)*

The next day, Gabriel worked on a better solution. This required folding out the shredded top of the mast stump and sliding the spinnaker pole inside. This took his speed up to 3 knots.

A day later he devised a still better plan of removing the existing mast base and building a completely new mast from the 12-foot-long section of upper mast lying on his deck. This required using a hacksaw to cut that mast section shorter. Ruben described how during the first cut, he broke the hacksaw blade. He had only one spare so knew he must be extremely careful. He said that his mind was very sharp and he was able to concentrate on every forward and backward motion of the saw to keep it straight inside the cut.

Gabriel had a particular frustration with the 12-foot mast section. He was able to raise it onto the deck step but was not able to secure it in place with lines. He attempted this many times over several hours. He had lines from the masthead running in all directions, held by blocks and clutches. But the moment he moved to secure one line, the mast fell in the other direction. After hours of failed attempts, he cut the mast height by 2 feet and was finally successful with the 10-foot section.

Gabriel's third mast fix entailed creating a new mast base from the 12-foot upper mast piece he had salvaged from the initial dismasting. After struggling for hours to stabilize the 12-foot piece, he finally shortened the spar by 2 feet and was able to secure it. *(Courtesy Ruben Gabriel)*

Mental Approach to Major Damage

We can learn several lessons from Gabriel's experience.

Regardless of the difficulty of circumstances and skipper's exhaustion, a major calamity can bring clarity of mind and a sharpness of focus that can last for several days. This ability to perform necessary repairs over an extended period is described by every singlehander in every situation of this nature. They commonly say that "adrenaline kicks in." However, adrenaline lasts only for a short period. The ability to concentrate and perform difficult tasks over many hours or even days is an indication that humans have more innate long-term performance abilities than we would normally consider. These abilities only come to the fore when faced with a very difficult task. This same level of energy was depicted by both John Hughes and Derek Hatfield when they also lost their masts.

Perhaps this is an attribute of singlehanded sailors, but the ability to never give up and keep moving toward the desired goal is necessary. After failing for several hours at his final solution, Gabriel could easily have gone back to the early spinnaker pole inside the mast stump. But he did not. Rather, he worked and worked at the 12-foot section. When this proved impossible, he simply adapted by cutting 2 feet off.

We have all faced similar situations while working on our boats. Because we are not experts in every aspect of boat construction, it often takes us many attempts over several hours to perform a task that an expert could do in a few minutes. This type of stubborn persistence is a necessary requirement for successful singlehanding.

Gabriel felt very lucky that the wind died completely during his final repair. He believes that he would not have been successful at all if the wind had stayed at its normal 15–20 knots in the region. Of course the wind remained dead for three more days after the repair was complete. It took 27 days for Gabriel to complete the voyage. He was down to scraps of food.

The final lesson of Gabriel's experience has been previously mentioned: don't throw anything away and certainly don't drop the mast overboard. It may come in handy later!

OTHER VARIETIES OF DAMAGE

Other misadventures include:

July 27: At 03:00 Skip Allen [aboard a Wylie Custom 27 *Wildflower*—whose abandonment was discussed in Chapter 13] was struck by a particularly strong squall. He was using two poles to fly his two headsails. A wind gust overpowered his windvane and his boat headed up into the wind. As a consequence I believe his port pole dipped into the ocean causing it to snap in two. Half the pole went flying overhead and wrapped in his outer shroud. The other end flew up and smashed his radar dome . . . while all this was happening Skip was hit by a flying fish. Now I know I'm having fun!

Here are instances of damage during the 2009 Solo Transat, collected by Jerry Freeman:

QII, **Open 35. Torn main sail**, the lowest full length batten had the batten car to mast track removed in error by sail makers' assistant. Point load opened to a hole that eventually ripped full width of sail on day 15, last 6 days sailed with 2 reefs in light conditions. **Cost 12 hrs.**

Spinning Wheel, **Open 40.** New plastic **rudder bearing pintles failed** on twin transom rudders in first 3 days. These bearings were fitted prior to start replacing long tested metal bearings that had completed the delivery from Italy with no problem.

De Franchsman, **Open 30.** Old **fore hatch fitting failed** on front-hinged hatch. Massive water ingress to cabin, floorboards cut to fix over hole. Consequential damage: nothing serious, but all clothing and fresh food wet. Cost: lost 4 hours repairing and recovering mainly due to reducing speed (down to about 1 or 2 knots) to minimize water ingress during the night. Remember it was a 30-knot beat in the Western Approaches.

Jbellino, **J/122. Lost all spinnaker gear over the side** on day 17 (Grand Banks ice/fog) in heavy running conditions and knockdown.

Also jib wrapped round forestay and flogged itself so that the vertical battens ripped the sail to shreds. Sail written off. Probable primary cause of this incident was lack of food—low blood sugar—and tiredness. It should have been a normal spin takedown but I changed the process and allowed the sail to drag in the water. Wind continued to increase. Boat gybed, sheets and guys tangled round rudder and more. Bad decisions at many points through the night. Solution—be aware of effects of low energy and tiredness and try to do minimum to stabilize situation. THEN eat and rest even if for short time. I failed to take this advice.

Pilot failure. New Raymarine Type 1 pilot (ram) failed after 35 hours. Used about 15 hours before race start so I believed that it had passed its failure phase. Problem was an assembly fault (Rob Craigie).

Katie Miller sailing her Figaro 2 *BluQube* (21 days 19 hrs) reports: The radar pole detached and fell into cockpit taking up a lot of space, a hazard. The pole was fitted 2008, radar never used. Cost about 36 hours? Loss of radar caused me to change planned route to avoid the Newfoundland banks and fog. Added extra distance and contrary current.

Water ingress to cabin caused by poor seal from companionway sliding hatch. **Cost about 5 hrs.** Immersed EPIRB in cabin—false alarmed causing distress at home.

Sail damage caused by loss of top batten. **Cost 2 hours.**

Rudder damage (20 cm of tip broken off) caused by collision with unidentified object. Most probably a container judging by shear on rudder. This lead to further more serious water ingress, the source of which could not be found during the race. Later found to be a tear in the rubber gaitor around the rudder stock.

Oscar Mead sailing *King of Shaves*, J/105: My first problem was that the cogs in the port side pit winch gave way before Lands End, as I made the change to the #4 jib in 25 knots of breeze, old cogs just sheered. Having contacted Harken on my arrival home they instantly guessed which winch it was before I told them, so it's a problem they have been dealing with.

The next real problem was SeaTalk, having been very happy with the pilot during the first part of the race and impressed at how it was coping it seemed fitting that this should be the next thing to break. It started with the speed instrument up by the 20/20s which began to flicker on and off, finally it turned off completely. Not a problem but the entire SeaTalk network crashed and the boat instantly rounded up, alarms going berserk. I got the boat back on track and used string and the wheel lock to keep her on course, but it wasn't fast, then I began to try and fix SeaTalk, I made an emergency call to Will Sayer as he knows Raymarine well. He suggested I look for breaks in the yellow SeaTalk wire, which I had already started. Going up wind in 25 knots with the spray hood and garage unscrewed and in the cockpit, all the headlining on the floor, was a frustrating few hours, but there was to be no sleep till it was fixed or I had some sort of solution. After about four hours it began to get dark, and I hastily re-wired the pilot without SeaTalk input using only one display, and with only heading data. This served but it was nowhere near as fast a wind angle, that definitely cost me, especially in the light, without the pilot playing the small shifts the boat simply stopped and I would go nowhere for an hour whilst I was asleep.

When the boat got back to the UK the problem proved to be water ingress into the main distribution panel in the wiring box, the panel had shorted and taken down the network, short of a replacement there wasn't any mending it.

However half way through the race and nicely mid Atlantic I found I was unable to charge the batteries at all, I checked all the terminals re did the fittings on the alternator and checked the boost system, all was ok. Finally I narrowed the problem down to the blocking diode in the split charging system, they had completely burned out, a quick rewire and they were removed, problem solved.

Damaged sails was another problem, by the time I reached Newfoundland I had a foot long gash just below the third reef, by the time the storm had gone through, I had a three-foot gash along and at least on and a half up, despite my best efforts with Kevlar tape, in the end I had to take the mainsail down three times and gaffa tape it into oblivion and that didn't really work either but I think it helped.

Will Sayer on *Elmarleen*:

Delivery to Plymouth: Wind generator started to spin excessively fast and developed a loud rattle as I sailed through the Needles—it was blowing 30 knots. Concerned that the generator was broken I contacted the manufacturer immediately on arrival in Plymouth. I was assured that it was fine and that it had over heated so it went into free spin. This was true but during the race it became apparent that the bearing had also gone resulting in hellish vibration and noise in anything over 15 knots. Noise was so great I couldn't sleep in a primary berth. No lost time but incredibly distracting.

During the race:

Day 3: On doing the first maintenance check around the boat since the beginning of the race I noticed that the port lower shroud had the majority of its strands broken at the top swage. A sound repair was required immediately otherwise I would have had to retire from the race. I had no spare lower, but I did have a spare inner forestay which was 6 mm dia rather than 7 mm. I also had a 6 mm Sta-Lok fitting. I used the 6 mm T on the spare inner forestay to attach it to the mast and cut the bottom to length with bolt croppers and used the Sta-Lok fitting to attach it through the body of the old bottle screw. It meant I could not tension the lower shroud but worked as a replacement for the remaining 20 days.

Two things to note: the Sta-Lok fitting unwound and nearly came loose after about a week. This was due to the difficulty in assembling it at sea. I reassembled it with a whole tube of Loctite. The second issue was on inspection in Newport, the backing plate in the mast had cracked as the 6 mm T terminal didn't fit the 7 mm backing plate. This could have resulted in the loss of my rig mid-Atlantic. **Time Lost: 2 hours**

Day 4: I am guessing the windvane rudder (Navik) hit an obstruction. This resulted in the trim tab on the trailing edge of the rudder breaking its lower pintle and being bent horizontal. I had a complete spare rudder paddle assembly which I swapped over two days later when the sea state had calmed down. In the mean time I sailed on using autopilot.

Day 5: Ripped my light-weight spinnaker. It caught inside the lower shroud and I continued to pull the halyard. Spinnaker was torn the full length and unusable for the duration of the race.

Day 10: I am guessing this happened when I was hit by a big wave beam on as I wasn't aware or the true extent of the damage until lifting the boat in Newport. When hand steering I felt the rudder get tight when I pushed it to port. The bearings were brand new and replaced in April but no sign of them being tight was evident before the race. This eased up as the race continued but was replaced with a clonking/knocking noise when the boat rolled. The bearings suddenly felt excessively worn when steering by hand. When lifted the rudder had been bent sideways 3–4 inches (measured at the bottom). This had resulted in the lower bearing breaking loose from the hull and wearing internally and externally excessively.

Other: I fought charging issues the whole way across. The wind generator with its damaged bearings appeared to have reduced output and the advanced alternator regulator tripped complaining of high battery temperature or high battery voltage nearly every time I charged. I replaced the alternator regulator at sea with no improvement. Since the race I have learnt it was the Sterling advanced alternator regulator at fault. **No time lost.**

Joe Harris reported this damage in his blog from the 2013 Bermuda 1–2:

We made good progress toward Newport and were about 70 miles offshore approaching the continental shelf, the wind built to 15 to 20 knots and a series of squalls began to come through bringing drenching rains. During one of the squalls, I was on deck trimming the sails when I heard a loud bang on the port side and the boat suddenly slowed from about 10 knots to about 2 knots to a dead stop. . . . I had hooked a large offshore lobster pot around the keel and the boat was stopped dead in its tracks. As this has happened to me before, I knew I was in trouble and most likely the only way to get the line off the keel was to dive under the boat and cut it. Since it was the middle of the night, pitch black, and raining with a pretty good sea state and 20-knot wind and I was alone, this did not seem like a very appealing option. So, I dropped all the sails and let the boat drift and contemplated my options. No good ones came to mind, so finally I got on the VHF radio and asked if there were any fishing boats in the area who might have a diver onboard. Remarkably, a captain from New Bedford came back and said he did not have a diver onboard but would come over and see if he could lend some assistance. Just as he arrived on the scene, after being hooked for about an hour, I heard another clang as the buoy unwrapped itself from the keel and the boat was free again! Unbelievable. I put the sails back up and was soon marching along again at 10 knots! A weird and scary experience.

What can a singlehander learn from these stories? The only important thing is that every part of the boat can break, even those parts that we can't imagine breaking.

THE ROLE OF INGENUITY AND HOW TO PREPARE FOR DAMAGES

The successful outcome in every story comes from a skipper who had enough ingenuity to come up with a fix. It would be impossible to consider every fix in advance, but it is possible to preplan and it is possible to arrive at a solution. We know from many examples that there is virtually no mechanical breakdown that necessarily stops a voyage and requires rescue.

Before a voyage, the skipper should spend a good 4 hours with a pad walking around and looking at every part of the boat. Then think about how to fix that part if it broke at sea. Starting from the bow, walk clockwise, examining anything that could break.

For example, at the bow, the following things might possibly break:

- Hitting a log or container smashes the bow at the waterline.
- Forestay breaks at the turnbuckle, any one of three components.
- Bow navigation light bulb burns out.

In this brief example, one item is life threatening but extremely rare, one item could stop the boat from sailing and is relatively common, and one item is just a little annoying but happens all the time. I am not asking the skipper to solve every single problem before it happens, but I am suggesting at least to give a moment's thought to every problem so that if it happens, it is not completely unexpected.

There are two considerations in this process.

Stanley Paris ripped the forestay on the 63-foot *Kiwi Spirit* during his attempt to become the oldest solo circumnavigator. *(Courtesy Stanley Paris)*

First, because we are concerned only with safely arriving at port, we do not need to be overly concerned with electronics. These are nice to have but (as we know from Chapter 7, Power Systems) not necessary for a safe voyage. A broken radar will not stop a voyage, though a broken forestay might. Second, by starting out with the idea of spending 4 hours on this assignment, the skipper will know how much time and consideration to spend on each item. This is not just a cursory glance—this is an in-depth examination with lots of thinking. By walking around the boat in this way, and by actually thinking about how each part could be repaired if broken, the skipper will have gained enough experience to handle nearly any problem that might arise.

My father tells the story of how, at age 5, he and his friends set out to build their own boat. Being a cautious group, they built the patches first. They didn't get much further, but at least they were ready for the worst possible disaster.

As my father's son, I developed my own emergency patch when I took a fist-size hole in the side of my Tanzer 22, just above the waterline, on day 1 of the National Championship. For day 2, I bought a corrugated plastic Beware of Dog sign from the local hardware store, along with Goop and some metal screws. I glued the sign over the hole and screwed it in place. This worked so well that I took a sign with me to Hawaii—just in case. Corrugated plastic is waterproof, bends nicely to the shape of the hull, and glues very quickly.

Lessons from *Yachting Monthly*— Dealing with Punctures

Yachting Monthly magazine performed a much more systematic study and evaluation of emergency puncture repairs. Their work is viewable on YouTube; search "Yachting Monthly's Crash Test Boat is holed." With a tremendous amount of effort they punctured a sailboat hull just below the waterline near the starboard bow. The ragged hole was about 3 inches across. It allowed about 2 tons of water to flood the boat over a 7-minute period.

Of particular note is the significant difficulty the *Yachting Monthly* testers had in creating the puncture, using a hammer, chisel, and grinder. Sailors must not think that their boat hull is liable to puncture at the slightest bump. As recounted in Chapter 8, I once ran into a dock at speed. I broke a wooden four-by-four on the dock, but this did nothing more than cause a scratch on the bow gelcoat. The movie *All Is Lost* presents a complete fantasy on this topic. In the movie, Robert Redford's character wakes up to water lapping at his bunk and finds a foot-wide hole in the side of his boat. Experts agree that such a hole would have required a very-high-speed collision, not the drifting bump depicted in the movie.

Yachting Monthly tested several methods of stemming the flow of water:

- A seat cushion jammed against the hole. In the test the user simply held the cushion against the puncture with his foot. This was very effective at reducing the water flow by at least 90%. Such a solution was immediately available and would certainly have saved the boat until a longer-term patch was possible. Obviously anything jammed into the hole is better than nothing: a seat cushion, pillow, sleeping bag, towel, or spinnaker. Any of these would be effective in the short term.
- A standard umbrella. They attempted to push the umbrella through the puncture to open outside the hull. The umbrella broke apart as it was being pushed, thus an utter failure.
- A special-purpose boat puncture umbrella known as Subrella, which is no longer on the market. This is an extra strong unit specifically designed for this purpose. The main drawback of the unit is that even when collapsed, the Subrella was considerably larger than the puncture hole. Thus pushing it through the puncture was both difficult and time consuming. More importantly, the process of pushing it through actually expanded the puncture. While this does indicate the strength of the Subrella, it seems to me that anything that expands the puncture is unadvisable. We are trying to

reduce water flow, not increase it. However, once through the hole, the Subrella did live up to its purpose and virtually stopped the water inflow.

- Inflatable life vest. The user covered a PFD with a towel and pushed it through the puncture, then pulled the inflation line. This was also very effective at reducing the water flow. However, the inflation force of the PFD expanded the cracks in the hull slightly. Watching the *Yachting Monthly* video, I noted that water flow was substantially reduced even before the PFD was inflated. It might have been nearly as effective to stop at this point, which would be very similar to pushing a seat cushion through.

Once the initial flow of water has been slowed, the skipper can make a longer-term plan. *Yachting Monthly*'s excellent video shows without question that a sheet of strong plastic strung under the boat will be pushed by water pressure into the puncture. This nearly eliminated the flow of water. They used a sheet of about 6 by 8 feet, with lines tied to each corner. Two men worked the sheet down to the puncture from the bow. This took some time, and the process would be difficult for a singlehander. It might be easier to tie one side to the toe rail on the puncture side of the boat and then move around the bow and pull the other side of the sheet back until the puncture is covered.

They tried the same solution with a storm jib, which was nearly as effective as the sheet of plastic. But the inherent shape of the sail left it bagging slightly over the puncture, and water continued to flow slowly as the boat rocked.

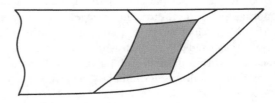

A patch from a storm jib or a sheet of plastic can be used to stem the flood of water from a puncture below the waterline.

Stay Afloat is a waxy putty that's ready for instant use to temporarily repair cracks, small holes, or broken throughhulls. It should be kept aboard for this type of emergency.

We have to assume that a serious puncture is not going to occur on a day with 5-knot winds and flat seas. So it would be very difficult for a singlehander to attempt a repair from outside the hull after jumping overboard into the water. In the most likely scenario, the puncture would occur in 20-knot winds with 15-foot breaking waves. The skipper must be prepared to make repairs under these most difficult conditions.

In another test, *Yachting Monthly* magazine evaluated a commercial emergency patching material called Stay Afloat (www.stayafloatmarine.com). It is a petroleum byproduct, a waxy putty that can be jammed into large or small cracks or broken through-hulls to stop leaks immediately. The videos on the website are impressive. Company President Gary Olson told me that it has been used to fill gashes in the hull up to 18 inches long and holes up to 3.5 inches in diameter. "Basically the more material you have the larger the hole you can plug, and it can be combined with other materials to plug very large holes." The product does not dry or harden over time. I asked if it would survive a trip to Hawaii, and Olson answered, "It will last a long time as it does not break down." But it is not designed as a permanent repair, more of a temporary patch to endure the voyage. The *Yachting Monthly* evaluation gave a similar recommendation. They used it very successfully to stuff a broken seacock with a diameter of 1.5 inches. Of course, any hole should be permanently repaired in port. Stay Afloat does have some adhesive qualities, so perhaps it could be used on a large hole with my Beware of Dog sign and some screws.

PUMPING OUT THE WATER

In the silly movie *All Is Lost,* the hapless Robert Redford character allows his boat to fill three quarters with water before plugging the large hole. Then he uses his manual cockpit bilge pump to slowly pump out the water a few ounces at a time. The movie depicts how exhausted he becomes during the many hours of this pumping ordeal. There is an age-old saying in the sailing world: "Nothing is faster than a scared man with a bucket." If the water below is more than ankle deep, a bucket is the only acceptable method of emptying the boat. The bilge pump should be used only when the water is too low for the bucket.

CASE STUDY: LOSING A HEADSTAY AND A RUDDER

Rob MacFarlane, who has sailed the Singlehanded Transpac multiple times, gave me the complete details of his experience during the 1996 race on his Newport 33. He suffered two major breaks, but a singlehander's ingenuity and persistence still got him to the finish line. Here's MacFarlane in his own words:

The Newport 33 uses as a stem fitting—a 1" wide or so stainless steel strap that runs vertically up the nose of the boat, has a bend to turn up around the hull-deck joint at the bow, and a bend aft to align with the headstay—normal typical setup for a smaller boat.

The problem is in the jib tack/anchor roller assembly that is "welded" to a portion of the stem fitting. The weld is horizontal, about an inch above the deck, and introduces a weak point in the stem fitting.

My failure occurred due to horizontal (side) loading of the headstay on the stem fitting, and the stem fitting cracked at the weld. During the race, while running deep, there is a lot of side-to-side rolling of the boat which introduces regular side-to-side loading on the stem fitting. The stem fitting failed entirely when the crack split across the metal, and then the last ¼"of stainless steel tore.

What was my state of mind when it happened—talk about freaking out! I'm sitting down below having dinner when there's a new

HITTING SUBMERGED ROCKS

In my overly extensive experience, there are two ways to hit submerged rocks: the "good" way and the "not-so-good" way. (There is a third way, the "bad" way, which I have only witnessed.) A submerged rock will most likely hit the keel, not the hull, so the greatest risk is not a puncture but a cracked hull.

The not-so-good way to hit a rock has the same feeling as stomping my foot down hard on a cement floor. My foot stops instantly and I can feel my bones shudder all the way up to my head. On the water, the boat stops instantly with a single "boom," and actually bounces slightly backward.

It is most likely that the boat is not stuck on the rock because it has bounced off. The skipper should first sail away from the danger, and then drop the sails and make an immediate check for water below. Likely there will be two cracks, one just forward and one just aft of the keel. These are probably not visible inside the boat, and perhaps not even outside. The damage is internal to the fibreglass structure. The only remedy is to haul the boat and have a professional repair completed. (As much as a do-it-yourselfer that I am, this is well beyond the abilities of anyone but an experienced professional.)

The good way to hit a submerged rock feels more like stamping my foot down hard on a grass lawn. My foot stops, but there is a slight give and my bones don't shake. On the water, the boat does not stop instantly but rather continues to move forward or sideways. And the boat leans over sharply because it is now sitting on top of the rock.

In the good-way-to-hit-a-rock case, my experience is that damage is limited to the mashed gelcoat and lead in the keel. So I don't see a reason to stop sailing immediately. Rather, I am more worried about further damage from scraping the hull on the rock, so my philosophy is to get the boat off of the rock. The only way to accomplish this is to lean the boat as much as possible and allow the keel to scrape its way off the ledge.

The only way to achieve this alone is to leave the sails up with the sheets tight. The wind can catch on the sails and (with the keel/rock joint acting as the pivot) heel the boat over and push it off the rock. I have used this method successfully with my genoa when sailing upwind and with my spinnaker when sailing downwind. It doesn't feel particularly good to have the keel scrape across a rock, but it's better than laying on a rock at a 50° heel in three-foot waves (not to mention a tide that might be dropping).

There is a third way to hit a rock, the "bad" way. I have not experienced it myself but I did watch a crewed boat sailing at 10 knots with the spinnaker up, pushed by another 3 knots of positive current, turn a corner just five feet too close, ripping the keel right off. The boat flipped immediately, throwing the entire crew into the water. The only questions for a singlehander are: can a PFD—if not already wearing one (when sailing inshore) or a liferaft (when offshore) be reached (or is yours rigged to self-deploy?) in this type of situation? What about a handheld VHF radio, PLB, or a flare gun?

BONK BONK BONK SCRAPE sound from up forward. Not loud, just different and new. So I poke around on deck for a couple of minutes and don't see anything wrong until I realize what I am hearing is the Harken roller furling drum being lifted by the filling downwind twin headsails until the drum strikes the bow pulpit, then it falls down again. The only thing holding the headstay to the deck was the roller furling retrieval line.

An hour later I have run the spinnaker halyards and spare jib halyard to the bow and ground them as tight as I could on the primary winches. And I felt miserable that my race was over from a competitive perspective. In the morning I got out my AC generator and big drill, to try and drill a new hole in the remaining metal up there and re-install the clevis pin that holds the headstay to the bow. The generator broke—ceramic magnet inside blew apart when I applied load by turning on the drill—tremendous racket and sudden silence from the generator. Bummer. I go to sleep.

Later in the afternoon I talk with Bruce Schwab over SSB, he points out that load pulling the mast forward is a good thing and Hanalei is downwind, so I cheer up and I think I set a spinnaker. (I do not believe the twins were usable as I did not want to try and unfurl them on the damaged headstay.)

Fast forward to the next evening, it's mellow conditions with 6-foot swell and perhaps 10 knots of wind and quite dark. I go to adjust the autopilot course and the boat slews 90 degrees off course. I disengage pilot and turn the wheel, the boat turns, and then continues turning to 90 degrees the other way. Aaahhhh! My mast! The spinnaker is pulling the wrong way! I run around the boat and get the kite down, worried entirely about the mast. We stop and continue slewing in the swell.

With a flashlight I peer in through a hatch at the quadrant, thinking a cable had broken—but they were all fine, as was the quadrant. I finally take a flashlight and look over the side and can see the blade swinging from side to side, it's still vertical but the blade is no longer connected to the stock. I am screwed. I am completely miserable. I now hate myself. I hate my boat. I think my boat hates me.

And at that moment the first ship of the race that I have seen comes steaming over the horizon, aiming more or less at where I am. This is a wonderful distraction from the problem of no rudder as now I don't want to get run over. I put out a security (I think) on the VHF, and the US Navy calls me back and asks if I want assistance. I imagine all the possibilities—they could crane my boat up on the deck, they probably have welders, we could fabricate something and then they would drop me back in the water. Wouldn't life be great? Instead I tell them I have a backup rudder that I will install in the morning, and would they mind repeating my position and lack of mobility and control over their much more powerful VHF radio, and they do and steam on by into the night.

In the morning I talk with The General (fellow SHTP racer Ken "The General" Roper) on the SSB and I suggest going under the boat to get rid of the now-useless blade. Ken says that would be a really stupid idea as I am not hurt now and if I got a finger pinched or crushed between the blade and the hull I would have a whole new set of problems to deal with. I agree, and do not go in the water.

Two hours later I have the monitor windvane removed from the transom and it is now sitting in the middle of the cockpit, a relatively large painful obstruction with lots of sharp pointy stainless steel bits that you have to watch out for. (Later Peter Hogg jumps in the cockpit in Hanalei and lands on the windvane with a severe ouch!) The backup rudder is installed, I hook it up to the autopilot, set the third reef of the main to help push and put the storm jib up forward to help pull, and we're off at 3 knots to Hawaii. I am so excited that I get on the SSB and tell everyone we're moving again!

Later I discover that the blade, freely swinging beneath the boat, will occasionally jam over to one side and cause the boat to do donuts before unjamming. This causes no end of frustration. We also hit 6 knots coming off a wave—that causes lots of concern that the backup rudder is going to break. And I worry a lot that if I lose my backup rudder then I will have a real problem.

So that's what happened.

The rudder failure can be explained as follows:

The Newport 33 uses a hollow stainless steel pipe as the rudder stock, an armature/flag is welded to the stock and the rudder blade (glass over foam) is attached to the flag. The pipe is not all that strong, so Capital Yachts (maker of the Newport 33) has developed what they call the "Alaskan" stock, as there have been 5 reported failures of their hollow stocks. The Alaskan stock has a solid slug of stainless driven into the stock to the point where the lower bearing is. Capital gave me instructions on how to do the work, materials, etc. and a stainless metal shop did the work.

The failure is this: the slug never perfectly contacts the surrounding pipe wall, water gets in, corrosion sets up, and the pipe continues to take all the torsional loads (the slug and pipe together take the shear loads). However, there is still room for a very small amount of play between the pipe and the slug, and just like bending a paper clip enough times will work harden the metal until it cracks, the pipe wall continues to do exactly the same thing (but at a much slower rate) despite the slug being installed.

Once across the finish line, the fix for the stem fitting was a replacement made back in California at Svendsen's Boatworks. They found another Newport 33 and copied what was there minus the welded roller/tack! The bolt holes did not line up perfectly with what I had, so at anchor in Hanalei several of us working in dinghies were able to redrill and install the part.

For the rudder we pulled the blade and stock out of the boat, and it was clear what had happened. There was a perfectly circular crack running entirely around the outer pipe and the pipe (stock) had broken into two halves (upper half attached to the quadrant, lower half attached to the blade). The only thing keeping the blade attached to the boat at all was the six inches of slug sticking down into the hollow stock encased in the blade and the buoyancy of the blade keeping it floating up against the boat.

At one point in the perimeter of the cracked and broken stock was a small detente in the metal, an ⅛" notch in the lower section and a matching tooth in the upper section—that was where the metal had torn rather than cracked. And that little notch and tooth was what would sometimes grab the swinging blade and jam it to one side and we would do donuts. I got quite good at doing donuts, and recovering from donuts.

Arne and Joakim, as subcontractors to Svendsen's, borrowed a rudder from another Newport 33 in San Francisco, the metal shop cranked out a replacement stock, Joakim built the blade, and it was air-shipped via United Airlines to Hanalei. All this happened while I was still headed for Hanalei at slow knots. When I got there the epoxy on the blade was still hardening. A gang of us went out to the boat with the new rudder and spent about two hours driving out the old blade and installing the new blade. Oh, and I needed to install a hole for the quadrant, there is a machine shop on the east side of the island and that fellow had a vertical milling machine—he thought it was pretty funny to be fitting an entire rudder onto the mill bed, but he matched the hole perfectly and all was good.

EMERGENCY RUDDER DESIGN

Building an emergency rudder can take on the complexity of a high-performance design, with all of the fiberglass and foam, or it can be a much more basic construction.

At the top end of the scale, I refer readers to several examples presented on the Singlehanded Transpac website. A good emergency rudder is required equipment in that race, and with several failures in the past they are fastidious during the prerace approval process. It would not be unusual to demand an on-the-water demonstration. The designs presented on the Singlehanded Transpac website are especially lightweight and take into account measurements of the force on the rudder based on the size and maximum speed of the boat.

A few general considerations:

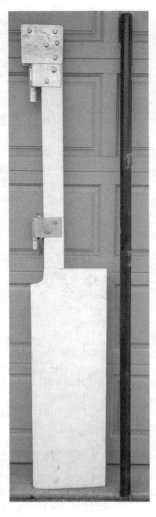

The emergency rudder for my Olson 30 is made from a 2 x 12 and designed to fit into the bottom of my outboard motor bracket.

Paul Kamen's soft rudder is essentially an underwater sail to steer the boat. *(Courtesy Paul Kamen)*

- The emergency rudder should be no smaller than half of the standard rudder.
- How will the emergency tiller fit through the pushpit and backstay?
- How will the rudder and tiller work with existing autopilot or windvane designs?
- A vertical rudder blade provides better steering control than a swept-back oar design.
- The greatest amount of force is not on the rudder but on the mounting points on the transom.
- The emergency rudder must be stored on the boat. Where will it fit?

- The design must be easy and quick to install, even in rough weather.
- What tools are necessary to eject the existing, damaged rudder?

Emergency Rudder Design Examples

I simply took a wooden 2 x 12 and attacked it with a bandsaw and belt sander to create a basic foil shape. The pintles were designed to fit into the bottom of my outboard motor bracket and the back of the extra solar panel bracket that I use for offshore voyages. I made the tiller extra long to fit from the rudder top all the way into the cockpit.

I welded a few pieces of aluminum together to create the brackets and pintles.

On the Singlehanded Transpac website, sailor Paul Karmen describes a soft rudder design for emergency use. It is essentially an underwater sail that steers the boat. Versions of this design have been used for boats 24–57 feet in length, so it obviously has some merit. Although some designs are created to make use of the boat's spinnaker pole as the primary the rudder spar, Karmen argues that this might be only half as strong as necessary under speed.

INSURANCE FOR THE SINGLEHANDER

When I was preparing for the Singlehanded Transpac, I contacted my insurance broker about the trip. This company, which is promoted by my yacht club, claimed to be specialists in marine insurance. They rightfully requested my sailing resume and, as expected, it showed extensive singlehanded experience. However, not only did they refuse to insure my race, they doubled my normal premiums because I singlehand my boat so much. It was obvious that they had no understanding of me or of singlehanding in general. I was appalled and dropped them immediately with severe prejudice.

Clearly, insurance is one of the major problems facing singlehanders. Many companies claim to be marine specialists, but very few have any understanding of singlehanding. It is not that we face extra risks, but that we face different risks that can be managed appropriately.

Fastnet Marine Insurance in the UK is one of the insurance leaders for singlehanded sailors and an official race partner of the Global Ocean Race. Fastnet is a broker; they seek out coverage on a policy-by-policy basis from insurance underwriters who provide the actual coverage. I posed a number of direct questions to Richard Power, the Director of Business Development.

They have been working diligently to develop support from underwriters for Class 40 boats in particular. "Fastnet has taken a close interest in the Class 40 Rule, the GOR's Notice of Race and—particularly—the Category Zero provisions. We have had Class 40s under close scrutiny since the 2008–09 GOR, logging and analyzing Class 40 performance and damage reports in all major offshore events including La Solidaire du Chocolat and the Route du Rhum. Our analysis of transoceanic races helps us to convince underwriters to insure a boat by demonstrating the class' relative reliability."

During the 2008–09 edition of the GOR, Fastnet dealt with a total loss claim for Nico Budel when the keel bulb on his Open 40 *Hayai!* began to detach from the keel fin, forcing the Dutch solo sailor to abandon his yacht and board a diverted bulk carrier in the high latitudes of the Indian Ocean. A few weeks later, the company also dealt successfully with claims by the doublehanded Class 40 duo, Jeremy Salvesen and David Thomson on *Team Mowgli*, following an 80-knot battering and equipment damage in hurricane-force winds off the remote Crozet Islands during Leg 2 of the Global Ocean Race. While they like to reassure underwriters about the seaworthiness and reliability of Class 40s, they are also determined to reform the traditional view of offshore racing yachts held by underwriters: "The nature of offshore racing produces a culture where yachts are often insured sporadically for individual races and events. This has no attraction for an underwriter as it presents a short term, high-risk environment, and any involvement is usually avoided, especially if the underwriter feels he is being 'selected against' by the yacht owner."

Coupled with the added complications of a high turnover of racing yacht ownership, the cost and availability of insurance in this field are seldom inexpensive or widespread. "We really want to encourage the teams to buy longer term policies, to include non-racing periods that are considered 'soft' and low-risk by underwriters, as this helps to balance the cost of cover for when the yachts are racing."

They are willing to attempt to find coverage for singlehanders located anywhere in the world, but they can do so only if the underwriters are licensed in that location. As such, they have struggled with yachts in the U.S. because there are only a few underwriters able to provide this coverage.

The role of the insurance broker is to develop

a proper relationship between the sailor and the insurance company. Like a marriage guidance counselor, the best way to do this is by ensuring that both parties are aware of "material facts" before they enter the relationship. From the insurance company's point of view, sailing or racing the boat singlehanded would definitely fall under the heading of material fact.

The singlehander is approaching any insurance company with a significant handicap. The hobby is certainly difficult and might even be considered illegal. Without advance planning, the skipper's negotiating position is virtually nil.

There is some level of truth to the idea that an insurance company will try to avoid paying out on large claims. The role of the insurance broker is to make this as difficult as possible—before the accident occurs.

It would be unwise for a sailor to simply announce to the company that he was a singlehander, without significant further qualification in terms of how the skipper manages the special circumstances. The skipper should list both his experience and the changes made to the boat particular to ensuring a claims-free singlehanded passage. The list should include:

- Watchkeeping equipment: AIS, radar, Sea-Me, etc. (See Chapter 10, See and Be Seen.)
- Redundancy in autopilot equipment.
- Knowledge of unpowered self-steering methods (see Chapter 6, Self-Steering Systems).
- Strength of the mast, renewed standing rigging, etc. (mast breakage is a major cost to insurance companies).

Insurance companies have clauses particular to marine insurance, and these have special significance to the singlehander. These are fundamental requirements, placed on the shoulders of the skipper, which should be considered paramount, as stated in the Allianz Yachting and Boating policy:

> You will exercise reasonable care to make the vessel seaworthy at the start of this policy, and you will exercise reasonable care throughout the period of insurance to make and keep the vessel in a seaworthy condition.

What is "seaworthy" on a crewed boat is different from what is seaworthy to a singlehander. The skipper needs to ensure a seaworthy singlehanded boat. Some insurers could legitimately state that keeping the vessel in a "seaworthy condition" includes making sure that it is properly manned and that a lookout is maintained at all times. To have any level of success, the skipper must put forth a valid counterargument in the application.

Some policies have strict limitations on singlehanded voyages. For example, according to the Navigators & General Yacht & Motorboat policy, "You are covered for singlehanded passages not exceeding 24 hours but not otherwise, providing the vessel is suitably equipped." And according to a Yachtsure 10/95 policy, "The vessel must only be sailed between the hours of sunrise and sunset local time and only for a cumulative total of 50 nautical miles per day unless she is manned by two people of adequate physical strength at least one of whom is competent to be in command."

But for all yacht insurance policy wordings, the insurers would not expect the yacht to be sailed, let alone raced, singlehandedly, unless they had agreed to this in advance.

The experience or inexperience of the sailor is generally reflected in the policy price. Richard Power emphasized that his company will try to avoid punitive pricing by gathering as much detail about the yacht preparations as possible. Skippers with relatively little experience are asked to provide extensive detail on proper yacht preparation, taking expert advice, taking courses, etc. Power commented that inexperience is not necessarily reflected in insurance pricing as long as the requested details are forthcoming.

In terms of pricing, singlehanders can expect to pay more than a similar crewed yacht—up to 50% higher premiums. For example, a Figaro II would be insured in the region of £1,250 to £1,500 for a year's coverage, including the SORC series and full racing risks.

However, it is with the deductible that the real differences appear. The skipper should expect a significantly increased deductible on actual damages when sailing singlehanded. Richard Power suggested that SORC entries should expect to pay a deductible of approximately 1% to 1.5% of the value of the yacht, compared to 0.5% or even less for a fully crewed yacht. There would not be much difference in this deductible for singlehanded cruisers versus racers, as long as the type of singlehanded sailing being done (i.e., cruising or racing) is specifically endorsed on the policy.

Power emphasized that singlehanded cruisers do not face the same risks as racers and can negotiate better rates. I asked if he would be able to provide insurance for "an extended cruise to many exotic ports around the world"? Power replied that as long as the skipper installed appropriate self-steering gear and other necessary equipment and maintained that gear throughout the voyage, coverage would not be a problem. If any breakdowns occurred, the skipper would be responsible to carry out repairs at the earliest opportunity—certainly not setting off on any voyage over 24 hours without full operation.

The more boat preparation and the greater detail provided, the better the broker is able to negotiate terms with the underwriter. For example, having the most modern watchkeeping equipment on board will be a factor in their discussions.

Insurance underwriters are adverse to skippers with a bad claims history. I would suggest from this that skippers should limit claims to only truly serious amounts, certainly amounts greater than the deductible. It would be better to eat a few thousand euros now than have insurance refused later.

As the most possible extreme in singlehanded sailing, I asked Power to consider the Global Ocean Race for Class 40 yachts. Fastnet has become a key supplier of insurance to these skippers. Obviously as a round-the-world race this is not indicative of the insurance most singlehanders require, but it does point toward the type of questions that all of us should consider. Fastnet's six-page questionnaire included the following information:

- Detail any accidents/claims/losses.
- Did the losses take place whilst racing?
- List all offshore *voyages* over 1000 nm, for each year, over the past 10 years; fully crewed, shorthanded, singlehanded.

- List all offshore *races* over 1000 nm, for each year, over the past 10 years; fully crewed, shorthanded, singlehanded.
- Include any information about your yachting experience which may affect potential insurer's judgment about your application.
- Detail your plans/program for the yacht over the next 12 months, including refit work, trials, qualification voyages and races, sponsor entertainment days, etc. Include the locations and indicate which voyages/races will be singlehanded, doublehanded, etc.
- Provide material and builder of the main components: hull, mast, rigging, rudders, engine.

Pricing for a round-the-world race will reflect the additional risks of total loss from a relatively minor event that would necessitate abandoning the boat. For example, a boat stricken in the English Channel can be towed to port. The same boat in the Southern Ocean is a write-off; the cost or even the possibility of salvage is unrealistic. Power suggested that premiums will be in the range of 3% to 4% of the boat's total value, or 2–3 times the normal rate.

On the other extreme, I asked Power to look at Mini 6.50 racers. He commented that they can't find any UK underwriter to cover them. He knows of only one company, in France, that provides this coverage. So Fastnet is not sourcing insurance for the Minis. "We have to draw the line somewhere."

My experience with insurance coverage has been good, even with significant claims. When I broke my mast, the total damage was significant: the mast sheared at the deck, rod rigging and all halyards cut, boom broken at the gooseneck, deck crumpled forward of the mast, lifelines cut in the tangle, masthead lights and windvanes destroyed, and my old spinnaker shredded for the fifth and no doubt last time.

I am well aware that insurance companies exist to earn a profit, and they achieve this by fighting excessive claims. Even before getting a repair quote, I recommended splicing the existing mast rather than replacing it, and I recommended wire rigging rather than rod. I am frugal by nature, with both

THE FATE OF YOUR GEAR

The purpose of the Coast Guard is to save lives, not necessarily to keep equipment in pristine condition. The Coast Guard cut my rod rigging and halyards into pieces while hauling my mast up on their dock. I have heard similar stories of this brute force approach from other sailors as well.

my own and other people's money. It seemed silly to spend a fortune to equip a 35-year-old boat with a brand-new mast and the best rigging. Even with these downgrades, the entire quote was $15,000, about three quarters of the value of the boat itself.

Allan Hart at Coast Claims said that the insurance company was thinking my mast break might

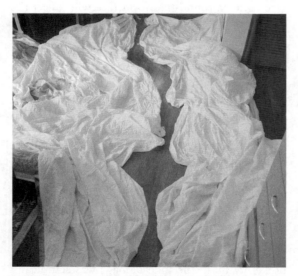

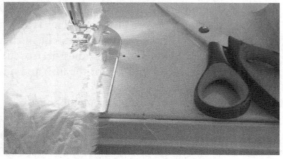

Lucky for me I'm handy with a sewing machine. I'll keep this chute for the next time I'm in really big winds.

have been caused by "wear and tear," which is not covered under most policies. However, from the very start I offered to do two thirds of the work myself, leaving only the mast repair and wire rigging for the professionals. Of course, I am not perfect at these things. The deck repair is not a perfect color match, and for the lifelines I used the Spectra cores from the old cut halyards. My sewing repair of the spinnaker is a mess, but it still works on a run. Looking back, I also could have spliced the mast myself if I had really tried.

Hart has no doubt that my offer turned the insurers in my favor. In the end they covered one third of the work done by the rigging company, all of the materials that I used for the repairs, and the new halyards and electrical wires that I bought in bulk and spliced myself. The insurers even waived my $1,000 deductible on the basis that my labor value was significantly greater.

We live in a world where self-sufficiency is lost in most things. With all of our technology and business degrees, we have lost the gumption to get our hands dirty. I have said elsewhere in this book that self-sufficiency is key to singlehanding. My experience with this repair is solid proof of my statement. Not only is self-sufficiency vital on the water, but my willingness to try, fail, and keep trying with all of these repairs was enough to convince the insurers to provide the coverage that I actually needed.

Of all of the stories about breakage and damage, I tip my hat to multi-voyage Singlehanded Transpac skipper Synthia Petroka, Race Chair for the 2008 edition. When speaking with Ruben Gabriel aboard *Sparky* shortly after he was dismasted 650 miles from Hawaii, she remarked, "You're a singlehanded sailor, so you'll figure it out!"

CHAPTER 13 **LIVING SINGLEHANDED**

I don't think there is anybody else in the world with more experience in living singlehanded than Jeanne Socrates, whom I have introduced earlier. A good friend of mine, Jeanne has completed three and a half solo circumnavigations, along with various side trips—like the voyages from San Francisco to Hawaii, Hawaii to Alaska, and Alaska to

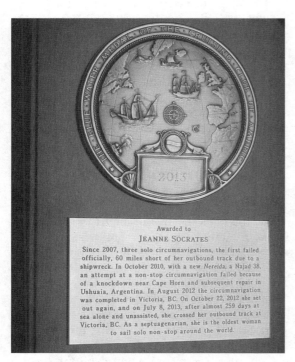

Jeanne Socrates won the 2013 CCA Blue Water Medal in recognition of her three solo circumnavigations. This is perhaps the world's most prestigious award for sailing. *(Courtesy Jeanne Socrates)*

Victoria! In all Socrates has covered some 80,000 nautical miles of open ocean alone. While there are a few racers who have completed more circumnavigations, these men (all men) were travelling at the highest possible speed. Jeanne takes a more leisurely pace. Her latest nonstop circumnavigation lasted eight and a half months. Now in her seventies, Jeanne certainly takes the record as the oldest female circumnavigator. I believe she may have also spent more days at sea actively sailing than any other person, male or female, ever. Socrates's list of accolades exemplifies her qualifications: Cruising Club of America Blue Water Medal, Cruising Association Duchess of Kent Trophy, Ocean Cruising Club Award of Merit and Rose Medal, shortlisted for the UK Yachtsman of the Year Award.

With this amount of experience Jeanne is extremely equipped to discuss the concept of living singlehanded.

FOOD

Our discussion started with the most basic: food. This book often refers to racing situations in which the skipper merely exists on pre-packaged, freeze-dried, meal-in-a-bag sustenance. With her latest circumnavigation lasting nearly nine months, Jeanne, by necessity took a very different approach.

Socrates felt that the most important thing she did was to have the widest possible variety of meals over the entire voyage. Her breakfast was the same as every day at home: cold cereal and milk, with juice before and coffee or tea after. She used vacuum-packed bags of cereal and UHT liquid milk in

1-liter containers. Others had suggested that liquid milk was heavy, and the more than 100 liters (26 gal.) that she carried certainly weighed more than an extra person on board, probably twice as much as Jeanne herself. However, she finds powdered milk unpleasant. She feels that a key to her successful voyage was to actually enjoy what she was eating.

Lunches were more casual. Depending on how busy or hungry Jeanne was, she might skip lunch altogether. A typical lunch could be a tin of tuna mixed in a bowl with mayonnaise and corn. Often she ate cheese and crackers. She carried vacuum-packed cheddar cheese along with tins of specialty Brie or other soft cheese. She also had bags of nuts and dried prunes or apricots handy at all times for snacking.

Supper was more varied. Socrates carried ten dozen fresh eggs on departure. Of special note is that these eggs had never been refrigerated. They were fresh from the hen. This is very important. Jeanne has found that fresh eggs, if turned over every day, will keep for up to four months. She did not coat the eggs in oil or wax but simply turned them every day. She stored all the eggs in a padded box with a simple rope tie with which she could turn them all over with one simple action.

She also carried fresh potatoes and onions, which will last for many months if stored away from light and kept dry. She ran out of potatoes before they turned bad and still had a few onions left after

eight and a half months. These were stored in crates lined with newspaper to absorb moisture.

Jeanne carried a variety of pasta and sauces, rice and Chinese sauces, curry paste, etc. In particular, she has a taste for good-quality tinned meats. As well as tinned ham, she mentioned chunky stewed steak or minced beef in gravy from Marks & Spencer in England. She loads her luggage up with this on every trip back from the UK. For a Christmas dinner, Jeanne had Marks & Spencer's chicken in white sauce with potatoes and petit pois. She had picked up the dried baby peas in New Zealand—delicious!

When expecting bad weather in the Southern Ocean, Jeanne made up a large batch of stew in her pressure cooker. She soaked dried beans overnight as the base for this stew, and added potatoes, fried onions, meat, and canned vegetables. With enough to last for at least three days, she was never without a good meal that was easy to heat up.

Her galley was equipped with a personal strap to hold her in place while working. However, in the roughest weather she found that even boiling water for coffee or tea could be a challenge, so she often stuck to juice and water. She always kept a large supply of nuts, dried fruit, and fresh water at the chart table.

Naturally, over the voyage she lost a couple of trouser sizes. She mentioned an occasional need to force herself to eat. Such a need was confirmed in her conversations with fellow English singlehanders Ellen MacArthur and Mike Golding.

I asked if she had planned each meal in advance of the voyage, and she had not done so. She stored all her tins of meat in one location, pasta in another, beans in another, crackers in another, etc., throughout the boat. She had found on previous trips that if every meal was presorted and stored, it quickly became a confused mess when she worked through multiple meal bags to find what she wanted. Of course, she now admits to having carried a lot of extra food that she is still working through, long after finishing the voyage.

Socrates's water was supplied by the Spectra Cape Horn watermaker. This unit is designed for the most rugged conditions and open ocean yacht

Jeanne Socrates raves about Marks & Spencer meals of minced beef along with dried peas. *(Courtesy Jeanne Socrates)*

Jeanne Socrates used Spectra's Cape Horn watermaker on her eight and a half month circumnavigation. *(Courtesy Spectra Watermakers)*

races. The two-diaphragm Clark pump system cannot be damaged by feed water intake aeration or by running dry.

With a 65-gallon (246 L) water tank, Socrates did not need to run her watermaker a lot, so often ran it a short while just to keep it in good order. She cooked with a mix of two thirds fresh and one third seawater to provide salt, and often prerinsed plates and pots in seawater, using fresh water to wash dishes and for coffee and drinking filtered tank water.

CLOTHING

On previous voyages, Jeanne had learned how quickly clothes become damp in the Southern Ocean. She used vacuum-packed bags to store fresh underwear, socks, and many thicknesses of intermediate layers of clothing. She noted how expensive these items of clothing can be. She broke open a new vacuum pack of dry clothing only every few weeks.

Jeanne carried several foul-weather jackets, two pairs of salopettes trousers, and extra lightweight splash pants. But once sailing in the far south, nothing could be done to keep these all from getting wet and staying very damp. She put them on damp and took them off again even damper. She also carried two pairs of Gore-Tex-lined boots.

Laundry was washed only in the tropic latitudes, done in a bucket in the cockpit. This was impossible in a rough sea or in cold weather. Likewise, personal showers were only possible in the tropics. In the Southern Ocean, bathing was a quick cleanup with baby wipes.

OTHER MATTERS

Jeanne's son is a dentist, so she had a thorough checkup before leaving dock. On his advice, she brushed with toothpaste alone—no water. But with frequently erratic sleep patterns, she often found it difficult to remember to do even that and had to remind herself.

Socrates had a complete set of sleeping bag and duvet on each side of the boat. She used a Mountain Equipment Co-op microfiber-filled bag rated for -10°C. In the cold, damp conditions of the Southern Ocean, she simply removed her foulies and crawled in, still wearing full bottom and middle layers.

To dispose of garbage, she tossed metal tins over the side to degrade in the ocean. All plastic, along with plastic film–coated milk and juice cartons, was rinsed in salt water, flattened, and stored in thick plastic bags. Sailing a 38-foot boat alone, Socrates had a relatively large amount of room for storage of food, equipment, and garbage. The boat was completely packed under the floorboards and in every other possible location. All storage areas were lockable, and all food crates were covered and tied down ready for rough seas.

COMMUNICATIONS

In Jeanne's mind, the most important aspect of "living" on board was human contact. She is licensed for every ham radio frequency she would possibly ever need, and it was not unusual for her to speak with other ham operators 1–2 hours every day. Her log for the voyage shows more than 4,600 contacts over the eight and a half months. She spoke to other operators both individually and in groups. She

MOBY-DICK

Sometimes in life, a coincidence is so profound as to provide positive proof of the hand of some superior sentient being. Such an event occurred as I enjoyed the light winds and sunshine of Cadboro Bay. It was a wonderful day when I set out singlehanded, as is my want, for an afternoon cruise. My Olson 30, *Foolish Muse*, is a racing boat, but on that day I was prepared for a stress-free bask in the sunshine with coffee in one hand, a salami sandwich in the other, and the tiller beneath my knee.

On such days I am usually found with an MP3 player hanging from my neck. I have grown to love classic audiobook versions of stories I find too long or too boring to actually read—but which are quite entertaining when presented by a pleasant voice with a British accent. Seafaring titles such as Carroll's *The Hunting of the Snark*, London's *The Sea Wolf*, and Barrow's *The Eventful History of the Mutiny and Piratical Seizure of H.M.S.* Bounty, are among my favorites. On this day I was determined to finish the final chapters of Melville's *Moby-Dick, or the Whale*. Melville's tome, all 135 chapters, had taken nearly 22 hours so far over numerous trips to approach the end. A slow beat now was the perfect setting to complete this task.

Chapters 133 and 134 of the book provide a nail-biting buildup toward the climax. They give the details of days one and two of the final chase of the white leviathan during which Ahab's favorite crewmember is lost, his ivory leg splintered, and boat smashed.

The event that shapes this story occurs exactly halfway through the climatic chapter 135. As we are all familiar, the great white whale exacts his final and deadly revenge on the *Pequod* and its crew. As I was listening to the book on my little craft, I heard a familiar Pfffffffft sound usually associated with a seal surfacing for a leisurely breath of fresh air. But today the sound was louder than usual—so loud that it penetrated past my earbuds. Thirty seconds later the Pfffffffft came again. This caught my attention. And in another 30 seconds my own whale, gray rather than white, surfaced only 40 feet off the starboard bow. At the very moment of my gray whale sighting, the white whale of my hearing was breaking the back of the *Pequod*.

What an unbelievable way to complete this book. While my whale was benignly enjoying the same sunshine as I, the final lines of the book wound down with Ishmael clinging to a makeshift casket/lifebuoy.

I have sailed some 4,000 hours over the past 10 years. While each and every one of those hours has been incredibly enjoyable, a few, just a very, very few, have proven to be life changing. I will remember the short interval from 1:30 to 2:30 on that afternoon until the day that I follow the *Pequod* into the beyond.

A distant photo showing one of a pair of blue whales I saw on my annual offshore vacation in the open Pacific, 50 miles west of Vancouver Island.

Jeanne Socrates's view from the top spreader of her 38-foot sloop, 1,000 miles north of Easter Island on day 41 of her circumnavigation, where she was attempting to repair the bent mainsail track, which left her stuck with two reefs for the remainder of the voyage. A rare view of her wind-vane, solar panels, wind generator, and radar. *(Courtesy Jeanne Socrates)*

special occasions. She feels that her ham radio was especially valuable for keeping in contact with the world at large after the other failures.

With her computers shot, Socrates lost the ability to receive weather GRIBs. Literally a lifesaver after this was her Furuno 408 Weather Fax Receiver with its own antenna. People might laugh at old-style weather faxes printed on paper, but without this Jeanne would have been sailing blindly into all kinds of nasty weather systems. Having it enabled her to avoid the bad storms of two very deep lows on their way to the Aleutians, as well as to avoid being headed by the changeable winds of frequent fronts. North of the Hawaiian chain, she was able to skirt along a front for several days, keeping going when she would otherwise have been badly headed. Nearing Vancouver Island, she was able to see when it was possible to head east rather than continuing north.

Paying attention to weather involved more than just avoiding storms—there were long straggling fronts that posed problems for heading east—see the path shown here—Jeanne wanted to head east as much as possible to get into the flow of south wind around the North Pacific High but was sometimes forced north-northwest or, at best, due north.

Jeanne learned a key lesson from the loss of her computers. (She had also lost use of two computers on a previous voyage from South Africa to New Zealand.) She told me that some vendors encouraged her to get a single centralized system to handle all aspects of boat operation and communications. She couldn't disagree more with this idea, and her own experience proves it. She has lost multiple computers over the years but has continued on to

made many lifelong friends over the air this way. Now on shore, she is surprised by how often people walk up and introduce themselves by their radio call sign. She knows them well—just not their faces.

Two months before finishing the voyage, Socrates's entire computer system became unusable due to broken screens. Her Iridium satellite phone had gone out long before. She could no longer send email or telephone her family on birthdays or

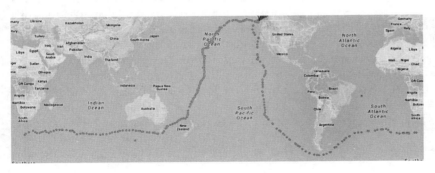

Jeanne Socrates's circumnavigation voyage shows an indirect route from Hawaii to Victoria.

Jeanne Socrates, singlehanding *Nereida*, nears Victoria, Canada, at the completion of her 259-day circumnavigation. Winds were very light, but she was stuck with two reefs in the main due to a bent sail track. *(Courtesy Ian Grant)*

The day after completing her third circumnavigation, Jeanne Socrates is already planning for her next voyage to the South Pacific. *(Courtesy Marylou Wakefield)*

complete voyages that could only be described as incredible. Could she have done so if a single circuit board failure had shut down her entire system?

As I mentioned earlier, with 80,000 nautical miles and literally years of singlehanded sailing under her keel, Jeanne is certainly one of the most experienced singlehanded sailors in all of history. When she makes an observation, no matter how much it flies in the face of opinions put forth by vendors, every singlehanded sailor would be very wise to listen carefully.

LOOKING AFTER THE BODY: FIRST, AVOID INJURIES

"I am a citizen of the most beautiful nation on earth. A nation whose laws are harsh yet simple, a nation that never cheats, which is immense and without borders, where life is lived in the present. In this limitless nation, this nation of wind, light, and peace, there is no other ruler besides the sea."

—Bernard Moitessier

When sailing with a crew it is easy to become cavalier about running around the boat. If a sailor falls, he has a crew member to pick him up and to take over his responsibilities. Injuries are fairly common on an active boat: broken ribs caused from falling onto a winch, sprained wrists from falling onto the deck, and sprained ankles from slipping on lines. While these might not be considered overly serious on a crewed boat, each would probably knock the sailor out of commission for several days, perhaps making it impossible to perform any work.

The singlehander cannot allow for this level of incapacitation. A relatively simple injury could lead to disastrous results, even during a day sail. For example, imagine jumping from the deck to the cockpit, catching a line, and spraining an ankle. This could cause the skipper to pass out for just a couple of minutes, which would be disastrous in a tight space. As a personal example, when sailing at night into the Juan de Fuca Strait, I was very tired when I stepped from the cabintop onto the ledge of the main hatch. I missed the ledge and fell—half through the hatch and half into the cockpit where I banged my head on the traveler. It took a couple of minutes to regain my bearings. I was lucky that the wind was light. Just a half hour earlier, before the wind died, this would have been a very serious incident as the boat continued to sail its course.

The rules laid out below are nothing more than commonsense, but commonsense alone can keep a sailor alive. These types of accidents are completely avoidable with proper caution. If we can avoid the obvious things, we can reduce the threat of accident by 90%. My hope is that after reading this chapter, the singlehander will pause and think for just a quarter of a second, long enough to adjust his behavior a bit to eliminate the risk. Perhaps the best way to put it is *learn from my mistakes*.

The first precaution: never run anywhere on the boat—walk quickly but deliberately. Look down at your feet when walking, not up at the sails or the mast or the rigging. There are dozens of threats to every step but almost nothing dangerous overhead.

The second precaution: never jump. Even jumping a short distance from the cabintop to the cockpit is an accident waiting to happen. Take deliberate, cautious steps from one level to another. Because the boat is a moving target, the chances of missing a proper step are very high. As much as possible, hold onto something solid at the same time. The old seaman's saying "one hand for the boat and one hand for yourself" is more than just quaint. The rule means that in any precarious situation, the sailor should use one hand to keep himself safe and one hand to operate the boat.

The third precaution: keep the working areas of the boat neat—especially at night. Take the time to clear the deck of any lines either coiled or loose, either neat or a mess. Any line will roll underfoot, which is very dangerous on a level boat and even more so on a boat at 30 degrees. At night the sailor will catch his feet on lines virtually every time he moves. Lines are everywhere around the boat. It is impossible to eliminate them but it is possible to make them manageable. The best way is to store the lines in exactly the same place every time. If every line is stored in the same place, the skipper will instinctively know how to avoid them. Even if he does catch a line on his foot, he will know how to shed it in the dark because he will have done it dozens of time in the light. Stuff halyards into a proper rope bag. Each halyard stuffed into a bag eliminates 30–60 feet of line in the cockpit. Loose jibsheets can be eliminated by using a single, continuous sheet rather than a pair of sheets. This one step removes 40 feet of line from the cockpit.

Every danger apparent during the day doubles in intensity at night. Obviously it is dark, making the danger impossible to see. For the most part, a singlehander is working the boat by experience and feel rather than by sight. All lines look the same at night. It is impossible to distinguish between a blue halyard, a green jib-sheet, and a red anchor line. Unless you know exactly where and how each of these lines is stored and how it will release, pulling into a tight anchorage at midnight would be a dangerous and embarrassing undertaking.

Here are a few excerpts from Glenn Wakefield's blog, written after a fall during his second westward round-the-world attempt. (Glenn seriously injured his elbow while pulling a line that unexpectedly released. The only way he could examine the injury was by taking a photograph. Stitches would have been advised, but were impossible in this position. His arm, from shoulder to knuckles, was badly swollen.)

Day 63: I woke with a very stiff left shoulder and elbow which is to be expected after my fall. I am happy with my conservative approach and I think *West Wind II* is fine with it as well.

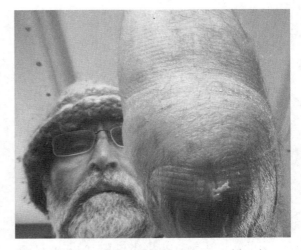

Glenn Wakefield, *West Wind II*, showing his elbow injury while on his west about circumnavigation attempt 2013–2014. (Courtesy glennwakefieldaroundtheworld.com)

Day 65: The wound on my elbow seems to be healing. Infection is the worst thing that could happen and so far so good. I change the bandage every day. I used some butterfly band aids and that seems to be working. It's my left hand so I've been using my right as much as possible. The motion of the boat makes it difficult. I have full movement of my fingers and hand so no problem there. I get some little notices if I do something it doesn't like. Turns out I'm a good first aid attendant.

Day 67: I hit my elbow yesterday which is to be expected. My dressing started to leak and while I was changing it, from what I can see with the aid of the camera, it's OK. I think it will take a while to heal in this environment. I must make something up to protect it from getting knocked, maybe a piece of Styrofoam with a hole in it that I can bandage to my arm.

Day 70: I'm resting today to give my arm a break. It's greatly improved today after a good solid 6 hours sleep last night.

Day 72: My elbow has settled right down these last few days. I will check the dressing a little later.

It is easy for us to read about this in a minute. But when we look back at his log, we understand that Wakefield was working with his bad elbow for nine days. That's nine days of working the sails on the open ocean on a moving boat. The injury takes on a new perspective in this light.

An even greater danger is that at three in the morning the singlehander is extremely tired, blurry-eyed, and making bad decisions. It is ridiculous to tell the singlehander to get some sleep—the boat must be sailed. The only step that can be taken is to make all of the actions required to sail the boat as robotic as possible. The skipper should not have to "think" at three in the morning—it's just not possible. Every action should be done by instinct, which requires that every piece of running rigging be perfectly stored in the correct place.

Do not store sails on deck in the walking areas. They will be in the way and they will be tripped on.

All sails should be stored belowdeck or secured in designated spaces on deck. I follow the rule that the working areas of my boat—the cockpit, cabin top, and foredeck—are all kept neat. These are the areas where I will be rushing to perform difficult tasks like gybing a spinnaker. Anything on the deck will catch either my foot or my tether. If the winds are so strong that I cannot pack the genoa into a bag, I just shove it down the main hatch in a big pile. I know that my working areas are neat, and if I step into the cabin I know that I'll be stepping onto a disorganized pile of sail and line. If I trip on something on deck and fall off the boat, I'll likely die. If I trip on something in the cabin and fall, I'll land on the bunk. The fact that I know the conditions makes this system work. Danger comes only when I don't know what I am stepping on.

Urinating

I am amazed to watch men urinate off the stern of a boat with one elbow wrapped around the backstay, holding himself in the other hand. It just seems insane to be in this precarious position, especially for a singlehander. Here is a paragraph from Ronnie Simpson's Singlehanded Transpac adventure, as published on SailingAnarchy.com:

> One most memorable instance, when I was on my knees pissing off the transom (still clipped in) and the boat decided to round up. So back up to the helm, board shorts still around my ankles, peeing all over myself and the cockpit, so that I can stop the pilot, dump the sheet, drive down, sheet back in, etc. But that's what singlehanding is all about. It's not always pretty, but you get there.

There is a simple solution. Use a 1-liter plastic bottle with a handle, such as a vinegar bottle. Cut the opening a little larger but leave the handle in place. Tie a cord through the handle with a large loop at the other end. Place the loop over a winch. Remaining safely in the cockpit, hold the bottle with one hand and hang onto something solid with the other. A man can just flop himself in the bottle, a woman hold the bottle between her legs. After urinating,

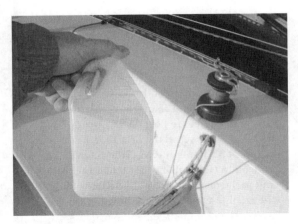

A simple and safe portable urinal—keep it tied in the cockpit.

toss the bottle overboard while zipping up. The bottle will be flushed in the wake. This is a safe solution to the problem.

Bowel Movements

The singlehander has two advantages over a crewed boat. First, he never need clean the head. Second, he can experience the delight of pooping outdoors, with the whole ocean in view. A simple 5-gallon bucket is the source of this joy. I glued a rubber mat on the bottom of my bucket so that it does not slip out from under me—a disaster. I also carry a 1-gallon pail on a rope to rinse out the larger one. I think it would dislocate my shoulder if I attempted to catch water in the 5-gallon bucket while traveling at 7 knots.

Diaper Rash—Not Just for Babies

For an adult, nothing is worse than a bad case of diaper rash. It is caused by too much moisture, for too long, in the nether regions. I strongly recommend that long-distance sailors pay the money for a really good, high-quality set of foul-weather gear. Once a person has experienced diaper rash, $1,000 for foulies will seem a cheap price.

However, in reality nothing can be done to eliminate moisture in the multiple folds of fabric and skin in the groin area. Singlehanders are likely to spend days on end sitting in the steady rain on a long voyage. When their foul-weather gear is wet from the outside, there is little chance for moisture from the inside to evaporate, even with the best gear.

Every singlehander should take a trip to the pharmacy and pick up a jar of strong zinc oxide diaper rash cream. It's messy stuff on a baby, and even more so on a hairy adult. But it should be applied any time that the sailor will be sitting in the rain more than a few hours. Simple corn starch is also invaluable for keeping the nether regions dry. (Corn starch is better than baby powder, which invariably contains perfumes that can cause an allergic reaction.)

Remember, the whole purpose of this book is to share with others the lessons that I gained through hard experience. Learn this one first!

Keeping Clean

Large boats have reasonably sized heads with sinks. Small boats don't. The best alternative to soap and water is premoistened towelettes, such as Wet Ones. These are stronger than normal baby wipes. They work equally well for wiping off sunscreen and after using the bucket.

Industrial-strength paper towels are handy for a quick cleanup after a day in the sun. I use them with water to wash my face and arms in the evening, when sunscreen is no longer necessary.

FIRST AID

Following is an account by my friend and yacht club mate Derk Wolmuth on *Béla Bartók* of his serious infection and request for medical evacuation during the 2012 Singlehanded Transpac:

> I departed singlehanded from Victoria BC June 21st 2012 on my sailing vessel *Béla Bartók*, a Vindö 40 (31'). This brought me into San Francisco Bay 3 days prior to the start of the Singlehanded Transpac. Soon after my arrival in San Francisco I was beset with an intense bout of stomach flu. Unable to eat for a day and a half I was still not feeling great on race day July 1st, although I decided to start. After the 3 days at sea, during the "sea leg" adjustment period where my food intake was reduced, feelings of fatigue and nausea persisted. After several more

days a welt appeared on my left buttock. This increased quickly to a large subsurface carbuncle rendering my leg painful and somewhat useless. The carbuncle arose not as a result of sitting in water, as has been speculated, but by a combination of a weakened immune system, a change in eating habits (during the first passage, the shoreside flu period, and the 3 days of "sea leg" adjustment), onboard challenge of maintaining hygiene, and limits to normal physical mobility. Fatigue, fever, and a general sick feeling accompanied me for the next 11 days.

On July 15th a mere 400 NM from Hawaii symptoms suddenly multiplied including nausea, dizziness, headache, weakness, breathlessness, and an unhealthy feeling in my heart. I made the decision to seek medical evacuation once I experienced the noticeably dramatic feeling of the infection moving into my chest cavity. Once my breathing became labored and my heart rate erratic, I realized it was time that I had to act and made a radio request for a medical evacuation.

I transmitted a mayday on frequency 2182 kHz of my single-sideband radio early in the morning of the 15th. After 30 minutes of transmission and failing to make radio contact with the Coast Guard I engaged my EPIRB. After another 20 minutes of distress radio calling I finally connected with the Coast Guard in Point Reyes. I was then given a medical evaluation and it was agreed that a medical evacuation was the best course of action. Third party radio contact with the freighter *Mokihana* (having just departed Honolulu on route to Oakland) ensued and a three-way conversation continued until the ship appeared on the horizon at dawn. The *Mokihana* was requested to perform the evacuation as it had an infirmary and medical officer onboard. I prepared my vessel by putting it on course to the Kauai Channel with a reefed headsail under windvane self-steering. Boarding the 800' *Mokihana* was challenging as I was without engine power. After the two vessels made contact my vessel scraped down the side of the ship and came close to being dismasted. Through the

small loading bay door at the aft end of the ship I was able to grab hold of cargo netting hung over the side and haul myself aboard. I was then directed to the infirmary. Unknown to me at the time, the captain of the *Mokihana* boarded the *Béla Bartók* and changed the self-steering course 15 degrees to port putting her on route with Maui. My vessel the *Béla Bartók* continued sailing at 3.5 knots and was later intercepted and sailed into Honolulu by SHTP race organizers and yachtsmen who were able to track her due to the satellite-connected race beacon installed as part of the race management logistics.

Needless to say I was very thankful for making it to the ship's infirmary where my vital statistics were recorded and then sent via satellite voice link to a coast guard flight surgeon stationed in Port Angeles who remotely assessed my condition. I subsequently received a slew of antibiotic injections performed by captain Thomas Crawford of the *Mokihana* which knocked back the infection. I am very grateful to the captain and crew of the *Mokihana* for working overtime and with increased risk to themselves to extricate me from this situation.

As I have had a chance to reflect on this journey I continue to learn and have recently upgraded my radio knowledge through passing the HAM radio licensing course and am also about to take a wilderness survival medical course. Needless to say I now also carry a full range of antibiotics and extended medical kit.

In hindsight, if I had carried a preventive stockpile of oral antibiotics onboard I am somewhat certain that I could have self-treated this condition so it didn't degenerate into a life-threatening situation. That said, singlehanded sailing is still a drive and passion and I will be embarking from French Polynesia to Fiji in the spring of this year.

On it goes. Count your blessings and live your dreams.

Derk Wolmuth

Wolmuth's story is particularly interesting because his medical condition was not "caused" by sailing, as we are more accustomed to reading. Rather, he would have faced the same problems on an extended cross-country ski trip in the Rocky Mountains or a canoe voyage in Northern Ontario.

The singlehanded sailor faces two key issues with regard to medical aid. Most "first aid" is given with the assumption that the patient can be transported to hospital within minutes, or at most a few hours. In nearly every first aid book in the world, the instructions for every serious ailment either start or end with "transport to hospital immediately."

When a sailor is offshore, the assumption must be made that formal medical assistance is 48 hours away at the absolute minimum. More realistically, professional medical assistance is 5–7 days away. I am not exaggerating with this figure, as it has been proved time after time.

Two factors lead to this long delay. First, if sailing anywhere more than 100 miles offshore, even near populated areas, it must be assumed that it will take 8–24 hours for a rescue vessel to reach the boat. If a sailor were to issue a mayday by VHF radio, he would have to hope and pray that a ship is passing within 20 miles to pick up the signal. If the sailor were to activate an EPIRB, it would take several hours for the Cospas/Sarsat system to verify the signal (which requires calling the sailor's contact person to verify that the signal is not a false alarm) and activate the emergency response. If the sailor were to attempt communication to the Coast Guard by single-sideband radio—good luck! Experience has shown this to be unreliable at best. (Remember Skip Allen's return to California from Hawaii, where he tried to contact them: "Coast Guard NMC Pt. Reyes, Kodiak, and Hono were not answering my radio calls on their published 4, 6, 8, and 12 mg frequencies, both simplex and duplex." See Chapter 11, Managing Heavy Weather, for more details.)

It is also unlikely that a casual sailor would go to the trouble of installing an SSB for a once-a-year offshore outing. A sat phone is the only way for a typical sailor to reliably and immediately contact emergency assistance. But the expense of purchasing or renting a sat phone means that many trips are done without them.

Second, in any type of rough weather evacuation will be impossible even once a rescue ship has appeared. Here is a brief excerpt (from http://www.kimchowaroundtheworld.com) about Glenn Wakefield's first westward round-the-world attempt:

But when he was about 300 miles northeast of the Falkland Islands and 750 miles from Cape Horn—his last big challenge before he turned the corner on the home stretch—a storm battered him, his boat, and his dreams. "I didn't look on the weather to be anything more unusual than what I'd already experienced," Wakefield said. "But as it turned out it was."

The boat was rolled by the fierce wind and enormous waves. Wakefield didn't think he'd perish, but said he realized his "capability to carry on was diminished."

"I was unconscious for a while, I had a gash, and was bleeding and the one side of my body was quite badly bruised so I have some nerve damage—nothing that time won't heal and I'm well on my way, but when you put that together with the fact that the life raft was gone, the solar panels were gone, the wind generator was damaged, and one hatch was gone, it just led you on a path that wasn't particularly great," Wakefield said. "As it turned out, it was the worst weather they'd had in the Falkland Islands in 25 years."

The Argentine coast guard pegged his situation immediately but getting a 450-foot naval vessel to him quickly was another matter. "It took them two days to get to me and then when they got to me it was so rough they couldn't get to me for 36 hours," Wakefield said. "It was too rough."

I know of several other examples with a similar long delay. The simple fact is, any offshore sailor must be prepared to live, and I do mean live, with emergency medical assistance at least 48 hours away under the best conditions and seven days away under the worst.

The second key issue the singlehander faces is that there are virtually no documentation and absolutely no courses available on "self first aid."

We live in a social world in which the loner really is alone. All first-aid manuals talk of treating "the patient" as a third person. (For example, even the excellent *Doctor on Board* reference book discussed below refers only to performing the Heimlich maneuver on another person, not on oneself.) And all books assume that the injured person will rest after the incident—a liberty not given to the singlehander.

Here are excerpts from the incredible story of Victor Yazykov, who performed self-surgery during the 1998 Around Alone (from www.SFGate.com as written by April Lynch, *Chronicle* staff writer, on November 19, 1998):

> Early in the race, he injured his right elbow. By November 10, he e-mailed Carlin, the race's on-call and online doctor, that his elbow did not look good.
>
> "It feels like dead," he wrote. "Waiting for your help."
>
> The arm problem grew worse, spreading to Yazykov's hand and making it tough to climb the mast, secure lines, or wrestle with the rigging. On November 12, Yazykov wrote, "The pulse in the wrist is OK. . . . All the fingers are moving, but it is still a bit colder and weak."
>
> The next day, Carlin decided that the infection needed emergency surgery. Yazykov, equipped with a few medical supplies, would have to do it on his own. Carlin e-mailed detailed instructions on how to puncture and drain the abscess with the scalpel. Yazykov would have to hold his arm over a mirror to see where the incision would go.
>
> Yazykov got the doctor's e-mail. Then, as the sun went down, his computer link died. He was on his own.
>
> The surgery was makeshift at best. Bungee cords, a bottle of red wine, and some chocolate became instant medical supplies for a sailor who had to become an instant surgeon almost entirely on his own.
>
> Holding his arm over the mirror, Yazykov cut into the infected area. As blood and fluid poured out of his arm, the sailor could no longer see the incision in the mirror and did not know

> where he should press to stop the bleeding. Panic started to set in.
>
> "It didn't take long to do all the doctor's instructions, but the bleeding was too frightening," he wrote. "So I have placed a (bungee) cord above the elbow," in a misguided attempt to stop the bleeding. "Watching as my life drop by drop (is) leaving me," he wrote in an e-mail Saturday.
>
> Cutting off the blood supply to the injured area could have cost Yazykov his arm. "The stakes were very high," Carlin said. "Losing his arm would have been a disaster."
>
> The tourniquet made the sailor's hand and arm go numb. The wound continued to bleed. The cabin was covered with blood. After two hours, Yazykov's arm turned cold and rubbery, and he took the tourniquet off. Slowly, the bleeding eased.
>
> "Blood was all over the cabin floor," he wrote. "The hand was white, cold and rubber-like. . . . I have been losing control. Getting out of power. Will finish later. Bye."
>
> He tried soaking the hand to coax some life back into it. Believing that red wine would help rebuild his blood supply, he drank half a bottle of it. He ate some chocolate. He took a couple of aspirin. Then he passed out.
>
> When he woke up, Carlin directed him by e-mail to apply direct pressure to the wound, which Yazykov did. He finished the first leg of the race, making it to Cape Town, and is expected to make a full recovery.

Medical References

Two books can provide the singlehander with good information for medical emergencies.

International Medical Guide for Ships is available for download from the World Health Organization at www.who.int. This volume should be printed and stored in a binder on the boat for the simple reason that it is the only large reference that actually uses the phrase "when evacuation is not possible"—i.e., it was specifically written for use at sea when help may be days away. The book was written for a ship's designated first-aid provider. As such, it assumes a basic level of medical competency.

This book has an excellent "medicine chest" section that describes in detail exactly what items should be carried in the boat's first-aid kit. Perhaps most important are the "What to Do" and "What Not to Do" instructions for every possible malady.

Dr. Laragh Gollogly, editor of the third edition, commented:

> Well, the same things happen to people on board a ship that happen on land. And because of the dangerous environment in which they are working a lot of other things that don't happen on land. So you have every gamut of problems you would see in an emergency room, from violent crime, to poisoning, to suicide attempts, to heart attacks, to falls from a height, with the addition of cold water exposure, drunkenness, diabetic crisis . . . everything you could imagine. And this book covers everything, essentially, it really does.

The International Sailing Federation specifically notes this book in the Offshore Special Regulations for Cat 0 and Cat 1 races: "In the absence of a national authority's requirement, the latest edition [of the *International Medical Guide for Ships*] is recommended."

Prior to a voyage, the singlehander should spend a few evenings browsing through the guide and reading the treatments for the most likely problems.

Doctor on Board, by Dr. Jurgen Hauert (2010), is a much more practical book for the typical sailor. It is an excellent quick-reference guide that also recognizes help may be days away. Most sailors find it easy to read because it uses normal, everyday terms and has many pictures. This 96-page book covers most of the traumatic injuries that might occur on board. It also has a concise list of medications and equipment for the medical kit.

Other Sources of Knowledge

Courses in remote first aid are available from the Red Cross, such as Wilderness and Remote First Aid (see www.wrfa.ca). An Internet search for "remote first aid" will show numerous courses from public and private institutions.

On a crewed boat, if one person has an accident, the others will be able to take 30 seconds to search the reference books for a resolution. But the singlehander cannot. It is very easy to imagine a sailor slicing a major artery on his hand while attempting to cut and release a spinnaker sheet that has jammed when the boat is broaching. Would this be a good time to search through the 469 pages of the *International Medical Guide*? A singlehander must have read and understood the instructions, at least in the *Doctor on Board* book (plus the self-Heimlich maneuver), before setting out on a voyage.

First Aid Kit Advice from the SHTP 2012 Seminar Series

With the guidance of a doctor, the Singlehanded Transpac website has posted this list of medications and a letter to be given to each skipper's doctor:

Mike's minimalist medical kit:
SAM splints—at least one of each size
Steristrip (or butterfly) closures
Gauze and nonadhesive pads
Tape
Ace bandage
Thermometer
Rubbing alcohol, hydrogen peroxide, benzoin
Emergency dental kit—$25 on Amazon
Meds (* means by prescription):
Pain meds: Aleve, Tylenol, Vicodin (hydrocodone)*
Cough med: Mucinex DM 1200 mg
Skin meds:
Burns, 1st degree = red skin, cool compresses
2nd degree = blisters, DON'T open the blister, if they become open use nonadherent dressing. Current recommendation is not to use Silvadene as it can delay healing, not good evidence of benefit from other prophylactic antibiotic creams, use if signs of infection occur.
3rd degree = get help ASAP
Topical antibiotics: Polysporin (not Neosporin due to allergy risk), Bacitracin
Allergies: Benadryl cream, 0.1% TAC*cream 30 gm (medium potency cortisone cream) otc HC isn't very useful
Sunscreen !!!!!!!

Antibiotics: discuss alternatives with your doc if you have allergies to any of these

Diarrhea—Cipro* 500 mg 3 times a day for 3 days 6 tabs

Skin infection—Keflex *500 mg one 4 times a day 40 tabs (nonresponse to Keflex suggests drug resistant staph, switch to Septra DS* one twice a day 20 tabs)

Productive cough—Azithromycin* 250 mg 2 day one then one a day for 4 days 6 tabs

Bladder infection—Septra DS* one twice a day for 10 days

Seasickness—whatever has worked for you—I use Transderm Scop* for myself and bring meclizine and Phenergan* (both oral and suppositories) for crew

Allergic reactions—Benadryl (I don't think the nondrowsy ones like Clariten are potent enough to bother with); Prednisone* 20 mg 3 for 3 days, 2 for 3 days, 1 for 3 days for severe allergic reaction 18 tabs (or whatever your doc's favorite tapering schedule is)

Eye problems:

Pink eye—ofloxacin* 2 drops 4 times a day for a week

Corneal abrasion—would NOT patch due to problems with only one eye at sea—use antibiotic eye drops as above

Vaccinations

All—be sure tetanus is up to date

Over 50—get the shingles vaccine

A sample note to one's physician on materials needed for offshore singlehanding:

Dear Doctor,
Your patient is about to embark on a sailboat race to Hawaii which will place them far from any medical facilities for 2–3 weeks. Halfway to Hawaii is as far as you can get from land anywhere on Earth, and they will be doing
this alone. In order for them to be prepared for the more common medical problems that may occur I've suggested they bring the following prescription medications:

Pain—injuries, especially rib fractures, are the most common problem and I consider 50–100 Vicodin or Percocet one of the higher priorities
ENT—Azithromycin, Cortisporin otic
Eye—Ocuflox
Skin—Keflex, Septra (for MRSA as well as UTI), Silvadene or Bacitracin for burns, medium potency steroid cream i.e., 0.1% TAC
GI—3 days of Cipro
Seasickness—whatever has worked for them i.e., Transderm Scop, Phenergan, Zofran; plus as backup should their usual med fail them Phenergan suppositories
Severe allergic reaction (i.e., Portuguese man-of-war) Medrol Dospak or prednisone

Anything else you might consider necessary for someone who will be far from medical help for over a month, especially if they have allergies to any of the above medications. They have been advised to also discuss any adjustments to their medical supplies required by any personal health problems.

This chapter has shown how commonplace injuries, such as banging the elbow hard, or commonplace sickness, such as a bout of the flu, can become drastically more serious when sailing alone on the open ocean. None of these would have been considered serious at all with a crew on board who could minister to the injured or at least provide food and rest. But sailing alone, they take on much greater consequences.

In the modern world, we have come to rely on ambulance service at our door in less than 3 minutes and emergency wards open to our every cut and bruise 24 hours a day. My hope is that skippers will not carry that blasé attitude out onto the water.

CHAPTER 14 RACING—GET INTO IT

Racing is the best way to learn to sail a boat well. It has been said that one year of racing experience is worth ten years of cruising. I believe that the difference is even greater. The reason is that in racing, boats are forced to take a route that is often uncomfortable and in worse weather than they would cruise. As well, when racing each skipper will be comparing the boat to all of the other boats—it's just human nature to want to do well. Sailing poorly is equivalent to driving a car with the emergency brake on. It is just inefficient. Sailing well is like driving a tuned car. Racing is the best way to learn to sail well.

Most regions have a limited number of singlehanded races, so we have no choice but to race singlehanded against fully crewed boats. I race every week—year-round. All but one or two of these races are against crewed boats. Over the last six years I've raced at least 250 times against fully crewed boats. I win few of these races, but I gain valuable experience every time.

For all of the reasons listed above and for the various issues listed below, a singlehanded boat is not as fast as a crewed boat. The only way to overcome this is for the singlehander to sail more intelligently than any other boat on the racecourse. The tips given below will assist in this endeavor.

HANDICAP ADJUSTMENT FOR SINGLEHANDING AGAINST CREWED BOATS

After racing for a full season, I found that I was very consistently racing bow on bow with another club boat that was rated at 13 seconds slower than my boat. At the annual club race meeting, I asked for, and was given, a PHRF handicap adjustment of 13 seconds per mile for singlehanding. Over the years since then I've found this to be quite fair. On corrected time I tend to do well on light-wind days, horribly on strong-wind days, and to finish in the middle of the pack on moderate-wind days. This is as fair as it can be. The tactics discussed below explain why a handicap adjustment is appropriate for the singlehander: it is either impossible or unsafe to sail as fast as a well-trained, crewed boat, and it's worth only 13 seconds per mile! Any more and the skipper is just not sailing well.

Distance races are ideal for singlehanders. These distance races might be just 5–7 miles long on weeknights or 15–25 miles long on weekends. A typical course is around a nearby island or navigation buoys with only one or two spinnaker runs. It may be necessary to ask the race committee for weekly distance races. The decline in interest in round-the-buoys races over the past decade is common knowledge. Distance races are a great opportunity to refresh the racing scene for all boats, not just singlehanders. Most club distance races are a more casual affair than round-the-buoys races, with less aggression by all. It's time to get off the merry-go-round.

Typical round-the-buoys racing has an extra challenge for the singlehander because of the need to keep clear of other boats at the rounding marks. This often means sailing 50 yards away from the windward mark before raising the spinnaker, and dropping the spinnaker 50 yards before the leeward mark. Obviously this is a huge racing disadvantage. But as a singlehander, you have an extra responsibility to keep clear of other racing boats. There are times to be aggressive and times to give way, even when not required by the rules. The best advice is to remember that as a singlehander you are probably not going to win the race anyway, so if you are generous with the rules, others are much more likely to be generous the next time. For example, I would never head a boat up into the committee boat at a starting line, because I know that next week the position may be reversed and I'll hope for the same consideration.

It is important to let other racers know that you are singlehanding. While it is unreasonable to expect any extra consideration (they will often give it anyway), it becomes a factor during tricky maneuvers. For example, in high winds I often hail a nearby boat to "keep an eye out" while I am raising a spinnaker just in case my boat rounds up sharply.

I've never hit another boat while racing singlehanded, but I've done so twice with a crew. I believe that as a singlehander you are much more aware of your surroundings than a crewed boat because you can never assume that someone else is watching out—there is no one else! It would be ridiculous to drive a car while asking the passengers to look for children crossing the road. In the same vein the singlehander is responsible for driving the boat and looking for hazards on the water. In retrospect it actually seems safer this way.

Flying the number 1 pennant (a red dot on a white background) is the best way to remind other boats that you are singlehanding. When asked, I remind people that the number 1 pennant is the universally unknown symbol of the singlehanded sailor.

THE STARTING LINE

Against Crewed Boats

The starting line is the one place where a singlehander can gain a significant advantage. The overriding philosophy at the line is "not to be in first place across the line—but to be in second place one minute later." This philosophy will keep the singlehander out of trouble, out of other boats' ways, and will give him a great start a majority of the time. This philosophy has worked so well for me that I've been complimented on having many good starts.

Arrive at the start line at least 5 minutes before the first warning gun. Take a good look at the line and figure out where all the other boats are going to be at the start. Most often in club races, all the boats will be crowding the committee boat end or the pin end, depending on the wind. So the first tactic is to avoid that end of the line completely. Why? There are three key reasons. First, there will be lots of jostling and calls to "head up" in the crowd. A singlehander has enough on his mind and does not want to get involved in this type of jockeying for the one top position. Second, only one boat will be first across the line and in club racing this is as much a matter of luck as skill. All the other boats will be sucking bad wind behind the first boat. Third, as we've discussed, in high winds a singlehanded boat makes significantly more leeway than crewed racers. So the skipper does not want to be sailing just slightly to windward of any other boats. He will drift down on them and need to drop behind to avoid a collision.

So a singlehander who avoids the crowd has, with this one tactic, put the boat into clear air and probably into second place 100 yards after the start. I can't say how many times I've used this tactic with success. I'm all alone in clear air and sailing full speed at the gun on the so-called "unfavored" end of the line while watching ten boats shouting at each other and sucking bad wind at the favored end of the line.

It is truly amazing to watch this phenomenon play out on downwind race starts where the boat that was first across the line in the crowd has its wind killed by the spinnakers of all the other boats behind it. Only on rare occasions should a singlehander get mixed in with the crowd at the start.

Another tactic that I've used well is to follow the others at the committee boat end but just slightly behind, and then tack immediately after the start. All the other boats on the line can't tack onto port until the lead boat tacks, and that skipper might not want to. Once again, I'm in clear air at full speed

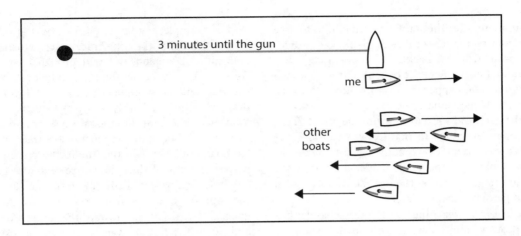

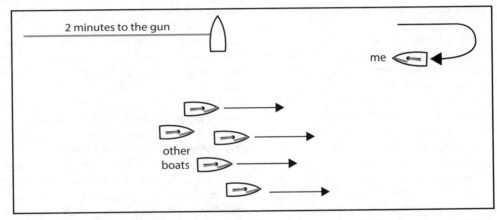

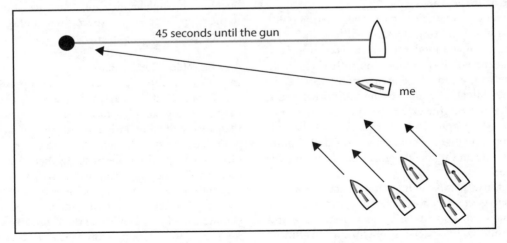

A starting sequence I have used to avoid the crowd when the committee boat end of the line is favored. However, this is only one of an infinite number of potential race starting sequences.

just moments after the start. It is difficult to foresee every starting tactic, but it remains the best advice to stay away from the pack.

Another example of the benefit of this approach occurs in handicapped races with upwind starts, where the biggest boat takes a position anywhere near the pack and soon moves into the lead. All the other boats are stuck in that leader's bad air. It is smarter to be well away from the pack in these situations. Remember, the singlehander does not want to be in first place across the line, he wants to be in second place one minute later.

So, before the warning gun the singlehander has figured out where the crowd will be and where he will be. Now is the opportunity to determine how to get there. As a first step, pick a route to take on the final run to the line. The goal is to hit the line at the gun at full speed. Perhaps the best choice is to run all the way down the line from the committee boat to the pin. Or perhaps the better choice is to run up from 100 yards behind the line, at a 45-degree angle. There have even been times when I've used a port start at the pin end because I knew all the others would be on starboard on the boat end.

It may be possible to sight on a crab pot, a small buoy, or a house on shore to use as a starting point for the final run. As a general thought, the starting point for the final run should be slightly less than 1 minute from the start.

Next, figure out how to get to that starting point. In most cases the singlehander will sail up to the starting point at a moderate speed. For example, if the final run will be from the committee boat down the line to the pin, the starting point will be the committee boat. The route to the committee boat is probably a direct line extension of the starting line. If the starting point is 100 yards back of the line, the skipper might choose to get to the starting point by sailing from the line downward. I'll call this the warm-up.

Next, use a stopwatch to time exactly how long it takes to get to the chosen starting point including both the warm-up and the final run to the line. It is important to be as precise as possible in this timing and include the time it takes to make the turn from the warm-up to the final run.

For example, say I've chosen to start at the pin end. I know that the other racers are favoring the committee boat end and will probably come up from 45 degrees below the line, so before the gun the line will be completely clear and I can run down the line easily. My warm-up will be to sail away from the committee boat for 1 minute, then gybe and sail back passing just below the committee boat, and then run the line to the pin end. To prepare for this, I time the entire sequence before the first warning gun. I click my stopwatch as I pass the committee boat, sail for exactly 1 minute and gybe, and then sail back toward the committee boat and down the line. I stop the stopwatch just as I head up at the pin. In a typical club race I've found that I sail out for 1 minute, back for 1 minute and 15 seconds, and then 45 seconds down the line to the pin. I've done these measurements so many times that I really don't need to do them before every race if I arrive late.

If performed reasonably well, this timing practice will put the singlehander exactly on the line at the gun. The amazing thing is that most other racers will not be doing this type of timing; they simply guess on their final run to the line and more often than not are wrong. By taking this simple extra step of timing the starting sequence, the singlehander will have a very significant advantage over the other boats. As a singlehander you must use your mind to make up for the many speed disadvantages faced in racing.

Against Singlehanded Boats

In a race of only singlehanders, the opposite approach is used at the start. Very few sailors do more than one singlehanded race each year. Because of this they tend to be rather shy in the normal congestion at the starting line. In a crewed race these same skippers would be pushing their way to the best possible starting position, but in a singlehanded race they float around nearly aimlessly.

An experienced, self-confident singlehanded skipper can take advantage of their timidity and use the same level of aggression at the start as in any crewed race, moving to the best possible position at the favored end of the line. The skipper who uses this tactic will be well ahead of every other boat in the fleet.

I have used this approach in every singlehanded race I have entered, and it has never proven wrong. Perhaps this would not be the case in a race like the Figaro Solo Race, but it is certainly the situation with normal club racing.

ROUNDING THE WINDWARD MARK

For the singlehander, rounding the windward mark requires extra attention because this is a key point where boats congregate. Unfortunately there is little that can be done to improve the situation without causing great distress to the crewed boats, which will not pay off in the long run. The overriding goal at a mark is to seek out clear water to engage the autopilot and raise the spinnaker. Nothing is more frustrating than being pinned into a crowded position watching other boats raise their spinnakers.

Most crewed boats enter the mark zone wide with a plan to turn tight around the mark. As a singlehander, your best strategy is to enter the mark zone tight with the idea of sailing wide after the mark. Although it may be legally permissible to force other boats wide as well, this would defeat the purpose of the maneuver because then you won't get the clear water you want. The idea of this tactic is to gain clear water to activate the autopilot and raise the spinnaker without danger of collision with other boats. Often the best strategy is to duck behind other boats, allowing them to lead around the mark but gaining clear water instead. Similar to the starting line strategy, you forgo fighting for the best possible position at the mark in favor of gaining a good position a minute later.

If your boat is properly set up and you are prepared, it should not take any longer to raise a chute than on a crewed boat. But this requires that you have the clear space necessary to do it. So, even if you are first to the mark, sail wide because following boats will quickly envelop you.

The amount of clear water required to raise the spinnaker depends entirely on the wind conditions. In light winds there is very little risk of a massive roundup when raising the chute, so only a small amount of clear water is needed.

In moderate winds, the danger of a roundup is greater until you've gained some experience. I will repeat the instructions I gave earlier: make sure that the spinnaker sheet has significant slack so that the chute does not fill when first raised. The chute should fill only when you deliberately trim the sheet with the intention of having the spinnaker fill. Obviously you do this only when you are confident that it is safe to do so.

In heavy winds the risk of an accident with the spinnaker is significant. Seek out a considerable amount of clear water, as much as 50 yards, before raising the chute. Sail wide around the windward mark to get this needed space. Other racers will almost certainly sail tight around the windward mark, attempting to get the best line to the next mark.

It is a tactical risk for the singlehander to mount the spinnaker pole before rounding the windward mark. In attempting to sail as close to the mark as possible, the skipper may misjudge and undercut, or a crowd at the mark may force the singlehander below the mark. In either case, the singlehander is forced into rapid turns to get back on course and back around the mark. These turns are impossible with the spinnaker pole in place.

It is also wise for the singlehander to consider gybing with jib and main only, before mounting the spinnaker pole and raising the chute. This is appropriate in heavy winds where the singlehander might not want to gybe once the spinnaker is up. Sacrificing one minute after rounding the mark is preferable to sailing a longer stretch without the spinnaker later in the leg.

THE LEEWARD MARK

A singlehander need not give any water at the leeward mark. He should be able to douse the spinnaker and round the mark every bit as fast as a crewed boat. There are a couple of conditions. First, he must ensure that the spinnaker halyard and guy are ready to run without any snags. If they do not run freely, he will not get the chute down by the mark.

A singlehander will not be able to do a windward takedown common to crewed boats because he cannot get the pole down before the mark. He

WHEN RACE BOATS MEET

Of course, singlehanders must adhere to the same port/starboard and windward/leeward rules when boats are crossing. Because you are alone, another boat's crew may assume that you have not seen them and shout "Starboard!" more than they would for another crewed boat. Acknowledge that you have seen them by shouting "I've got you" or "No problem" in return so that they don't keep shouting. I've found that just a hand wave is not enough to acknowledge a shout.

must douse the chute beneath the boom into the main hatch, and leave the pole up, thus staying on the same tack, until after he has cleared the mark and stabilized his position on the upwind leg. Only once he is at full speed on the windward leg should he drop the pole. Naturally he will not be able to tack until the pole is down.

Some singlehanders launch and douse from the foredeck. This is much slower than from the cockpit because it must be done far ahead of the mark, leaving the boat with only a small headsail in the final boat lengths before the mark. I usually leave my chute up until the very last moment on a downwind leg. This is not possible if dousing to the foredeck because the skipper must give himself time to return to the cockpit.

CHAPTER 15   MAINTAINING A WINNING ATTITUDE FOR THE DURATION OF A LONG-DISTANCE SINGLEHANDED RACE

A hundred years ago the marathon was considered a survival race. Early Olympic film shows wobbly legged men collapsing at the finish line in a state of advanced delirium. Just finishing was considered remarkable. A century later and hundreds of thousands of average people run marathons all over the world, with dozens of high-level, potential winners in every race. The most popular books on running concentrate on how to win rather than merely finish.[1]

Long-distance, singlehanded sailboat racing appears to be stuck in the mindset of the early marathon runners—that finishing is enough to be remarkable. Until now, all academic studies on the subject have concentrated solely on coping with the numerous stresses of the sport, such as lack of sleep, hallucinations, solitude, etc.[2] Even the most popular books on the great singlehanded races have barely touched on the concept of winning, focusing instead on the survival aspects of the voyage.[3] One of the most often repeated statements in singlehanded racing is "In order to win, you first have to finish."[4] While this is obviously true, it reveals the mindset of the sport, even at the highest level.

The time has come to move beyond the notion of simply finishing the race. Competitive singlehanded sailors need to understand and master the concepts that will take them from the finish line to the top of the podium. There are many schools where one can learn to sail a boat fast, even while singlehanded (see the sidebar on Artemis Offshore Academy on page 41), but it is apparent that no one has studied the mental and psychological requirements necessary to win a transatlantic or transpacific race. This chapter attempts to fill the void and move racing to the next level of competition.

There are no other sports realistically comparable to long-distance, singlehanded racing. A typical event lasts two weeks, nonstop, 24 hours a day, in complete isolation other than intermittent radio chat. The skippers eat, sleep, perform bodily functions, read, chat on the radio—and yes, even sail their boats—all while racing. The closest comparable sport is the Iditarod Trail Sled Dog Race[5] in Alaska, which similarly involves a single person in isolation (although competitors meet up after each leg) and a very difficult and unpredictable environment. The results of a personality study of Iditarod mushers are presented later in this chapter.

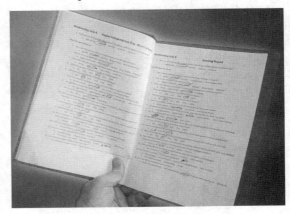

The twice-daily questionnaire was easy to fill out.

(Endnotes for this chapter may be found on page 228.)

Much of this analysis is based on my psychological study involving seven of the twenty-three racers in the 2012 Singlehanded Transpac,[6] a biannual race from San Francisco to Kauai, Hawaii. This is considered the preeminent singlehanded race in North America. The study participants completed prerace, postrace, and twice-daily questionnaires on "maintaining an aggressive/winning attitude for the duration of a long distance singlehanded race."

It is important to note that the sailors completed their twice-daily reports before their radio check-in to ensure that their feelings in the reports were based only on their perception of their own performance in isolation, not as compared to other racer's reported positions.

As a point of comparison, boats in the Vic-Maui International Yacht Race, a biannual crewed race from Victoria, Canada, to Hawaii, agreed to undertake a similar study. The basic survey difference between the singlehanded and crewed versions is the reference to "you" in the singlehanded race and "on deck crew" in the crewed race. For example, "what percentage of time did you feel energetic?" versus "what percentage of time did the on deck crew feel energetic?"

This analysis is also based on my own knowledge and experience from some 900 afternoon singlehanded sails, including 250 races and the 2006 Singlehanded Transpac, as discussed throughout this book. In the 2006 race I placed second overall, missing first place by less than 2.5 hours, or 0.1 knots of average boat speed. I am in full knowledge that this 0.1 knot failure came not from a lack of sailing skill but resulted completely from psychological factors influencing my acceptance of sailing at significantly less-than-full potential speed. I initiated this study in an attempt to understand and correct this 0.1 knot speed differential.

THE MOST IMPORTANT POINT: SAIL HARDER

The saying "In order to win, you first have to finish," is the most dangerous statement in this sport. I have never heard of a team entering the Super Bowl saying, "In order to win we will block a little softer so we don't get injured." I have never heard of a runner entering the Olympic 100-meter dash saying that she's going to slow down so she won't pull a muscle. I never heard of Muhammad Ali saying that he was going to take it easy so that he could last the entire 12 rounds. Every top athlete in every sport knows that the only way to win is to put everything they have, and more, out on the field of play. The line should read: **"In order to win, you have to sail harder than every other boat on the water."**

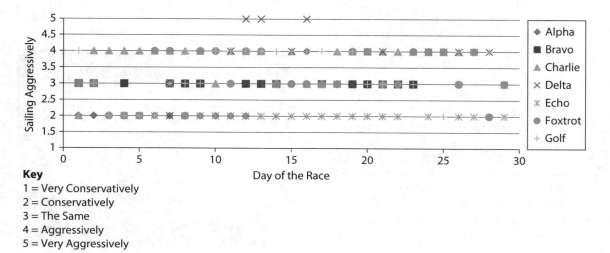

Key
1 = Very Conservatively
2 = Conservatively
3 = The Same
4 = Aggressively
5 = Very Aggressively

Question 8. Individual responses to the question "How aggressively did you sail compared to a normal afternoon race or cruise?"

The study proves this to be true. Question 8 of the twice-daily survey asked, "Compared to normal afternoon races or cruises near your home club, have you sailed: (1) very conservatively, (2) conservatively, (3) the same, (4) aggressively, (5) very aggressively." The results are presented in the graphic on page 206.

Average Self-Assessment of Sailing Aggressiveness (Question #8) Compared to Home Races, by Each Racer vs. Final Race Rank

Racer	Question #8 Score	Race Finish Rank
Charlie	3.8	1
Delta	3.5	7
Foxtrot	3.2	2
Golf	3.2	3
Bravo	3.0	5
Alpha	2.4	4
Echo	2.1	6

The average scores for each racer, from highest to lowest, along with their relative finish race ranking is shown in the above table. We can see from the table that there is a medium 43% correlation between reported aggressive sailing and finish ranking, reading 1, 7, 2, 3, 5, 4, 6.[7] If we remove the outlier boat Delta from the calculation, the reported results have an astounding 86% correlation, reading 1, 2, 3, 5, 4, 6. (Delta's result is interpreted below.)

This correlation was the most significant finding of the study and leads to the most important recommendation for any racing singlehanders: **The skippers' final ranking is directly correlated to how aggressively they feel that they are sailing compared to a usual afternoon race or cruise.** A skipper who feels that he sails more aggressively,

more consistently than any other boat in the race, has the greatest chance of winning.

It is interesting to note that the level of aggressive sailing is not being judged by an independent third party, but by the skippers themselves. What an inexperienced skipper reports as "aggressive" might be considered "neutral" or "conservative" by an experienced skipper. But this did not change the correlation results for the race. It is the skipper's own perceptions of his sailing that proved important.

Referring in particular to boat Charlie, the overall race winner out of 23 boats: the graph shows a very consistent reading of "aggressively" with only two drops down to "the same" after the first day of the race. While other boats had peaks into "aggressively" and even "very aggressively," they had greater variability of reported results during the race with a large number of results in "the same" or "conservatively" categories.

Question #1 of the survey asked, "How are you feeling right now, in terms of pushing hard for the highest possible speed: nervous (1), cautious (2), neutral (3), assertive (4), aggressive (5)?" This accompanying graph (next page) shows the average responses for all seven racers every 12 hours.

There is a large dip at the 36-hour point when exhaustion is kicking in, but then levels climb through midrace, and then drop toward the end as racers understand their final positioning. Of note is the good 50% correlation between responses to this question and those to question 8 on how aggressively each skipper sailed over the previous 12 hours.

As a check on Question 8 about sailing aggressively, Question 9 asked, "Did you push beyond your comfort limit: (1) no, (2) once, (3) several times, (4) many times?" Overall there was only an 18% correlation between the two questions. Thus sailing aggressively does not mean sailing beyond the skipper's comfort zone.

It is important to understand, as seen in the accompanying view of the vessel's routes in the race, that the race result was independent of the course taken by the skipper. That is, as long as the skipper did not make a significant mistake in routing,

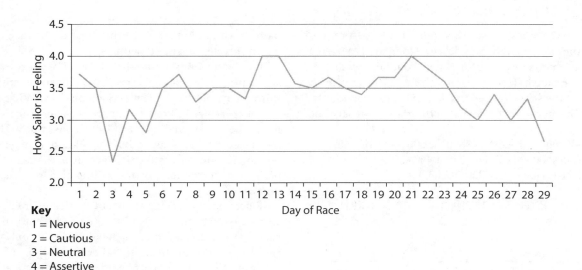

Key
1 = Nervous
2 = Cautious
3 = Neutral
4 = Assertive
5 = Aggressive

Question 1. The average of seven sailor's self-assesment regarding how nervous or aggressive they felt on each day of the race.

the course chosen was much less important than sailing aggressively in the final race results. This might be taken to indicate that excess time spent on weather forecasting and course routing is wasted.

It should also be noted that each boat's potential speed, as measured by its handicap rating, did not appear to impact on final race ranking. For all 23 competitors in the race, there was a negative 11%

correlation between handicap rating and race ranking. It is often thought that the weather during a particular race favors fast boats or slow boats, but this was not the case with the 2012 Singlehanded Transpac.

Boat Delta. On the accompanying route chart, boat Delta is the southernmost track when nearing Hawaii. A record of the course heading of each

The Transpac 2012 routes. Boat Delta is the southernmost boat; boat Alpha is the northernmost track, sailing with an asymmetrical spinnaker.

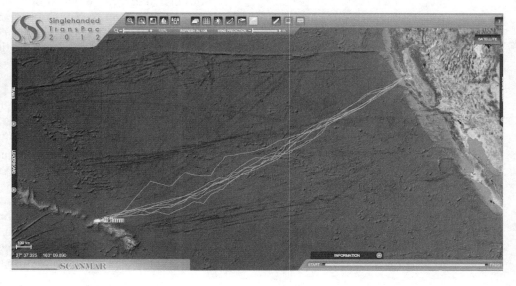

boat, taken every 12 hours through the entire race, provides a look at course deviation, measured in degrees, as shown in the table below. Boat Alpha, on the northernmost track when nearing Hawaii, used an asymmetrical spinnaker that required taking a very zigzag course in the directly downwind trade winds. So Alpha should be ignored in comparing course deviations. Boat Delta has a much higher deviation in course heading compared to the other symmetrically rigged boats (8 degrees greater than the average). Thus Delta sailed a much longer distance than the other boats. This might be a reason why Delta ranked poorly in spite of a high "aggressive" sailing report in survey Question 8.

Standard Deviations to Course Headings

Charlie	15°
Foxtrot	15°
Golf	10°
Alpha	23°
Bravo	13°
Echo	9°
Delta	22°

SAILING COMPARED TO THE IDITAROD

The Iditarod is an annual dog sled race from Anchorage to Nome, Alaska. Running for 1,112 miles, the race typically takes under two weeks to complete, about the same length as the Singlehanded Transpac. The Iditarod trail passes through a landscape of spruce forests and tundra, over hills and mountain passes, and across rivers. Most of the trail is through widely separated towns, villages, and small settlements. Although the racers can see people all along the route and there are numerous stopping points, it is a solitary adventure, much like long-distance singlehanded sailing. Given that the dogs are doing the work (like the sails on a boat) and the musher is along for the ride (like a singlehanded skipper), the Iditarod is perhaps the closest comparable sport to long-distance racing from our point of view.

An extensive study of the personality profiles of twenty-four Iditarod racers was performed during the 1988 and 1989 races.[8] The standard 16PF[9] multiple-choice personality questionnaire was used to measure sixteen fundamental traits of human personality. The test was completed by each musher a few weeks before the race began. After the race, the results were categorized according to how each finished in the race: 1–10, 11–20, 21–30.

The first ten finishers showed by a wide margin the highest score of all groups for the aggressive Factor E. Factor E ranges from submissive (1) to dominant (10). The top 10 finishers scored an average of 9, compared to the 5 averaged by the middle group of racers and the average of 4 by the slowest group. I believe that this is an overwhelming match with the results of the singlehanded study discussed here: the direct correlation between aggressive sailing and finish rank. Accordingly, a sailor must not only be more aggressive during the race but must have a more aggressive personality in general.

The top ten Iditarod finishers also had a very high average score of 8 for Factor F, which is a ranking from sober (1) to enthusiastic (10). Racers in the middle group ranked an average 5, and racers in the slowest group have an average 4 on this scale.

With Factor H, a ranking from shy (1) to bold (10), the top ten finishers averaged 8.5, compared to 5 for racers in the middle group and 4 for the slowest racers.

Perhaps surprisingly on Factor Q3, a ranking from group-oriented (1) to self-sufficient (10), the top ten racers averaged 3, which is far more group-oriented than the others: 8 for both the middle and slowest groups. The Iditarod race has checkpoints including mandatory rest stops and supply restocking. Perhaps during these periods, being team-oriented is significantly more valuable than being self-sufficient. This might be a cue for round-the-world singlehanded sailors, such as the Global Ocean Race, where teamwork and cooperation during stopovers are an important part of winning.

It is interesting to note that all the Iditarod mushers, regardless of their final placing, can be described as being extremely "cool, reserved" versus the opposite of "warm, outgoing." It would seem that this is a trait necessary to even enter the race. I would agree that this compares well with singlehanded sailors.

ASSESSING SINGLEHANDED RACING FACTORS

Experience

In the Singlehanded Transpac study, among the prerace questions were three that attempted to measure experience:

- "How many times have you sailed singlehanded in the past two years: 1–5, 6–20, 21–40, 41–70, 70+?"
- "How many times have you raced or cruised to Hawaii on crewed boats?"
- "How many times have you flown a spinnaker while singlehanded in 15–20, 20–25, 25+ knots of wind?"

The answers are presented in the table below, in order of finish.

It is apparent that there is no correlation at all between race ranking and any one criterion of experience, although when all the items are put together, there is a general feeling that the more experience the better.

Is winning important? I was told several times during this study that skippers were racing only for the experience, rather than the podium—that they were simply making a checkmark on their bucket list. The study itself refutes this point. In the prerace questions, four of the seven respondents indicated a desire to "Hopefully Win," and two wished to "Finish Respectfully." Only one skipper wished to "Just Finish."

Another often-held idea is that skippers use their first entry into the race as a learning experience or practice for future success. Of these seven participants, boat Bravo had sailed the race eleven times previously and Delta had sailed it one other time. This was the first Singlehanded Transpac for the five other boats. All but Echo answered a strong "Yes" when asked, "Do you have the financial resources

Race Experience and Spinnaker Flying Experience Prior to the Transpac

	Times Singlehanding	Times to Hawaii	15–20 knots	20–25 knots	25+ knots
Charlie	1–5	14	Many times	A few times	Once
Foxtrot	41–70	0	A few times	A few times	Once
Golf	6–20	2	A few times	Once	Never
Alpha	6–20	1	A few times	A few times	Never
Bravo	1–5	19	Many times	Many times	A few times
Echo	6–20	1	Never	Never	Never
Delta	41–70	0	Many times	A few times	Never

and vacation time to do this race several times over the coming years, if you desired: Yes, Possibly, Difficult, No?" Even the skippers themselves might be thinking of their first attempt at the Transpac as a practice. But the race records have proven this to be a false hope. In the history of all Singlehanded Transpac races, 75% of skippers complete the race only one time. The Mini Transat race has an even higher attrition rate, in which 90% complete the race only one time. In spite of the skipper's wishes, it is apparent that the financial expenditure and effort required for the race are too high for repeats.

Thus we are left with the idea that (to quote from beer commercials) this is the skipper's one shot at glory, his one chance to grab the brass ring. While simple completion of the race will be talked of at the yacht club bar for several years, winning the race would be a point of pride for the skipper for the rest of his or her life. At the very least, all skippers would want to finish the race knowing that they tried their absolute best, that they left everything they had out on the water, and that they could not have possibly have done better.

Confidence

Survey Question 14 asked, "How confident are you that the boat can finish the race with no significant breakage?" There was a medium 41% correlation between the responses and those to Question 8 on sailing aggressively.

The open ocean is a lonely place for a singlehanded sailor. He has no one to rely on but himself if any of the many things that can go wrong does. In this edition of the Singlehanded Transpac, one racer was rescued by a passing ship when he reported a life-threatening case of blood poisoning. In previous races masts have been broken, a rudder was lost, a boat hull cracked, and a storm led to a rescue on the return trip.

These are typical events in the life of a singlehander and all are perfectly valid reasons why a rookie might have some worries. Regrettably, given the requirement for aggressive sailing in winning, any lack of confidence in the boat must be overcome before race start.

Boat Echo provides one extreme on the proof of this thread. Echo had the lowest level of confidence in his boat, the lowest number of times when he pushed beyond his comfort limit, and the lowest reported aggressive sailing rating. This led to Echo placing second to last among the group and an overall dissatisfaction with his racing performance. He reported that he "stopped racing and started enjoying" the trip after just the first couple of days. In the prerace survey, Echo reported that he had singlehanded six to twenty times in the previous two years and had never flown a spinnaker singlehanded in over 15 knots of wind.

On the other extreme, Delta had the highest confidence in his boat and the second highest aggressive report. Delta had sailed singlehanded forty-one to seventy times in the previous two years and had flown the chute many times in 15–20 knots and a few times in 20+ knots.

Confidence can be gained only on the water in challenging conditions. Singlehanded sailing in 10-knot winds teach a skipper to sail fast. But only sailing in 20, 25, or 30 knots will give the skipper confidence. Race winner Charlie reported, "I had the chute up 24 hours a day for ten straight days. Rode out every squall (maybe 15 of them?) with the chute up." Charlie had gained his confidence in fourteen previous trips to Hawaii, albeit with crew. He had a clear understanding of what a boat can handle, and he pushed it to the limit. Charlie was only in the middle of the confidence ranking but was at the top of the aggressive ranking. This shows that he pushed beyond even his own confidence level. This is what it takes to win a race—having high confidence and pushing beyond it in addition.

Self-Sponsorship

All but a very few transoceanic singlehanded skippers are amateurs. However, many (particularly in transatlantic races) do gain some level of sponsorship from corporations to help offset expenses. Nonetheless, there is no question that each skipper has invested a very large amount of his own money and an even larger amount of work effort in getting to the starting line. Thus the skipper himself or perhaps his wife might be considered his sponsors. So in addition to the concept of making a checkmark on his own bucket list, each skipper must also consider the demands of the sponsor (even if that sponsor is himself). Will a sponsor be happy with anything less than an absolute, full effort? At the end of the race, can each skipper face a sponsor and say, "I gave it everything I had. I could not possibly have done any better."

The survey participants spent an average of about $20,000 to complete the Transpac. This works out to $9.43 per nautical mile or about $65 an hour for 24 hours a day, sleeping and awake, sailing, cooking, reading. Each skipper must ask, "Based on the amount of money it is costing, will my sponsor be happy with my effort over the past day, the past hour, the past 10 minutes? Perhaps each singlehanded skipper should post a big sign in the cockpit: "**$9.43 per nautical mile**"

THE DISCONNECT: SINGLEHANDERS NEED TO ACTIVELY SAIL THE BOAT FOR SUCCESS

Watching videos of the Volvo Ocean Race, considered the highest level of crewed long-distance racing, I noticed a huge disconnect with singlehanded racing. In every VOR video there was a crewman hunched over the grinder. Every 30 seconds or so, this crewman would grind the sheets in or out, making small adjustments to sail trim to increase boat speed. When significant events, such as broaches, occurred, the crewman would immediately jump up and get back on the grinder.[10] I asked a VOR crewman how he was able to maintain his motivation to stand at the grinder many hours a day. He replied that if he didn't do it, there were a thousand other sailors at the next stopover waiting to take his place.

On the other hand, videos of the Vendée Globe, considered to be the highest level of singlehanded long-distance racing, show the complete opposite. Videos show the skipper sitting at the nav station belowdeck or gazing off into the distance at the scenery. As mentioned earlier in this book, during her famous 2000–01 Vendée Globe race, Ellen MacArthur blogged that she was spending 8 hours a day at her nav station, forecasting weather. I sent her an e-mail asking what she was doing in 8 hours that could not be done in half an hour? She replied,

"Nothing." (MacArthur placed second in the race and later set a world record for singlehanded circumnavigation.) It appears that sitting at the nav station was considered to be acceptable sailing. Another sailor friend, Bruce Schwab, circumnavigated in the 2002 Around Alone and 2004 Vendée Globe races. When asked if he helmed the boat, he replied that he did so for short periods, but then went below to "get back to racing."

The question becomes obvious: if constant attention to sail trim is not important for boat speed, could Volvo Ocean Racers significantly reduce cost and weight by cutting their crew size by half? On the other hand, if constant attention to sail trim is important, why are singlehanded sailors ignoring it? Why are singlehanders relying on the autopilot to perform the same functions as the entire on-deck crew?

Skippers must understand that while the autopilot steers the boat, it does not sail the boat. The most advanced autopilots have functions that enable them to learn and adapt to wave movements, but no autopilot has any understanding of boat speed. The autopilot does not know that the wind has dropped by 1 knot and boat speed has fallen by a half knot, or that wind speed has increased by 1 knot and VMG has fallen by a quarter knot. The autopilot does not know that chop has increased so the boat is slowed by half a knot with each wave and that it takes 30 seconds to get back up to full speed. If set according to wind angle, the autopilot does not understand that a 10-degree shift in wind direction adds 1% to distance traveled. The autopilot does not know that surfing a wave is a good thing or that turning down a few degrees in choppy water can increase VMG. And if set according to compass direction, the autopilot does not understand that a 5-degree wind shift can decrease boat speed by 10% or more.

Sailing Faster

It is very easy to study and test these conditions. During an afternoon with normal fluctuations of wind speed and direction, a skipper can set the autopilot, trim the sails, and watch boat speed rise and fall. For example, a skipper might know from the boat's polars[11] that maximum boat speed is 5.5

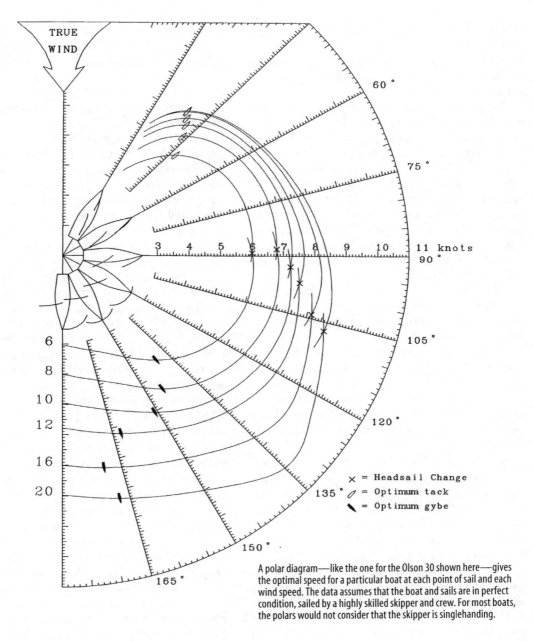

TRUE WIND

60°

75°

3 4 5 6 7 8 9 10 11 knots
90°

105°

6
8
10
12
16
20

120°

× = Headsail Change
⟋ = Optimum tack
◣ = Optimum gybe

135°

150°

165°

A polar diagram—like the one for the Olson 30 shown here—gives the optimal speed for a particular boat at each point of sail and each wind speed. The data assumes that the boat and sails are in perfect condition, sailed by a highly skilled skipper and crew. For most boats, the polars would not consider that the skipper is singlehanding.

knots when beating into 8 knots of true wind, so the skipper hand steers to the correct wind angle, sets sail trim perfectly, gets boat speed up to 5.5, and sets the autopilot to apparent wind angle. Then the skipper notices that boat speed has dropped down to 5.3 knots with no changes in the wind conditions—this

is just a normal fluctuation, but it represents a half day more on a trip to Hawaii. Then if the true wind speed fluctuates within a normal range and drops to 6 knots, the boat speed falls dramatically to 4 knots. This is a 25% decrease in boat speed and represents an extra three days on a trip to Hawaii. Then if the wind picks up to 10, the boat heels over and the GPS notes that the VMG drops by half a knot because the boat is making extra leeway. As well, the autopilot has pushed the tiller to windward, adding extra braking power to the rudder.

After watching the autopilot perform as above for a half hour, the skipper starts steering manually. Once again she steers up to 5.5 knots in 8 knots of wind. Every time a small wave approaches ahead, she heads down a little to build power and keeps the speed steady. A really energetic skipper might also work the backstay to maintain power. Of course, every time boat speed changes, the apparent wind speed also changes, and she makes tiny adjustments to sail trim to keep boat speed up at the highest level. When the wind speed drops to 6, she watches the telltales and sails down by 4 degrees to keep boat speed at 5. (The polars show that the boat can beat into 8 knots about 4 degrees closer than it can beat into 6 knots, so rather than allowing the autopilot to pinch, the skipper gains an extra knot of speed.) When the wind increases to 10, the mainsheet and jibsheets are eased a few inches to add twist and maintain the optimum boat heel, and the boat can now head up by 2 degrees and increase in speed to 6 knots. This also serves to reduce pressure on the tiller, enabling the light touch that ensures no braking and maximum speed.

Heading back home, the skipper turns downwind and launches the spinnaker. The polars show the boat can travel at 5.5 knots at the optimum wind angle of 140 degrees in 8 knots, so the skipper sets the autopilot and watches. The only way to allow the autopilot to sail the boat is to trim the spinnaker sheet until the chute does not collapse with a normal small wind shift. But this means that for the 90% of the time that the wind is not shifting or gusting, the sheet is too tight. This in turn means that the boat is sailing slower than possible. So our intrepid skipper is never able to reach the polar boat speed of 5.5. The boat gets only up to 5.2 knots as the skipper continues to watch. When the wind drops to 6 knots, boat speed drops to 4 knots. But then the wind gusts to 10, the first thing that happens is the boat rounds up in a broach. Of course it will—the big spinnaker is trimmed for a higher

point of sail and the boat will always head up to where the sail is trimmed. After regaining control (which takes a couple of minutes), boat speed rises to 6, which seems good until another boat passes by sailing 8 degrees farther downwind.

Once again taking the tiller and sheet manually, the skipper gets up to 5.5 boat speed at 140 degrees in 8 knots. Every time the chute starts to curl she trims by a few inches, and then eases when the luff tightens again, keeping speed exactly at 5.5. When the wind drops to 6 knots, the skipper heads up by 5 degrees according to the optimum heading on the polars and boat speed drops only to 4.7. When the wind gusts up to 10, easing the sheet to dump wind maintains complete control. Then the skipper heads down by 7 degrees and increases speed to 6.2 knots.

All of the numbers above are based on the polar diagrams and experience with my own boat. This is a very accurate description of a typical afternoon on the water. Wind speed fluctuations of 1–2 knots and wind shifts of 10 degrees happen every few minutes under normal conditions. These examples show that even if the boat is sailing perfectly, the skipper who sets the autopilot and goes below is giving up a very significant amount of boat speed, boat control, and VMG to the skipper who is actively involved in sailing the boat. In addition, boat polar diagrams work on the assumption that the sails are trimmed perfectly. Every change in wind speed does not require simply a change in boat direction but also a change in sail trim. Any experienced skipper knows the joy of watching boat speed rise by half a knot just because the main sheet has been eased by 3 inches.

The facts about boat speed are clear, even to the racers themselves. Perhaps the most telling question of the survey was: "If you had been in the perfect racing frame of mind and had sailed as fast as possible with your abilities while you were awake, could you have increased your 12-hour average speed by: 0 knots, 0.1 knots, 0.5 knots, 1 knot, 2 knots?"

From the accompanying chart showing all the boats, it can be seen that boats Bravo and Charlie (the race winner) consistently show a potential speed increase of only 0.1 knots. Bravo had sailed this race thirteen times, and Charlie had sailed to Hawaii in crewed races fourteen times. But

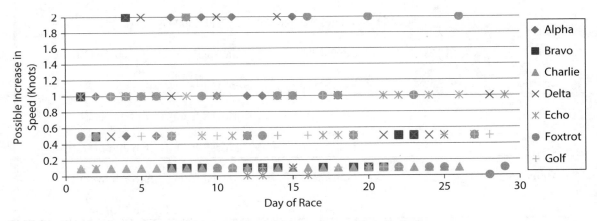

The graph shows sailors' answers regarding whether they could push their boats more aggressively. Charlie, the boat that won, felt little increase in speed was possible—he was pushing the boat all he could.

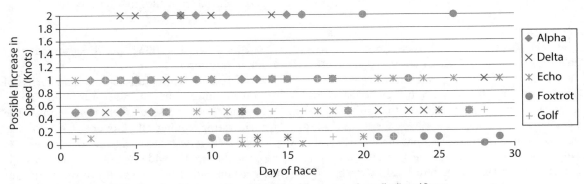

The survey results concerning whether sailors felt they could push their boats, after removing boats Charlie and Bravo.

removing them from the study to show the less experienced skippers is more revealing, as shown in the chart above.

The vast majority of reports from less experienced skippers indicate potential speed increase of 0.5 knots or 1 knot, with significant numbers at 2 knots. (Note that boat Delta reported the second highest average potential speed increase of 0.9 knots, second only to Alpha's 1.3. Alpha is a much faster boat with handicap rating of -123, compared to the average of 141. Delta's 0.9 knot response, along with its wide variation in course, might indicate a general dissatisfaction with course selection and speed achieved.)

Do these numbers make a difference? The Mini Transat has the greatest number of entrants, with seventy-five competitors in two boat classes. An examination of the results of the past four races shows that an increase in speed by just over 0.2 knots would improve the average placement by ten positions. Is it worth the extra effort of 0.2 knots of boat speed to move from seventeenth to seventh? Most racers would think so.

We should also look at what the above potential speed increases would have meant to each boat in miles, time reduction, and final ranking (assuming that each boat had met its potential speed in isolation), when compared to all twenty-three boats in the Transpac. The results are shown in the table on the next page.

Adjusted Finish Times Using Responses to Question 13

Boat	Miles	Time Reduction	Change from Potential Speed Increase
Charlie	31	4 hours saved	Actual 1st overall
Foxtrot	266	33 hours saved	Moved from 7th to 1st overall
Golf	173	22 hours saved	Moved from 10th to 2nd overall
Alpha	222	29 hours saved	Moved from 13th to 7th overall
Bravo	66	9 hours saved	Moved from 14th to 12th overall
Echo	200	27 hours saved	Moved from 17th to 8th overall
Delta	268	38 hours saved	Moved from 18th to 6th overall

In the Vic-Maui crewed race, skippers reported that they could not increase their speed at all, other than in a few boat damage situations. That is, every boat in the Vic-Maui was reported to be racing at 100% of potential for nearly the entire race. I believe, and my own extensive experience racing against crewed boats shows, that there is no reason why a singlehander should be sailing at anything less than the boat's full potential, at least while the skipper is awake.

A significant question in the survey asked, "What percentage of awake time were you in 'the zone' of sailing, able to concentrate on trimming, helming, etc. and not get distracted by other things? 10%, 25%, 50%, 75%, 100%?" See the accompanying graph of responses.

Two results jump out. The vast majority of responses indicate that the racer was "in the zone" of sailing 50% or less of their awake time. The average rating among all skippers was 35%. The highest average was 66% and the lowest was 8%. Also notable are the wide swings within each skipper's results, jumping up and down by significant amounts between reports. This returns us to the earlier question: by how much could each racer have improved his average speed if he had been "in the zone" for an extra 25% or 50% of their time on the water?

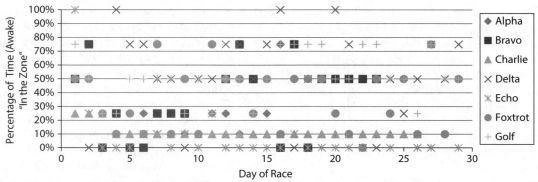

Sailors' responses regarding their sailing "in the zone."

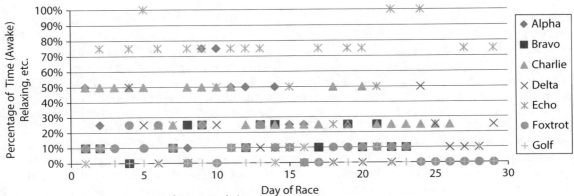

Sailors' responses regarding the percentage of time spent relaxing.

The opposite behavior was also studied with this question: "What percentage of awake time did you relax/read/watch movies/radio chat or just chill out?"

It is abundantly clear from the survey results and from my own experience that there is a very strong tendency to let the autopilot "sail" the boat, rather than just "steer" the boat.

Given the relatively low percentage of time in the zone of sailing and the relatively high percentage of time relaxing, the question of each skipper's satisfaction with his performance comes to the fore. Question 2 asked, "How satisfied are you with your performance over the past 12 hours: very disappointed (1), disappointed (2), neutral (3), satisfied (4), very satisfied (5)? The twice-daily results are averaged in the accompanying table, together with the relative race ranking.

Alpha had the highest satisfaction rating at 3.79, even though he placed thirteenth overall in the race. Even the race winner, Charlie, was only slightly higher than "neutral" about his performance over the duration of the race. Not one racer even reached the point of "satisfied" on average. The results show only a mild 30% correlation between performance satisfaction and final results. It appears that the skippers are reasonable but not excellent judges of their own performance.

More importantly, it shows that the mind-set of the race acknowledges "neutral" as acceptable. This race is costing the skippers on the order of $9.43 for every passing mile, but not one of them

Skipper's Satisfaction with Performance vs. Race Ranking

	Relative Race Ranking	Satisfaction with Performance
Charlie	1	3.35
Foxtrot	2	3.07
Golf	3	3.34
Alpha	4	3.79
Bravo	5	2.87
Echo	6	2.88
Delta	7	3.21

drove himself or his boat hard enough to be "satisfied" with his performance. Perhaps if the racers had been in the zone of sailing for longer periods, had hit their potential speed more often, and had relaxed a little less, they would have been more satisfied with their performance.

Having completed some 250 afternoon and evening races singlehanded, there were very few in which I was not satisfied with my performance even though I have rarely won. After each race I would know if I had tried my best and would analyze my performance for the next time. This is the type of strategy that should be undertaken after each 12-hour reporting period of a long-distance race. Skippers should make a decision about their level of satisfaction and adjust their performance over the next period accordingly. In the postrace report, Golf commented, "I compared what I was doing/seeing with my ideal of what should be done and then analyzed the gaps."

Question 3 then asked, "How do you feel about the coming 12 hours: highly motivated, determined, relaxed, discouraged, dejected?" Did the responses to this pan out in the next 12 hours? The vast majority of responses were "Determined." However, there was a 38% correlation between these responses and the following 12-hour period response to Question 2. This is a medium correlation level for this type of question. It appears to some extent that skippers did adjust their performance. However, there was no correlation at all between each skipper's responses to Question 3 and their final race ranking.

Much of this chapter has promoted the idea that a boat should be actively sailed to reach its potential speed. I believe this would be true even for the race winner, Charlie. Even though he reported a potential for only 0.1 knot of extra speed, one wonders if his laissez-faire approach would have held if he had faced a competitor 100 meters away—if another skipper in an identical boat had been stuck on his starboard bow. Would Charlie have sailed that little bit harder to get away from the mystery boat? A tenth of a knot makes a significant distance when measured over 15 days. For me, 0.1 knot was the difference between my second place and the top of the podium.

Energy and Lethargy

Surprising to first-time long-distance singlehanded racers is just how boring it can be. Once the initial euphoria of starting the race has passed, skippers have only their own company for days on end. This may be the first time in their life with a total lack of someone to talk with. For many, "small talk" makes life bearable for the social human animal. When this boredom is added to the general lack of sleep prevalent in all singlehanded races, as well as the heat of the tropical sun, it becomes a self-perpetuating cycle of energy drain and lethargy.

Lethargy is not the same thing as feeling tired, although they are related. Feeling tired can be cured with sleep, but we understand that lack of sleep is integral to singlehanded sailing (see Chapter 2, The Mental Challenges). It is also possible to be tired and energetic at the same time, if necessity pushes the skipper to activity. In his first circumnavigation, Derek Hatfield was well past exhaustion nearing Cape Horn: "He had been at the helm for almost twenty-four hours and was so exhausted he could barely think . . . ."[12] But just a short time afterward Hatfield pitchpoled and had enough of an adrenaline boost, lasting over several hours, to detach the broken mast and rigging and motor into the islands, all while fighting against 40-foot waves.

Lethargy is better defined as being lazy, sluggish, or indifferent. Lethargy is what a man feels when he lays on the chesterfield on a Saturday afternoon watching NASCAR on TV and is too much of a sloth to get a beer from the fridge, so he asks his wife. The problem is not lack of sleep—it is lack of motivation.

Lethargy is an absolute killer of boat speed because it pulls the skipper away from the tiller and sheets for long periods of time. Every time a skipper watches the telltales flutter, but knows that the situation will correct itself in 30 seconds or a minute, he is experiencing lethargy. Even worse, lethargy tells the skipper to go and read a book in the shade of the mainsail rather than sit in the hot sun in the cockpit.

The study asked, "What percentage of time did you feel energetic?" and "What percentage of time did you feel lethargic?" The accompanying graph presents the average results (with the boat Golf removed, as explained below).

In this graph of the average results, the odd numbers on the bottom represent the evening reports covering the previous daytime. The even numbers on the bottom represent the morning reports covering the previous night times.

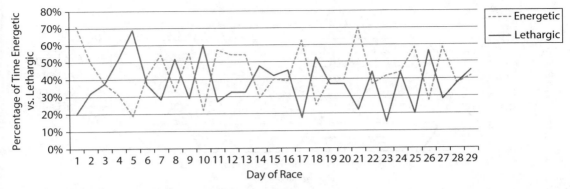

Average of the sailors' responses regarding their feeling energetic versus lethargic.

Moving from the left on the graph, the first noticeable trend is the decrease in energy during the first three days of the race when skippers were facing rough weather and operating on adrenaline, thus getting very little sleep and draining energy rapidly. Next is the clear decrease in energy and increase in lethargy each night, as noted by the up and down swings of the two lines. The peak at point 17 represents the evening report at the time when the largest number of boats is nearing or has just passed the midway distance of the race and boat Alpha is arriving at the finish. The energy level is evenly spread between 50%, 75%, and 100%. At point 21, four of the five boats left in the race reported 75% energy. The other boat reported 50% energy. This was the most consistently high energy level in the race.

Energy level has a medium (32%)[13] correlation with sailing aggressively when all data points are compared. This jumps to 43% if Charlie is ignored. Charlie reported the highest level of aggressive sailing. However, he noted,

Heavy boat that doesn't surf is relatively easy to keep at full speed—a 0.1 change in boat speed for a non-surfing boat is quite a bit. I also noted from discussions with others that very few people had full sail area 24 x 7 (full main, big jenny, then chute). Lots of folks mentioned reefing in day 2 and 3—and taking down the chute for hours each day if not all night. I had the chute up 24 hours a day for ten straight days. Rode out every squall (maybe 15 of them?)

with the chute up (though takes specific squall strategy to make this work). Basically I had all the same sails up as I would if fully crewed. Also my autopilot with gyro helms better than most of my typical PacCup crew. The boat was set-up to sail near full speed without my being at the helm—and the reduced crew weight made her faster than in a crewed race in many conditions.

So it appears that Charlie was able to sail very aggressively without a high energy level.

Improving Energy

The skipper of Golf reported the highest energy and lowest lethargy levels by a wide margin. Before the race and as a part of the study, Golf's skipper was instructed in three techniques for improving energy. The next graph is a comparison between Golf and the other racers. Clearly he was showing far more energy and far less lethargy than any other racer. This result is a very significant part of the study and should be clearly understood by all future racers.

One month prior to the race, I asked skipper Golf to undertake a simple program of iron supplements, nuts, and moderate exercise.

Iron[14]

Iron is an essential component of the proteins involved in oxygen transport. A deficiency of iron limits oxygen delivery to cells, resulting in fatigue,

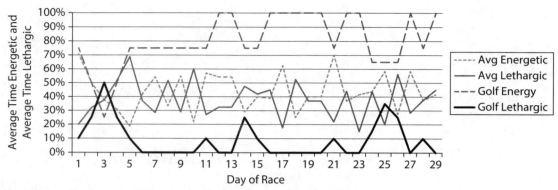

Golf's responses regarding times of energy and lethargy compared to the average of the other skippers.

poor work performance, and decreased immunity. Almost two thirds of iron in the body is found in hemoglobin, the protein in red blood cells that carries oxygen to tissues. Golf took off-the-shelf multivitamins with iron for the three weeks prior to and during the race.

Nuts[15]

Nuts are loaded with protein, a great source of energy, but it tends to work more slowly than carbohydrates. Protein does not provide a quick energy fix, but it keeps us going for the long haul.

Another nutrient found in nuts is coenzyme CoQ10. This nutrient helps our cells produce energy. It is also an antioxidant, which means that it protects our cells from damage caused by oxidative stress. Our bodies produce some CoQ10 naturally, but the amount decreases with age.

Nuts also contain omega-3 fatty acids, a category of unsaturated fats that provide energy to the muscles and organs. They also store energy for the body and help lower LDL, the so-called "bad" cholesterol. Nuts are one of the best sources of this class of fatty acids.

Golf ate a cup of cashews, almonds, and peanuts daily as his snack food.

Moderate Exercise[16]

Exercise helps increase energy levels in both the long and short term. In the short term, doing a little exercise helps greatly by getting the blood pumping around the system and the oxygen flowing. If a

racer is feeling lethargic, then chances are that the system is static and not pumping that blood around. Jumping around a bit "kick starts" the body back into action, and one starts to feel vigorous again.

I have found a very significant immediate energy boost simply from walking in place in the cockpit for just 10 minutes, even lifting my feet only a few inches. The goal is to get blood moving to the brain without exhausting the body. Thus moderate exercise is more appropriate for the long-distance singlehander than vigorous exercise. Golf reported increased energy from daily running in place in the cabin while holding onto the ceiling grab rails.

Ginseng Root

Another natural energy supplement, but not tested during this study is ginseng root.[17] A Mayo Clinic study found that high doses of the herb American ginseng over two months reduced cancer-related fatigue in patients. At four weeks, the pure ginseng provided only a slight improvement in fatigue symptoms. However, at eight weeks, ginseng offered cancer patients significant improvement in general exhaustion—feelings of being "pooped," worn out," "fatigued," "sluggish," "run-down," or "tired"— compared to the placebo group. "After eight weeks, we saw a 20-point improvement in fatigue in cancer patients, measured on a 100-point, standardized fatigue scale," Dr. Barton says. The herb had no apparent side effects, she says.

The lethargy experienced during a long-distance race may be comparable to that felt by a cancer patient, so the Mayo Clinic study's findings about the benefits of ginseng are appropriate for singlehanders. Ginseng is the active ingredient in the energy-boosting drink Cheetah Power Surge that promises rapid energy with "no caffeine and no caffeine crash."[18]

Carnitine

Carnitine[19] was also not a part of this study. "Patients taking chemotherapy drugs can deplete levels of carnitine, a natural substance in the body. Scientists at the Urbino Hospital in Italy found that a pineapple-flavored drink containing a compound called levocarnitine, which the body converts into carnitine, helped most patients recover from their fatigue within a week." Carnitine is also available in energy-boosting drinks.

In the crewed Vic-Maui race, skippers reported that their crew on deck were operating 100% energetically for most of the reports, with the occasional dip down to a 75% energy level. This is obviously substantially higher than the reports for the single-handed race and may be a key reason that there was no room for speed improvement in the Vic-Maui boats. Clearly energy is important to racing, and any steps a skipper can take to increase energy not only improves boat speed but will also substantially improve the skipper's emotional state during the race.

MINDFULNESS

The current state of the art in the psychology of athletic performance enhancement includes the concept of "mindfulness." In brief, mindfulness is a condition in which the athlete is able to engage in a present-moment focus on the task at hand for extended periods without distraction from extraneous factors. Being mindful does not attempt to block these extraneous factors but, rather, allows them to pass through the athlete's mind with no effect. That is, they are simply passing events no more important than a bird flying overhead. If a sailor can allow a seagull to fly past with no impact on his concentration, can he allow other thoughts also to fly past with no distraction?

Consider driving a car for a long distance, perhaps an 8-hour trip of steady driving with just one bathroom break. For the length of this trip you can concentrate on keeping the vehicle between the white lines just a yard to either side, while driving at 65 mph with other cars driving in the opposite direction just a few yards away. Somehow thousands of drivers, in particular long-haul truck drivers, perform this act of mindfulness every day.

During this 8-hour trip a thousand thoughts pass through your mind. "Do I need to move money into the checking account to make the mortgage payment?" "My arm aches." "I've got to fix that leaky gutter." Each of these thoughts passes and is considered briefly before being shunted elsewhere. Our mind has given itself the ability to complete an incredibly complex task of driving at a high speed with many thoughts passing harmlessly and not impacting the necessary concentration. At any moment we can react immediately to a deer running across the highway.

However, once in a while a more significant thought enters the mind. "Is my wife having an affair? She seems to be on the phone every night and has been spending a lot of time at the yacht club. What is she doing right now?" During such a period when we do not have the solution within our own consciousness, the world seems to pass by without notice. All of our concentration is focused on the issue and not on driving. These are the times when we hit a deer or drift across the white line into oncoming traffic. This is also the reason that talking on a cell phone while driving is so dangerous: it allows extraneous factors to become the "present-moment focus" instead of remaining engaged in the act of driving. Distracted driving is virtually tied with alcohol and speed as the leading cause of traffic deaths. One can imagine how difficult it would be for a golfer to hit the perfect shot if someone in the crowd shouted, "Your wife is having an affair!"

In some activities, mindfulness must be taken to the extreme. For example, in professional golf the athlete must be absolutely perfect for the 10 seconds up to and including the swing. A golfer who is only 99.9% perfect would never reach the professional ranks. On the other hand, for professional truck drivers and the rest of us, engineers have designed roads and vehicles to allow for a significantly lower threshold of acceptability. How much more mindful would drivers need to be if the highways were two meters narrower?

In the same way, mindfulness also refers to attention to the present moment rather than allowing the mind to wander into the past or future. Returning to our roadway example, 5 minutes ago the driver needed to cross the centerline while passing a group of cyclists. Similarly, if the weather forecast calls for heavy rain this afternoon, the driver will need to be more cautious. The driver's thoughts of these past and future situations does not result in driving off the road now. The driver's mindfulness of the current situation allows for safe driving for every moment of the trip.

Thankfully, in singlehanded sailing the threshold of required mindfulness is even lower than for driving. The autopilot enables us to completely ignore sailing altogether. We can actually go to sleep while the boat continues to sail. But this is a two-edged sword. In high-performance racing, technology has become a problem rather than a complete solution. In allowing us to walk away from the tiller, it has also allowed us to walk away from all the aspects of sailing that make the boat go fast.

An interesting comparison can be made with the America's Cup World Series. The level of concentration required by the entire crew in those short-duration races equals that of professional golf. For example, if a crewman were to fumble pulling in the jibsheet because he was distracted by thinking about his wife's affair, his boat might fall behind by just one boat length—enough to lose the race. Even at the highest level, long-distance singlehanded sailing does not require the mindfulness of a golfer about to make the perfect swing or an America's Cup crewman in mid-tack. It would be more accurate to say that a long-distance singlehanded sailor is very well served with the mindfulness of a truck driver. All that is needed is to stay within the white lines (i.e., keep the inside and outside telltales flying with each change in wind direction) while adjusting the pressure on the gas pedal for every hill and valley (i.e., trim or ease the sheets with each change in wind strength). Thankfully, the singlehander is not likely to cause

an accident and death even if ignoring the telltales completely.

Mindfulness-Acceptance-Commitment (MAC) Approach

In earlier years, sports psychologists considered that optimum performance could be obtained by avoiding destructive thoughts; that is, negative thoughts or emotions should be controlled, eliminated, or replaced. This was based on studies that showed high-performance athletes are less anxious and more confident, and experience fewer negative thoughts. This led to the assumption that interventions should work to replace negative thoughts with positive thoughts. Unfortunately, subsequent studies did not show that a reduction in negative thoughts consistently resulted in enhanced performance. In fact, they showed that the suppression of one negative thought actually resulted in a triggering process whereby the athlete actively searched for signs of negative cognitive activity and then brought this to the forefront in order to suppress it; i.e., the mind was being trained to seek out and destroy negative thoughts. But this only ended in more seeking and thus more finding of negative thoughts. The result was that rather than concentrating on the important task at hand (swinging a golf club), the athlete's mind was more concerned with the seeking-destroying process. Further difficulty arose from the tendency of people to connect these internal negative thoughts with the behavior with which they occurred. For example, if negative thoughts were summoned during practice sessions, an athlete would avoid practicing in order to avoid the negative thoughts.

The current approach is to accept rather than suppress these destructive thoughts. Thoughts are viewed as naturally occurring events that regularly come and go in normal experience. Mindfulness-based techniques emphasize the development of nonjudgmental attention to all thoughts. That is, all thoughts are noticed but not evaluated as being good or bad, right or wrong. This allows thoughts to pass without impacting performance. To give an extreme example, the thought "My wife is having an affair" is given the same value as "I need to move money from savings to checking to make this month's mortgage payment" or "I need to fix the gutter"—that is, they all have no value at all. None of them is good or bad. None of them is right or wrong. Thoughts remain simply thoughts—words in our heads. Our present-moment focus, then, can more easily be trained on our actions: sailing the boat.

Of course, it is not only thoughts from outside the race that can lead to distraction. A hundred considerations within the race itself can lead to the same negative effect. "I'm hungry." "This seat is damned uncomfortable." "Jim has gotten way ahead and I'll never be able to catch him." "I screwed up on my weather forecast and went too far south." "I'm worried about squalls tonight." Each of these might distract skippers and take their mind off the key goal of sailing fast. But the skipper who practices concepts of mindfulness will let each current issue pass by without any value judgment and will concentrate on the here and now rather than dwell on past mistakes or future worries.

Emotional flare-ups are common in long-distance singlehanding. Racers report intense crying jags lasting several hours during which real or imagined external and internal factors take control of the mind (see Chapter 2). This is exactly the type of situation where mindfulness can be of benefit. The skipper can learn to allow the thought "I miss my wife" to pass by attaching no more value to it than to the seagull flying overhead.

Once we accept the premise of this chapter, that it is better to actively sail the boat than to let the autopilot do all the work, the ideas behind mindfulness allow the singlehander to stay at the helm or on the sheets for longer periods. If the skipper is able to maintain the level of mindfulness of a long-haul trucker, with his eyes on the telltales and his hands on the sheets or tiller, he will be able to sail much faster than the skipper who allows himself to be constantly distracted.

I am not proposing that singlehanders hand steer for the entire race. I am suggesting that skippers share the load with the autopilot for as long as possible, in the same way that the pit-crew shares the load with the helmsman on a crewed boat. There are times when allowing the autopilot to steer while working the sheets would be most beneficial. There are other times when hand steering would add the greatest speed.

THE ROLE OF COMPETITION

One of the most common maxims in sailing is that a race occurs any time two boats are in sight moving in the same direction. Every skipper has a natural inclination to show that he is as good as or better than the skipper in the next boat. In almost any sport, racers are told to train against a partner because that calls out the natural competitive instinct of every human being. Unfortunately, the corollary would be no race occurs when there is no other boat.

A significant problem in long-distance sailing is the lack of any visible competitor. After the first few hours of the race, each boat is on a seemingly empty ocean with nothing on the horizon but seagulls. The facts that each boat is taking a different route to the finish and that each boat is racing with a different handicap rating add to the problem. It is exceedingly difficult to maintain a competitive attitude in these circumstances. Twice-daily position reports, with latitudes and longitudes handwritten on a pad or plotted on a chart, do not offer a level of incentive to racers.

It is thought that on a crewed boat, energetic crewmates push each other to higher performance, with different crewmates taking the encouraging

COMPETITION IN THE MINI TRANSAT

In the 2013 Mini Transat, Craig Horsfield and another racer stayed in sight in fierce competition, pushing each other, for ten solid days. Only on the last day of the race did they split apart. This undoubtedly helped with Horsfield's tenth-place finish. This approach of cooperating to beat the competition is a standard part of bicycle racing. Taking it to sailing is a natural progression.

role at different times and no crewman wanting to be seen as slacking. This is another reason why crewed boats in the earlier study were energetic nearly 100% of the time and could not add to their average speed by being in a perfect racing frame of mind. They were already in that frame of mind.

Steps to Increase Active Racing

Racers can take several steps to increase their feeling of active racing and thus keep themselves at the highest level of performance.

First, while seated in the cockpit with a hand on the tiller or on the sheets, skippers must keep a constant eye on the knotmeter. It is very easy for speed to drop by a half knot or more with no audible change in water passing by the boat. Speed drops at this level are a constant part of sailing, even with an autopilot. Skippers must watch the knotmeter and make immediate corrections to sail trim and heading to maintain top speed. A few minutes here and there with the speed at a knot below optimum can quickly add up.

Second, each skipper must have a copy of her boat's polars on hand and must push to sail to the polars. These graphs represent the best possible speed for each boat design and will give the skipper immediate feedback on her sailing ability.

Third, sail to the best possible speed for the moment. I find it best to watch the knotmeter looking for spikes of speed, and then sail to match these spikes. For example, if while sailing at 5.9 I notice a spike to 6.2, I will do everything possible to regain and maintain that speed. I say to myself, "If I can reach 6.2 once, why can't I do it continuously?"

Racing Against Other Boats' Reported Positions

Most races allow for only twice daily reporting of positions. It is vitally important for a skipper to record all of the competitors' positions so that he has a ready reference to how he is doing. Nothing could be more disappointing than to lose a race by a small amount only because the skipper did not even know how close he was. Such a record might not be useful to close a 10-hour gap, but it would certainly be useful to discover a 1-hour gap that could be overtaken.

Handicap racing has an extra challenge in that the closest competitor's boat might be a day or two in front or behind. The final result will be known only when the corrected time is calculated. For example in the Singlehanded Transpac, the overall difference between the third and fourth boats was only 2.5 hours on corrected time, or a speed difference of 0.1 knots. However, the handicap ratings were such that the third-place boat finished two and a half days after the fourth-place boat. I have

First Half of Race	PHRF	Actual Distance Travelled	Actual Average Speed	Corrected Time (minutes)	Corrected Speed	Corrected Distance
Bandicoot	128	740	6.22	5547	8.00	953
Champ	156	653	5.49	5199	7.54	897
Darwind	240	639	5.37	4153	9.23	1099
Flight Risk	97	780	6.55	5933	7.89	939
Frolic	154	714	6.00	5223	8.20	976
Galaxsea	145	710	5.97	5335	7.98	950
Green Buffalo	132	804	6.76	5497	8.78	1044
Harrier	184	653	5.49	4850	8.08	961
Hope For the Warriors	152	687	5.77	5248	7.85	935
Indefix	99	775	6.51	5908	7.87	937
Moon Shadow	160	700	5.88	5149	8.16	971
Mouton Noir	119	729	6.13	5659	7.73	920
Rainbow	184	758	6.37	4850	9.38	1116
Red Sky	133	757	6.36	5485	8.28	985
Rushmore	152	641	5.39	5248	7.33	872
Scaramouche	92	775	6.51	5995	7.76	923
Slacker	140	796	6.69	5398	8.85	1053
Taz	129	649	5.45	5535	7.04	837
Team Open	115	769	6.46	5709	8.08	962
Tortuga	199	667	5.61	4663	8.58	1021
Truth	-123	1220	10.25	8671	8.44	1005
Turbo Camper	84	812	6.82	6095	7.99	951

My spreadsheet showing the positions of the competition data after day 5 of the 2012 Singlehanded Transpac. After calculating for individual boat ratings, *Rainbow* and *Darwind* are in the lead.

developed a spreadsheet that calculates with the handicap rating to allow boats to know their standing at any point in the race.

Here's the calculation:

1. At each report of the race, take the actual miles sailed toward the finish line by each boat up to that point in the race. This can be done by subtracting the total race length from the Distance to Finish (DTF). (We are concerned only with each boat's speed toward the finish, not any extra miles they cover to gain a weather advantage.)

2. Take all of these numbers and average the result for all the boats. Set this average mileage as a "Standard Race."

3. Divide the actual distance traveled toward the finish line by the actual time of the race to find the Actual Speed of each boat on the race to date.

4. Based on their Actual Speed, calculate each boat's corrected finish time for the Standard Race.
   - Use the normal Time-On-Distance formula (TA) to calculate each boat's Corrected Time for the Standard Race.
   - The time-on-distance formula is: TA = (Standard Race Length x PHRF)/60
   - Actual Time – TA = Corrected Time
   - At this point we have the Corrected Time for each boat in the Standard Race.

5. Divide the actual distance traveled by each boat by its Corrected Time. This gives the Corrected Speed for each boat.

6. Multiply the Actual Hours since the start of the race by each boat's Corrected Speed. This gives a Corrected Distance traveled by each boat.

7. Compare the Corrected Distance for each boat to determine the relative placing of each boat at any point in the race. This should give a fairly good indication of how many corrected miles are between each boat in the race.

The above calculation is long, but it can easily be set up in a spreadsheet before the race, and then only the DTF figures need be entered at each report. The spreadsheet will instantly output the result.

Racing Against Herself

Top-level marathon runners use this method when competitors are out of view.[20] Runners know their own potential speed (like the polars of a boat) and use a stopwatch when passing mile markers on the race at a specific rate. They can break a race down to individual miles of running and then work to match their best possible performance for each mile. A singlehander can use the MOB (man-overboard) feature on their GPS and a stopwatch to help with this process by setting up a continuous series of 20-minute races.

With this method, the skipper pushes the MOB button and takes one of two approaches: She can watch for a specific distance to pass, such as 2 nautical miles, and time the duration of her race. Or she can sail for a set period, such as 20 minutes, and watch the distance covered. She must immediately write the result down on a white board in the cockpit. This is important to provide a challenging visual competitor. After she does this once, she immediately does it again, and then again, and again, and again continuously. Ideally, the distance or time differences for each race segment will be very close to each other. Think of short around-the-buoys races where competitors are only separated by a boat length or two.

Each past race segment represents a new competitor against whom she is racing in the current segment. If she betters the last race segment, she wins that little race. If she does not match the last segment, she loses the race and must try harder the next time. She should do a series of nine of these race segments over 3 hours before taking a break. Each segment represents a new competitor's boat on her course, so she must write down every segment result on the white board. After nine segments in the morning, she can take a sanity break to get something to eat, before starting the process again for her afternoon race series.

She should look at each 3-hour period as an intense set of races, just like a set of round-the-buoy

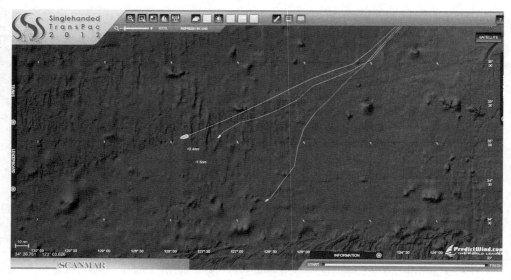

The track showing *Hotel's* course change southward while the skipper slept and the autopilot drove. *(Courtesy Yellow-brick Tracking Ltd.)*

races at her yacht club. And she should dedicate the same level of concentration and intensity to it.

Two considerations are important. The distance or duration of each race segment must be sufficiently short that it does not allow the skipper to leave the tiller and do other functions, like get coffee. These periods are intended to be intense, short duration races where the skipper concentrates solely on boat speed. However, they should be long enough that normal fluctuations in wind do not impact performance over the entire duration of the race. Within each segment she can watch the knot meter to try to match her highest speed, knowing that more important than staying at 6.2 knots is cutting down the time needed to cover 2 nautical miles.

Sea and wind conditions might change over the entire 3-hour race period, but they will not change sufficiently from one segment to the next to nullify the comparison.

Also the skipper should not make any course changes during the 3-hour race series. This idea is to cover the greatest possible distance on a particular point of sail. A runner would not include a flat and a hill within a 1-mile measurement. Likewise, a sailor should not include any course changes. A course change would slow the boat, and the race result would not be measurable against the other segments.

THE AUTOPILOT: THE WEAKEST LINK IN THE CHAIN

There is a second reason why sailors must understand the need for not relying on the autopilot: it is the least reliable piece of equipment on the boat. In some cases, the autopilot cannot handle the wind and wave conditions the boat faces. This was the situation facing the boat *Hotel* in the Transpac. Quoting from the logs, "I was so exhausted last night I let the boat go way south in exchange for 3 hours of solid sleep. On my planned heading, the autopilot kept rounding up every time a gust or big wave hit, which meant no sleep."

This change in direction to head south cost *Hotel* 40 nautical miles in distance to finish compared to *India*, and 27 nautical miles compared to *Juliette*, over the next 14 hours. (See the accompanying course chart.) All three boats were in close proximity and facing the same weather conditions before *Hotel* headed southward.

In other situations, the entire electrical system fails. Boat *Kilo* reported: "With no solar power and fully depleting my batteries in the first two [hours], I was left to hand steer with no other real alternative if I wanted to keep racing. I hand steered 60 out of 72 hours for a 20 hour/day average over 3 days. I hit my mental and physical breaking point a few times, dropping both sails and collapsing in the cockpit."

It is difficult to imagine how a marathon runner could expect to win if he decided to stop running and rest on the park bench for a couple of minutes. The solution in this situation is amazingly simple and well known, requiring nothing more than a $3 piece of surgical tubing. While this emergency self-steering system is not as fast as an autopilot, it is a lot faster than dropping sails and sitting adrift. (See Chapters 5 and 6.)

The autopilot fails in other situations. Here are more comments from the logs: "Wind! Finally it decided to show up! 18–22 knots. Boat speed averaging in mid to upper 8s all night, recklessly over-canvassed. Autopilot could not keep up and would begin oscillating the boat horribly." Another: "Autopilot was too slow to drive with spinnaker in moderate seas and 20 knots of breeze. I remember being below, feeling a roundup coming and sticking my head out to look at the autopilot and yell: 'You got that?' Much of the time, the answer was no." And another: "When one of the squalls passes the wind speed picks up and the boat wants to round up and the autopilot can't handle so I jump on to hand steer again." And still another: "The autopilot is leaving a bit to be desired with the spinnaker up. So far, I figure that I'm about 20% faster than the pilot on average. That really hurts when it comes to standings in the race." My own experience is very much the same. All autopilots have limits when a boat is being pushed to its maximum. Competitive racers must accept that there will be many hours when they must steer with one hand and keep the other on the sheet. The speed of the boat must be determined only by what the boat, sails, and skipper can handle, not by the autopilot—the weakest link in the chain.

Included in the prerace questions was: "Are you confident that you can handle a significant event, such as breaking the mast half way up?" Three racers answered "Very Confident," three answered "Confident," and one answered "Neutral." So it was surprising to see that the skippers were prepared to manage the very rare and traumatic event of breaking a mast but seemed not at all prepared to manage the very common problem of an electrical system or autopilot failure.

Skippers must understand the overwhelming requirement that in order to win, they must keep moving fast toward the finish line. Small equipment failures are a normal part of racing, and every skipper must be able to handle them without slowing.

IMPROVING COMFORT

If one wanted to design a method of torture, sitting on a hard piece of plastic covered in 40-grit sandpaper 16 hours a day in soaking wet pants would be an effective starting point. Round-the-world singlehanded racers are known to install very comfortable executive chairs reminiscent of Captain Kirk's inside the cabin. This only encourages the skipper to spend more time out of the cockpit and away from actually sailing the boat. It is rare for singlehanders to make even the smallest adaptation to the cockpit to allow for comfortable seating for hours on end. Professional race cars install ergonomic seats designed specifically for each driver in a race that lasts only 3 hours. But singlehanded sailors are expected to sit on a section of ridged, stippled plastic for the duration of a transoceanic race. The sheer pain of it will drive even the hardiest skipper away from the tiller after a few hours.

If we accept that effective racing includes actually sailing the boat for extended periods, then skippers must take steps to improve cockpit comfort for long-duration sitting. Such seating must be comfortable on the bum, provide proper back support, allow for movements necessary to sail the

A seat cushion sewn from an old sail and some closed-cell packing foam prevents back pain after a long day on the water.

boat, and have sufficient drainage to remove water immediately. Homemade solutions include cutting the legs off a plastic deck chair and adding wooden cross-slats with carpeting on the bottom. Another solution is a beanbag chair using closed-cell foam pellets and lawn chair fabric. West Marine offers a Go-Anywhere seat that seems to provide back support.

FINAL THOUGHTS ON LONG-DISTANCE RACING

The study reported in this chapter is the first in-depth analysis of the psychological factors required to win a long-distance singlehanded sailboat race. There is a strong correlation between sailing aggressively and final race ranking. This conclusion aligns with a study of the Iditarod Trail Sled Dog Race showing that the most aggressive mushers had better finishes than less aggressive mushers.

The study also showed that typical singlehanded skippers are "in the zone" of sailing only a third of the time of boat crews in a similar race. By increasing their time "in the zone" and by actively sailing the boat to achieve small increases in average speed, skippers can significantly improve their final result. Records show that even slight, incremental increases in average boat speed can improve race ranking by as much as ten positions.

ENDNOTES

(See the Bibliography for full citations.)

1. E.g., Matthew Fitzgerald, *Iron War: Dave Scott, Mark Allen, & the Greatest Race Ever Run*; Hal Higdon, *Marathon: The Ultimate Training Guide*.
2. E.g., Glin Bennett, "Medical and Psychological Problems in the 1972 Singlehanded Transatlantic Yacht Race"; Neil Weston, et al., "Stress and Coping in Single-Handed Round-the-World Ocean Sailing"; H.E. Lewis, et al.,"Voluntary Solitude: Studies of Men in a Singlehanded Transatlantic Sailing Race."
3. E.g., Ellen MacArthur, *Taking on the World: A Sailor's Extraordinary Solo Race Around the Globe*; Adam Mayers, *Sea of Dreams*; Nicolas Tomalin and Ron Hall, *The Strange Last Voyage of Donald Crowhurst*.
4. www.Gitana-Team.com, "Gate Hopping in the Deep South," 2008.
5. http://iditarod.com.
6. www.singlehandedtranspac.com.
7. A correlation of 0.5 might be regarded as strong in social science situations (e.g., where the measures are based on 5-point Likert scales) wiki.answers.com/Q/Would_a_0.5_correlation_be_considered_weak_modest_strong_or_very_weak.
8. G. O Dean, et al., "Personality Profiles of Iditarod Mushers as Compared by Finish Group."
9. http://en.wikipedia.org/wiki/16PF_Questionnaire.
10. www.youtube.com: "Telefonica Big Wave Crashes, Volvo Ocean Race 2011–2012."
11. Boat polars: a graph produced for a particular boat showing the maximum possible speed for every wind angle, wind speed, and sail combination assuming all other conditions are optimum. See http://www.pro-charter.com/english/polar.htm.
12. Adam Mayers, *Sea of Dreams*.
13. It becomes challenging to measure the correlation between two data sets that are both based on reported opinions. A 50% correlation would be considered weak in a strict mathematical comparison, but is considered stronger in social science situations.
14. U.S. National Institutes of Health, Office of Dietary Supplements, "Dietary Supplement Fact Sheet."
15. http://www.workingwellness.com/fitness-&-excercise/nuts-to-increase-energy.php
16. http://www.healthguidance.org/entry/16197/1/Fighting-Lethargy.html
17. http://www.mayoclinic.org/news2012-rst/6907.html
18. http://www.cheetahpowersurge.com/
19. http://www.prescriptiondrug-info.com/drug_details.asp?title=Levocarnitine&ad=true http://health.groups.yahoo.com/group/experimentalandunconventional/message/460. Also See BBC's Story on this June 12, 2002.
20. Timothy Noakes, *The Lore of Running, 4th Edition*.

CHAPTER 16

THE SPIRITUAL SIDE OF SINGLEHANDING

How rare it is that a man can spend time alone with his thoughts. We have always been a social animal; in fact we have been taught from our earliest days the importance of "getting along with others." Those of us who enjoy being alone are thought of as odd, even peculiar. But, speaking as one of those peculiar people, perhaps we are the ones who will reach new insights into the universe.

In his best-known book *Walden*, Thoreau wrote of his voyage of spiritual discovery during a two-year stay in a 10- by 15-foot cabin (about the size of a typical sailboat) on the edge of his hometown. Thoreau rhapsodized about the beneficial effects of living solitary and close to nature:

> I find it wholesome to be alone the greater part of the time. To be in company, even with the best, is soon wearisome and dissipating. I love to be alone. I never found the companion that was so companionable as solitude.
>
> Society is commonly too cheap. We meet at very short intervals, not having had time to acquire any new value for each other. We meet at meals three times a day, and give each other a new taste of that old musty cheese that we are. We have had to agree on a certain set of rules, called etiquette and politeness, to make this frequent meeting tolerable and that we need not come to open war. We meet at the post-office, and at the sociable, and about the fireside every night; we live thick and are in each other's way, and stumble over one another, and I think that we thus lose some respect for one another. Certainly less frequency would suffice for all important and hearty communications. It would be better if there were but one inhabitant to a square mile, as where I live. The value of a man is not in his skin, that we should touch him.
>
> I have a great deal of company in my house, especially in the morning, when nobody calls. Let me suggest a few comparisons, that someone may convey an idea of my situation. I am no more lonely than the loon in the pond that laughs so loud, or than Walden Pond itself. What company has that lonely lake, I pray? And yet it has not the blue devils, but the blue angels in it, in the azure tint of its waters. The sun is alone, except in thick weather, when there sometimes appear to be two, but one is a mock sun. God is alone—but the devil, he is far from being alone; he sees a great deal of company; he is legion. I am no more lonely than a single mullein or dandelion in a pasture, or a bean leaf, or sorrel, or a horse-fly, or a bumblebee. I am no more lonely than the Mill Brook, or a weathercock, or the north star, or the south wind, or an April shower, or a January thaw, or the first spider in a new house.

As a final thought on Thoreau, I'll go with this quote: "If a man does not keep pace with his companions, perhaps it is because he hears a different drummer. Let him step to the music which he hears, however measured or far away."

A singlehanded sailor is freed from the shackles of socialization, freed from the need to maintain polite conversation, the need to say "good morning" and not say "you're a twit." Where else in our life can we get this freedom? Socialization is not a bad thing, but is it really necessary 24 hours a day, every day of our life? For a few hours a week, or a few weeks a year, can we not get away from all human contact, even away from the potential for human contact?

Maslow is most famous for his "hierarchy of needs." In his theory, Maslow proposes that a person must meet lower-level needs before being able to move up to a higher level. In order, from the lowest to the highest level, these are: physiological needs (food, sleep, etc.); safety and security needs (personal, financial, etc.); social needs (love and friendship); esteem needs (respect and self-respect); and self-actualization (the realization of one's full potential).

The beauty of singlehanded sailing is that it allows the skipper to pass over the four lower levels and move directly to self-actualization. Once at sea, the physical and safety needs are met by the boat—nothing else is needed. There is no one else to be loved by and no one else to be respected by. The singlehander has love for himself and self-esteem, for without these, he would not have set out in the first place. (How can anyone on a crewed boat get past the love and esteem levels of the hierarchy?) The only thing left for the singlehanded skipper is self-actualization. Alone with his thoughts he can realize his full potential; there is nothing and no one to stop him from doing so.

During the first of his circumnavigations, Webb Chiles wrote, in *Storm Passage*: "I have always psychologically, and for the past several years physically, lived on the edge of the human herd. All I have wanted from society is that it be well enough structured so that I can find its edge and live there. Yet, even on the edge, I was a part of the herd life; and only now have the days at sea cleansed me. . . . As I naively—yet accurately—began this log: I was born for this. More than I knew I was born for this. There is nothing ugly out here but me; and at this moment when I want for nothing, when I am no longer striving, when I am not in a process of becoming but of being, when I am whole, complete, one, transcendent, I am also transcended and do not exist, except

as an essential part of the beauty around me. How incredible that this should happen here as I enter the Forties. How incredible that it should happen anywhere."

Buddhism discusses the concepts of nirvana and enlightenment. According to Buddhist texts, Siddhārtha Gautama realized that a meditative state was the right path to awakening. He discovered a path of moderation away from the extremes of self-indulgence and self-mortification. Gautama was seated under a tree—now known as the Bodhi tree—when he vowed never to arise until he had found the truth. After forty-nine days of meditation he is said to have attained enlightenment. From that time, Gautama was known to his followers as the Buddha or "Awakened One."

When a man knows the solitude of silence, and
feels the joy of quietness, he is then free from
fear and he feels the joy of the dharma. Happy is
he who lives contented in solitude, is well-versed
in the Doctrine and who has realized it. Happy
is he who lives in this world free from ill-will,
and is benevolent toward all beings. Happy is
he who lives in this world free from passion,
has overcome sensual enjoyment, and who has
attained mastership over the conceit of "I am."
This indeed is the highest happiness.

Enlightenment is sometimes described as complete and perfect sanity or awareness of the true nature of the universe. After attainment, it is believed that one is freed from the cycle of birth, suffering, death, and rebirth.

These thoughts about the advisability of silence are echoed in "The Solitude and Silence of Jesus," adapted from a sermon by Tom Shepard:

There is great value in seeking silence and
solitude in our lives. In this fast-paced world—it
is not uncommon for most of us to miss tranquil
times of quiet. Jesus used silence and solitude
quite a bit during His life and ministry. He did
not get away by Himself just to get away from
people—He wanted to hear that "still small
voice" of The Father speak to Him. So—He
sought solitude and silence—so that He could
hear God's voice clearer.

The scripture tells us: "Jesus was led up by the Spirit into the wilderness to be tempted by the devil."

I would never advise anyone to go out and try to pick a fight with Satan. However, I also believe that there are times when Satan will try to pick a fight with you. Silence and solitude—your quiet time with God—will help you resist.

The second example is right before He goes out and chooses the twelve apostles. "Now it came to pass in those days that He went out to the mountain to pray, and continued all night in prayer to God. And when it was day, He called His disciples to Himself; and from them He chose twelve whom He also named apostles." It is never a bad idea to pray before making major decisions in your life—Jesus did!

Next: You recall the story of John the Baptist: When Jesus heard about the beheading of John, He withdrew from there in a boat to a secluded place by Himself." Jesus sought solitude and silence.

The storms of death will more than likely touch each and every one of our lives, and it is times like those that we may need to seek silence and solitude with our Father in heaven. We need His strength and support as we travel through "the valley of the shadow of death."

As the popularity of Jesus increased—so did the demands placed upon Him. "The report went around concerning Him all the more; and great multitudes came together to hear, and to be healed by Him of their infirmities. So He Himself often withdrew into the wilderness and prayed."

Daily demands can drain us. There are times we all need to seek silence and solitude to help us recharge our batteries for the challenges that may lie right around the corner.

None of us knows when we are going to die. We really don't know for sure what tomorrow holds. You may be going through good times right now—or hard times. You may be walking through the valley of the shadow of death—or walking on cloud nine. You may have your future all planned out—or you may be living one day at a time. But the most important thing you can do is build a relationship with God.

The psychologist Carl Jung wrote:
The sea is the symbol of the collective unconscious because unfathomed depths lie concealed beneath its reflecting surface. Those who stand behind have burst into the terra firma of consciousness like a flood. Such invasions have something uncanny about them because they are irrational and incomprehensible to the person involved. They bring about a momentous alteration of his personality since they immediately constitute a painful personal secret which alienates and isolates him from his surroundings. Isolation causes an activation of the unconscious, and this produces something similar to the illusions and hallucinations that beset lonely wanderers in the desert, seafarers and saints.

Looking over my years of singlehanding, I really can't say with confidence whether I fall into the class of lunatic, seafarer, or saint. The one thing I know is that the best chance any person has of conversing with God is to put himself in a position to do so, give deep consideration to issues of morality, and hope that God has a free moment to talk. It happened to me once, for a very brief conversation. But that is all it took. Now that I have actual knowledge of the existence of God and have received the answer to a universal question of morality, there is not much more that I need out of life. In the words of Maslow, I have achieved self-actualization; in the words of Buddha, I have achieved Nirvana; in the words of Christ, I have achieved peace. All of this thanks to singlehanded sailing.

—Tandem Solus—

BIBLIOGRAPHY AND READING REFERENCES FOR SINGLEHANDERS

BOOKS

Bruce, Peter. *Adlard Coles' Heavy Weather Sailing*.

Chiles, Webb. *Storm Passage: Alone Around Cape Horn*, 1977.

Dashew, Steve and Linda. *Surviving the Storm, Coastal & Offshore Tactics*.

Fike, Matthew. *The One Mind: C.G. Jung and the Future of Literary Criticism*, 2014.

Fitzgerald, Matthew. *Iron War: Dave Scott, Mark Allen, & the Greatest Race Ever Run*. Velo Press, 2011.

Gollogly, Laragh, ed. *International Medical Guide for Ships, Third Edition*. World Health Organization.

Goss, Peter. *Close to the Wind*.

Hauret, Jurgen. *Doctor on Board: A Guide to Dealing with Medical Emergencies*, 2010.

Higdon, Hal. *Marathon: The Ultimate Training Guide*. St. Martin's Press, 1999.

Hughes, John. *The Sailing Spirit*.

Lundy, Derek, *Godforsaken Sea*.

Mayers, Adam. *Sea of Dreams*. McClelland & Steward, 2006.

MacArthur, Ellen. *Taking on the World: A Sailor's Extraordinary Solo Race Around the Globe*. International Marine/McGraw-Hill, 2003.

Moitessier, Bernard. *The Long Way*.

Noakes, Timothy, *The Lore of Running, Fourth Edition*. Human Kinetics, 2002.

North Sails/North University, *Performance Racing Trim*.

Shane, Victor. *Drag Device Data Base*.

Thoreau, Henry David. *Walden*. (Several editions exist.)

Tomalin, Nicholas and Ron Hall. *The Strange Last Voyage of Donald Crowhurst*. International Marine/McGraw-Hill, 2003.

JOURNALS/MAGAZINES

Australian Transportation Safety Bureau, "Independent investigation into the collision between the Australian registered yacht *Ella's Pink Lady* and the Hong Kong registered bulk carrier *Silver Yang* off Point Lookout, Queensland, 9 September 2009." http://www.atsb.gov.au.

Bennet, Glin. "Medical and Psychological Problems in the 1972 Singlehanded Transatlantic Yacht Race." *The Lancet* 2, 1973.

_____ "Psychological Breakdown at Sea: Hazards of Singlehanded Ocean Sailing." *British Journal of Medical Psychology*, 47, 1974.

Caldwell, John A., *An Overview of the Utility of Stimulants as a Fatigue Countermeasure for Aviators*. Brooks AFB, Texas: United States Air Force Research Laboratory. (19–24). February 2003.

Dean, G.O., N.M. Dean, and A. Turner. "Personality Profiles of Iditarod Mushers as Compared by Finish Group." University of Alaska/Anchorage: Arctic Sports Medicine/ Human Performance Laboratory, 1989.

Gooch, Tony. "Albert Takes on Otto, Offshore Sailing," *Cruising World*, 2004.

Lewis, H.E., J.M. Harris, D.H. Lewis, and C. deMonchhaux. "Voluntary Solitude: Studies of Men in a Singlehanded Transatlantic Sailing Race." *The Lancet* 1, 1431–1435, 1964.

Maister, David. "The Psychology of Waiting Lines." 1985, http://davidmaister.com/articles/the-psychology-of-waiting-lines/

U.S. National Institutes of Health, Office of Dietary Supplements, "Dietary Supplement Fact Sheet."

Weston, Neil. J. V., Thelwell, R. C., Bond, S. and Hutchings, N. "Stress and Coping in Single-Handed Round-the-World Ocean Sailing," *Journal of Applied Sport Psychology*. 21, 460–474. United Kingdom/University of Portsmouth, 2009.

HARDWARE MANUALS AND WEB RESOURCES

Manual for the Monitor Self-Steering System http://www.selfsteer.com/pdfs/Monitor-Manual.pdf

Walt Murray's Homemade Windvane, http://tinyurl.com/4mvxpg6/

INDEX

Numbers in **bold** indicate pages with illustrations